SHONEN JUMP ADVANCED MANGA

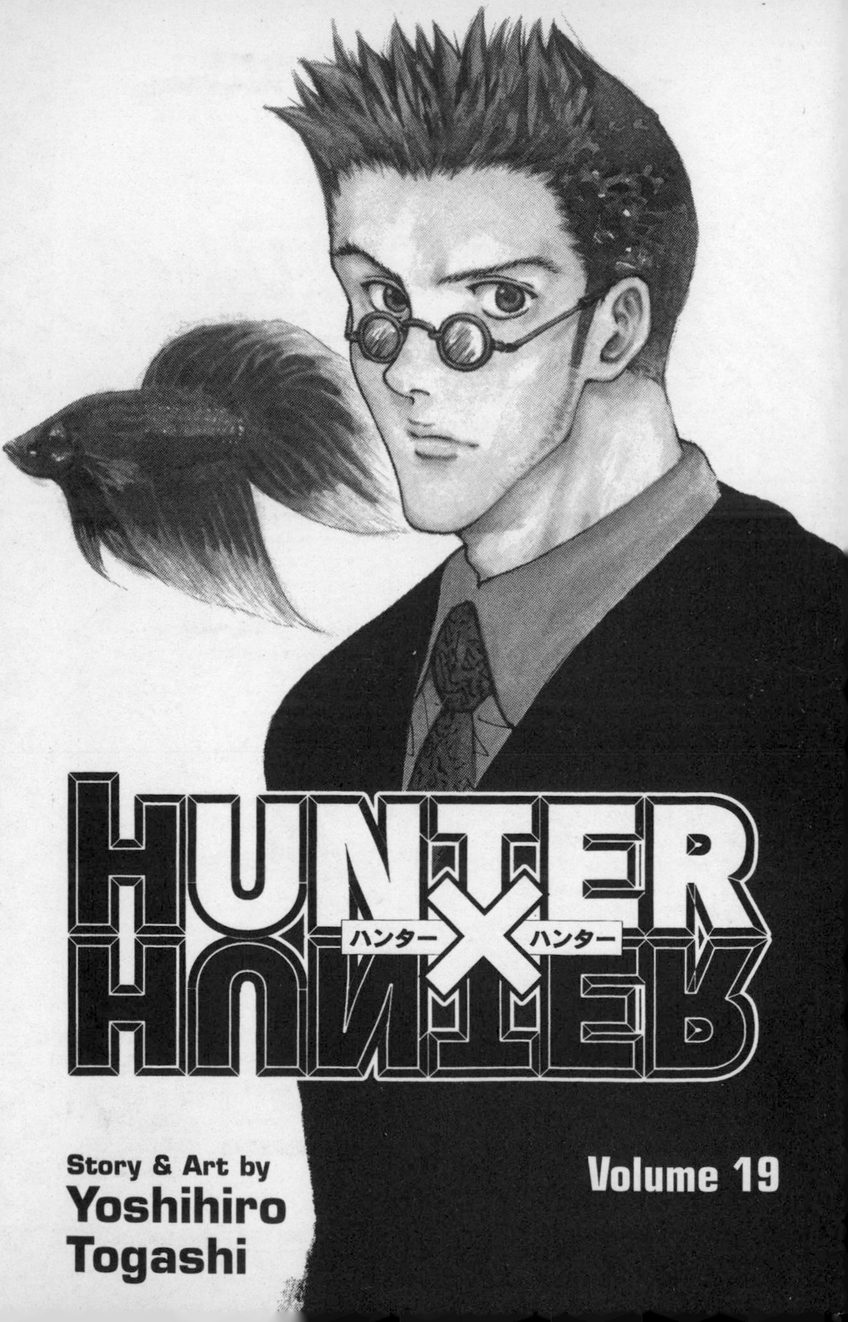

HUNTER × HUNTER

ハンター × ハンター

Story & Art by
Yoshihiro Togashi

Volume 19

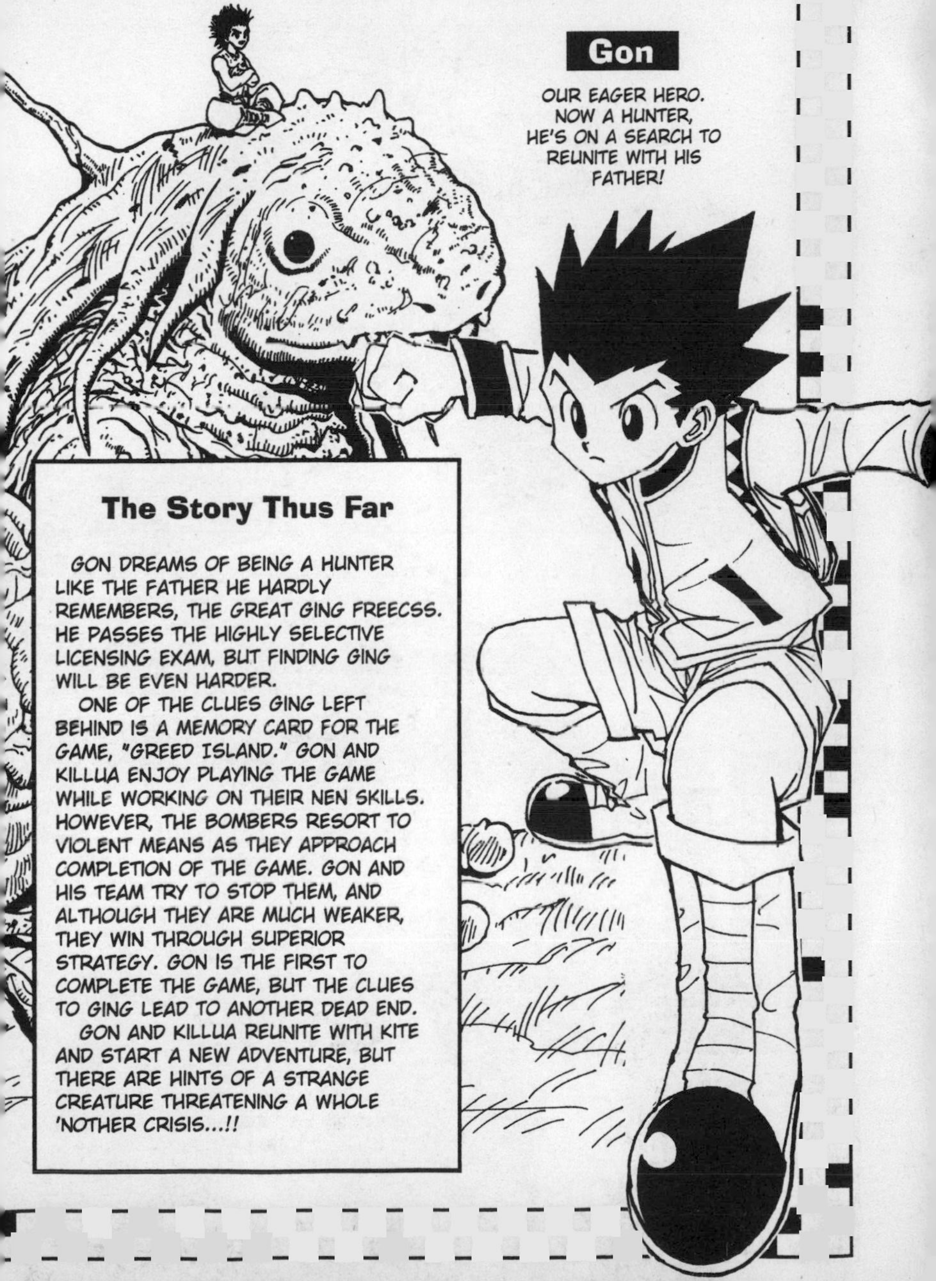

Gon

OUR EAGER HERO. NOW A HUNTER, HE'S ON A SEARCH TO REUNITE WITH HIS FATHER!

The Story Thus Far

GON DREAMS OF BEING A HUNTER LIKE THE FATHER HE HARDLY REMEMBERS, THE GREAT GING FREECSS. HE PASSES THE HIGHLY SELECTIVE LICENSING EXAM, BUT FINDING GING WILL BE EVEN HARDER.

ONE OF THE CLUES GING LEFT BEHIND IS A MEMORY CARD FOR THE GAME, "GREED ISLAND." GON AND KILLUA ENJOY PLAYING THE GAME WHILE WORKING ON THEIR NEN SKILLS. HOWEVER, THE BOMBERS RESORT TO VIOLENT MEANS AS THEY APPROACH COMPLETION OF THE GAME. GON AND HIS TEAM TRY TO STOP THEM, AND ALTHOUGH THEY ARE MUCH WEAKER, THEY WIN THROUGH SUPERIOR STRATEGY. GON IS THE FIRST TO COMPLETE THE GAME, BUT THE CLUES TO GING LEAD TO ANOTHER DEAD END.

GON AND KILLUA REUNITE WITH KITE AND START A NEW ADVENTURE, BUT THERE ARE HINTS OF A STRANGE CREATURE THREATENING A WHOLE 'NOTHER CRISIS...!!

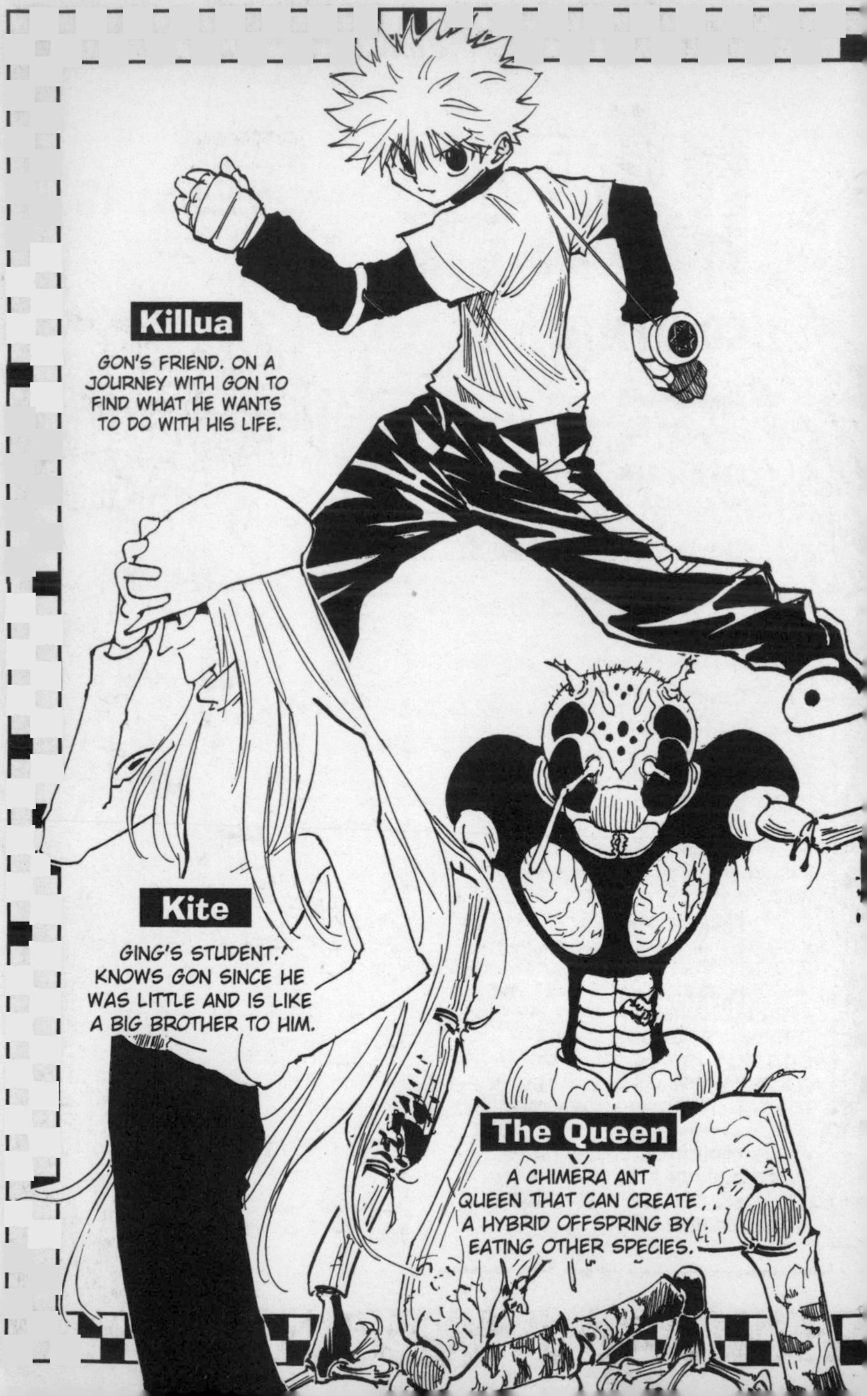
Killua
GON'S FRIEND. ON A JOURNEY WITH GON TO FIND WHAT HE WANTS TO DO WITH HIS LIFE.
Kite
GING'S STUDENT. KNOWS GON SINCE HE WAS LITTLE AND IS LIKE A BIG BROTHER TO HIM.
The Queen
A CHIMERA ANT QUEEN THAT CAN CREATE A HYBRID OFFSPRING BY EATING OTHER SPECIES.

HUNTER × HUNTER

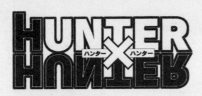

Volume 19

CONTENTS

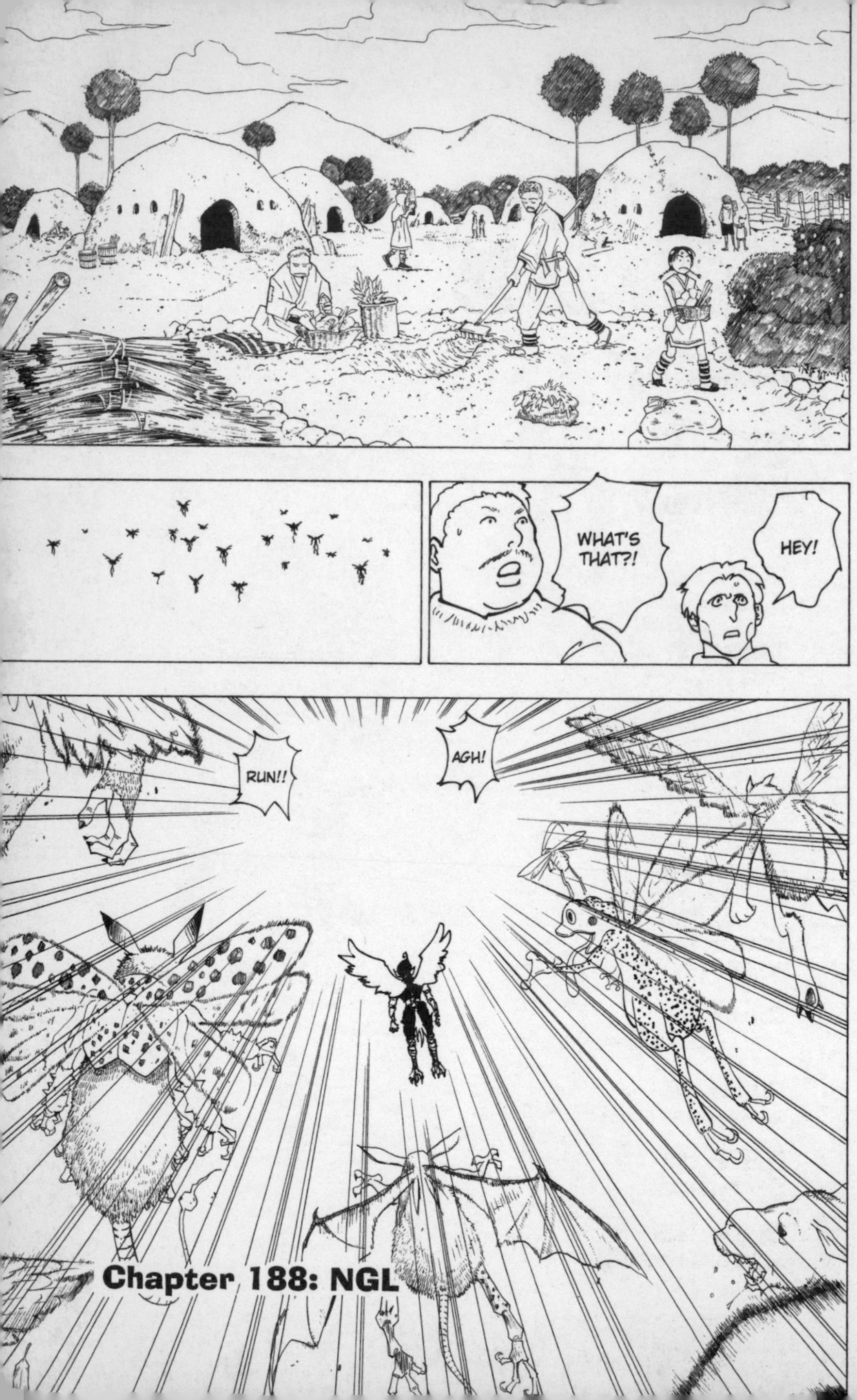
HEY!
WHAT'S THAT?!
AGH!
RUN!!

Chapter 188: NGL

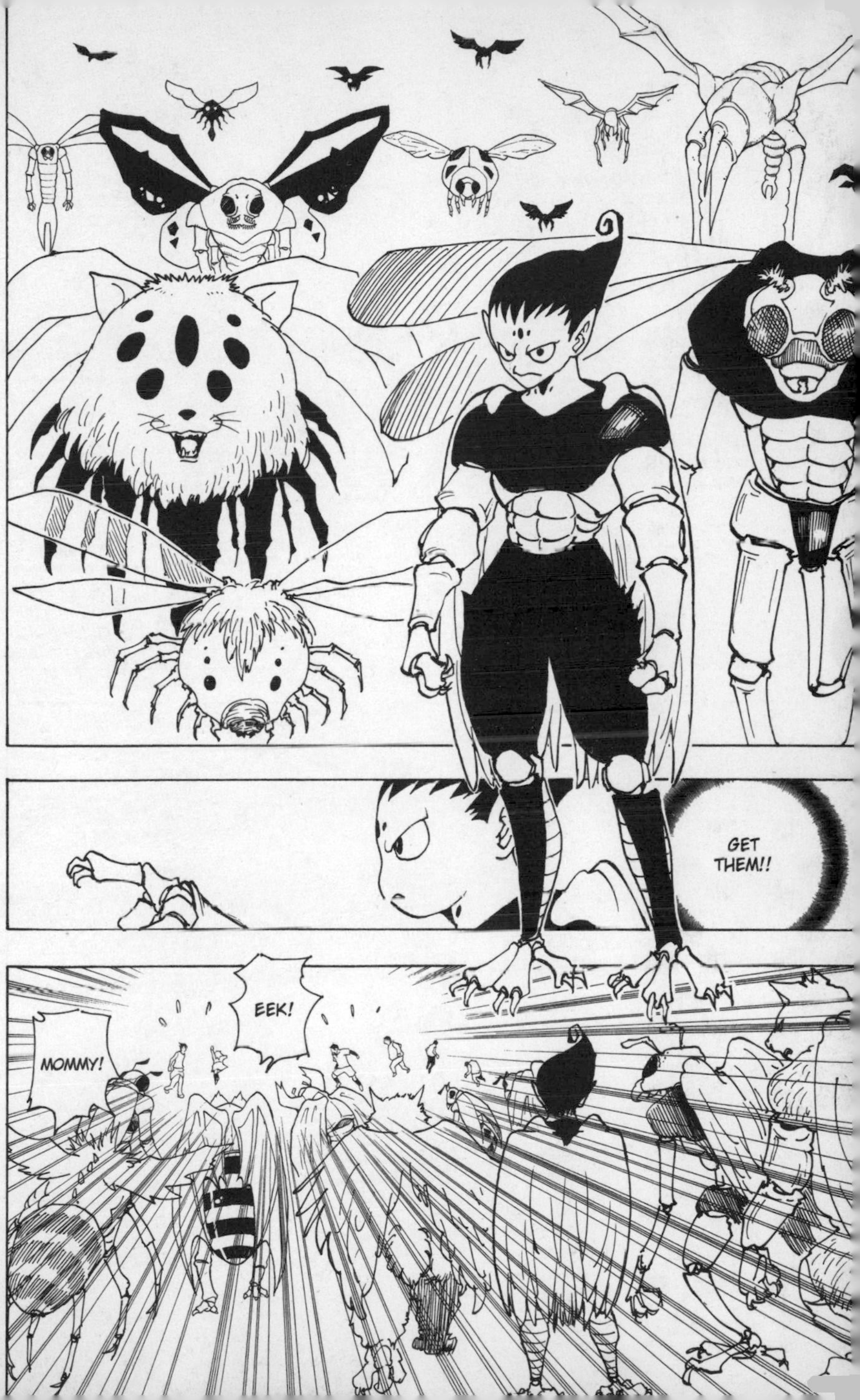
GET THEM!!
EEK!
MOMMY!

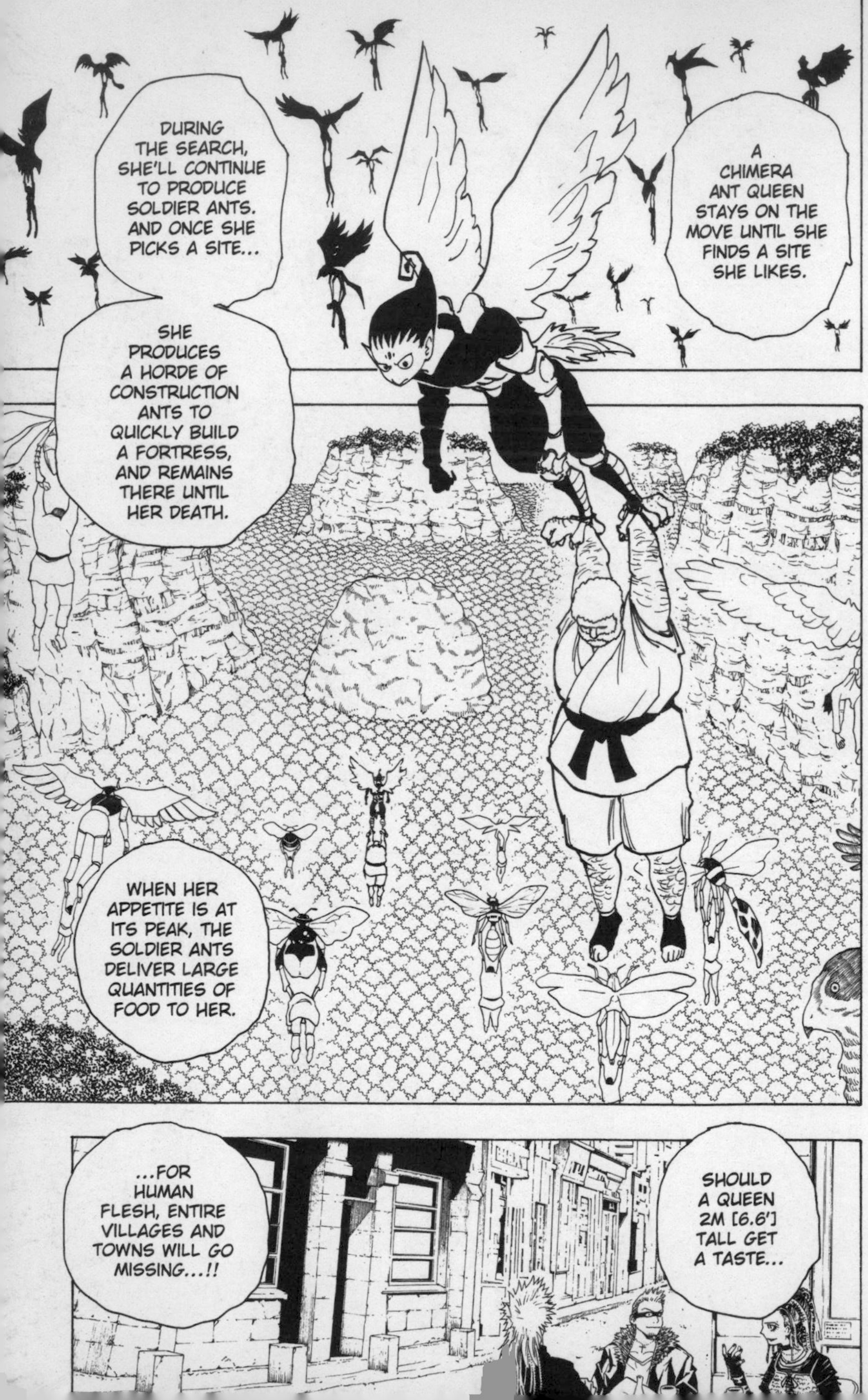
A CHIMERA ANT QUEEN STAYS ON THE MOVE UNTIL SHE FINDS A SITE SHE LIKES.
DURING THE SEARCH, SHE'LL CONTINUE TO PRODUCE SOLDIER ANTS. AND ONCE SHE PICKS A SITE...
SHE PRODUCES A HORDE OF CONSTRUCTION ANTS TO QUICKLY BUILD A FORTRESS, AND REMAINS THERE UNTIL HER DEATH.
WHEN HER APPETITE IS AT ITS PEAK, THE SOLDIER ANTS DELIVER LARGE QUANTITIES OF FOOD TO HER.
SHOULD A QUEEN 2M [6.6'] TALL GET A TASTE...
...FOR HUMAN FLESH, ENTIRE VILLAGES AND TOWNS WILL GO MISSING...!!

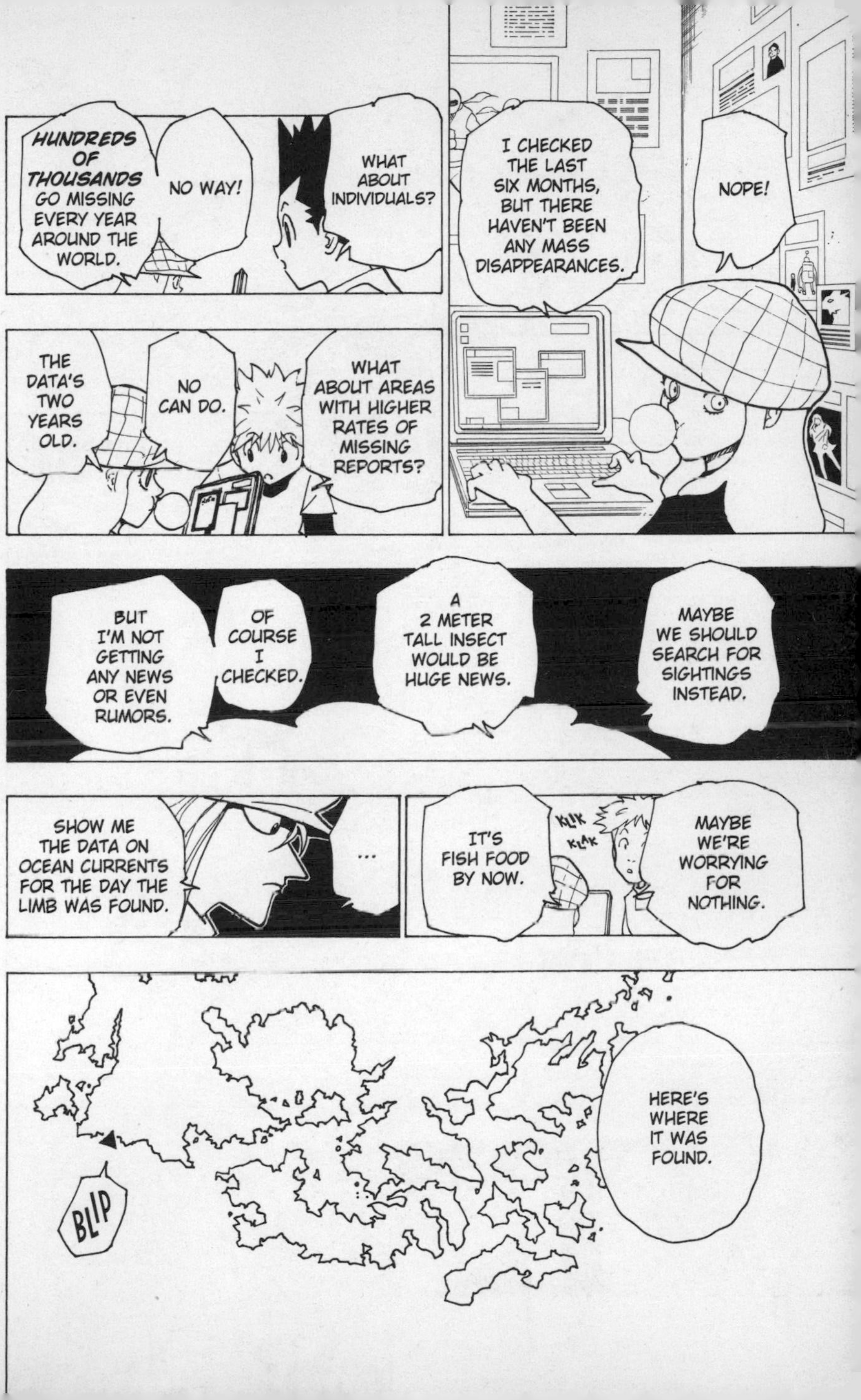
NOPE!
I CHECKED THE LAST SIX MONTHS, BUT THERE HAVEN'T BEEN ANY MASS DISAPPEARANCES.
WHAT ABOUT INDIVIDUALS?
NO WAY!
HUNDREDS OF THOUSANDS GO MISSING EVERY YEAR AROUND THE WORLD.
WHAT ABOUT AREAS WITH HIGHER RATES OF MISSING REPORTS?
NO CAN DO.
THE DATA'S TWO YEARS OLD.
MAYBE WE SHOULD SEARCH FOR SIGHTINGS INSTEAD.
A 2 METER TALL INSECT WOULD BE HUGE NEWS.
OF COURSE I CHECKED.
BUT I'M NOT GETTING ANY NEWS OR EVEN RUMORS.
MAYBE WE'RE WORRYING FOR NOTHING.
KLIK
KLAK
IT'S FISH FOOD BY NOW.
...
SHOW ME THE DATA ON OCEAN CURRENTS FOR THE DAY THE LIMB WAS FOUND.
HERE'S WHERE IT WAS FOUND.
BLIP

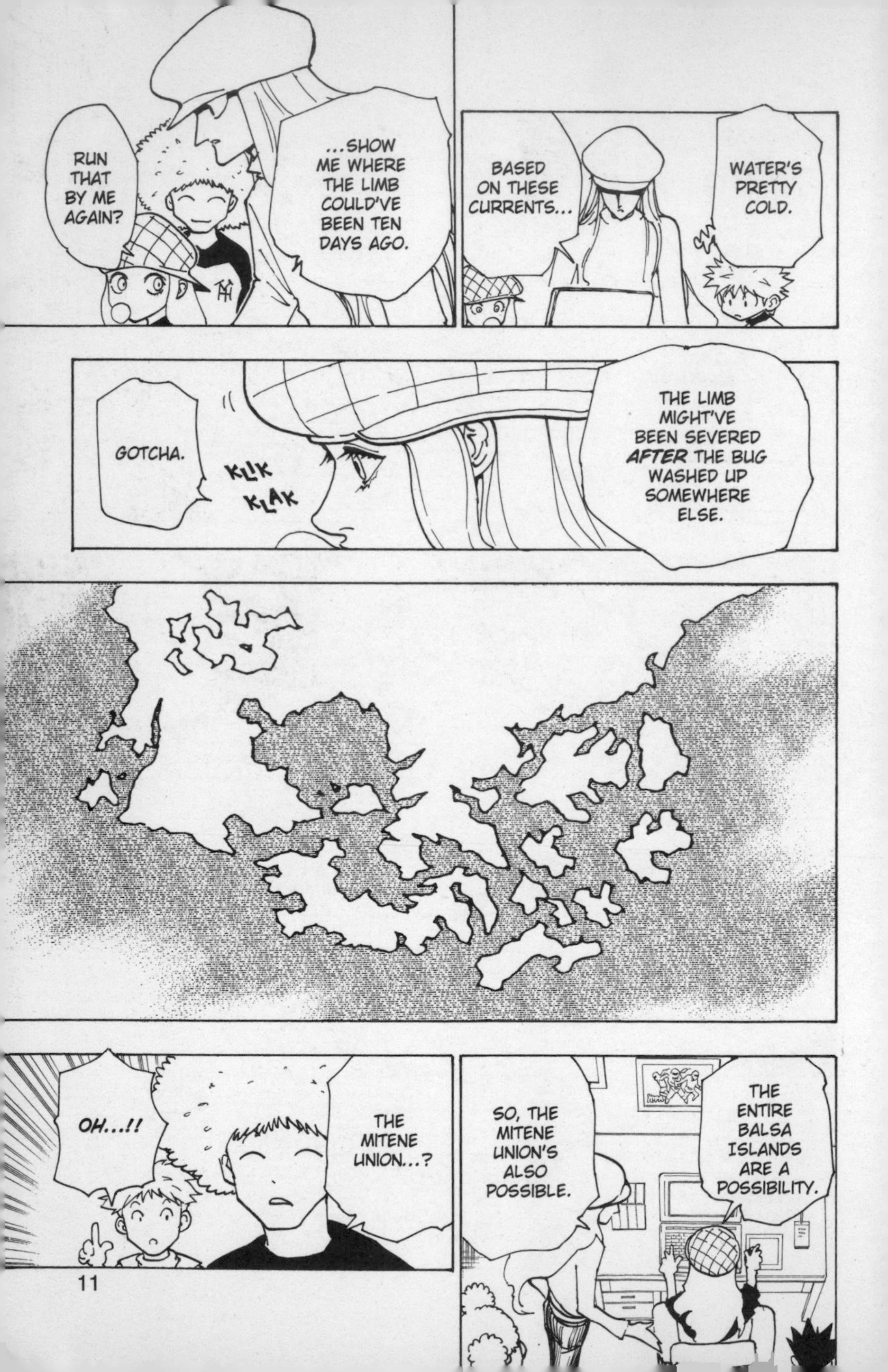
WATER'S PRETTY COLD.
BASED ON THESE CURRENTS...
...SHOW ME WHERE THE LIMB COULD'VE BEEN TEN DAYS AGO.
RUN THAT BY ME AGAIN?
THE LIMB MIGHT'VE BEEN SEVERED AFTER THE BUG WASHED UP SOMEWHERE ELSE.
KLIK KLAK
GOTCHA.
THE ENTIRE BALSA ISLANDS ARE A POSSIBILITY.
SO, THE MITENE UNION'S ALSO POSSIBLE.
THE MITENE UNION...?
OH...!!

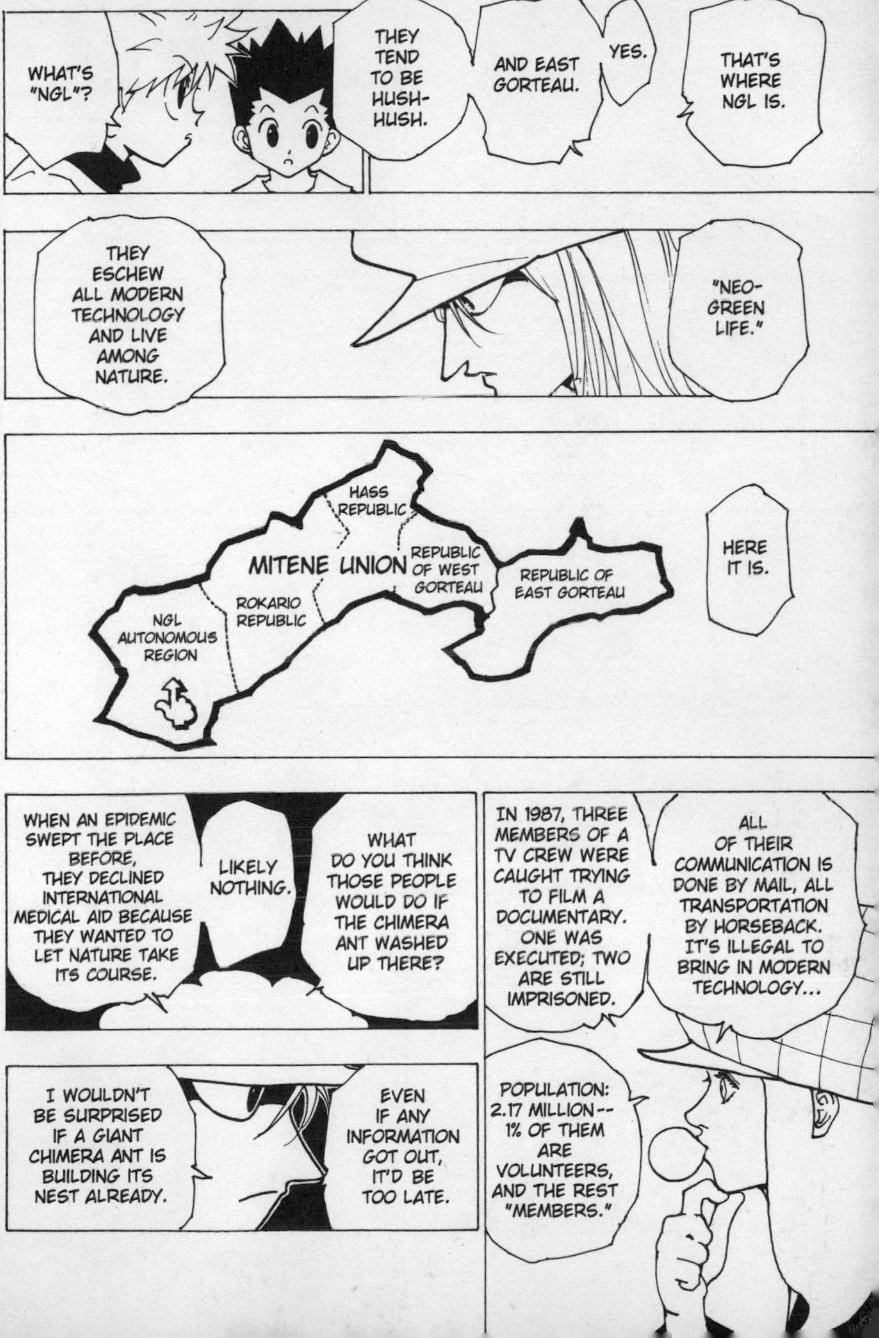
THAT'S WHERE NGL IS.
YES.
AND EAST GORTEAU.
THEY TEND TO BE HUSH-HUSH.
WHAT'S "NGL"?
"NEO-GREEN LIFE."
THEY ESCHEW ALL MODERN TECHNOLOGY AND LIVE AMONG NATURE.
HERE IT IS.
HASS REPUBLIC
MITENE UNION
REPUBLIC OF WEST GORTEAU
REPUBLIC OF EAST GORTEAU
ROKARIO REPUBLIC
NGL AUTONOMOUS REGION
ALL OF THEIR COMMUNICATION IS DONE BY MAIL, ALL TRANSPORTATION BY HORSEBACK. IT'S ILLEGAL TO BRING IN MODERN TECHNOLOGY...
IN 1987, THREE MEMBERS OF A TV CREW WERE CAUGHT TRYING TO FILM A DOCUMENTARY. ONE WAS EXECUTED; TWO ARE STILL IMPRISONED.
POPULATION: 2.17 MILLION-- 1% OF THEM ARE VOLUNTEERS, AND THE REST "MEMBERS."
WHAT DO YOU THINK THOSE PEOPLE WOULD DO IF THE CHIMERA ANT WASHED UP THERE?
LIKELY NOTHING.
WHEN AN EPIDEMIC SWEPT THE PLACE BEFORE, THEY DECLINED INTERNATIONAL MEDICAL AID BECAUSE THEY WANTED TO LET NATURE TAKE ITS COURSE.
EVEN IF ANY INFORMATION GOT OUT, IT'D BE TOO LATE.
I WOULDN'T BE SURPRISED IF A GIANT CHIMERA ANT IS BUILDING ITS NEST ALREADY.

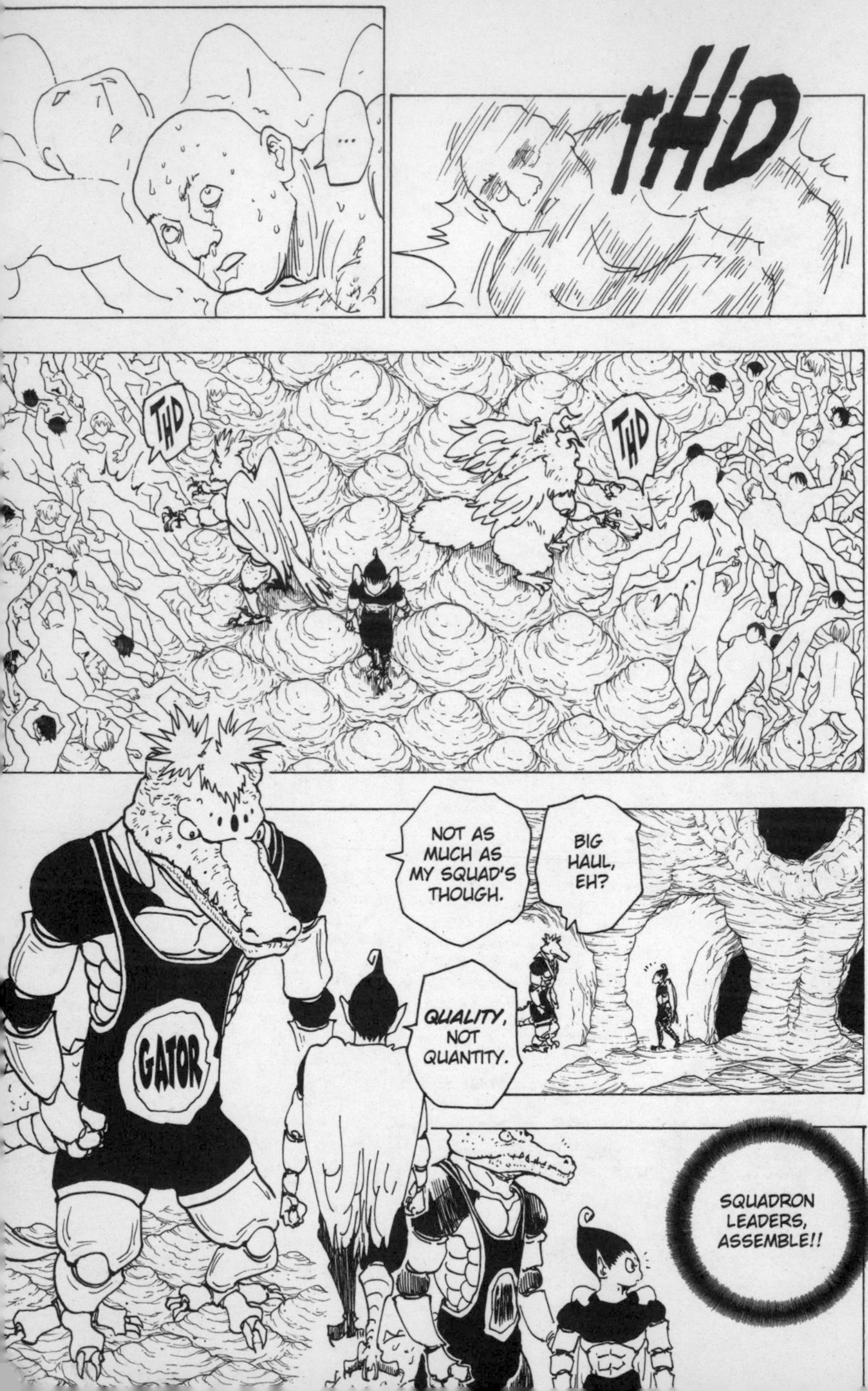
THD
...
THD
THD
BIG HAUL, EH?
NOT AS MUCH AS MY SQUAD'S THOUGH.
QUALITY, NOT QUANTITY.
GATOR
SQUADRON LEADERS, ASSEMBLE!!

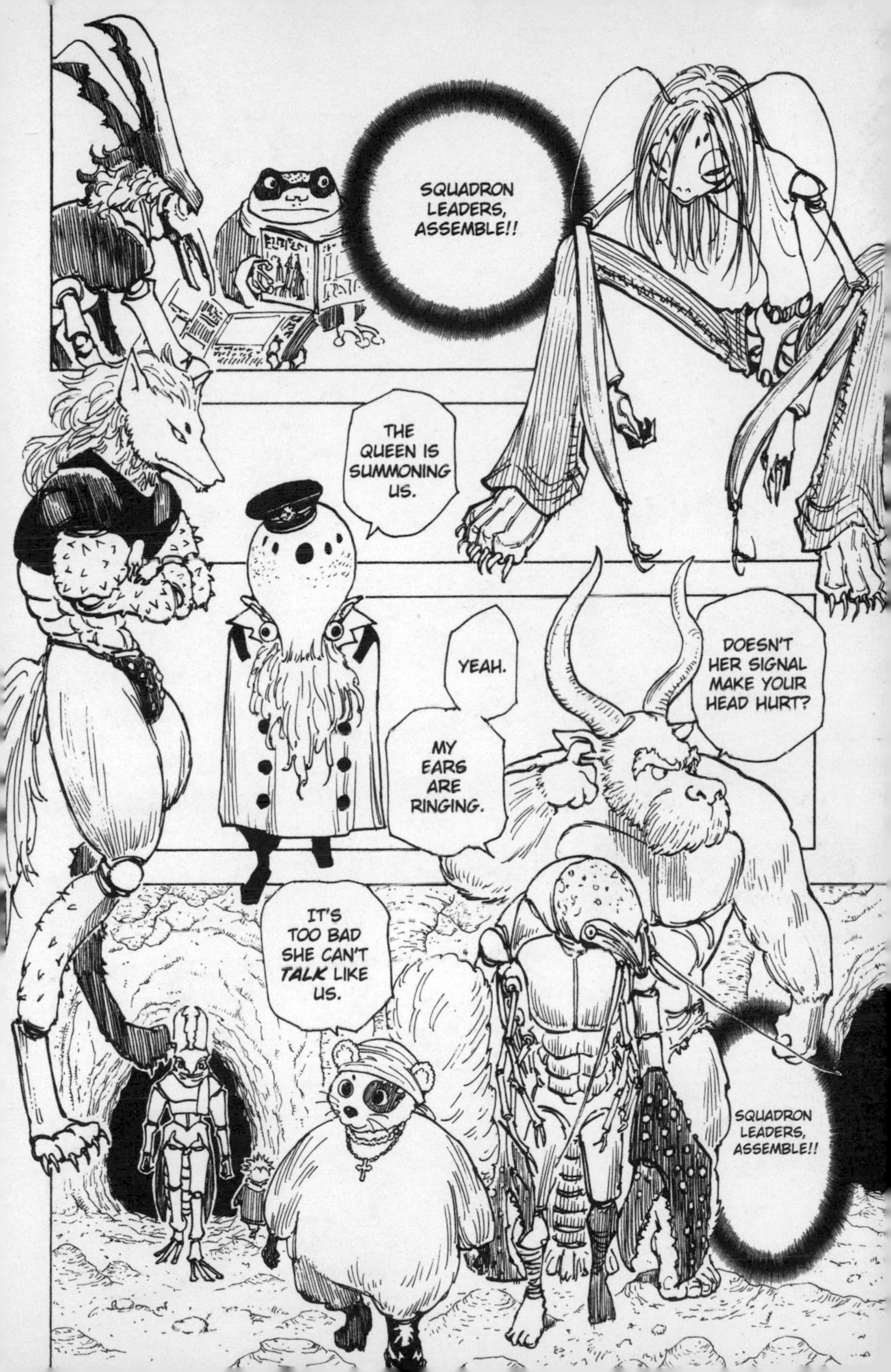
SQUADRON LEADERS, ASSEMBLE!!
THE QUEEN IS SUMMONING US.
DOESN'T HER SIGNAL MAKE YOUR HEAD HURT?
YEAH.
MY EARS ARE RINGING.
IT'S TOO BAD SHE CAN'T *TALK* LIKE US.
SQUADRON LEADERS, ASSEMBLE!!

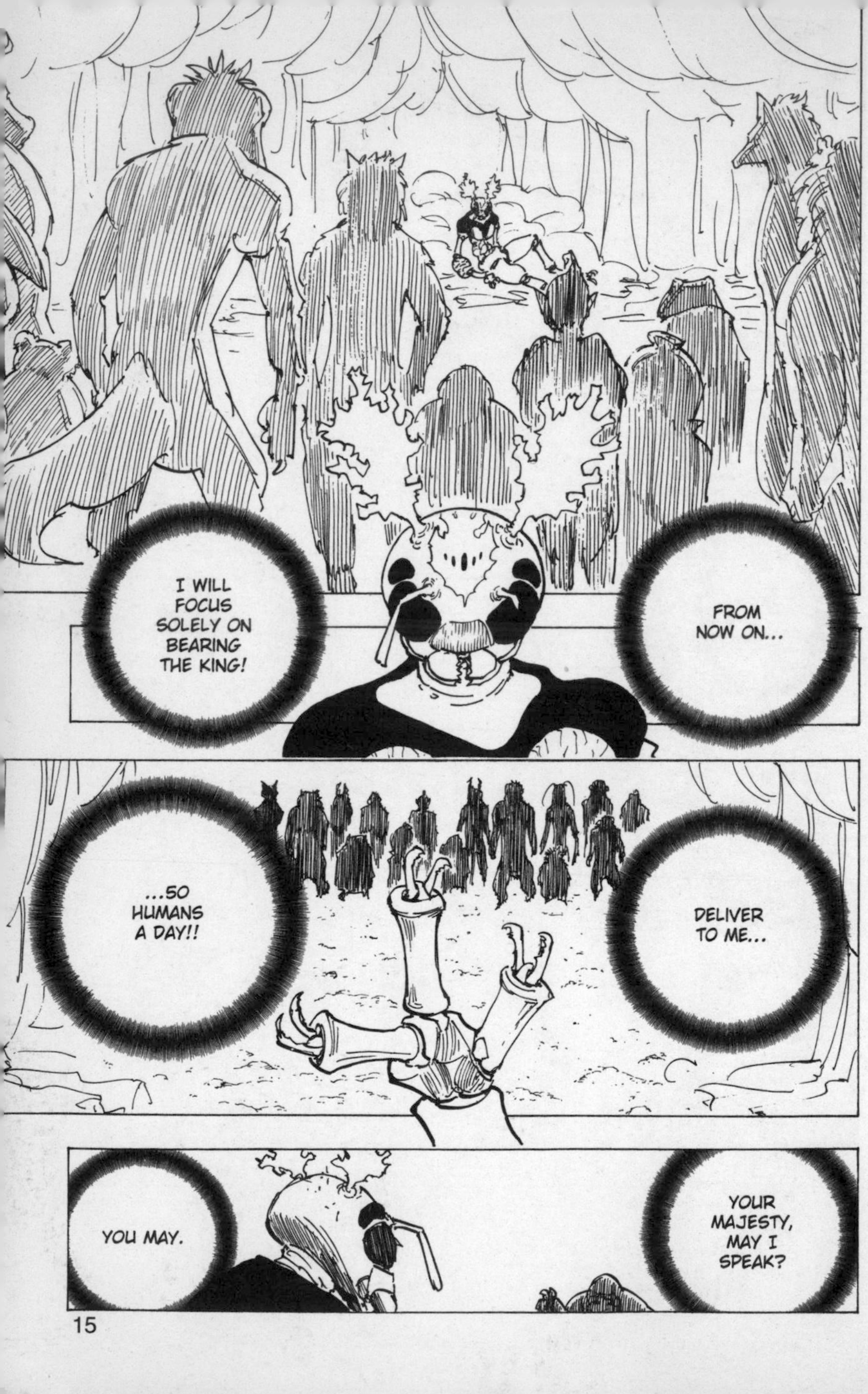
FROM NOW ON...
I WILL FOCUS SOLELY ON BEARING THE KING!
DELIVER TO ME...
...50 HUMANS A DAY!!
YOUR MAJESTY, MAY I SPEAK?
YOU MAY.

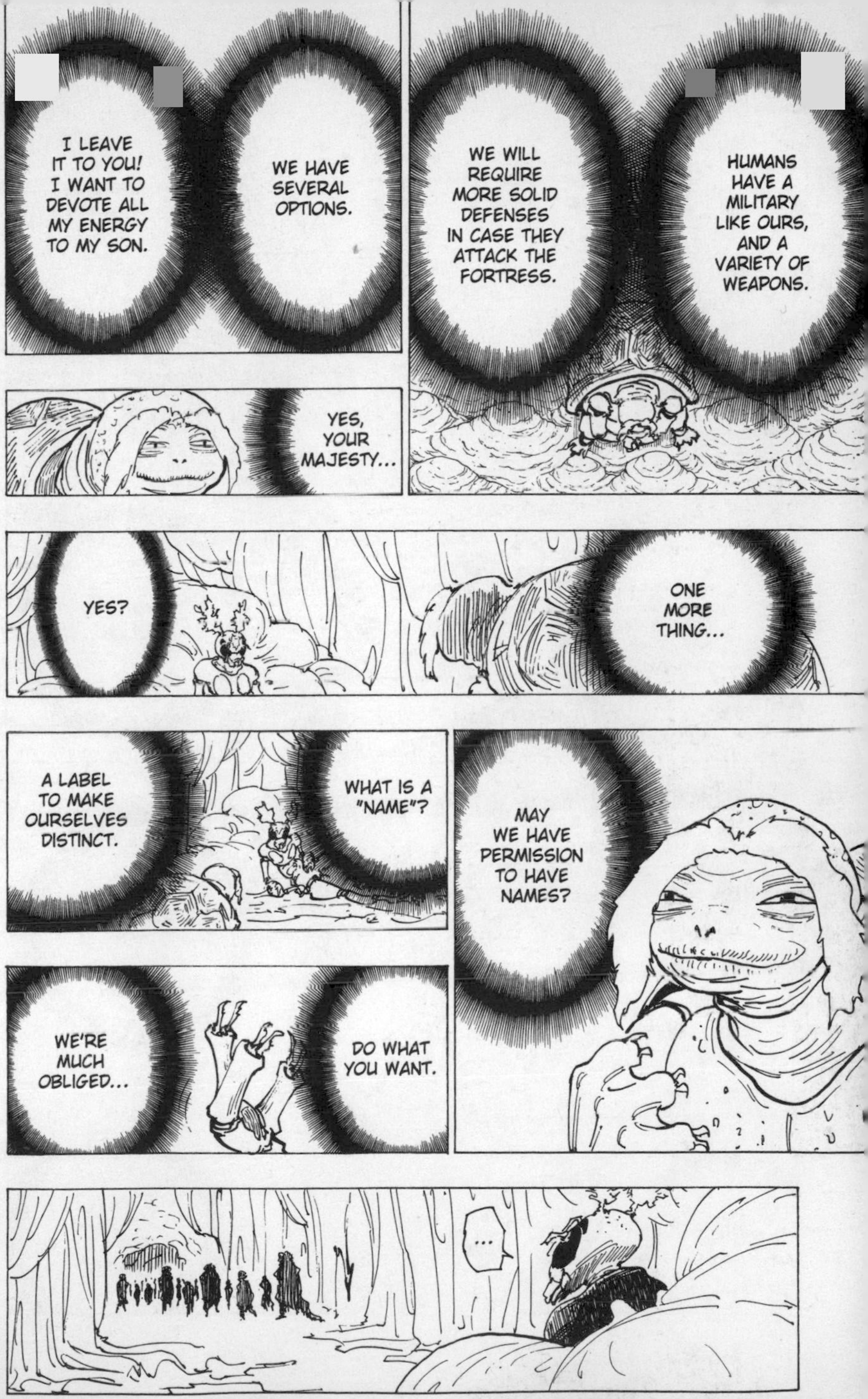
HUMANS HAVE A MILITARY LIKE OURS, AND A VARIETY OF WEAPONS.
WE WILL REQUIRE MORE SOLID DEFENSES IN CASE THEY ATTACK THE FORTRESS.
WE HAVE SEVERAL OPTIONS.
I LEAVE IT TO YOU! I WANT TO DEVOTE ALL MY ENERGY TO MY SON.
YES, YOUR MAJESTY...
ONE MORE THING...
YES?
MAY WE HAVE PERMISSION TO HAVE NAMES?
WHAT IS A "NAME"?
A LABEL TO MAKE OURSELVES DISTINCT.
DO WHAT YOU WANT.
WE'RE MUCH OBLIGED...
...

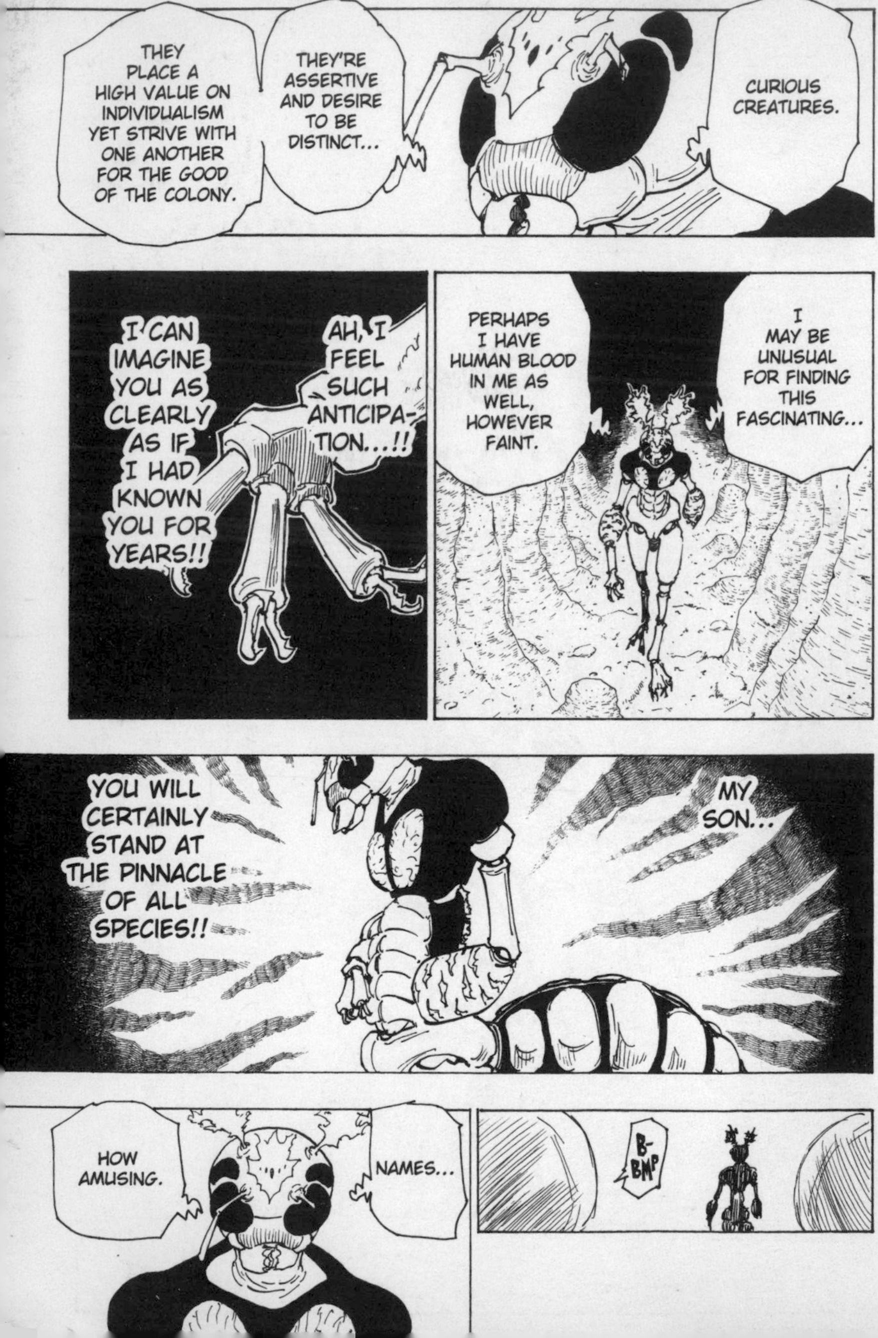
CURIOUS CREATURES.
THEY'RE ASSERTIVE AND DESIRE TO BE DISTINCT...
THEY PLACE A HIGH VALUE ON INDIVIDUALISM YET STRIVE WITH ONE ANOTHER FOR THE GOOD OF THE COLONY.
I MAY BE UNUSUAL FOR FINDING THIS FASCINATING...
PERHAPS I HAVE HUMAN BLOOD IN ME AS WELL, HOWEVER FAINT.
AH, I FEEL SUCH ANTICIPA-TION...!!
I CAN IMAGINE YOU AS CLEARLY AS IF I HAD KNOWN YOU FOR YEARS!!
MY SON...
YOU WILL CERTAINLY STAND AT THE PINNACLE OF ALL SPECIES!!
B-BMP
NAMES...
HOW AMUSING.

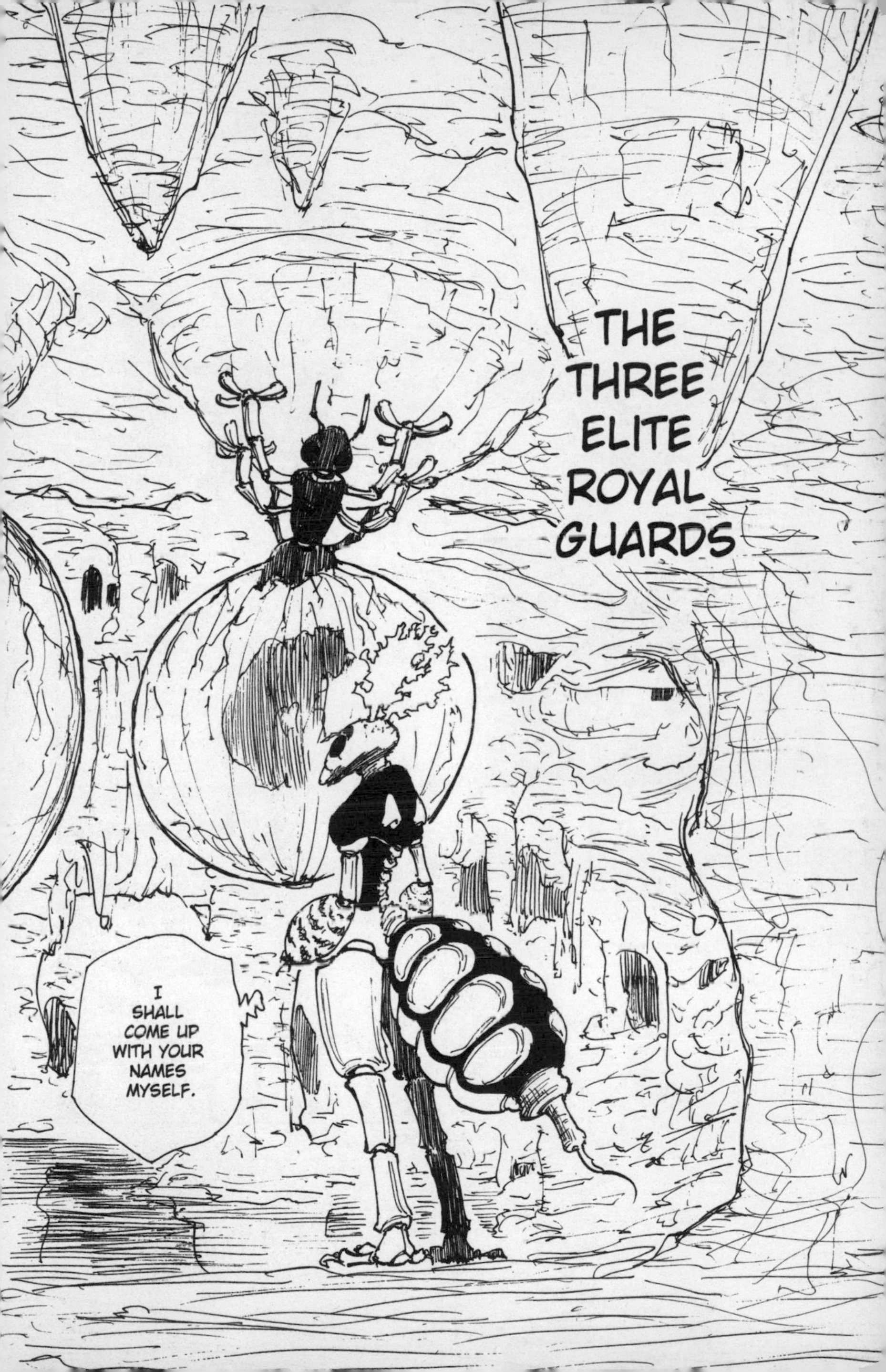
THE THREE ELITE ROYAL GUARDS
I SHALL COME UP WITH YOUR NAMES MYSELF.

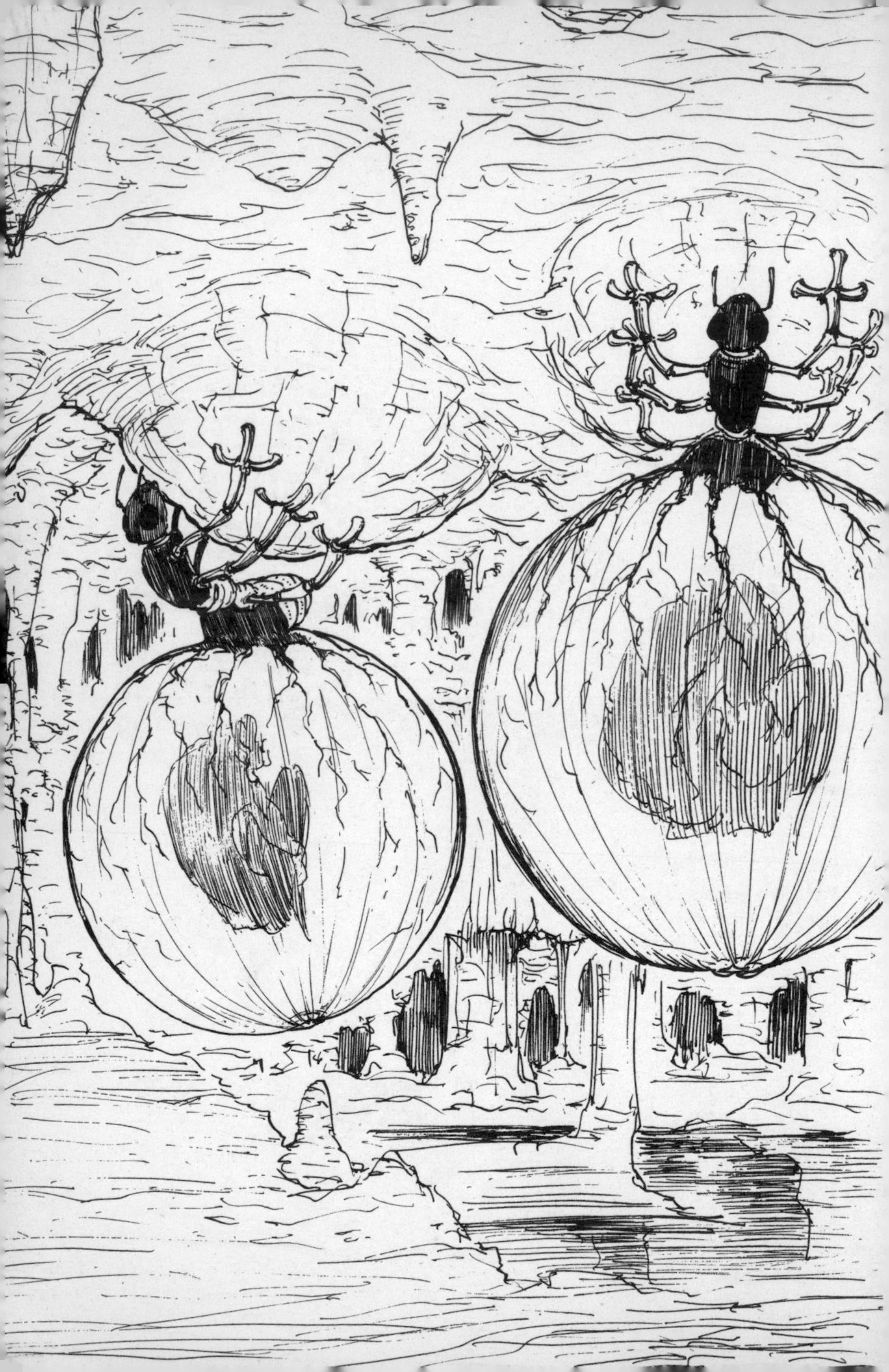

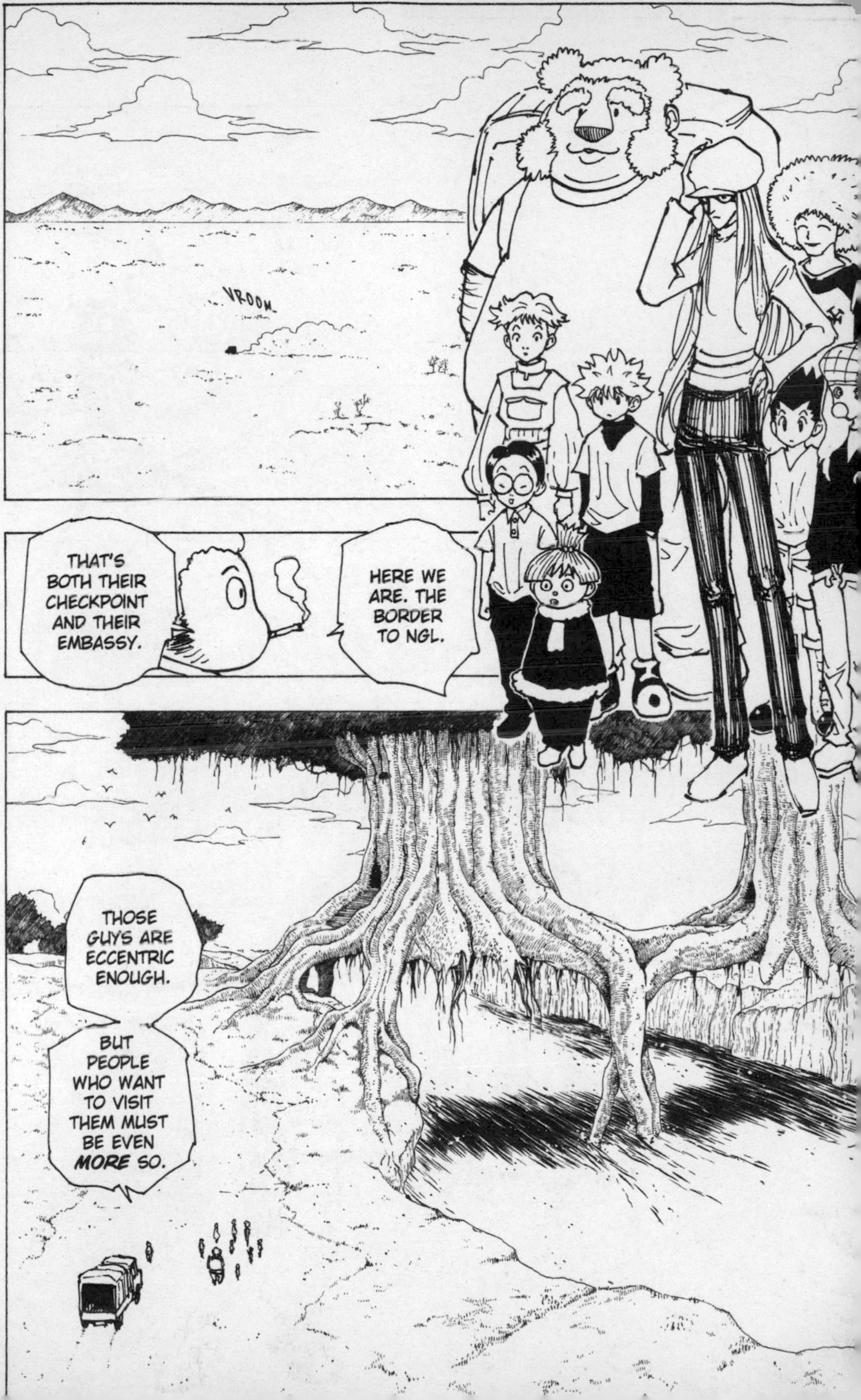
VROOM
HERE WE ARE. THE BORDER TO NGL.
THAT'S BOTH THEIR CHECKPOINT AND THEIR EMBASSY.
THOSE GUYS ARE ECCENTRIC ENOUGH.
BUT PEOPLE WHO WANT TO VISIT THEM MUST BE EVEN MORE SO.

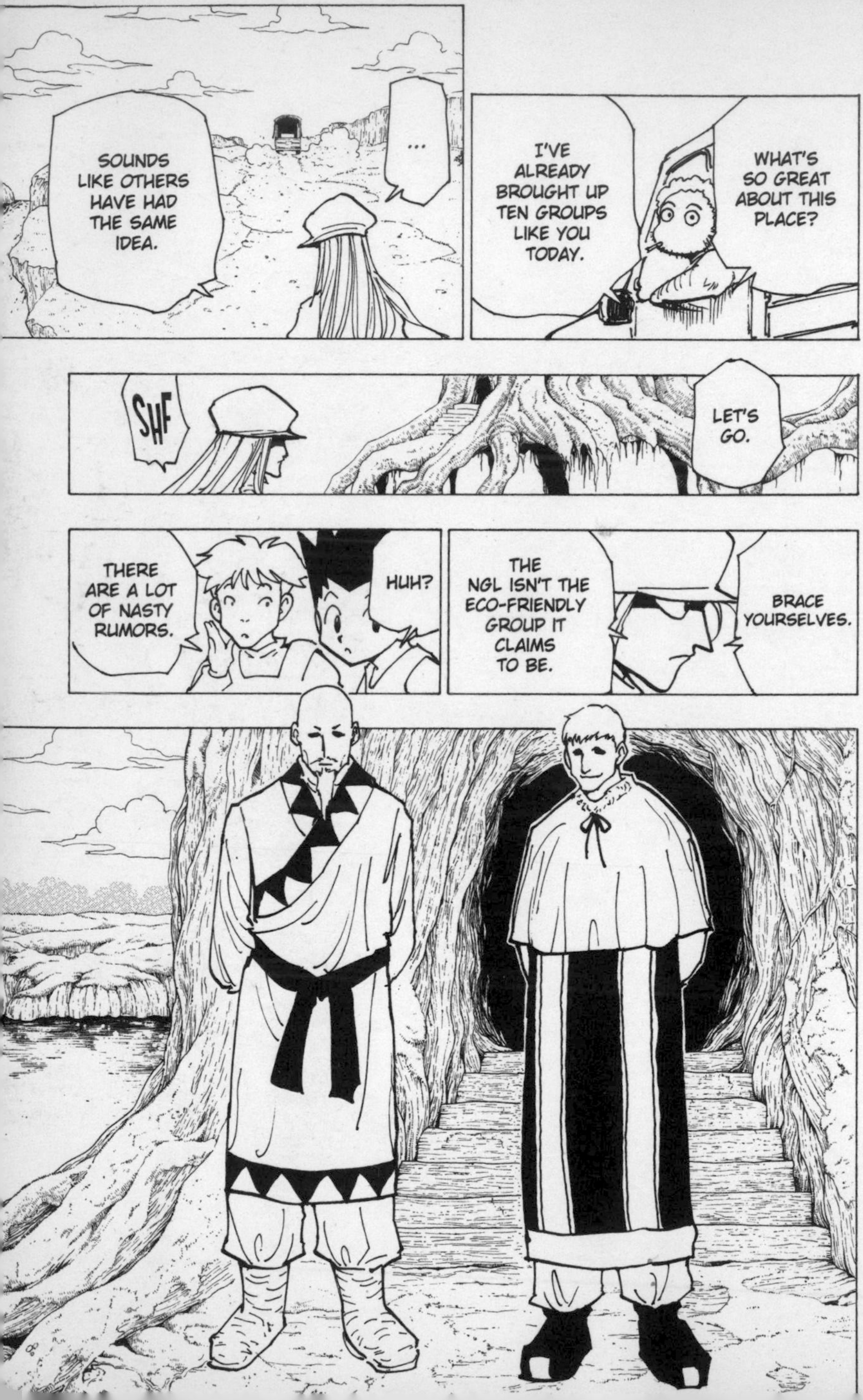
WHAT'S SO GREAT ABOUT THIS PLACE?
I'VE ALREADY BROUGHT UP TEN GROUPS LIKE YOU TODAY.
...
SOUNDS LIKE OTHERS HAVE HAD THE SAME IDEA.
LET'S GO.
SHF
BRACE YOURSELVES.
THE NGL ISN'T THE ECO-FRIENDLY GROUP IT CLAIMS TO BE.
HUH?
THERE ARE A LOT OF NASTY RUMORS.

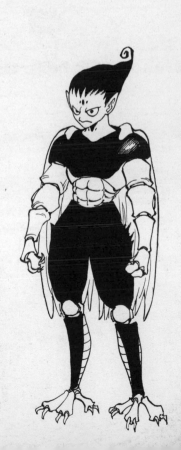

Chapter 189: Infiltration

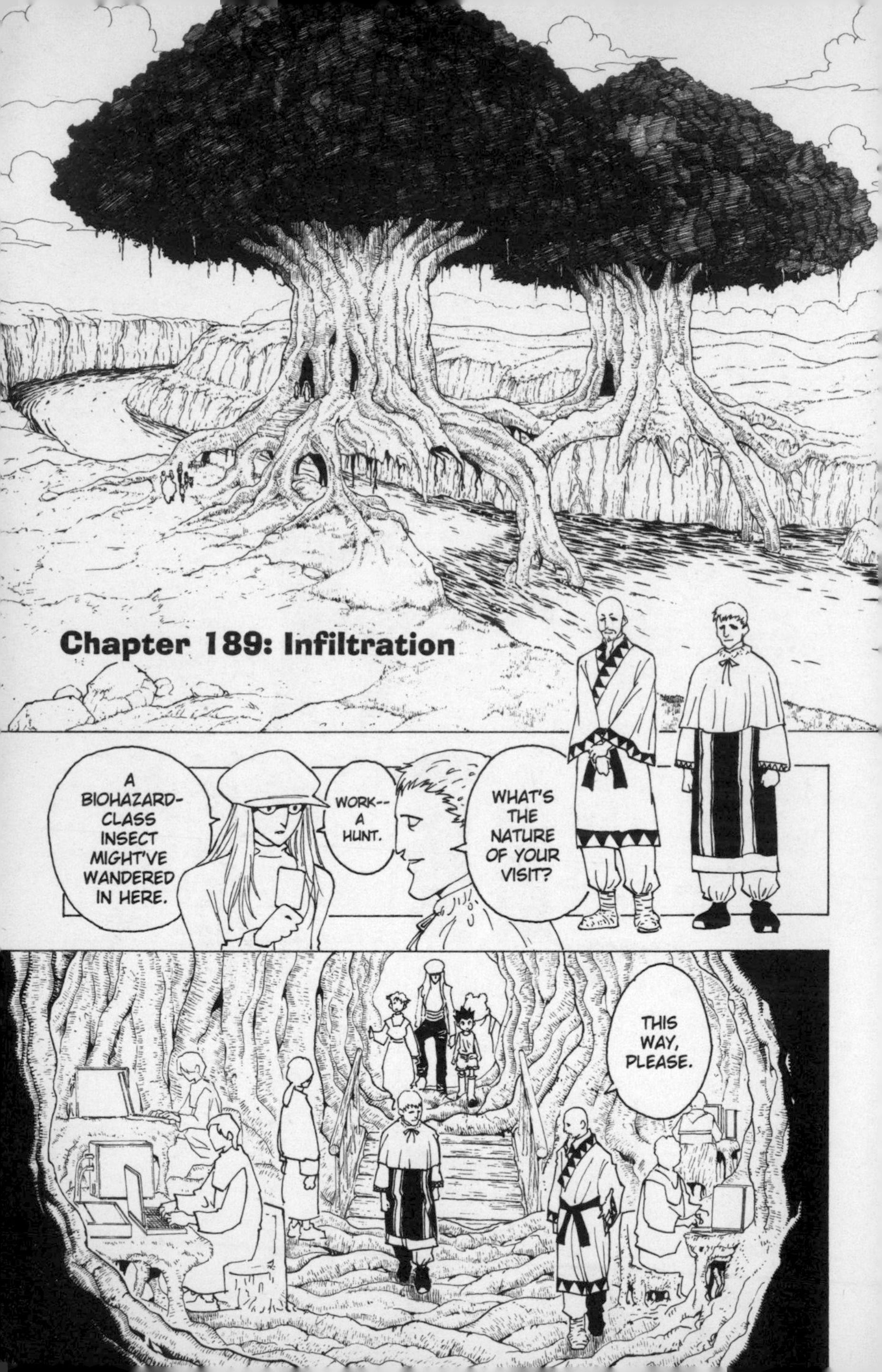
WHAT'S THE NATURE OF YOUR VISIT?
WORK-- A HUNT.
A BIOHAZARD-CLASS INSECT MIGHT'VE WANDERED IN HERE.
THIS WAY, PLEASE.

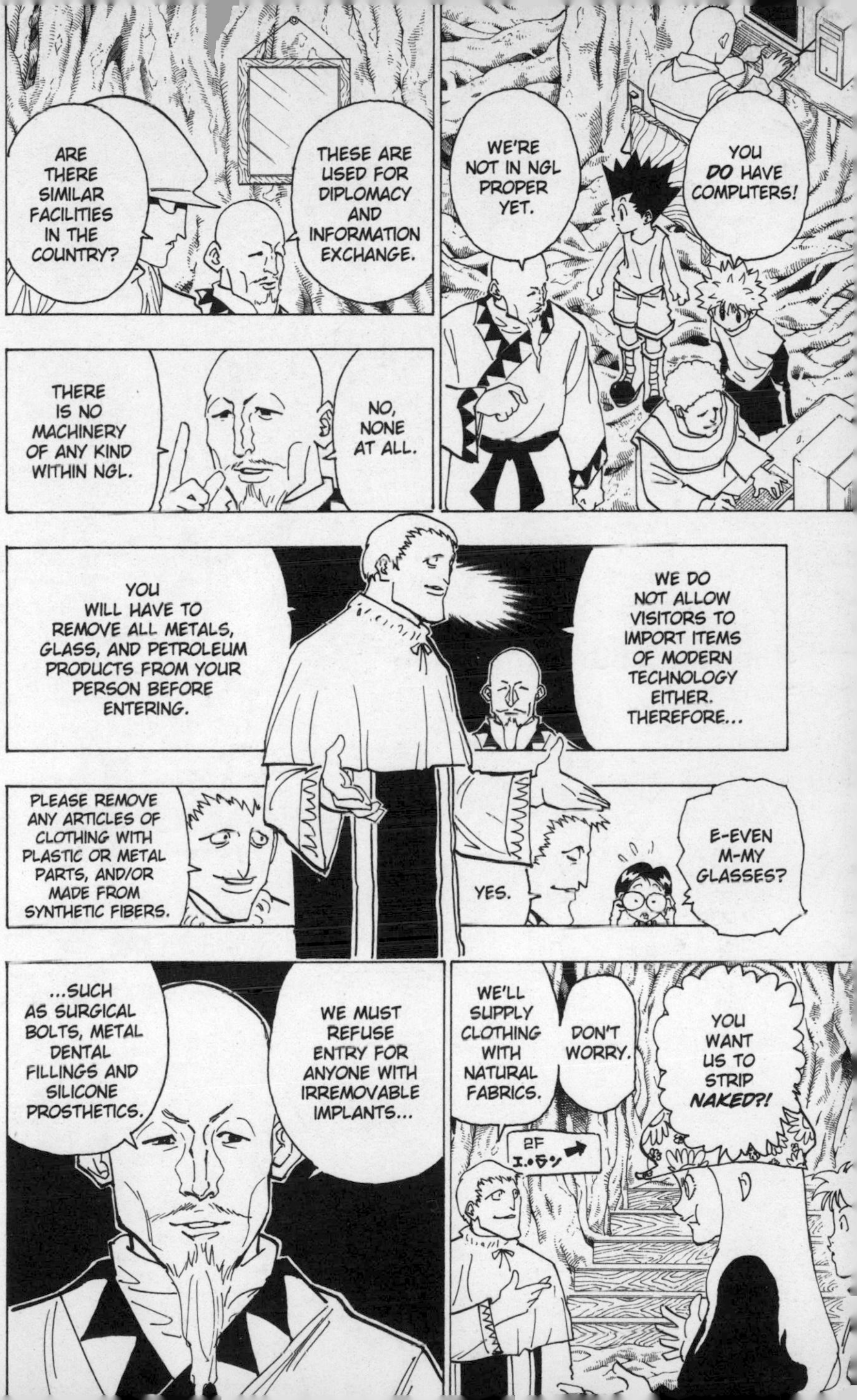
YOU DO HAVE COMPUTERS!
WE'RE NOT IN NGL PROPER YET.
THESE ARE USED FOR DIPLOMACY AND INFORMATION EXCHANGE.
ARE THERE SIMILAR FACILITIES IN THE COUNTRY?
NO, NONE AT ALL.
THERE IS NO MACHINERY OF ANY KIND WITHIN NGL.
WE DO NOT ALLOW VISITORS TO IMPORT ITEMS OF MODERN TECHNOLOGY EITHER. THEREFORE...
YOU WILL HAVE TO REMOVE ALL METALS, GLASS, AND PETROLEUM PRODUCTS FROM YOUR PERSON BEFORE ENTERING.
E-EVEN M-MY GLASSES?
YES.
PLEASE REMOVE ANY ARTICLES OF CLOTHING WITH PLASTIC OR METAL PARTS, AND/OR MADE FROM SYNTHETIC FIBERS.
YOU WANT US TO STRIP NAKED?!
DON'T WORRY.
WE'LL SUPPLY CLOTHING WITH NATURAL FABRICS.
2F
WE MUST REFUSE ENTRY FOR ANYONE WITH IRREMOVABLE IMPLANTS...
...SUCH AS SURGICAL BOLTS, METAL DENTAL FILLINGS AND SILICONE PROSTHETICS.

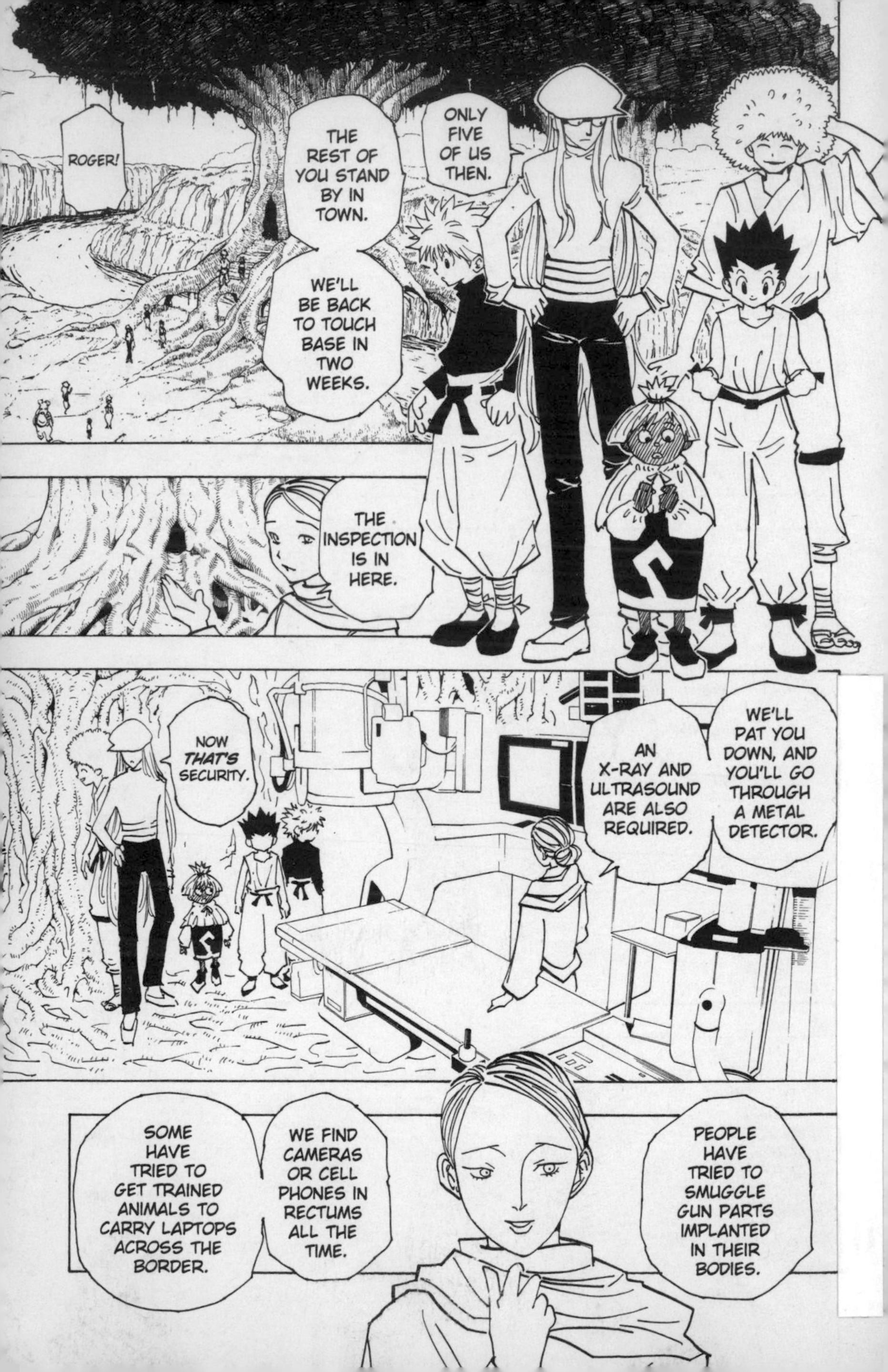
ONLY FIVE OF US THEN.
THE REST OF YOU STAND BY IN TOWN.
WE'LL BE BACK TO TOUCH BASE IN TWO WEEKS.
ROGER!
THE INSPECTION IS IN HERE.
WE'LL PAT YOU DOWN, AND YOU'LL GO THROUGH A METAL DETECTOR.
AN X-RAY AND ULTRASOUND ARE ALSO REQUIRED.
NOW *THAT'S* SECURITY.
PEOPLE HAVE TRIED TO SMUGGLE GUN PARTS IMPLANTED IN THEIR BODIES.
WE FIND CAMERAS OR CELL PHONES IN RECTUMS ALL THE TIME.
SOME HAVE TRIED TO GET TRAINED ANIMALS TO CARRY LAPTOPS ACROSS THE BORDER.

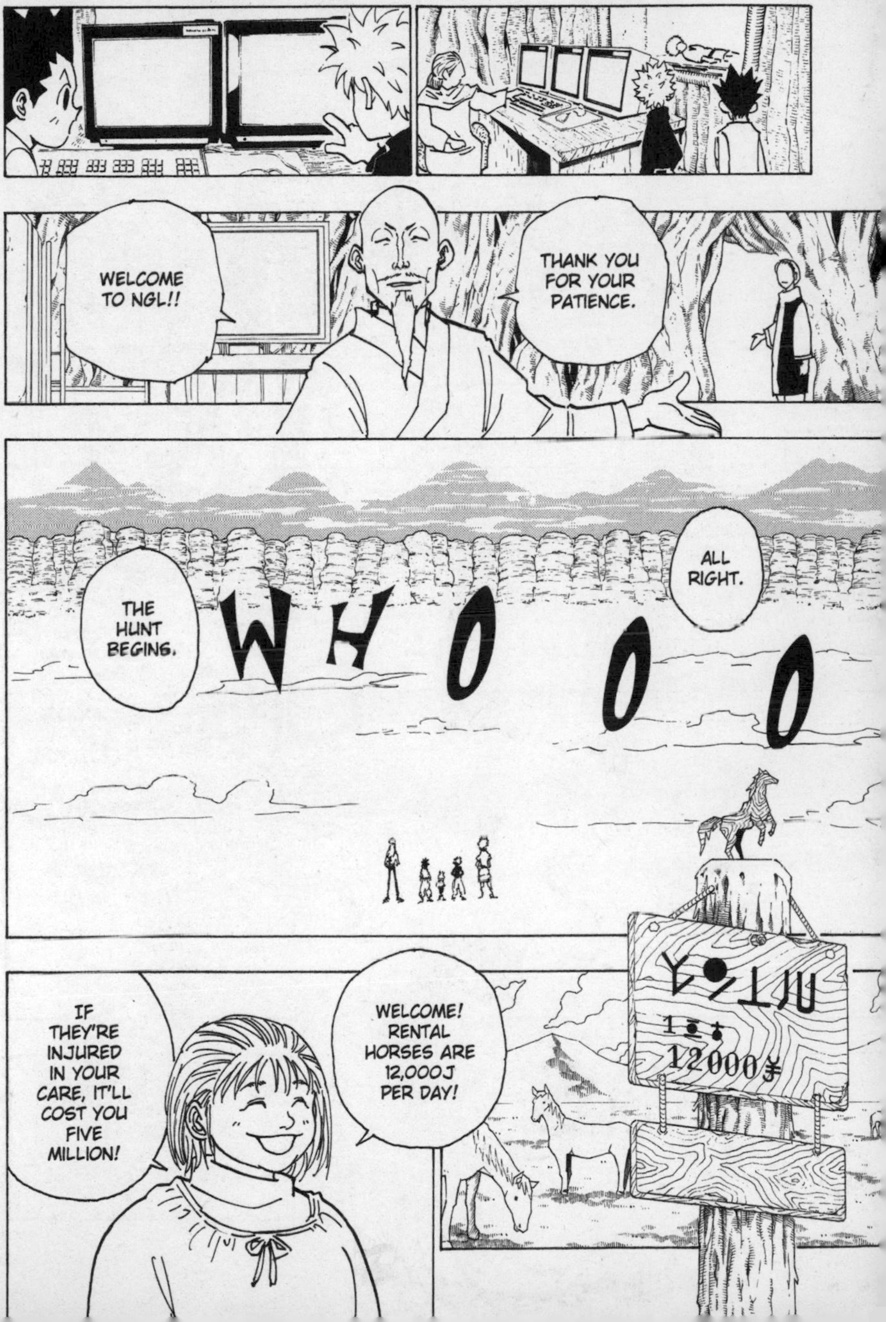
THANK YOU FOR YOUR PATIENCE.
WELCOME TO NGL!!
ALL RIGHT.
WHOOOO
THE HUNT BEGINS.
12000
WELCOME! RENTAL HORSES ARE 12,000J PER DAY!
IF THEY'RE INJURED IN YOUR CARE, IT'LL COST YOU FIVE MILLION!

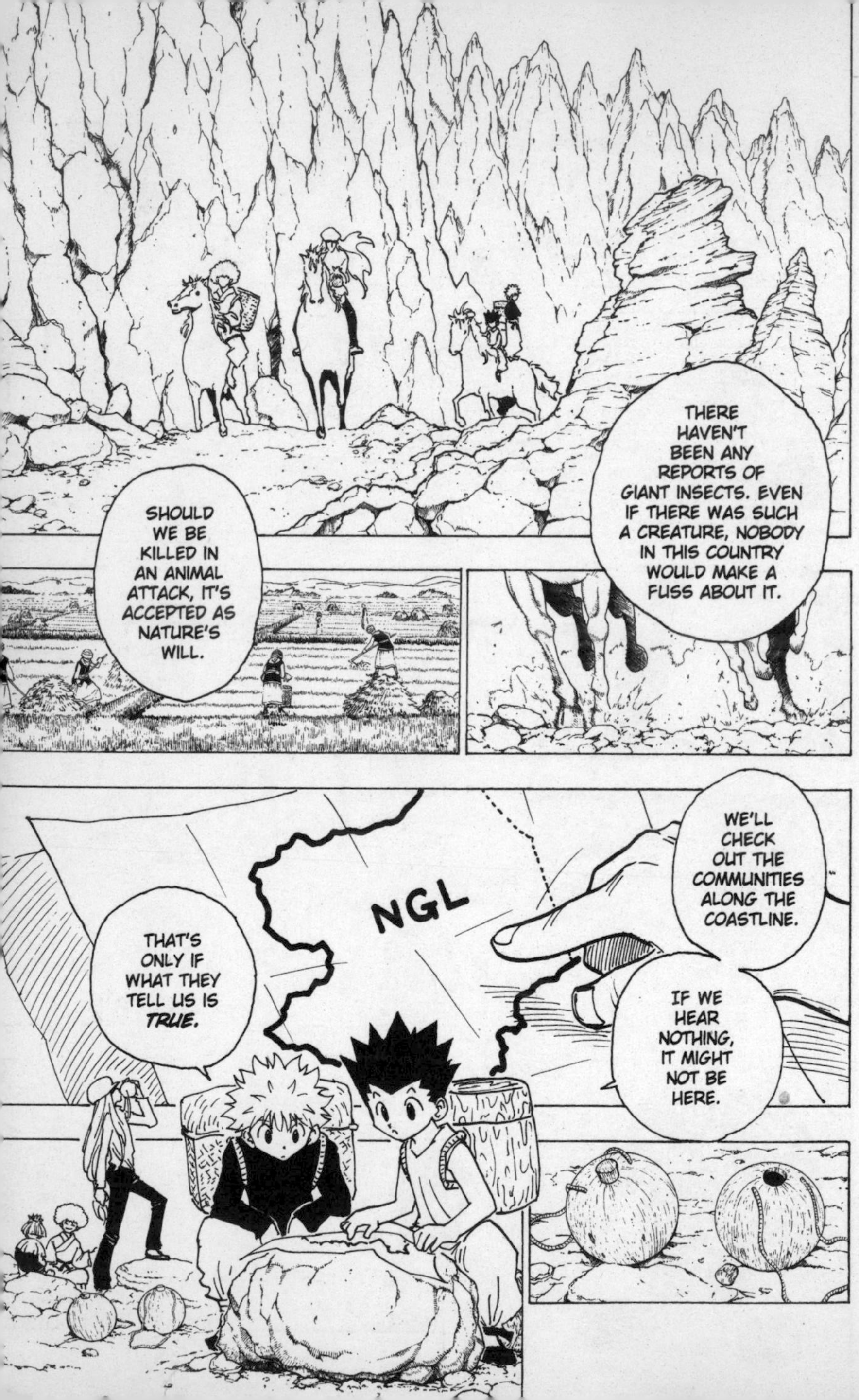
THERE HAVEN'T BEEN ANY REPORTS OF GIANT INSECTS. EVEN IF THERE WAS SUCH A CREATURE, NOBODY IN THIS COUNTRY WOULD MAKE A FUSS ABOUT IT.
SHOULD WE BE KILLED IN AN ANIMAL ATTACK, IT'S ACCEPTED AS NATURE'S WILL.
WE'LL CHECK OUT THE COMMUNITIES ALONG THE COASTLINE.
IF WE HEAR NOTHING, IT MIGHT NOT BE HERE.
NGL
THAT'S ONLY IF WHAT THEY TELL US IS *TRUE*.

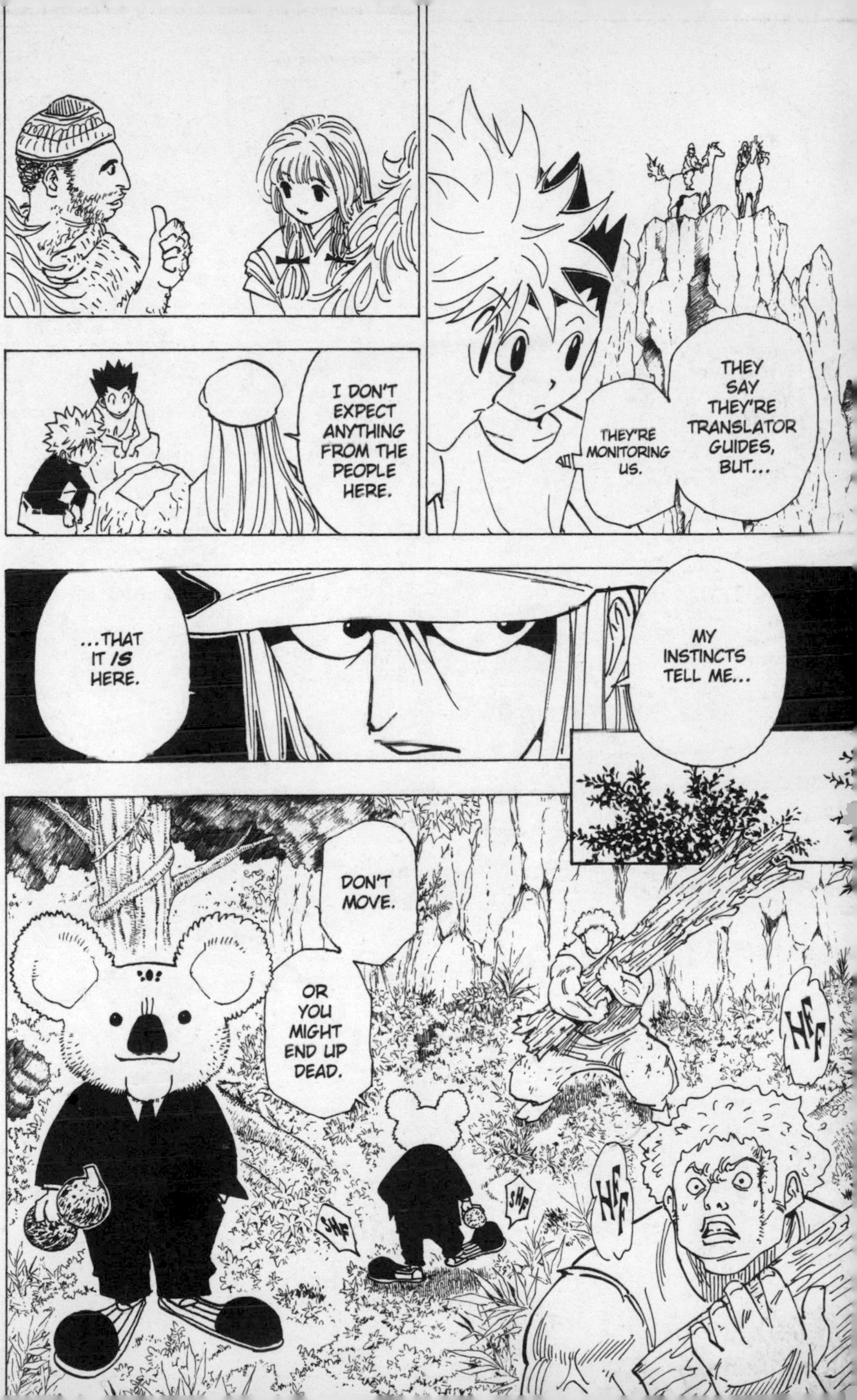
THEY SAY THEY'RE TRANSLATOR GUIDES, BUT...
THEY'RE MONITORING US.
I DON'T EXPECT ANYTHING FROM THE PEOPLE HERE.
MY INSTINCTS TELL ME...
...THAT IT *IS* HERE.
HEF
DON'T MOVE.
OR YOU MIGHT END UP DEAD.
HEF
SNF
SNF

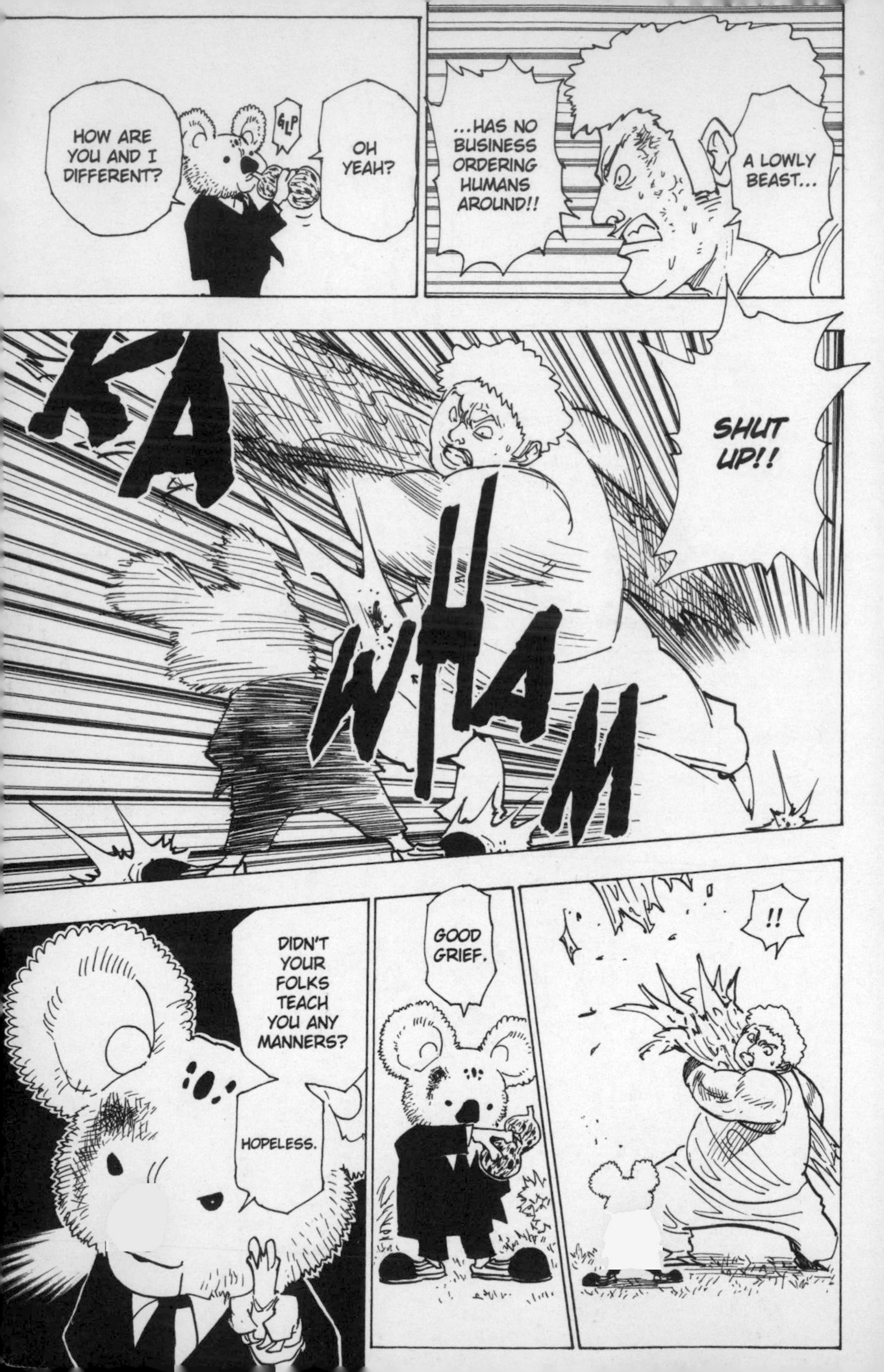
A LOWLY BEAST...
...HAS NO BUSINESS ORDERING HUMANS AROUND!!
OH YEAH?
GLP
HOW ARE YOU AND I DIFFERENT?
SHUT UP!!
WHAM
KA
!!
GOOD GRIEF.
DIDN'T YOUR FOLKS TEACH YOU ANY MANNERS?
HOPELESS.

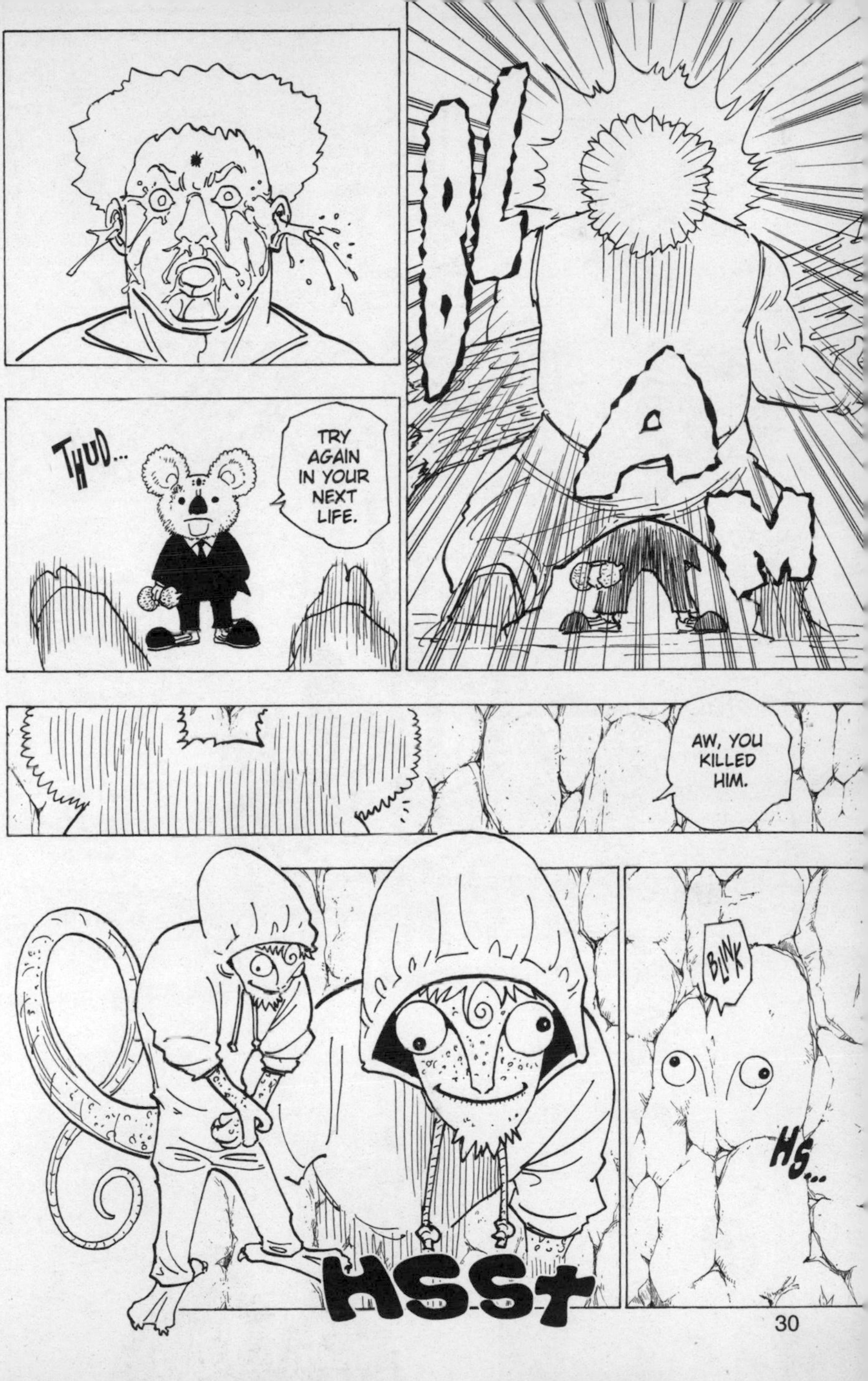
BLAM
THUD...
TRY AGAIN IN YOUR NEXT LIFE.
AW, YOU KILLED HIM.
BLINK
HS...
HSST

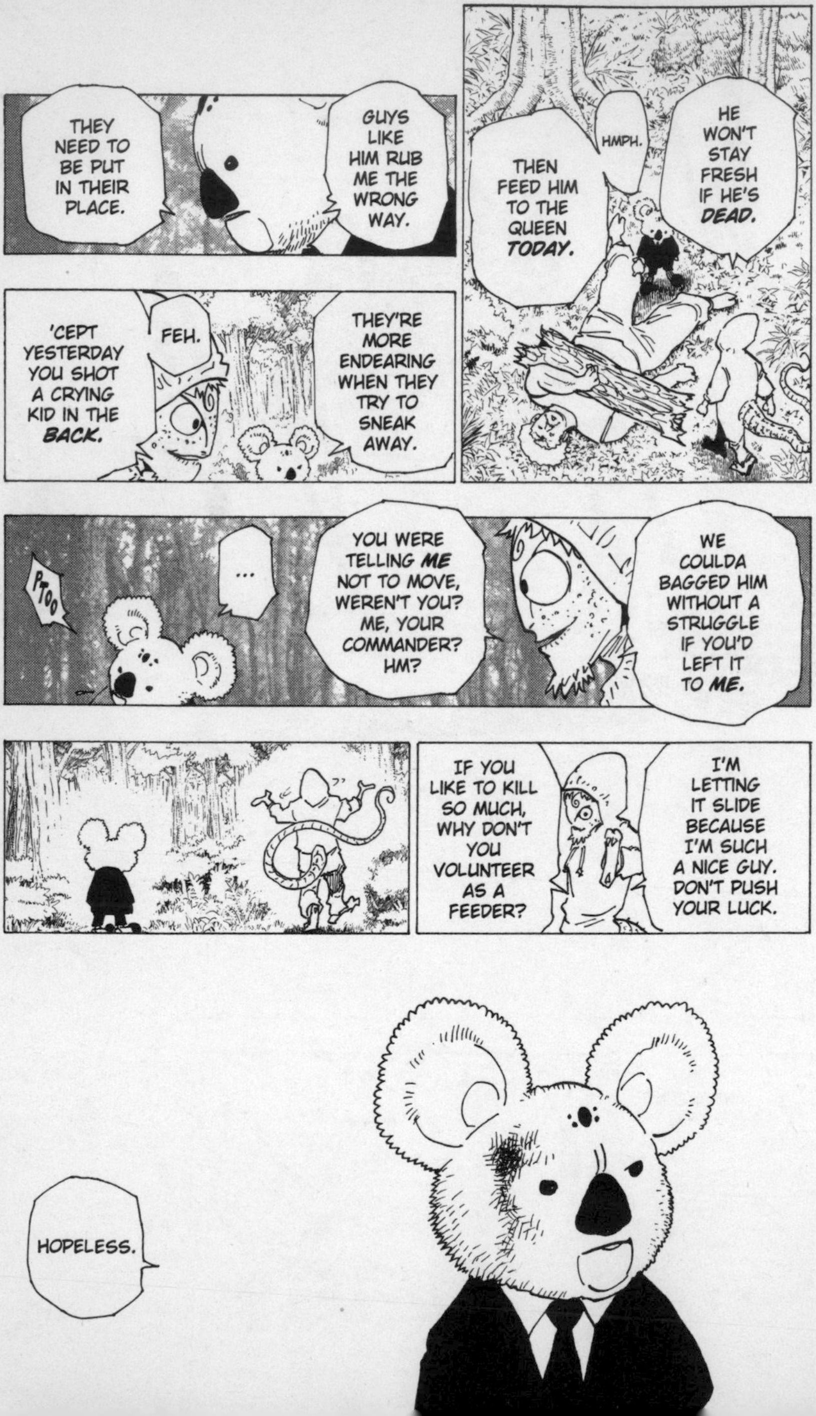
HE WON'T STAY FRESH IF HE'S DEAD.
HMPH.
THEN FEED HIM TO THE QUEEN TODAY.
GUYS LIKE HIM RUB ME THE WRONG WAY.
THEY NEED TO BE PUT IN THEIR PLACE.
THEY'RE MORE ENDEARING WHEN THEY TRY TO SNEAK AWAY.
FEH.
'CEPT YESTERDAY YOU SHOT A CRYING KID IN THE BACK.
WE COULDA BAGGED HIM WITHOUT A STRUGGLE IF YOU'D LEFT IT TO ME.
YOU WERE TELLING ME NOT TO MOVE, WEREN'T YOU? ME, YOUR COMMANDER? HM?
...
PTOO
I'M LETTING IT SLIDE BECAUSE I'M SUCH A NICE GUY. DON'T PUSH YOUR LUCK.
IF YOU LIKE TO KILL SO MUCH, WHY DON'T YOU VOLUNTEER AS A FEEDER?
HOPELESS.

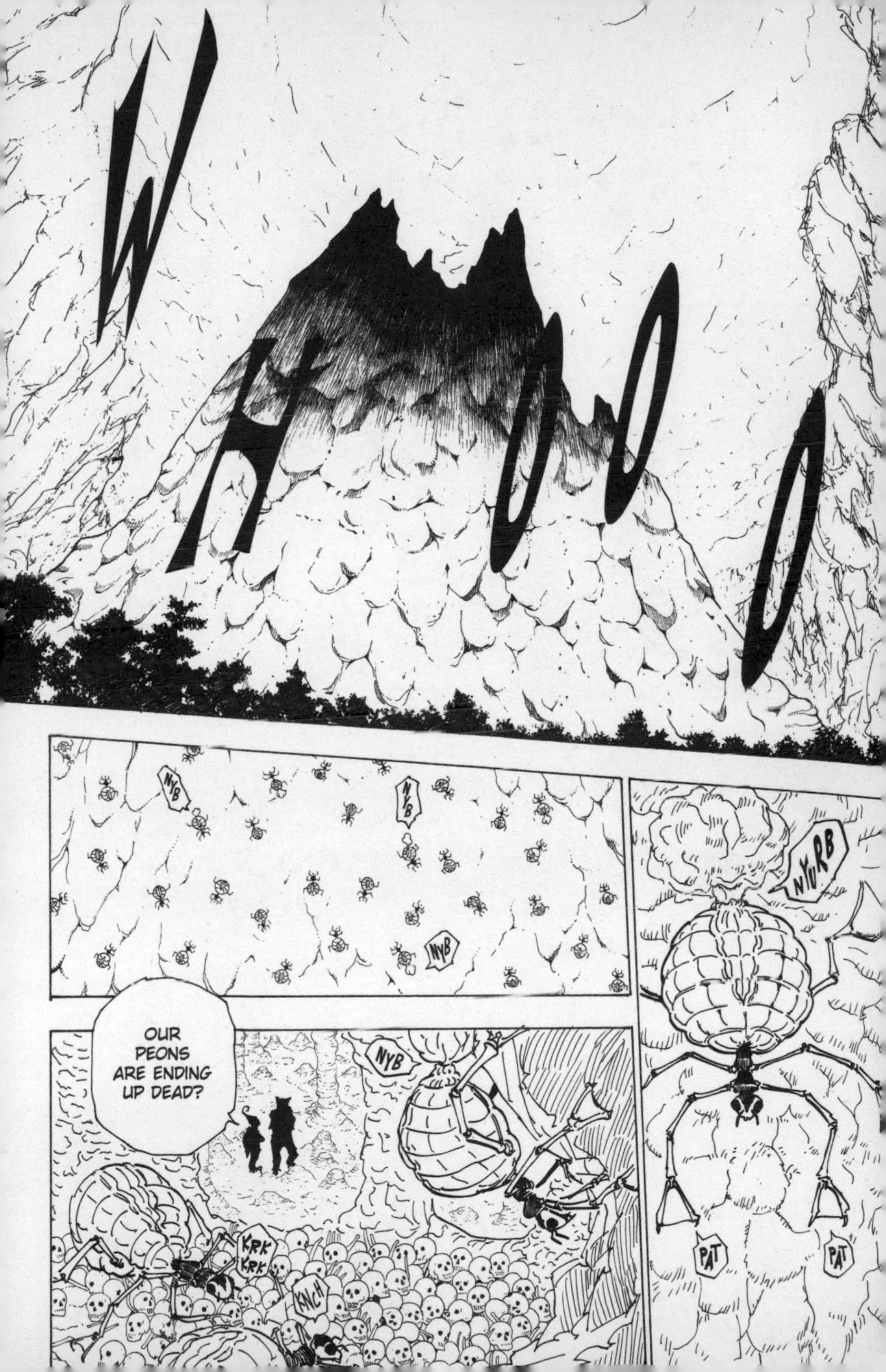
WHOOO
NYURB
PAT
PAT
NYB
NYB
NYB
NYB
OUR PEONS ARE ENDING UP DEAD?
KRK KRK
KNCH

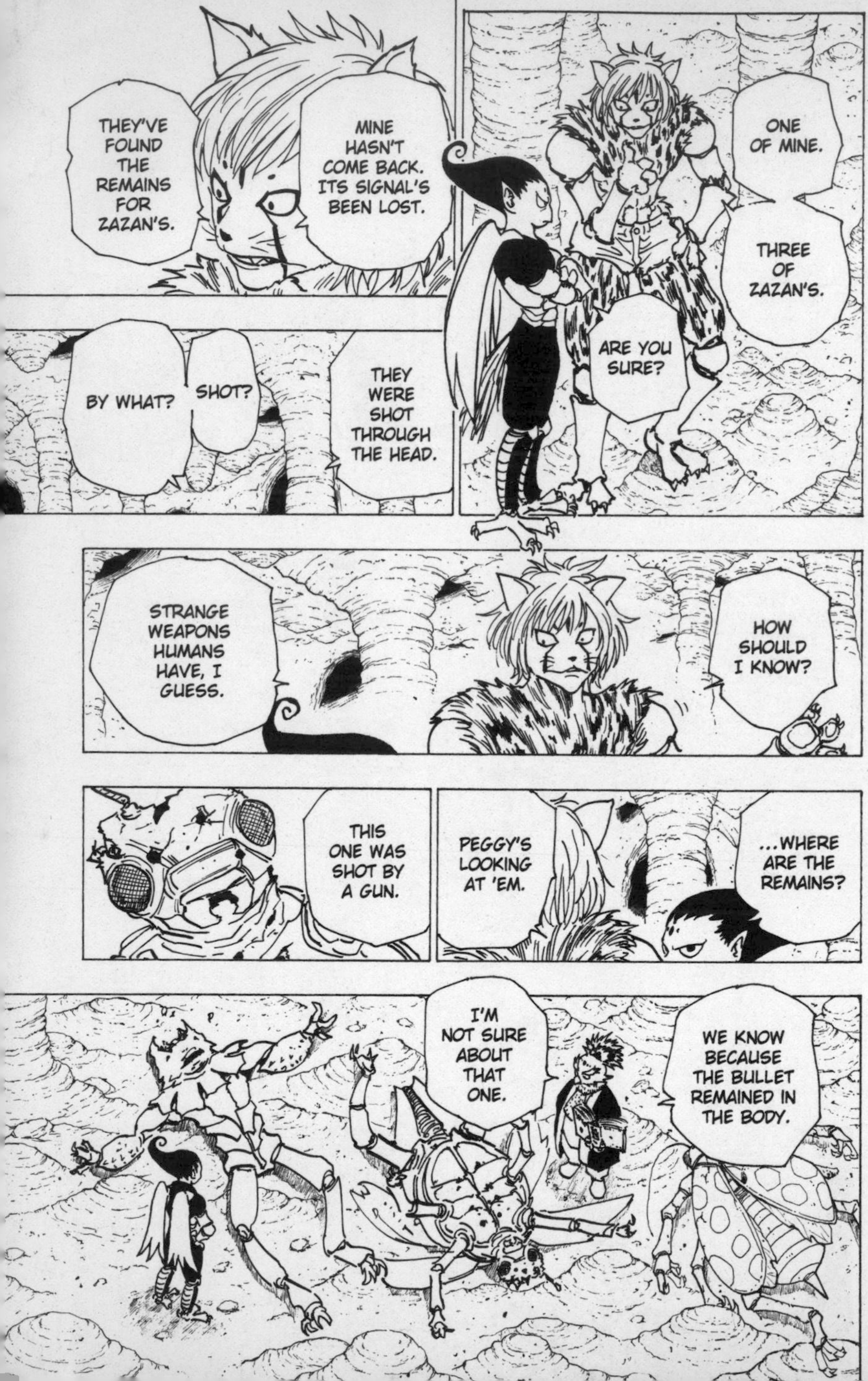
ONE OF MINE.
THREE OF ZAZAN'S.
ARE YOU SURE?
MINE HASN'T COME BACK. ITS SIGNAL'S BEEN LOST.
THEY'VE FOUND THE REMAINS FOR ZAZAN'S.
THEY WERE SHOT THROUGH THE HEAD.
SHOT?
BY WHAT?
HOW SHOULD I KNOW?
STRANGE WEAPONS HUMANS HAVE, I GUESS.
...WHERE ARE THE REMAINS?
PEGGY'S LOOKING AT 'EM.
THIS ONE WAS SHOT BY A GUN.
WE KNOW BECAUSE THE BULLET REMAINED IN THE BODY.
I'M NOT SURE ABOUT THAT ONE.

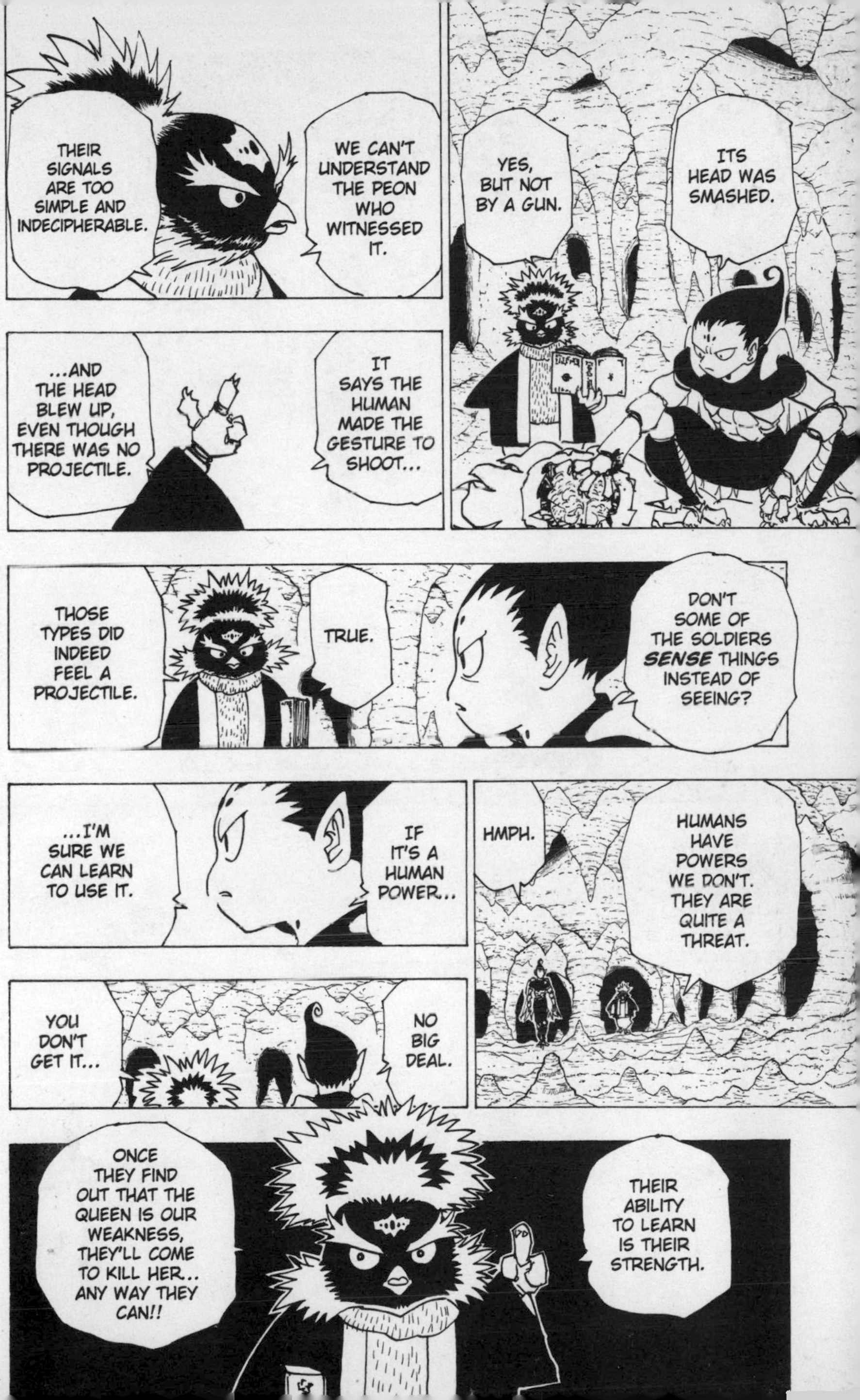
ITS HEAD WAS SMASHED.
YES, BUT NOT BY A GUN.
WE CAN'T UNDERSTAND THE PEON WHO WITNESSED IT.
THEIR SIGNALS ARE TOO SIMPLE AND INDECIPHERABLE.
IT SAYS THE HUMAN MADE THE GESTURE TO SHOOT...
...AND THE HEAD BLEW UP, EVEN THOUGH THERE WAS NO PROJECTILE.
DON'T SOME OF THE SOLDIERS **SENSE** THINGS INSTEAD OF SEEING?
TRUE.
THOSE TYPES DID INDEED FEEL A PROJECTILE.
HUMANS HAVE POWERS WE DON'T. THEY ARE QUITE A THREAT.
HMPH.
IF IT'S A HUMAN POWER...
...I'M SURE WE CAN LEARN TO USE IT.
NO BIG DEAL.
YOU DON'T GET IT...
THEIR ABILITY TO LEARN IS THEIR STRENGTH.
ONCE THEY FIND OUT THAT THE QUEEN IS OUR WEAKNESS, THEY'LL COME TO KILL HER... ANY WAY THEY CAN!!

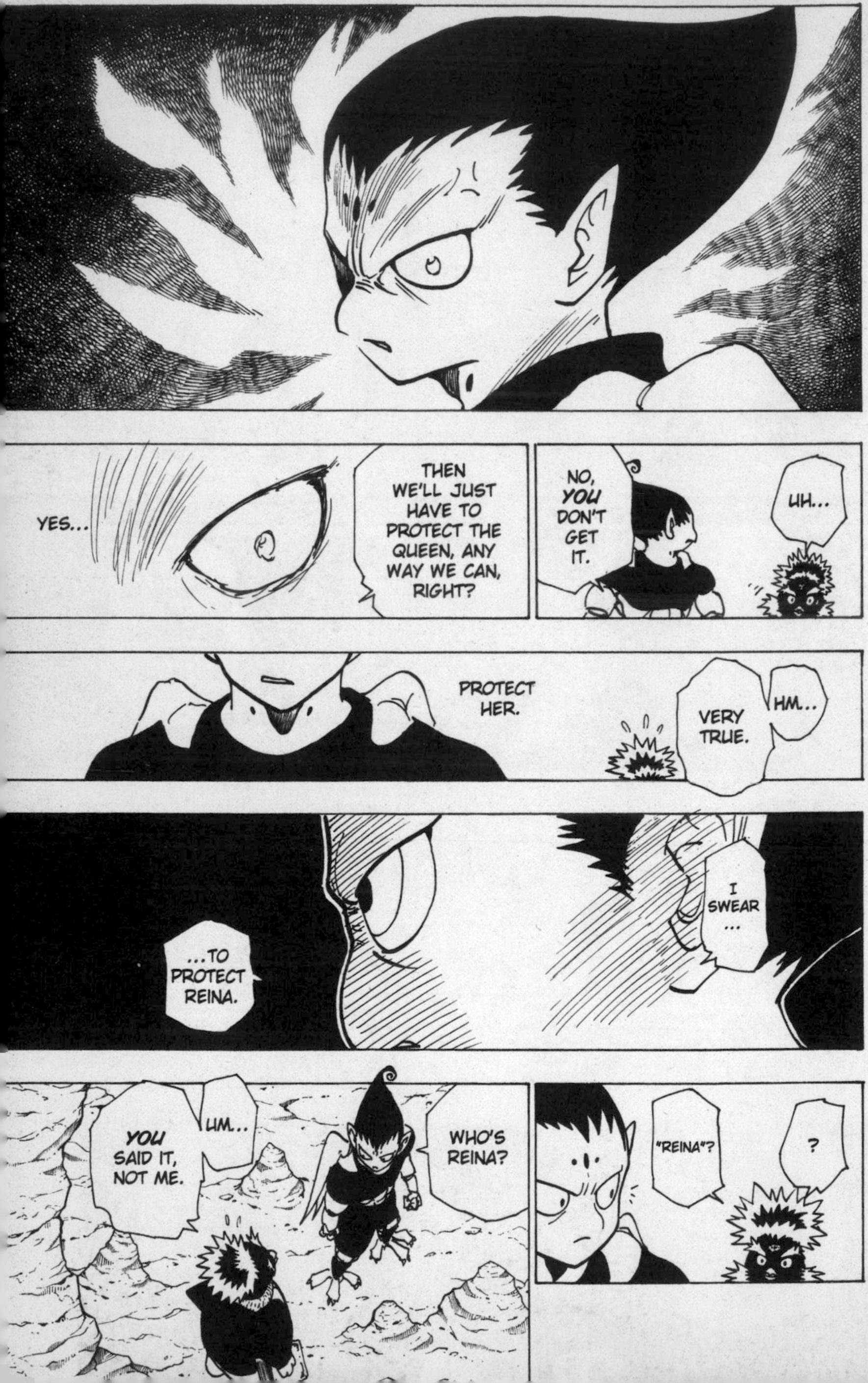
UH...
NO, YOU DON'T GET IT.
THEN WE'LL JUST HAVE TO PROTECT THE QUEEN, ANY WAY WE CAN, RIGHT?
YES...
HM...
VERY TRUE.
PROTECT HER.
I SWEAR...
...TO PROTECT REINA.
?
"REINA"?
WHO'S REINA?
UM...
YOU SAID IT, NOT ME.

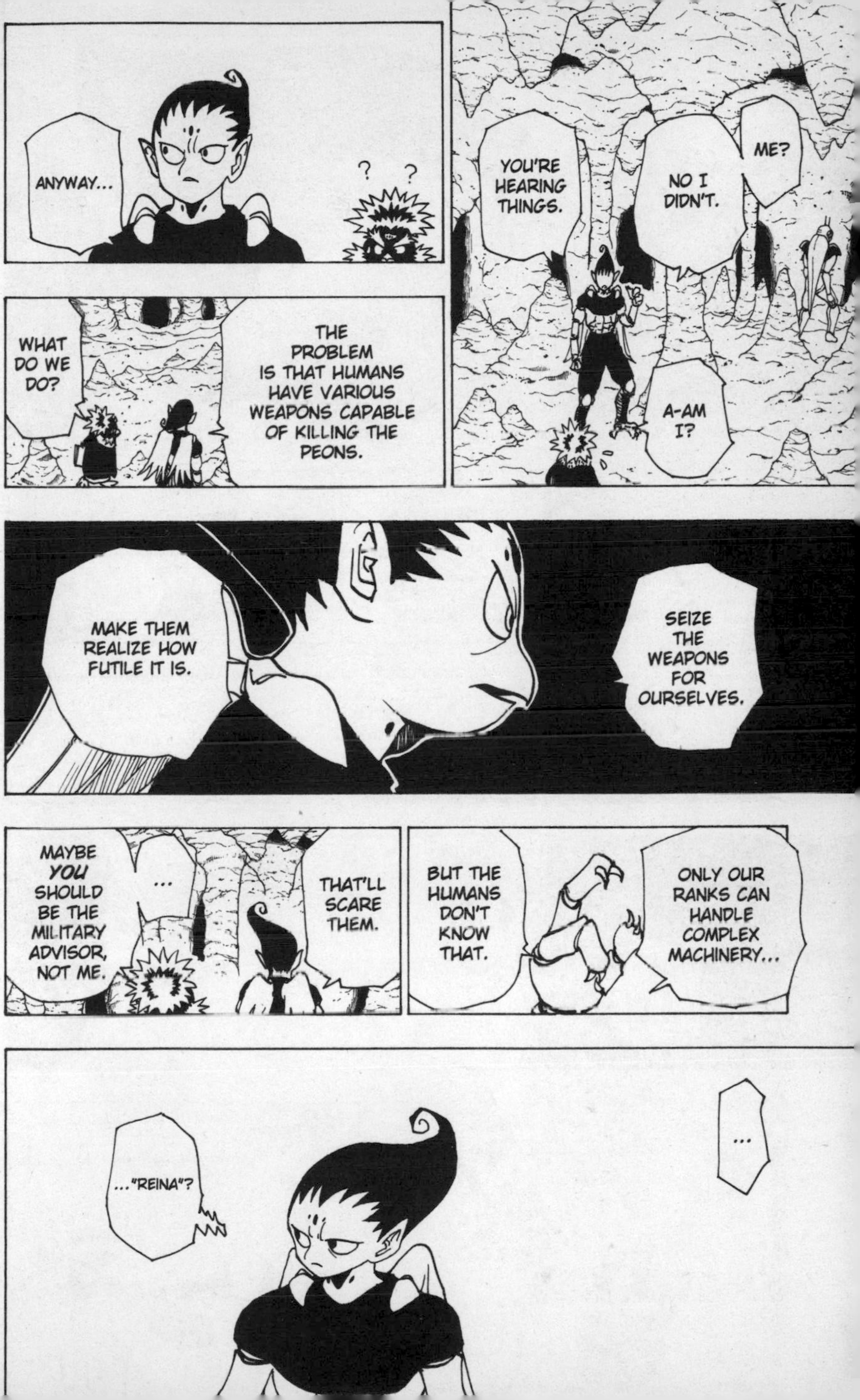
ME?
NO I DIDN'T.
YOU'RE HEARING THINGS.
A-AM I?
ANYWAY...
? ?
THE PROBLEM IS THAT HUMANS HAVE VARIOUS WEAPONS CAPABLE OF KILLING THE PEONS.
WHAT DO WE DO?
SEIZE THE WEAPONS FOR OURSELVES.
MAKE THEM REALIZE HOW FUTILE IT IS.
ONLY OUR RANKS CAN HANDLE COMPLEX MACHINERY...
BUT THE HUMANS DON'T KNOW THAT.
THAT'LL SCARE THEM.
...
MAYBE *YOU* SHOULD BE THE MILITARY ADVISOR, NOT ME.
...
..."REINA"?

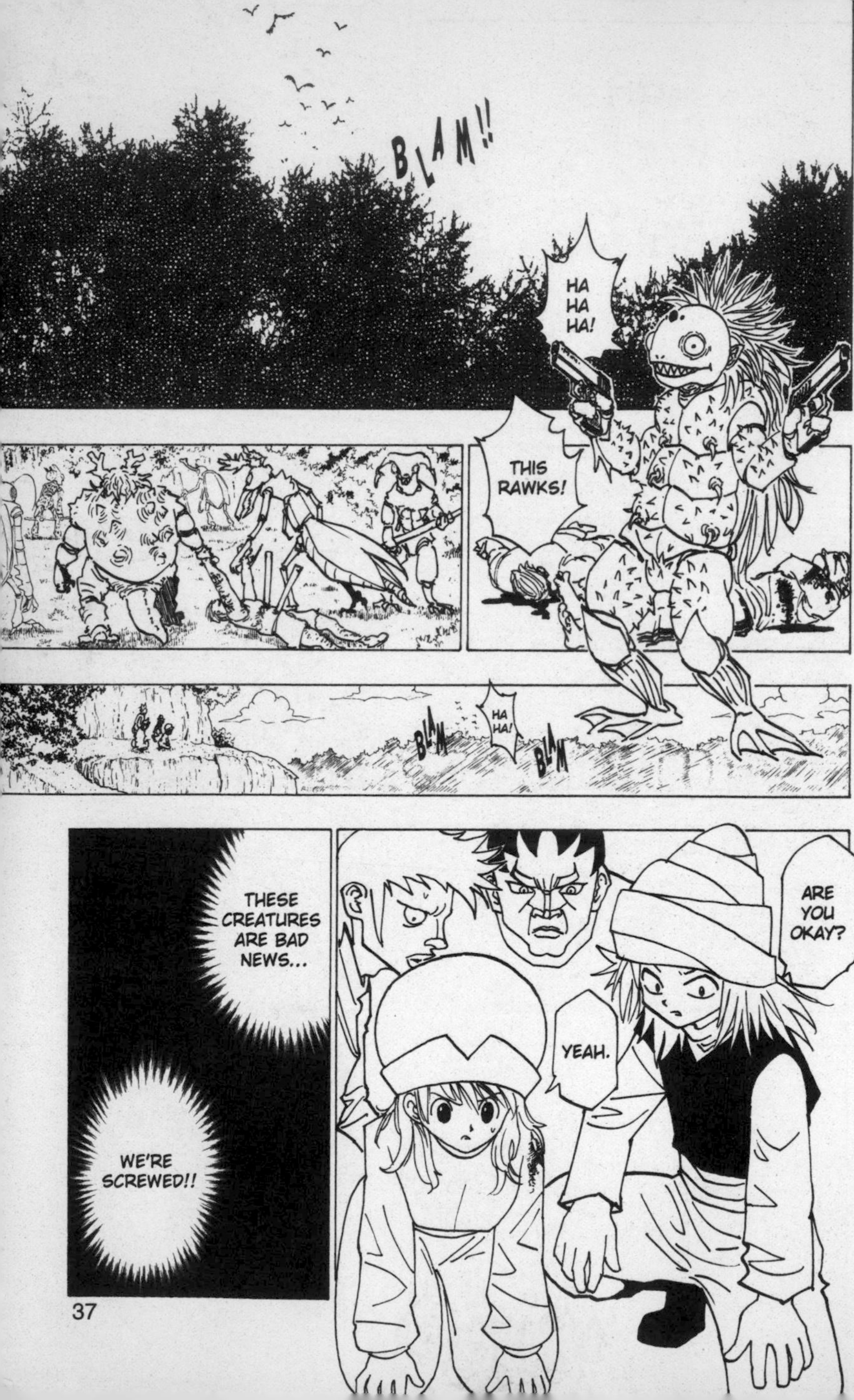
BLAM!!
HA HA HA!
THIS RAWKS!
BLAM
HA HA!
BLAM
ARE YOU OKAY?
YEAH.
THESE CREATURES ARE BAD NEWS...
WE'RE SCREWED!!

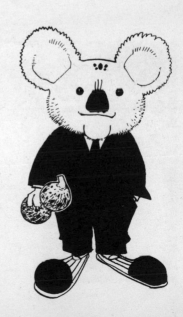

Chapter 190: The Hunt

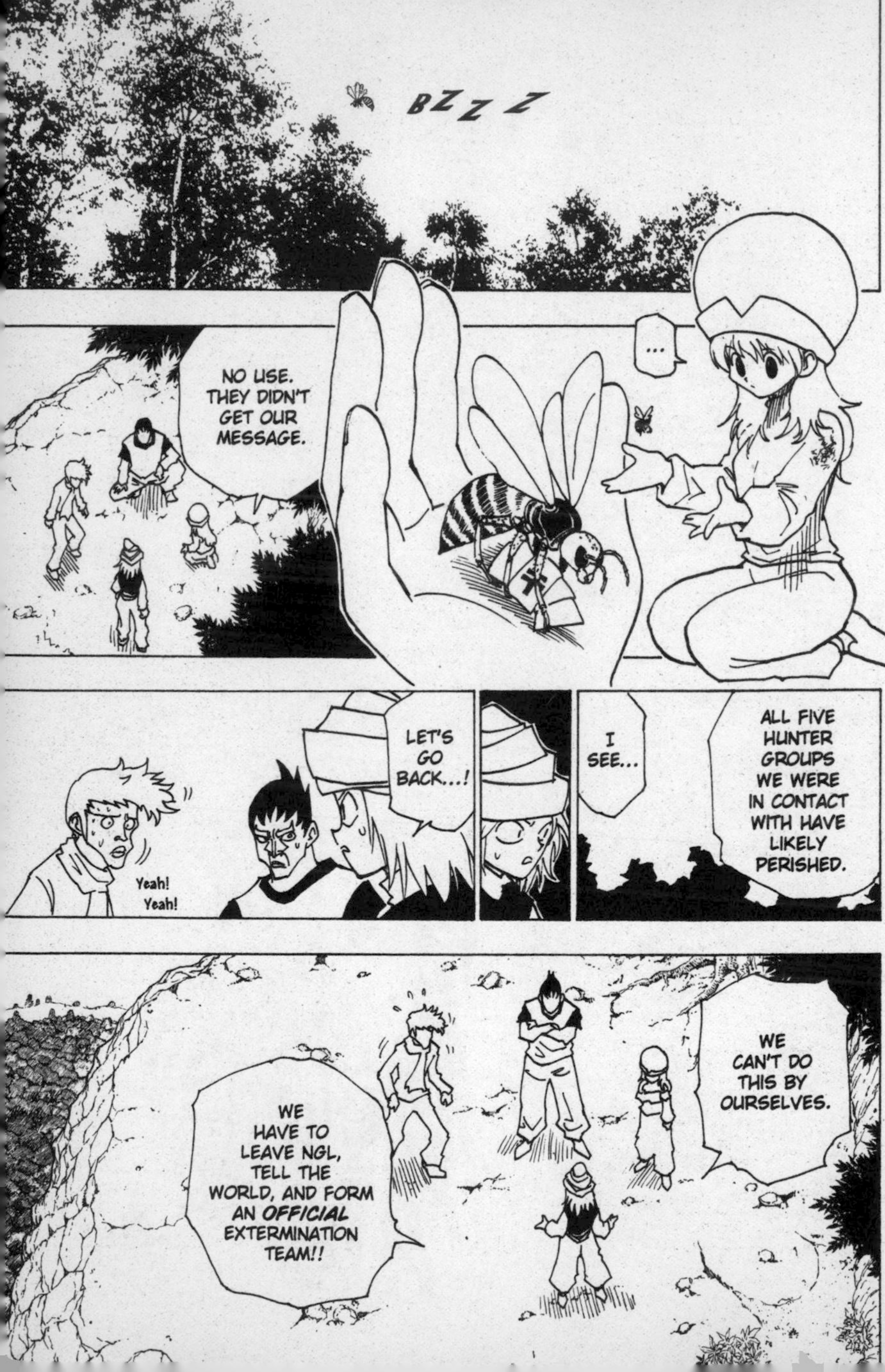
BZZZ
...
NO USE. THEY DIDN'T GET OUR MESSAGE.
ALL FIVE HUNTER GROUPS WE WERE IN CONTACT WITH HAVE LIKELY PERISHED.
I SEE...
LET'S GO BACK...!
Yeah! Yeah!
WE CAN'T DO THIS BY OURSELVES.
WE HAVE TO LEAVE NGL, TELL THE WORLD, AND FORM AN *OFFICIAL* EXTERMINATION TEAM!!

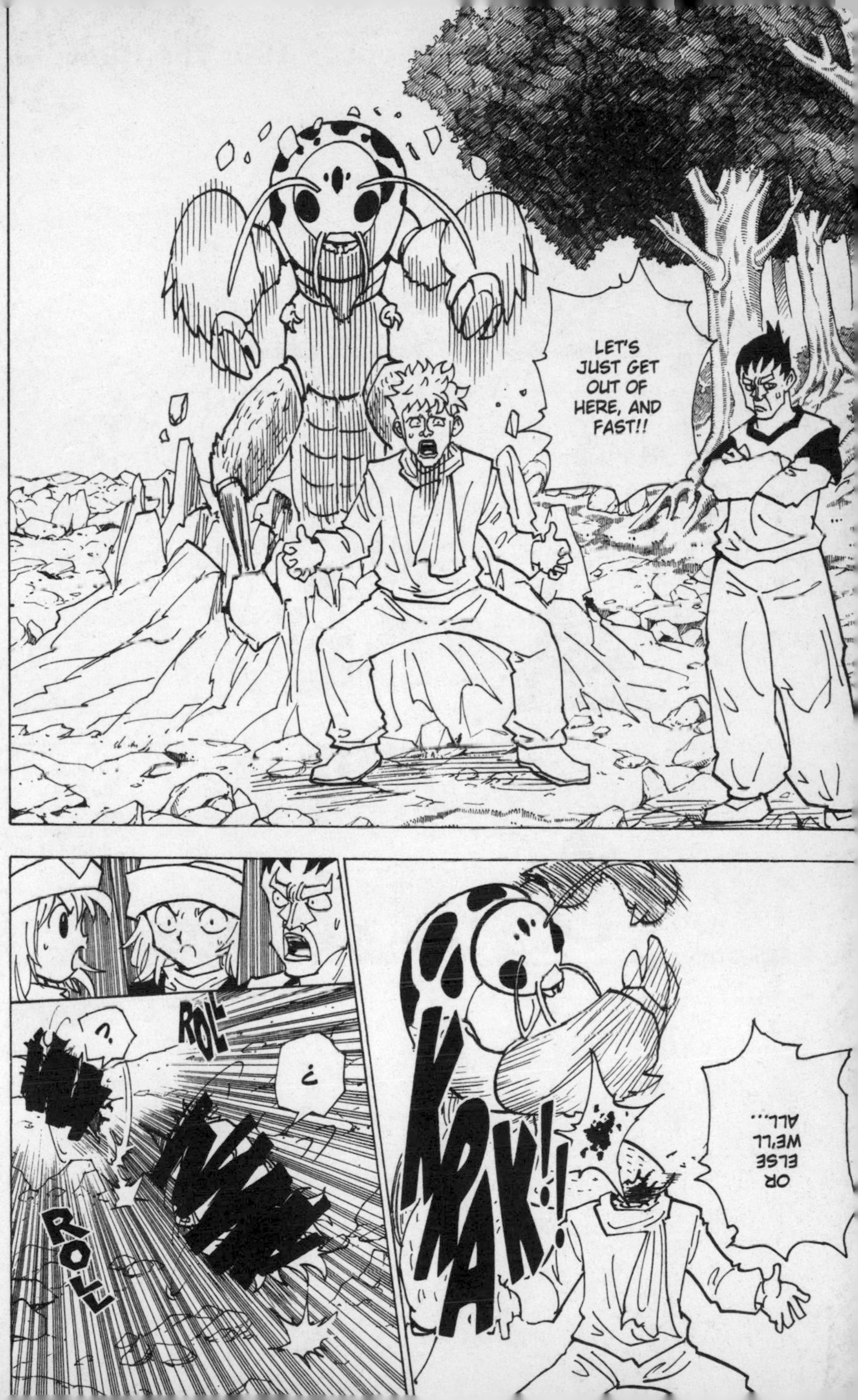
LET'S JUST GET OUT OF HERE, AND FAST!!
...
OR ELSE WE'LL ALL...
WHAK!!
?
ROLL
?
ROLL

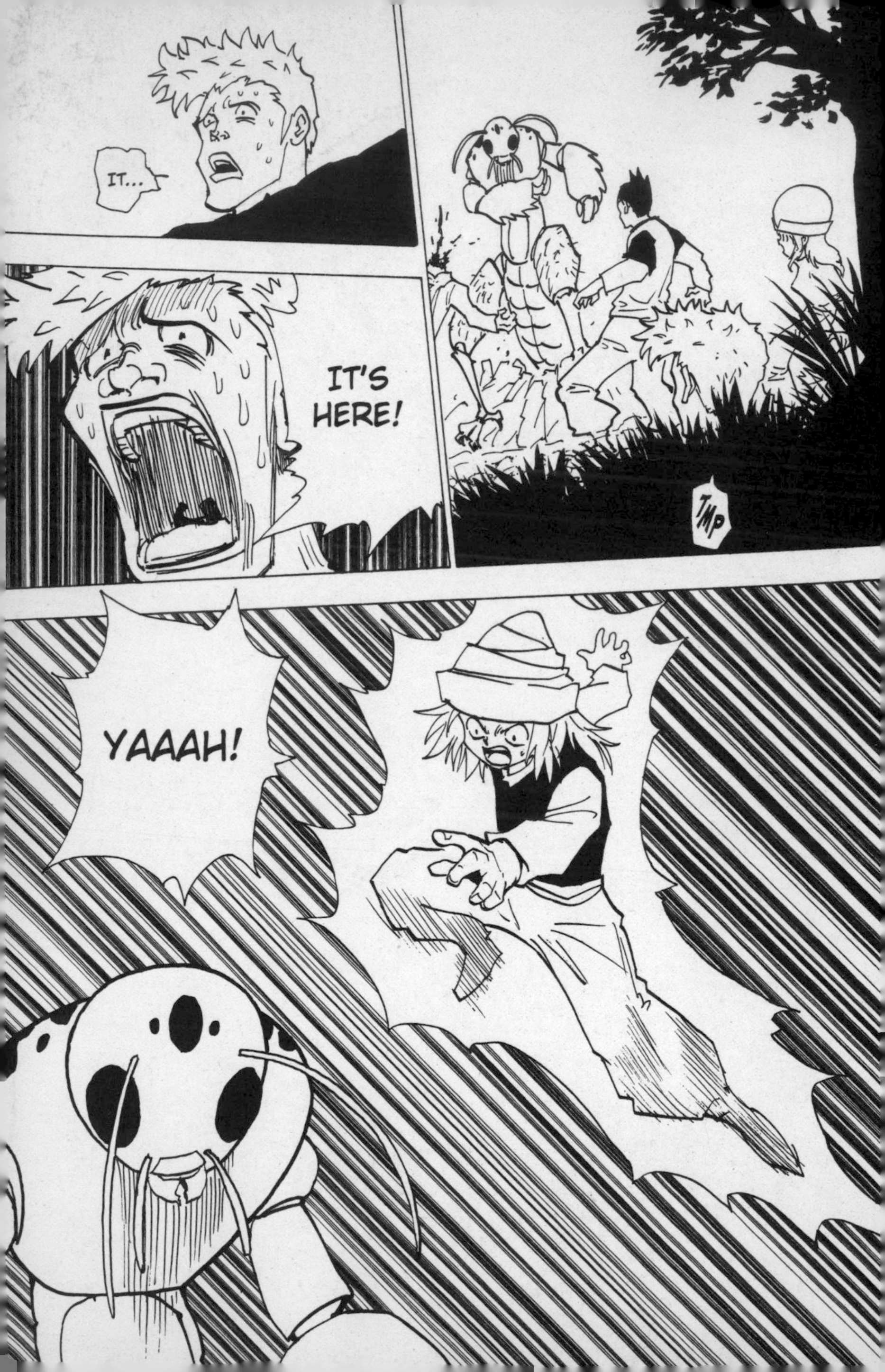
TMP
IT...
IT'S HERE!
YAAAH!

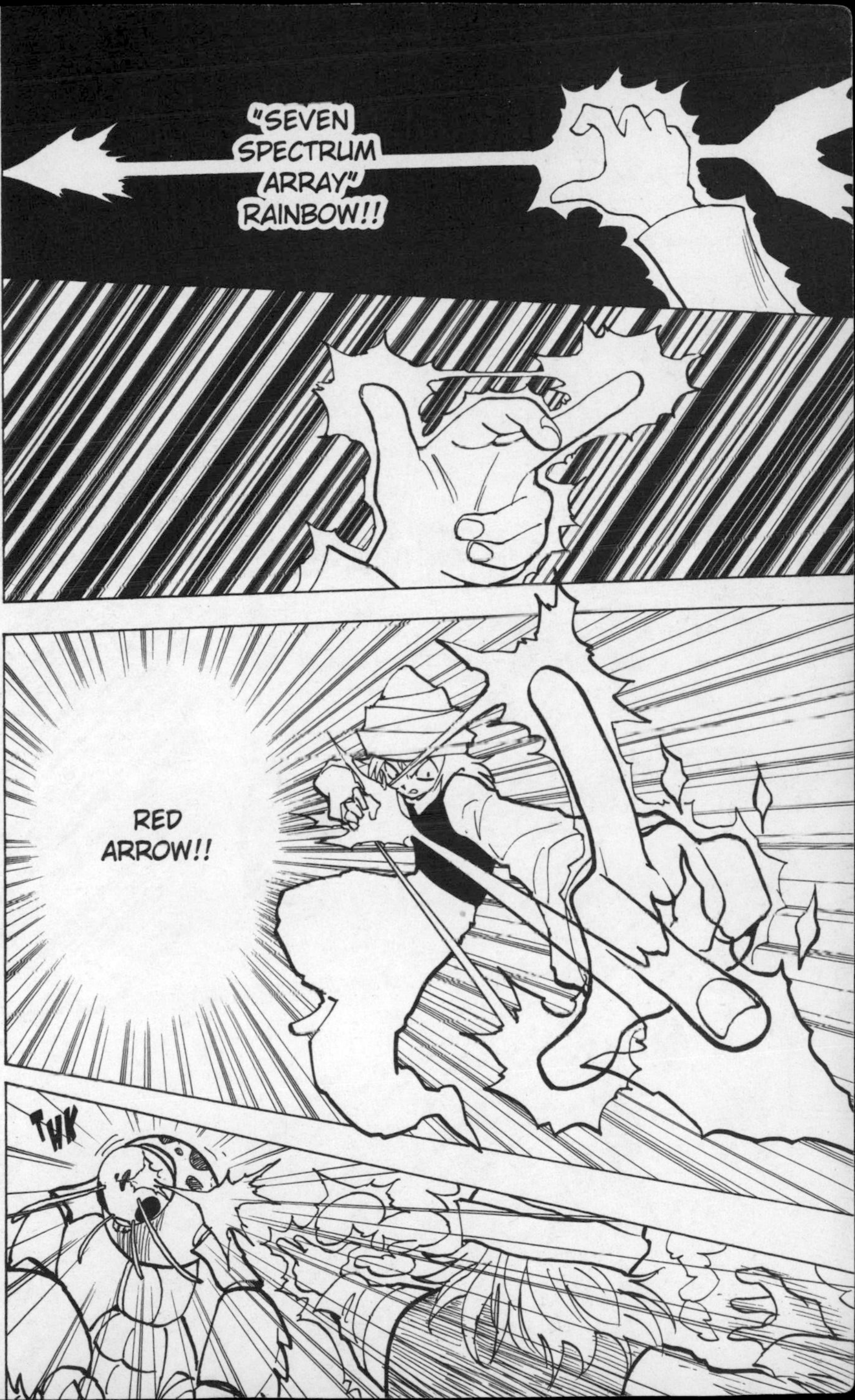
"SEVEN SPECTRUM ARRAY" RAINBOW!!
RED ARROW!!
THK

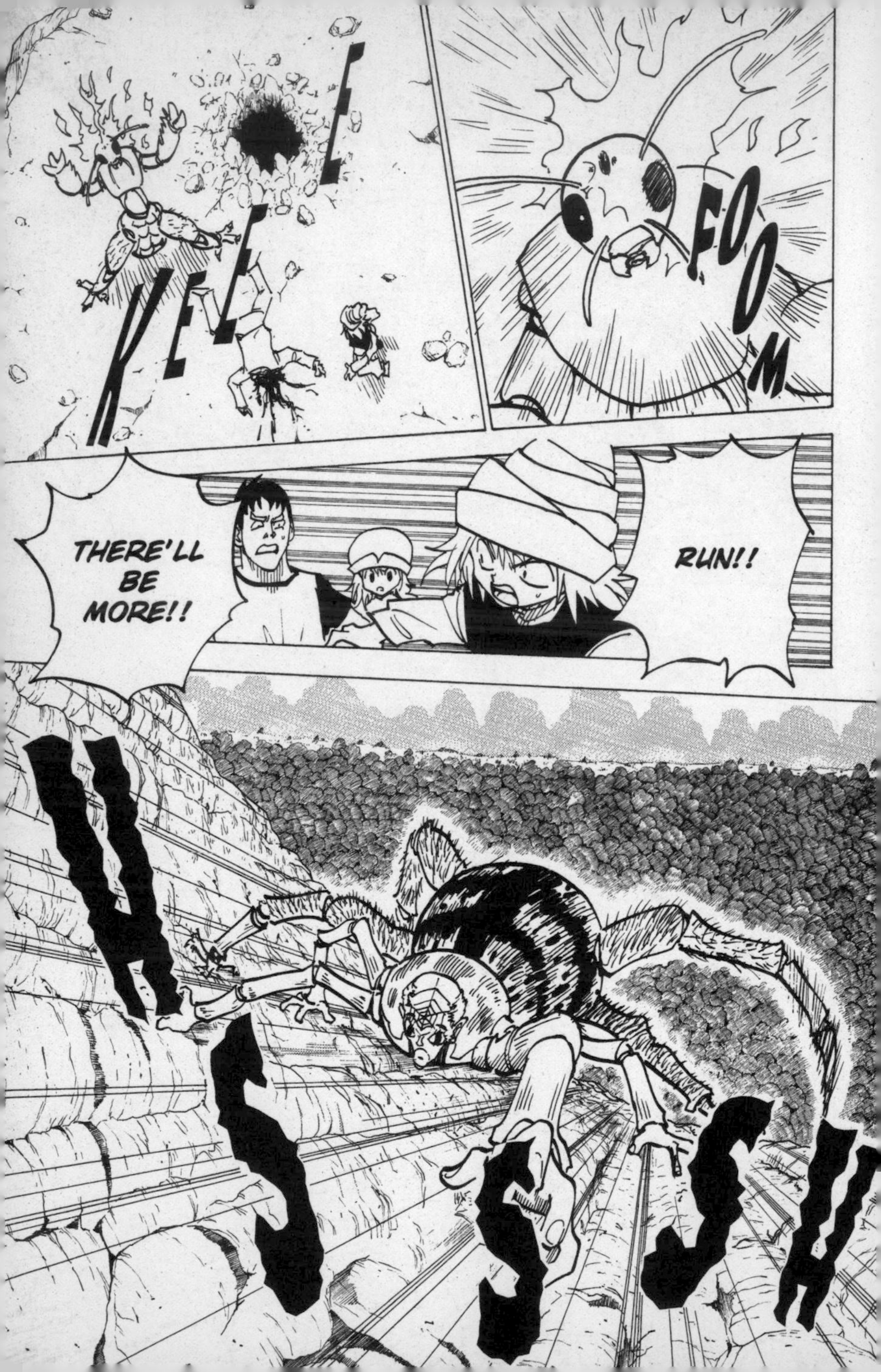
FOOM
KEEEE
RUN!!
THERE'LL BE MORE!!
HSSSH

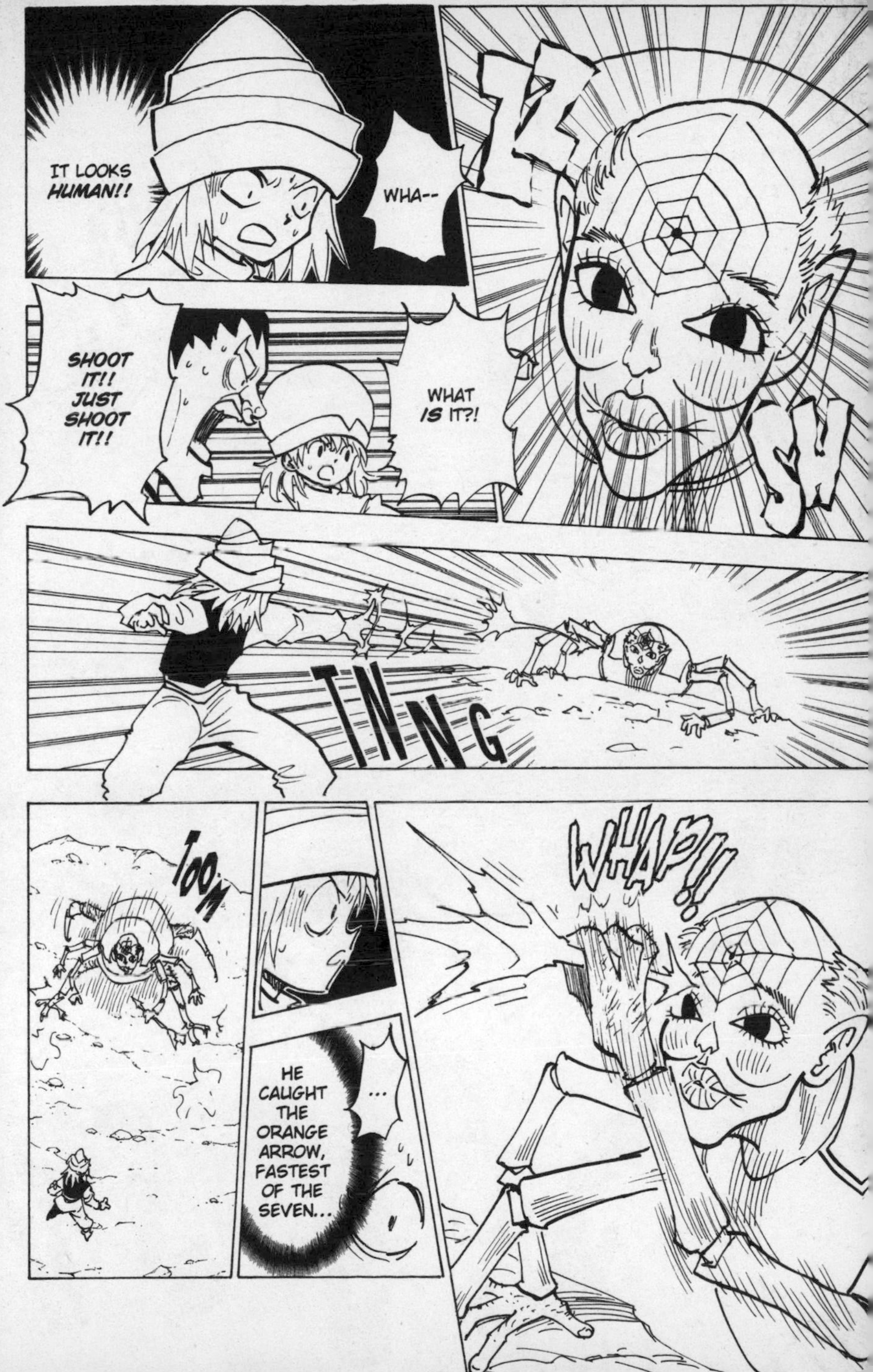
WHA--
IT LOOKS HUMAN!!
WHAT IS IT?!
SHOOT IT!! JUST SHOOT IT!!
TNNG
WHAP!!
...
HE CAUGHT THE ORANGE ARROW, FASTEST OF THE SEVEN...
TOOM

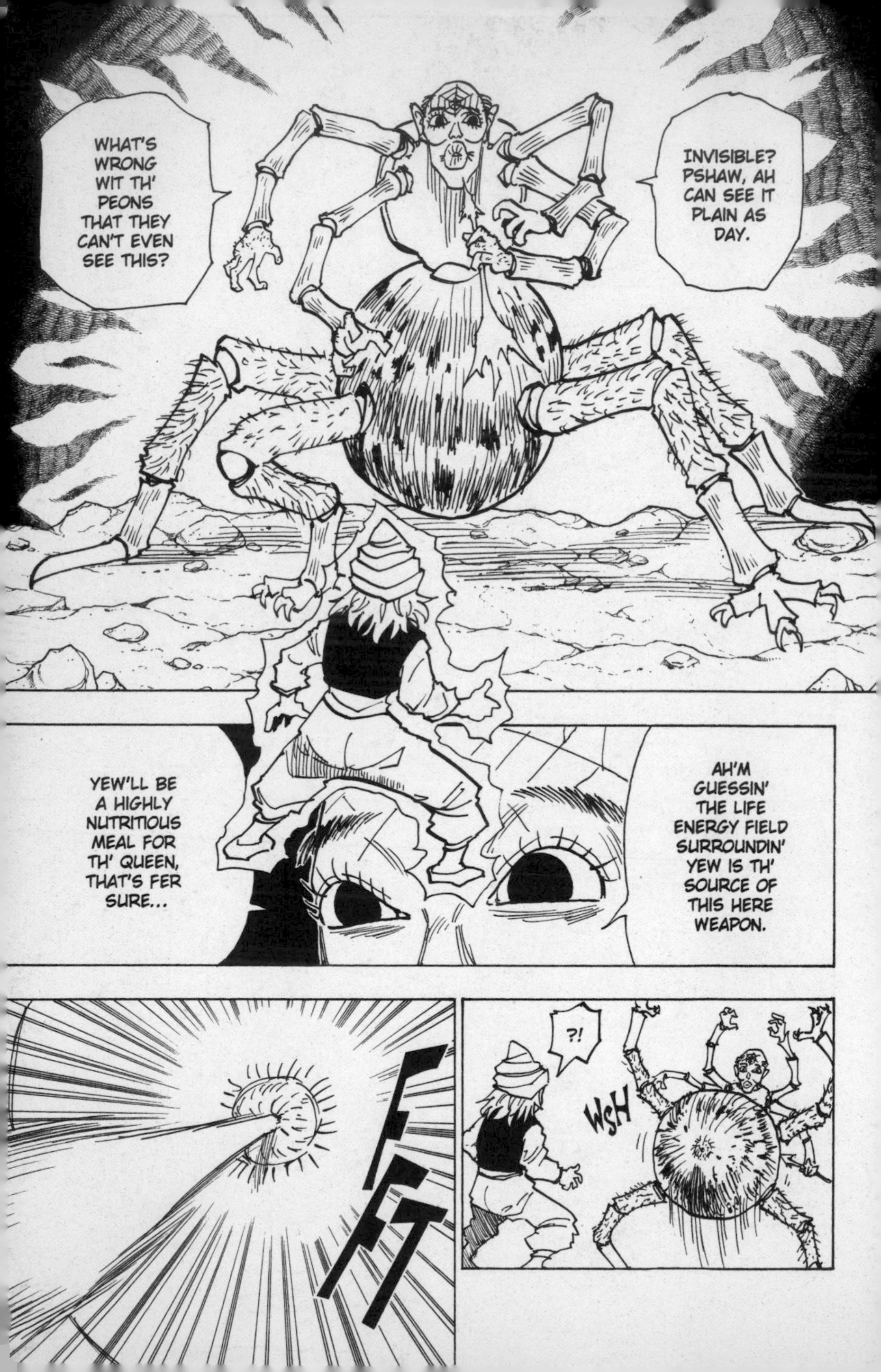
INVISIBLE? PSHAW, AH CAN SEE IT PLAIN AS DAY.
WHAT'S WRONG WIT TH' PEONS THAT THEY CAN'T EVEN SEE THIS?
AH'M GUESSIN' THE LIFE ENERGY FIELD SURROUNDIN' YEW IS TH' SOURCE OF THIS HERE WEAPON.
YEW'LL BE A HIGHLY NUTRITIOUS MEAL FOR TH' QUEEN, THAT'S FER SURE...
?!
WSH
FFFT

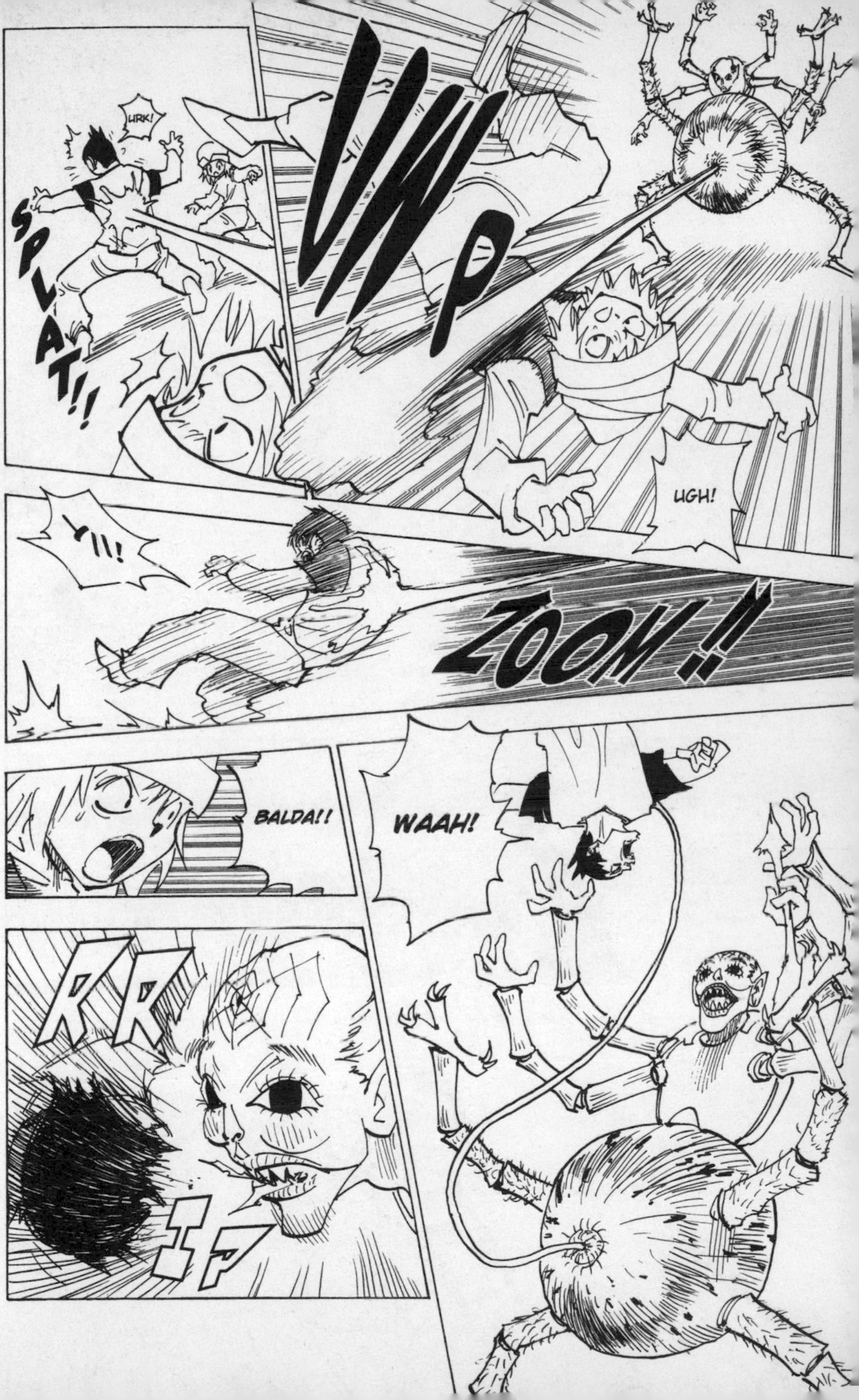
WHP
UGH!
URK!
SPLAT!!
ZOOM!!
WAAH!
BALDA!!
RRIP

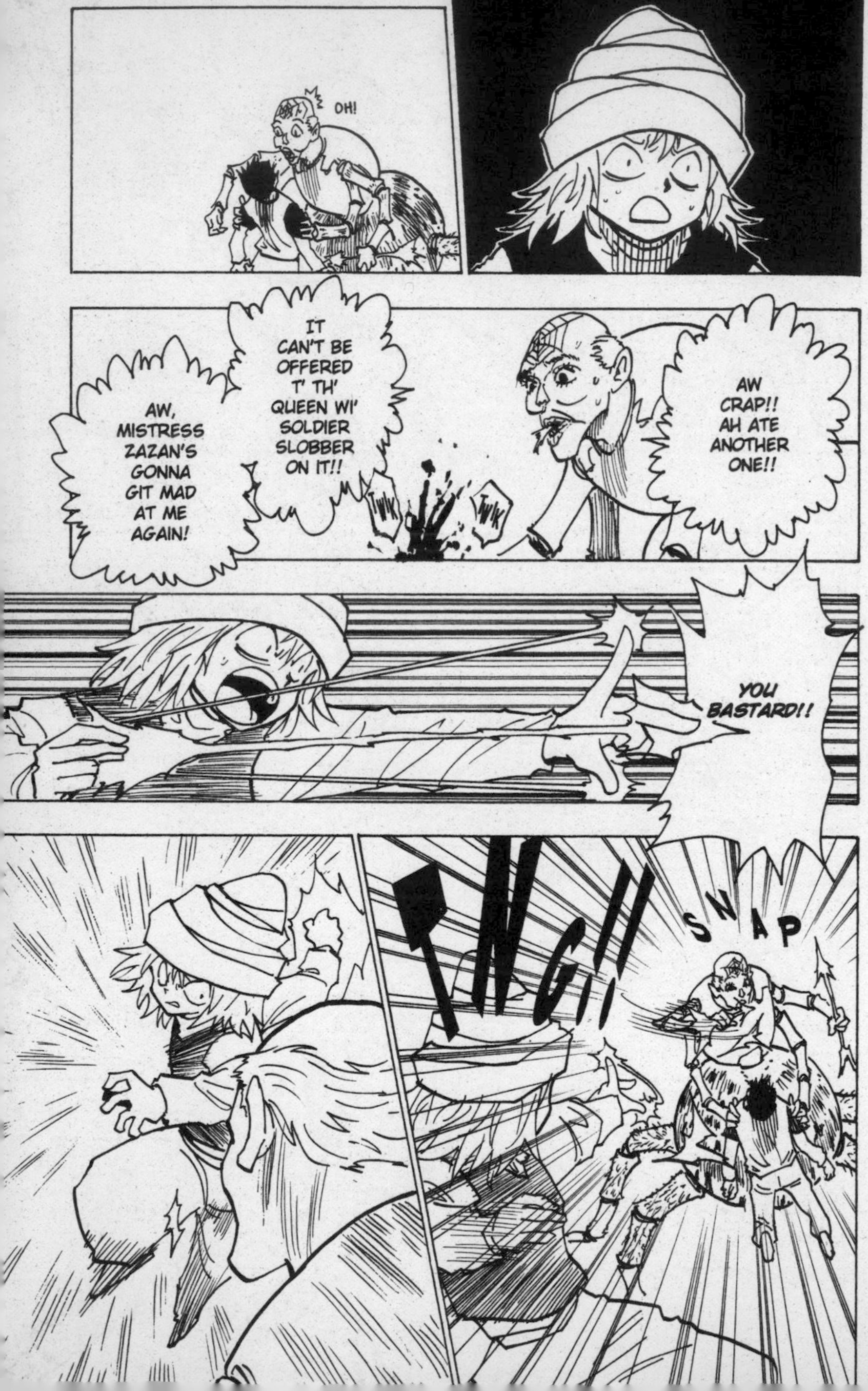
OH!
AW CRAP!! AH ATE ANOTHER ONE!!
TWIK
TWIK
IT CAN'T BE OFFERED T' TH' QUEEN WI' SOLDIER SLOBBER ON IT!!
AW, MISTRESS ZAZAN'S GONNA GIT MAD AT ME AGAIN!
YOU BASTARD!!
SNAP
PING!!

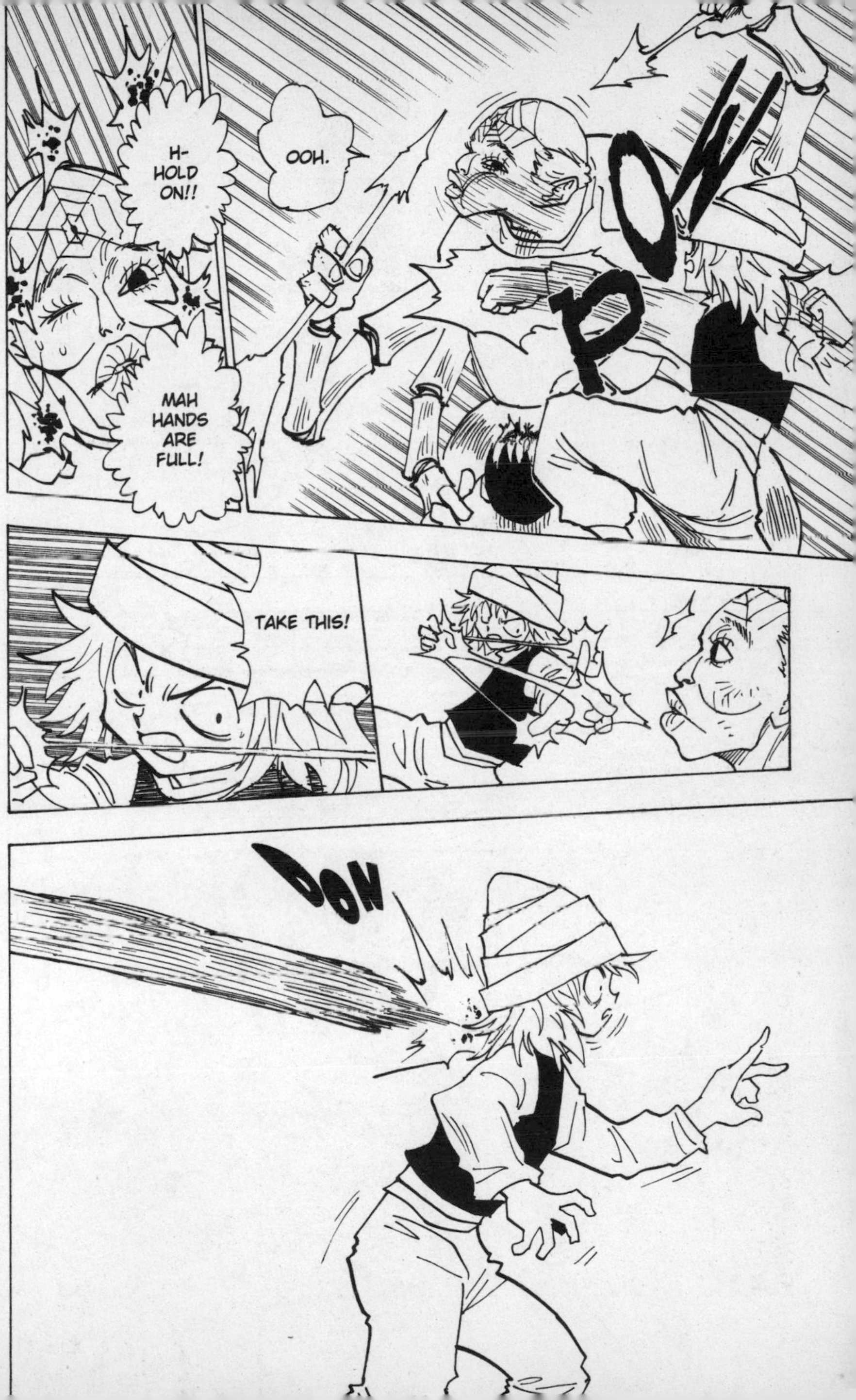
POW
OOH.
H-HOLD ON!!
MAH HANDS ARE FULL!
TAKE THIS!
DON

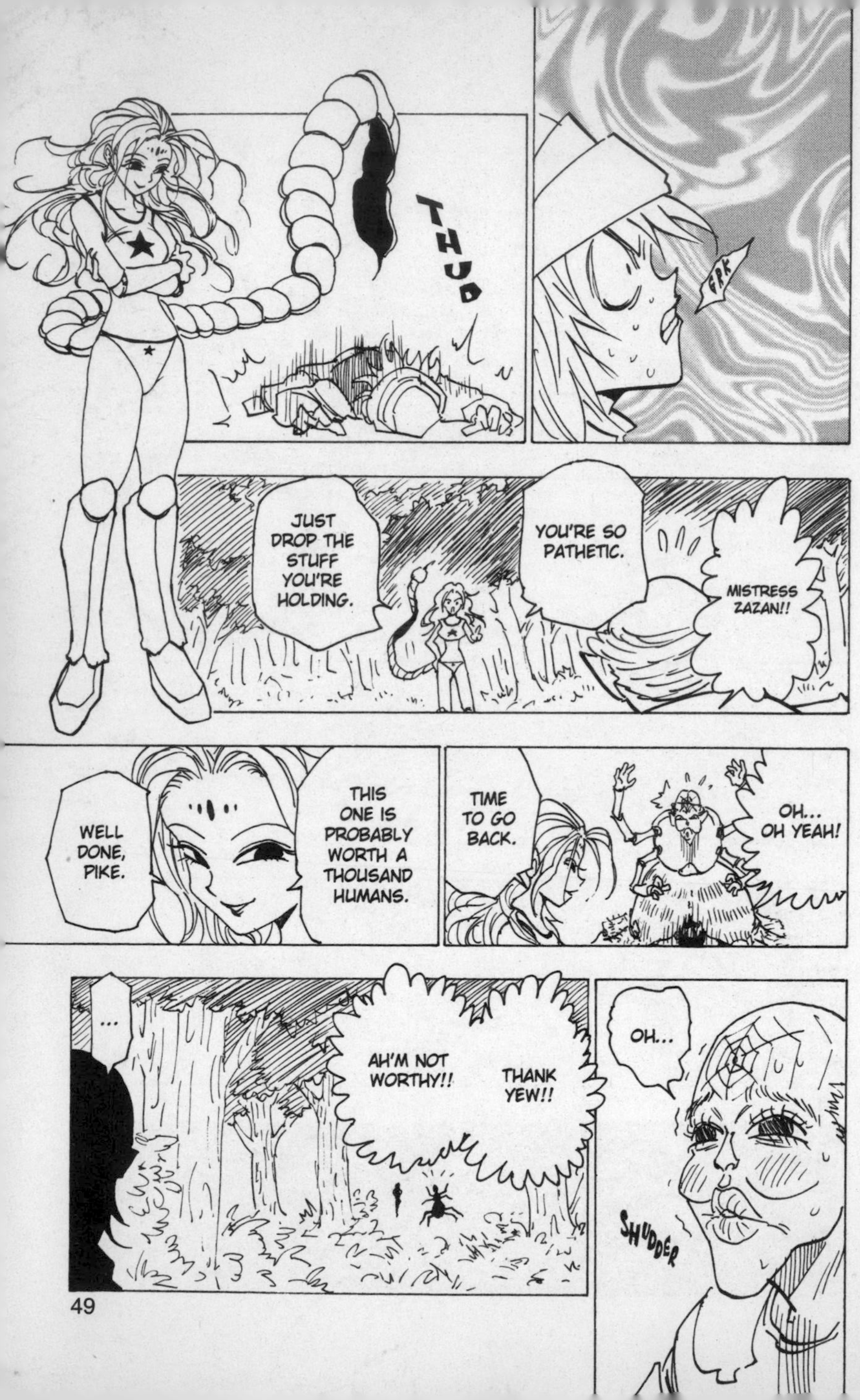
GRK
THUD
MISTRESS ZAZAN!!
YOU'RE SO PATHETIC.
JUST DROP THE STUFF YOU'RE HOLDING.
OH... OH YEAH!
TIME TO GO BACK.
THIS ONE IS PROBABLY WORTH A THOUSAND HUMANS.
WELL DONE, PIKE.
OH...
SHUDDER
AH'M NOT WORTHY!!
THANK YEW!!
...

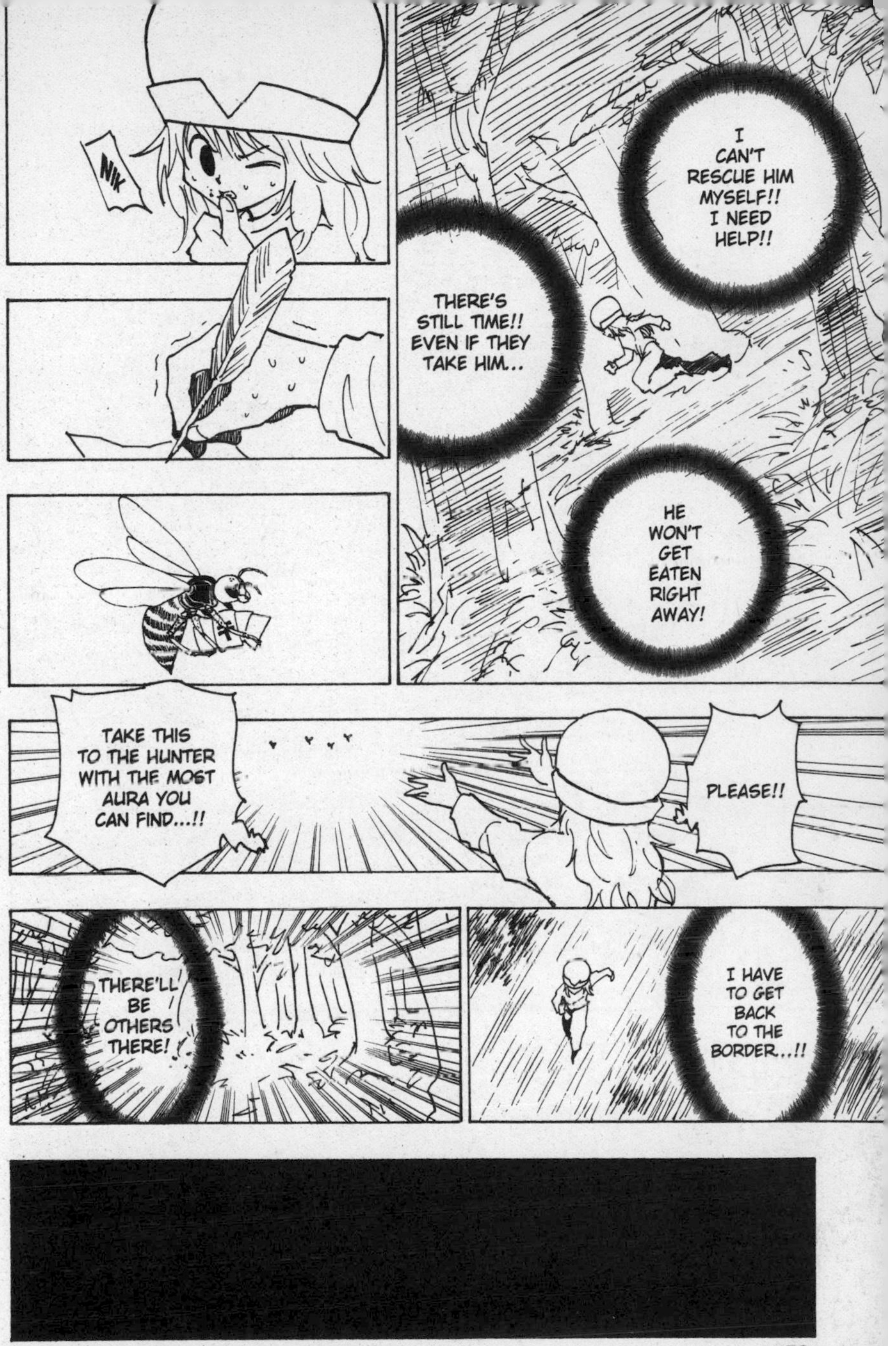
I CAN'T RESCUE HIM MYSELF!! I NEED HELP!!
THERE'S STILL TIME!! EVEN IF THEY TAKE HIM...
HE WON'T GET EATEN RIGHT AWAY!
NIK
PLEASE!!
TAKE THIS TO THE HUNTER WITH THE MOST AURA YOU CAN FIND...!!
I HAVE TO GET BACK TO THE BORDER...!!
THERE'LL BE OTHERS THERE!

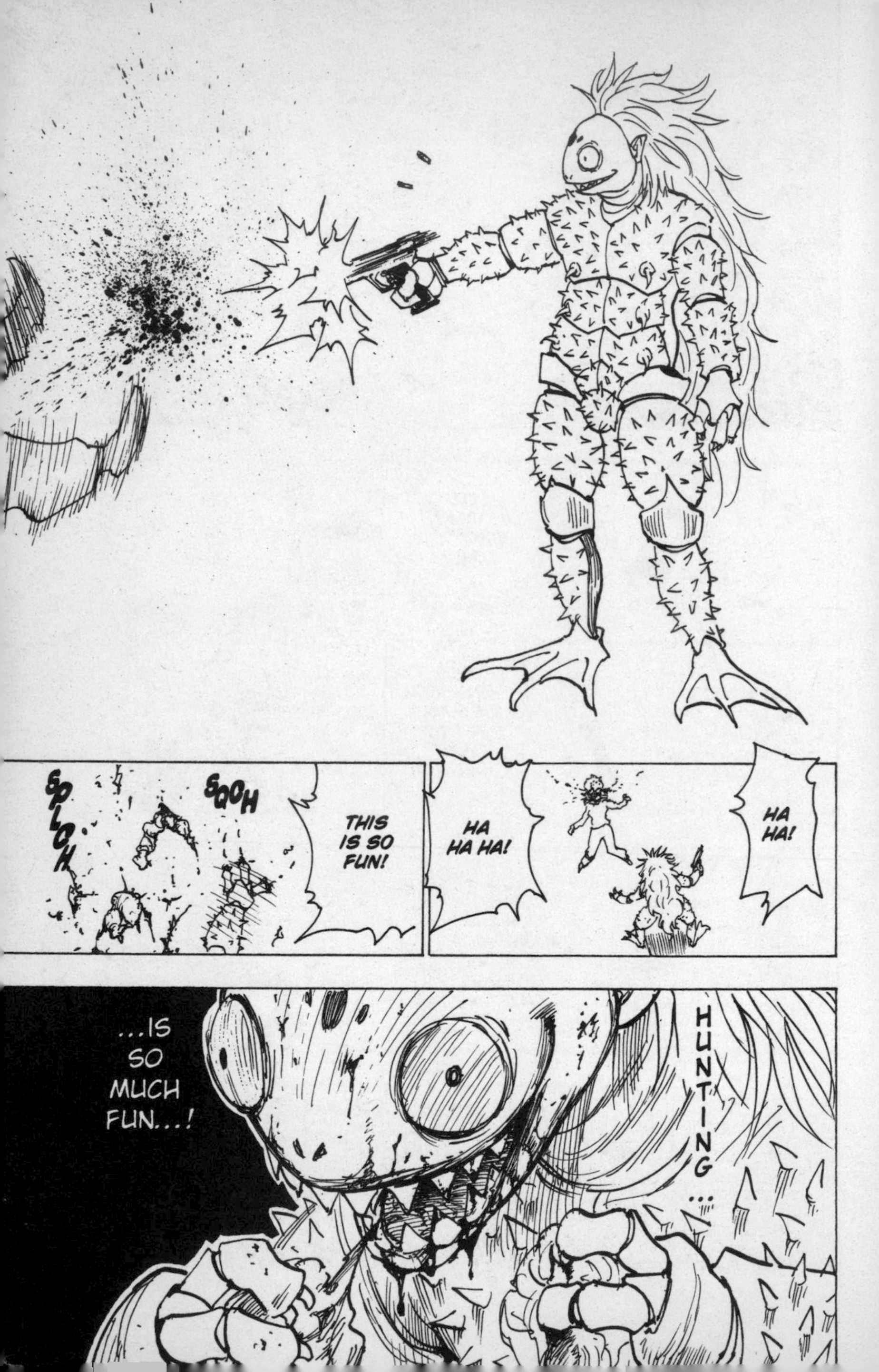
HA HA!
HA HA HA!
THIS IS SO FUN!
SQOH
SPLOCH
HUNTING...
...IS SO MUCH FUN...!

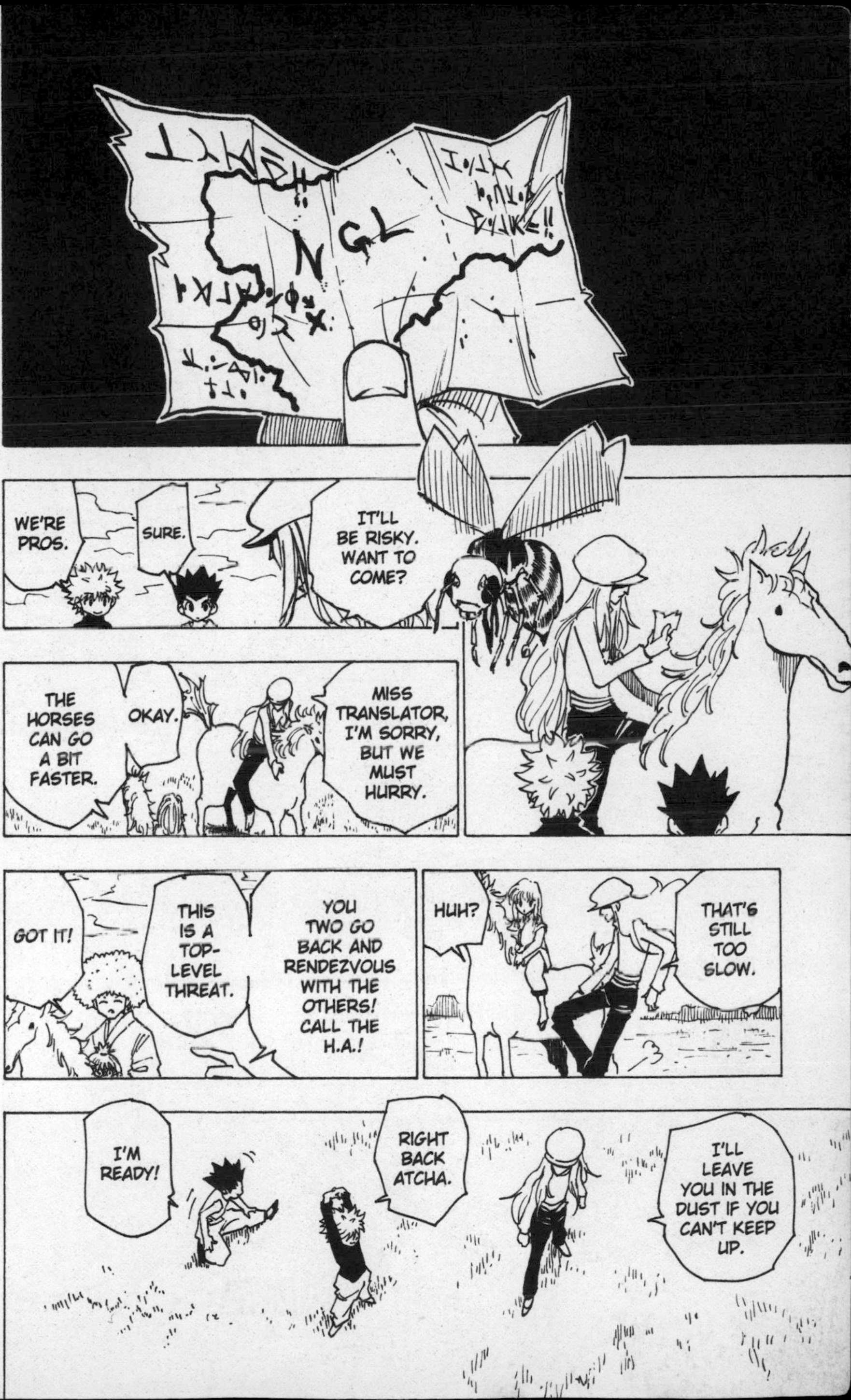
NGL
IT'LL BE RISKY. WANT TO COME?
SURE.
WE'RE PROS.
MISS TRANSLATOR, I'M SORRY, BUT WE MUST HURRY.
OKAY.
THE HORSES CAN GO A BIT FASTER.
THAT'S STILL TOO SLOW.
HUH?
YOU TWO GO BACK AND RENDEZVOUS WITH THE OTHERS! CALL THE H.A.!
THIS IS A TOP-LEVEL THREAT.
GOT IT!
I'LL LEAVE YOU IN THE DUST IF YOU CAN'T KEEP UP.
RIGHT BACK ATCHA.
I'M READY!

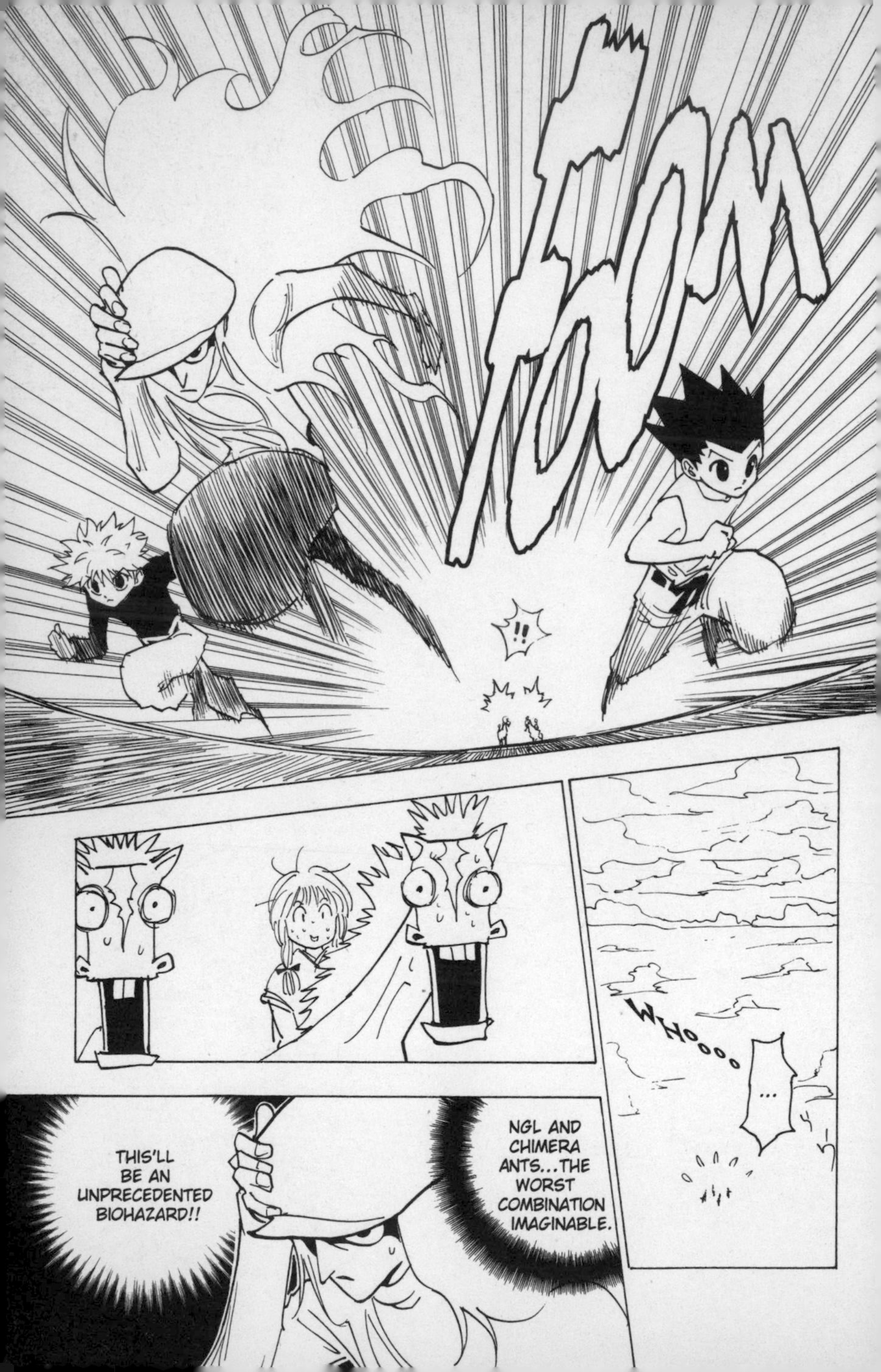
FOOM
!!
WHOOOO
...
NGL AND CHIMERA ANTS...THE WORST COMBINATION IMAGINABLE.
THIS'LL BE AN UNPRECEDENTED BIOHAZARD!!

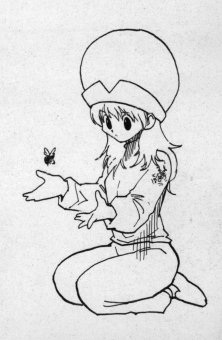

Chapter 191: Pros

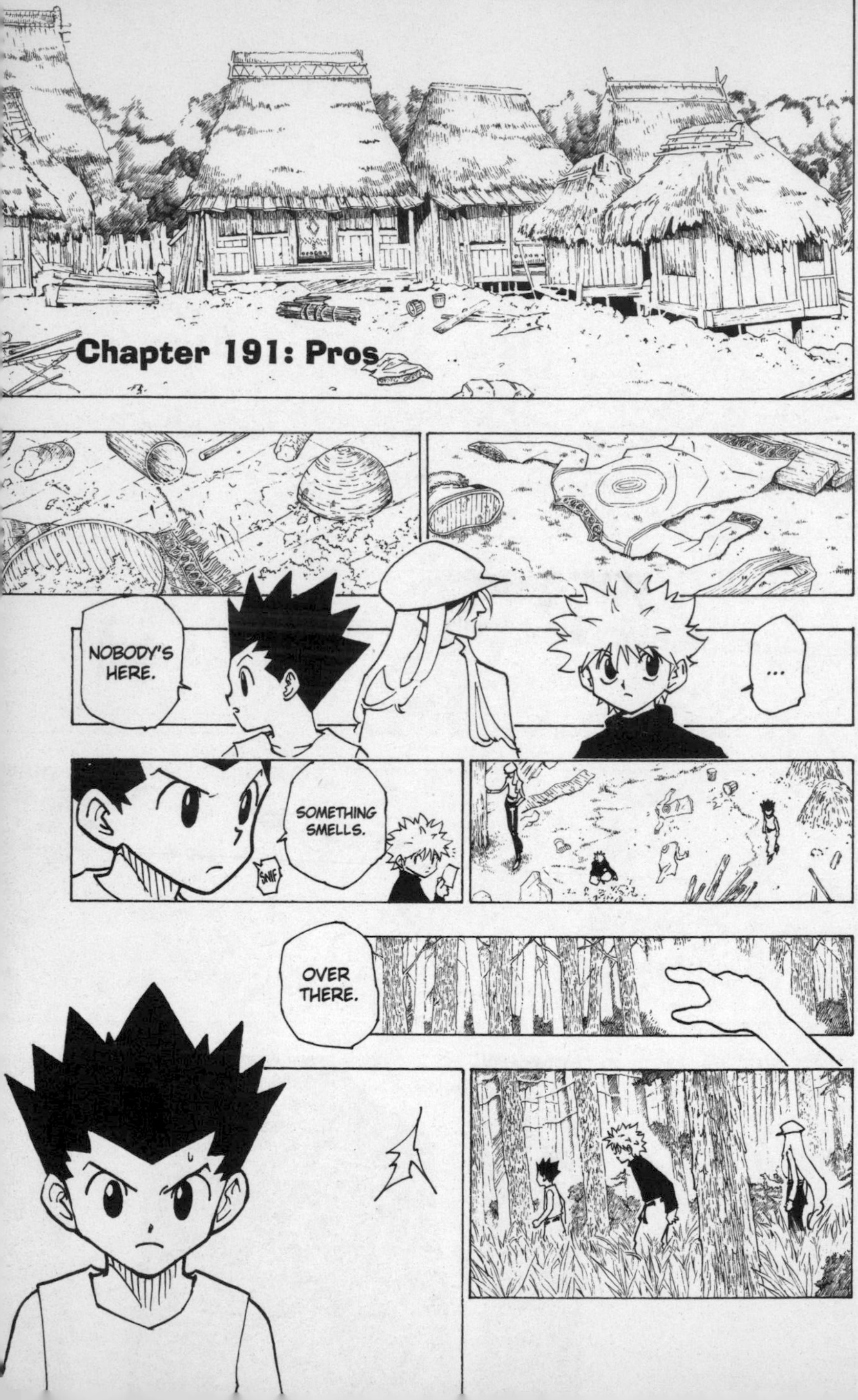
...
NOBODY'S HERE.
SOMETHING SMELLS.
SNIF
OVER THERE.

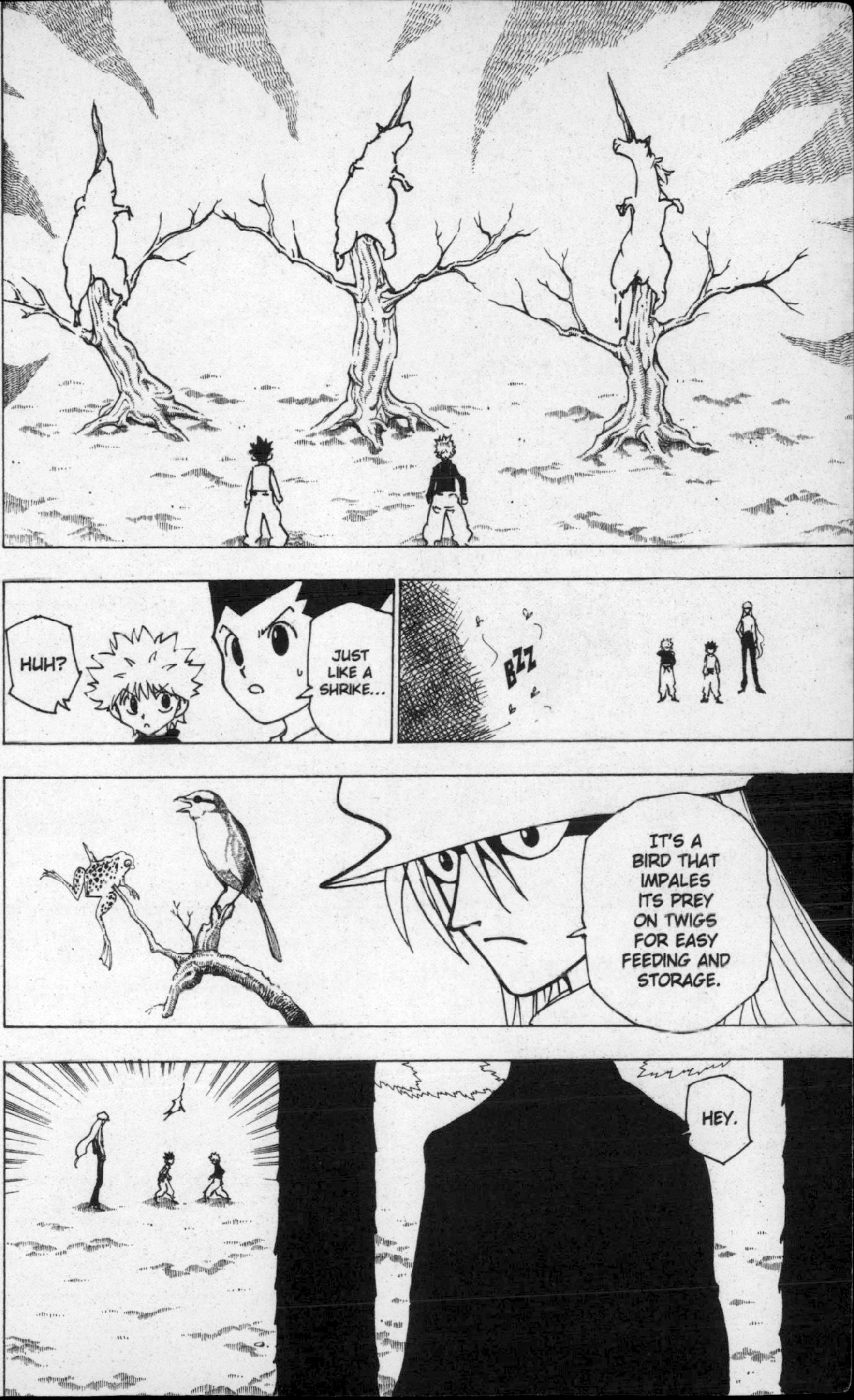
BZZ
JUST LIKE A SHRIKE...
HUH?
IT'S A BIRD THAT IMPALES ITS PREY ON TWIGS FOR EASY FEEDING AND STORAGE.
HEY.

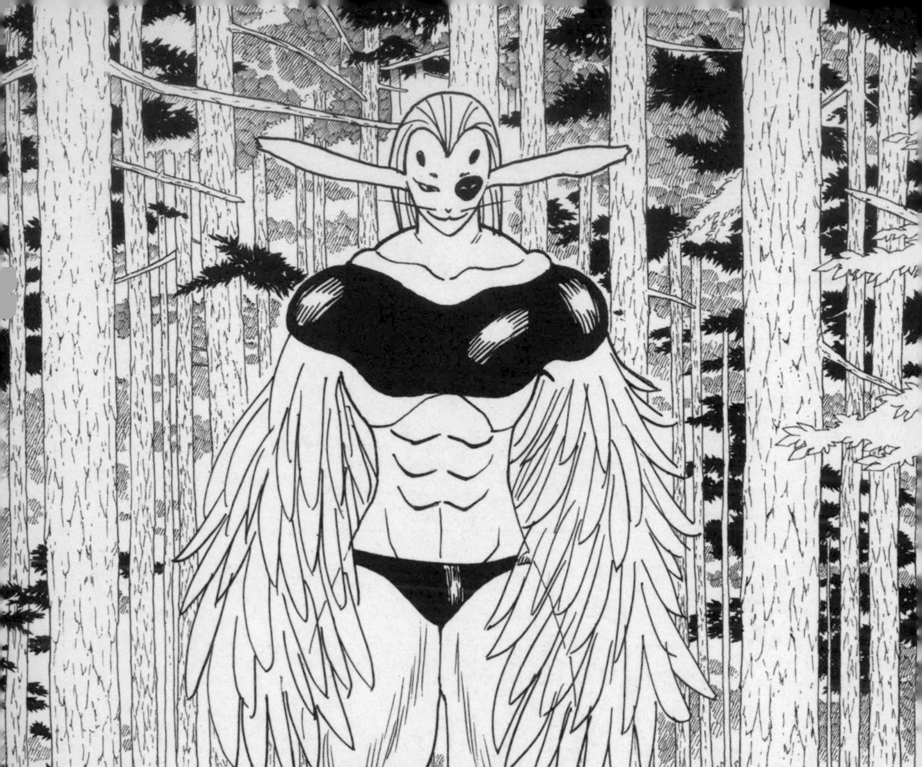

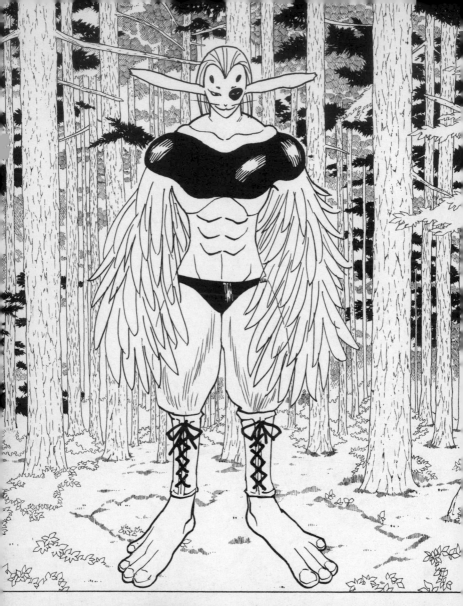

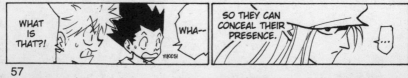

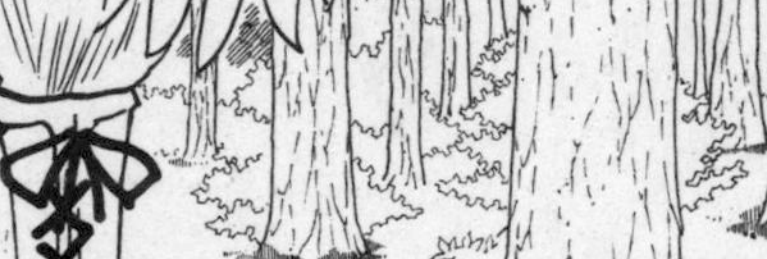
...
SO THEY CAN CONCEAL THEIR PRESENCE.

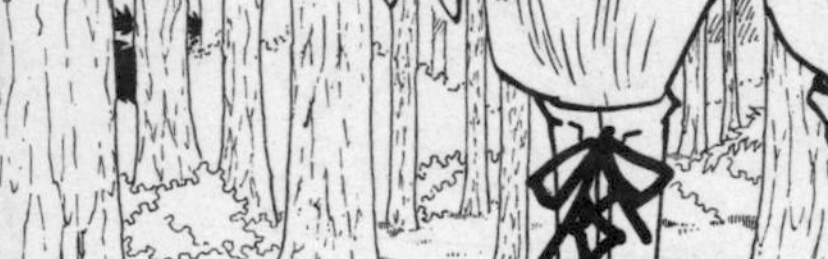
WHA--
WHAT IS THAT?!
YIKES!

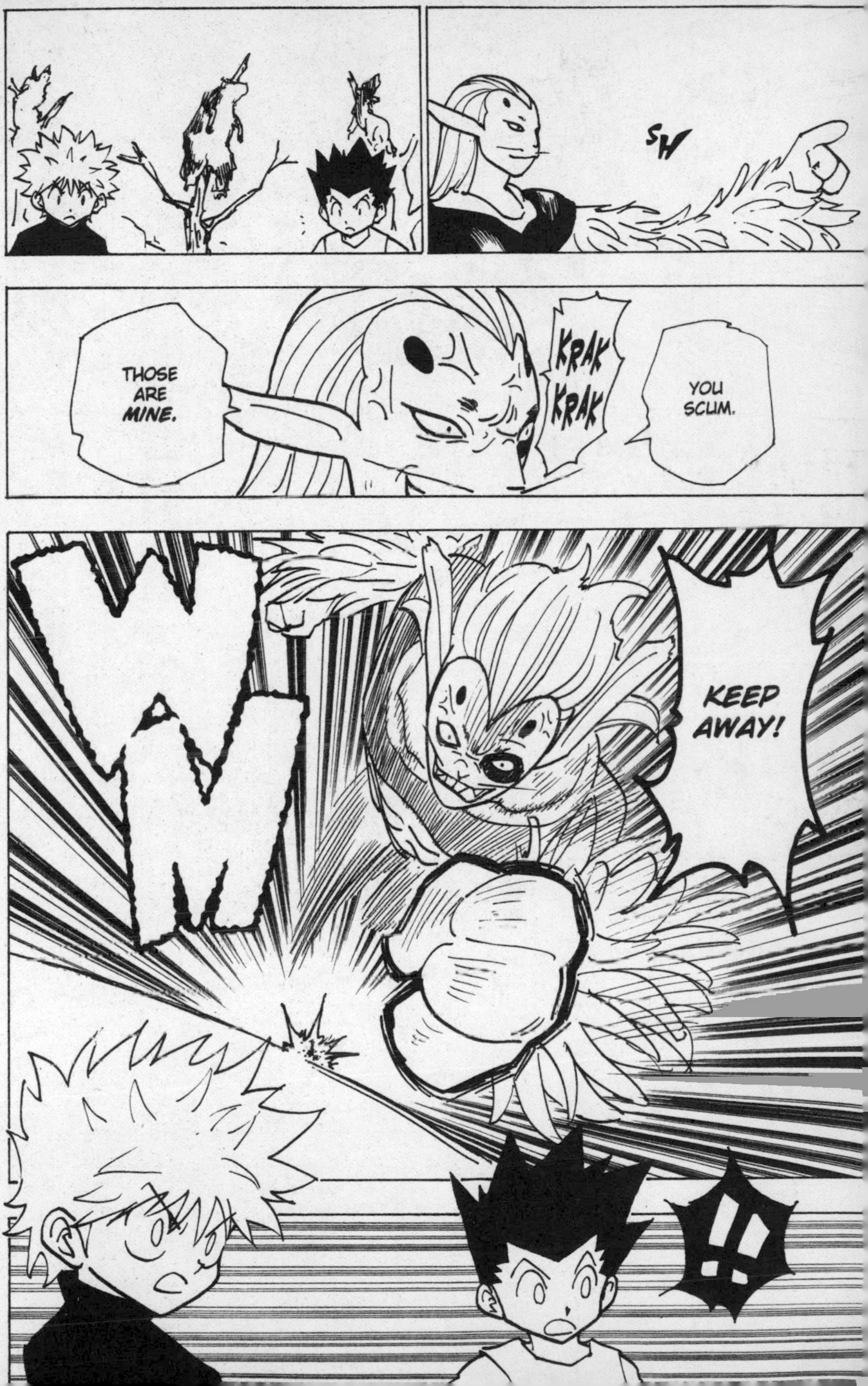
SH
YOU SCUM.
KRAK KRAK
THOSE ARE MINE.
KEEP AWAY!
WM
!!

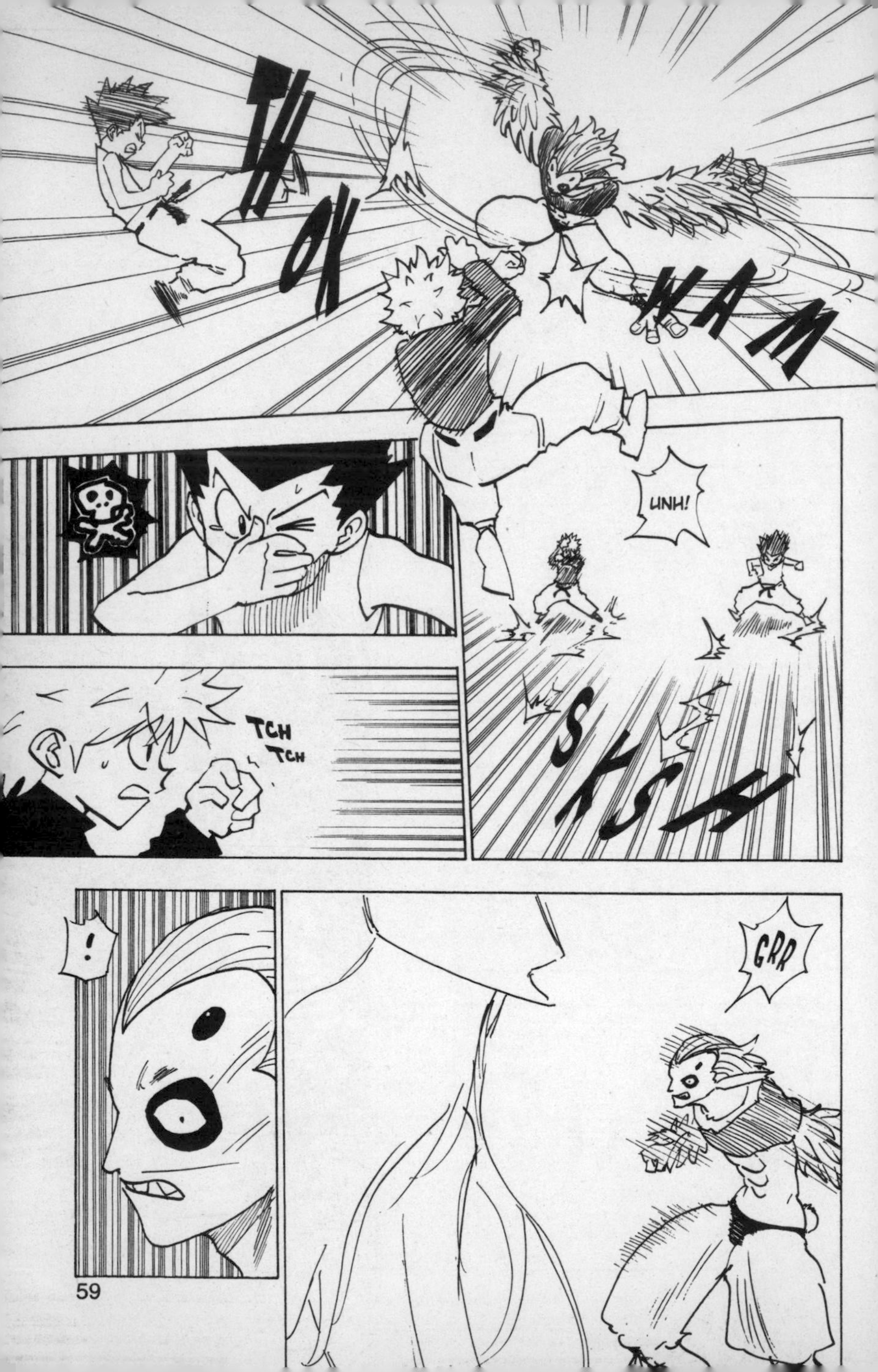
WAM
THWOK
UNH!
SKSH
TCH
TCH
GRR
!

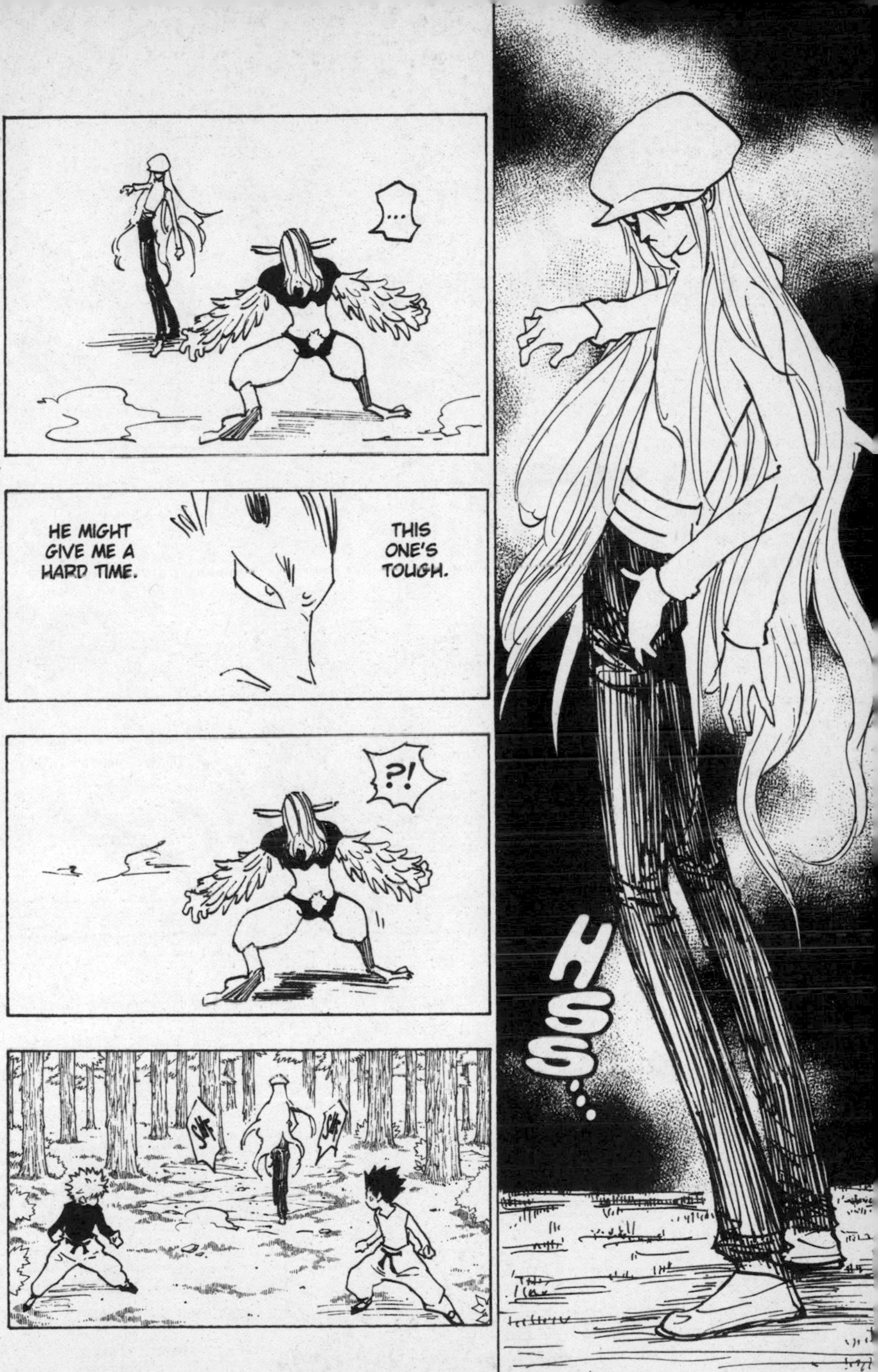
HSS...
...
THIS ONE'S TOUGH.
HE MIGHT GIVE ME A HARD TIME.
?!

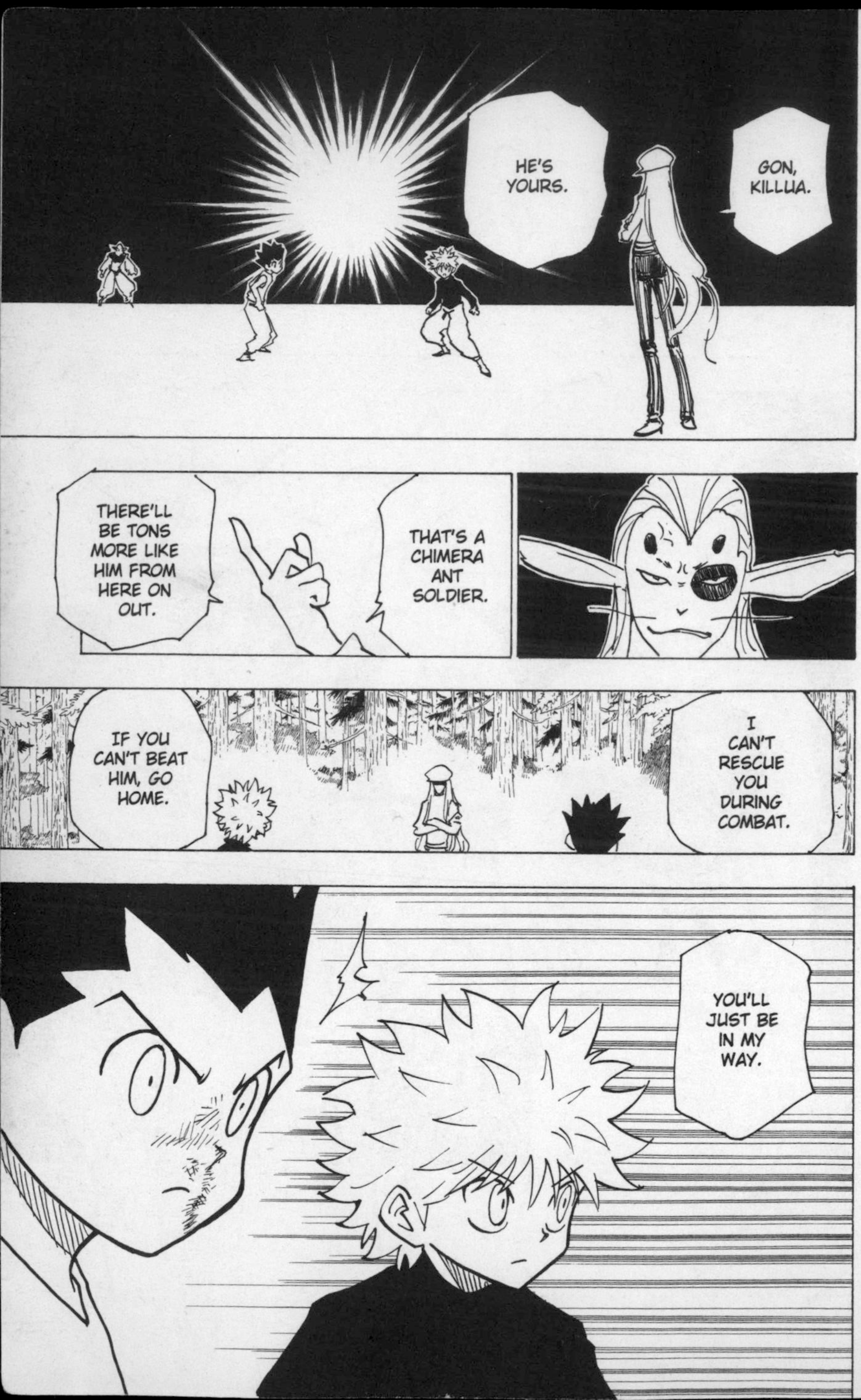
GON, KILLUA.
HE'S YOURS.
THAT'S A CHIMERA ANT SOLDIER.
THERE'LL BE TONS MORE LIKE HIM FROM HERE ON OUT.
I CAN'T RESCUE YOU DURING COMBAT.
IF YOU CAN'T BEAT HIM, GO HOME.
YOU'LL JUST BE IN MY WAY.

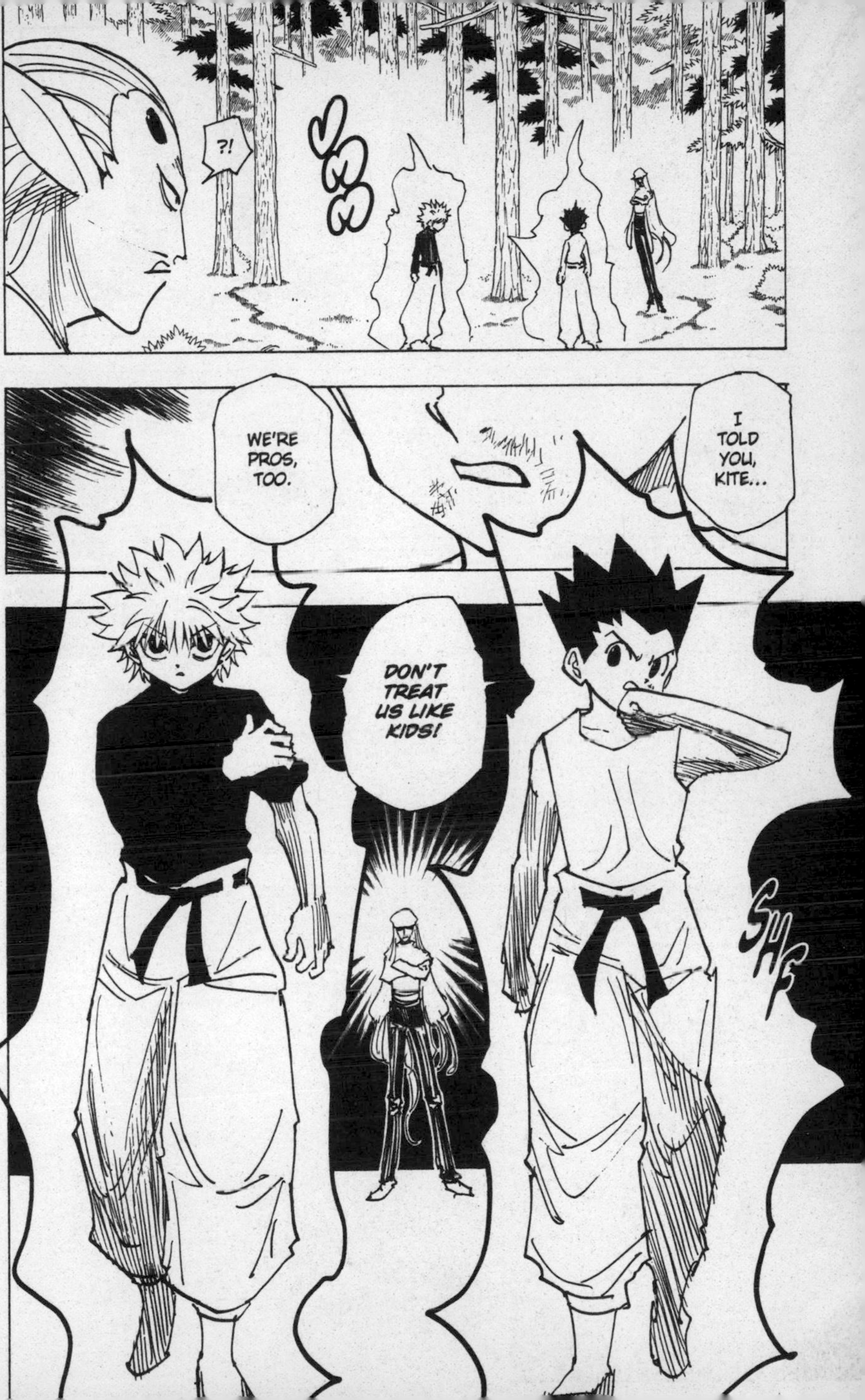
?!
I TOLD YOU, KITE...
WE'RE PROS, TOO.
DON'T TREAT US LIKE KIDS!

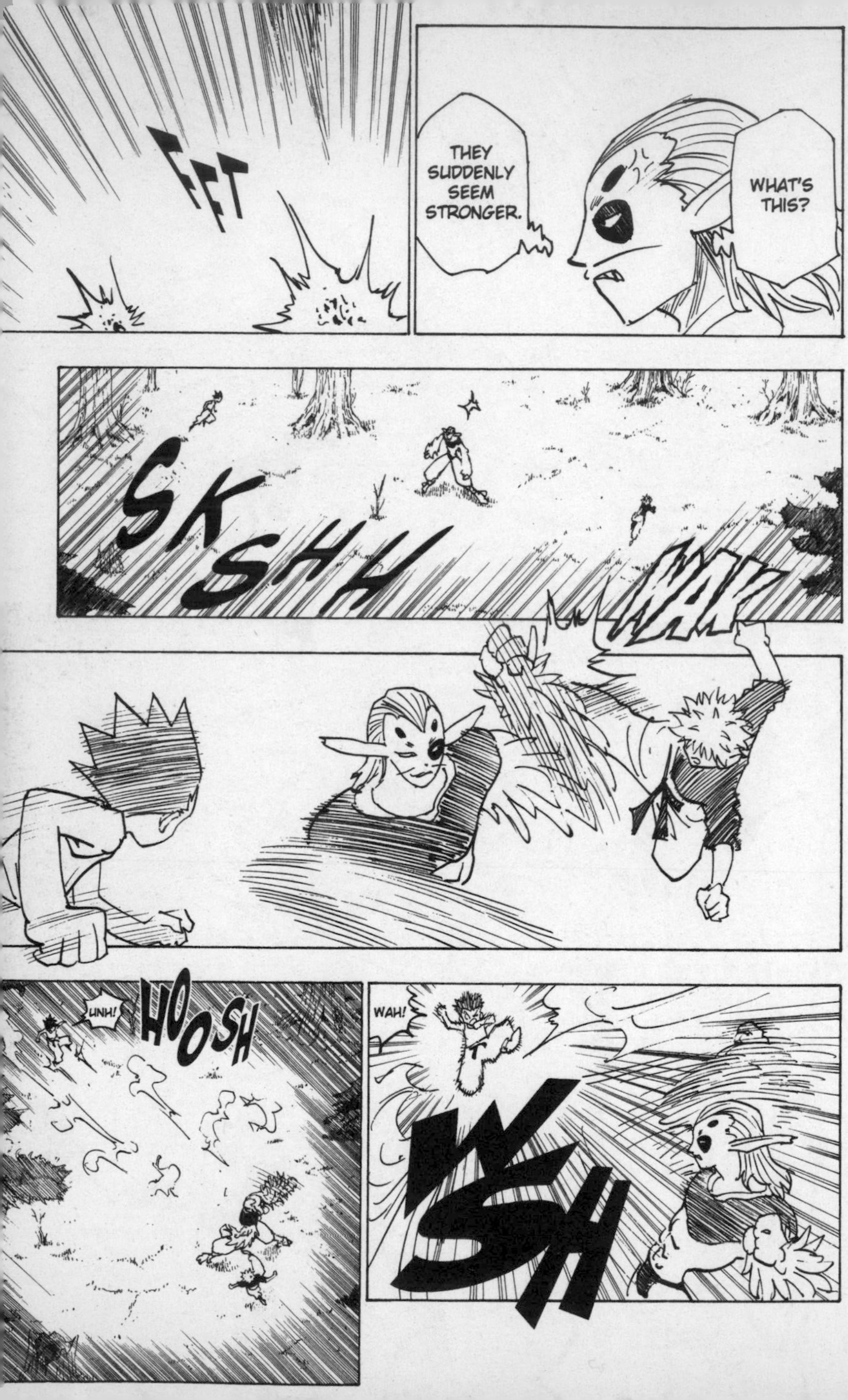
WHAT'S THIS?
THEY SUDDENLY SEEM STRONGER.
FFT
SKSHH
WAK
WAH!
WSH
UNH!
HOOSH

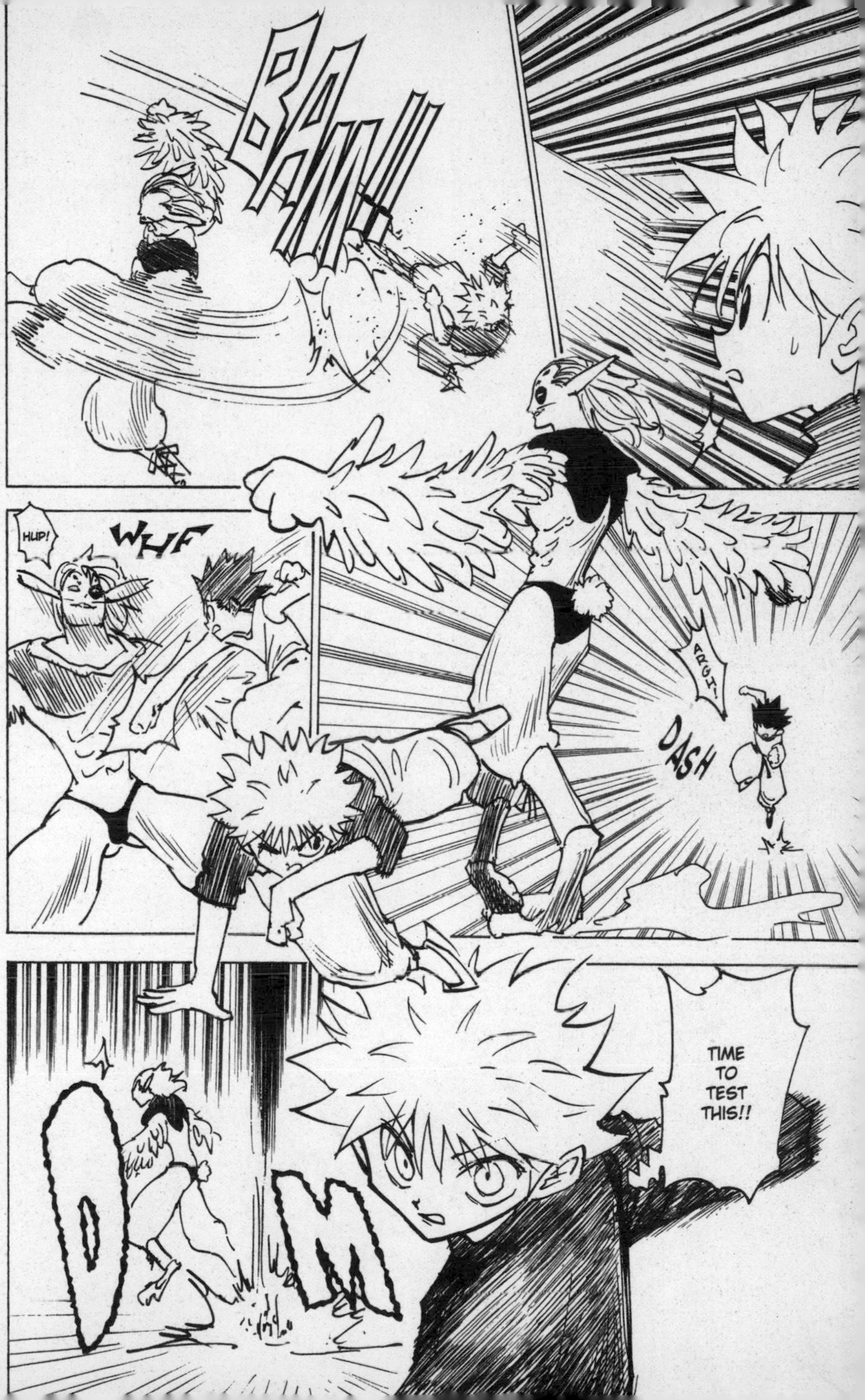
BAM
WHF
HUP!
ARGH!
DASH
TIME TO TEST THIS!!
DOM

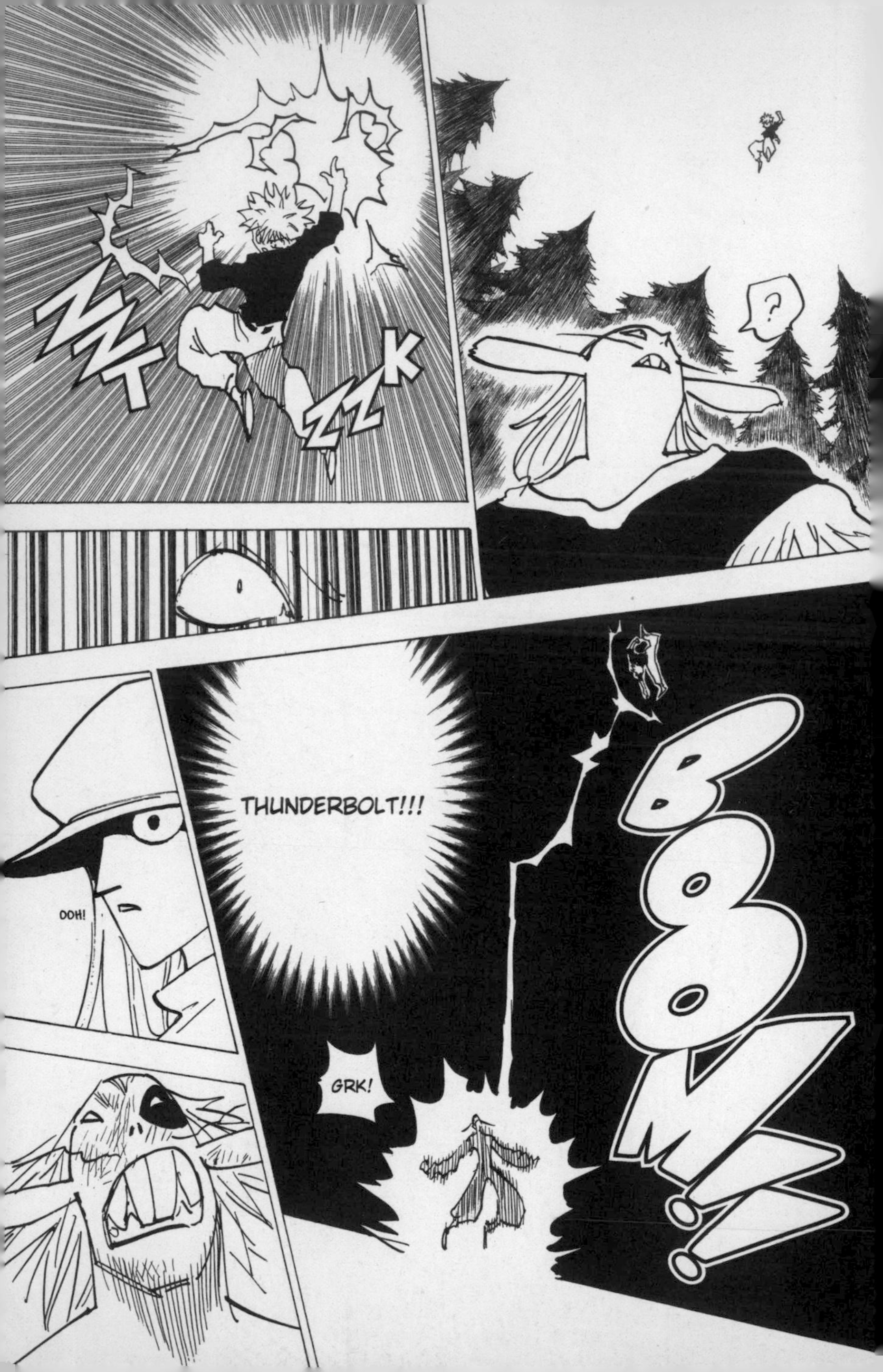
?
NNNTZZZK
THUNDERBOLT!!!
BOOM!!
GRK!
OOH!

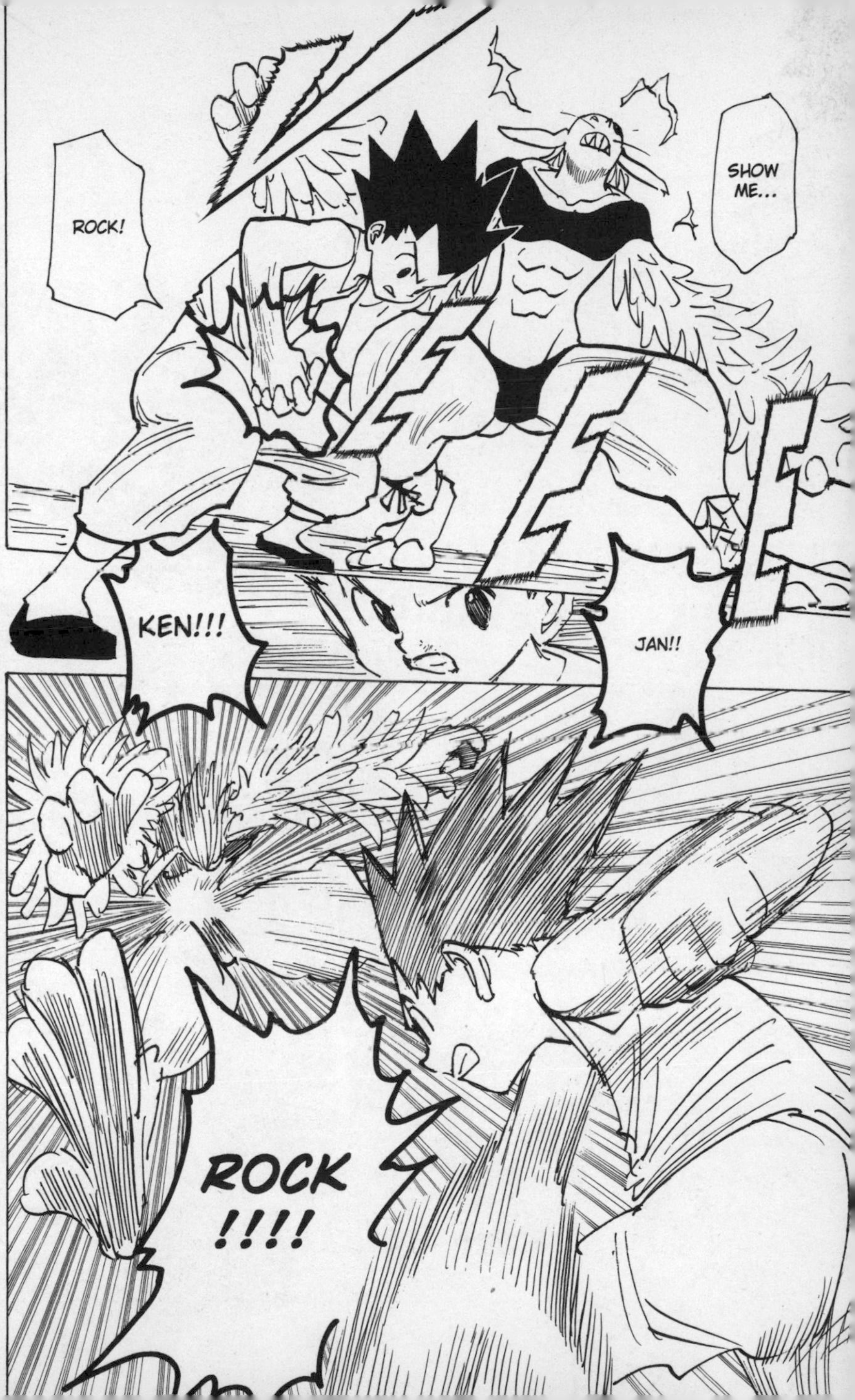
SHOW ME...
ROCK!
JAN!!
KEN!!!
ROCK !!!!

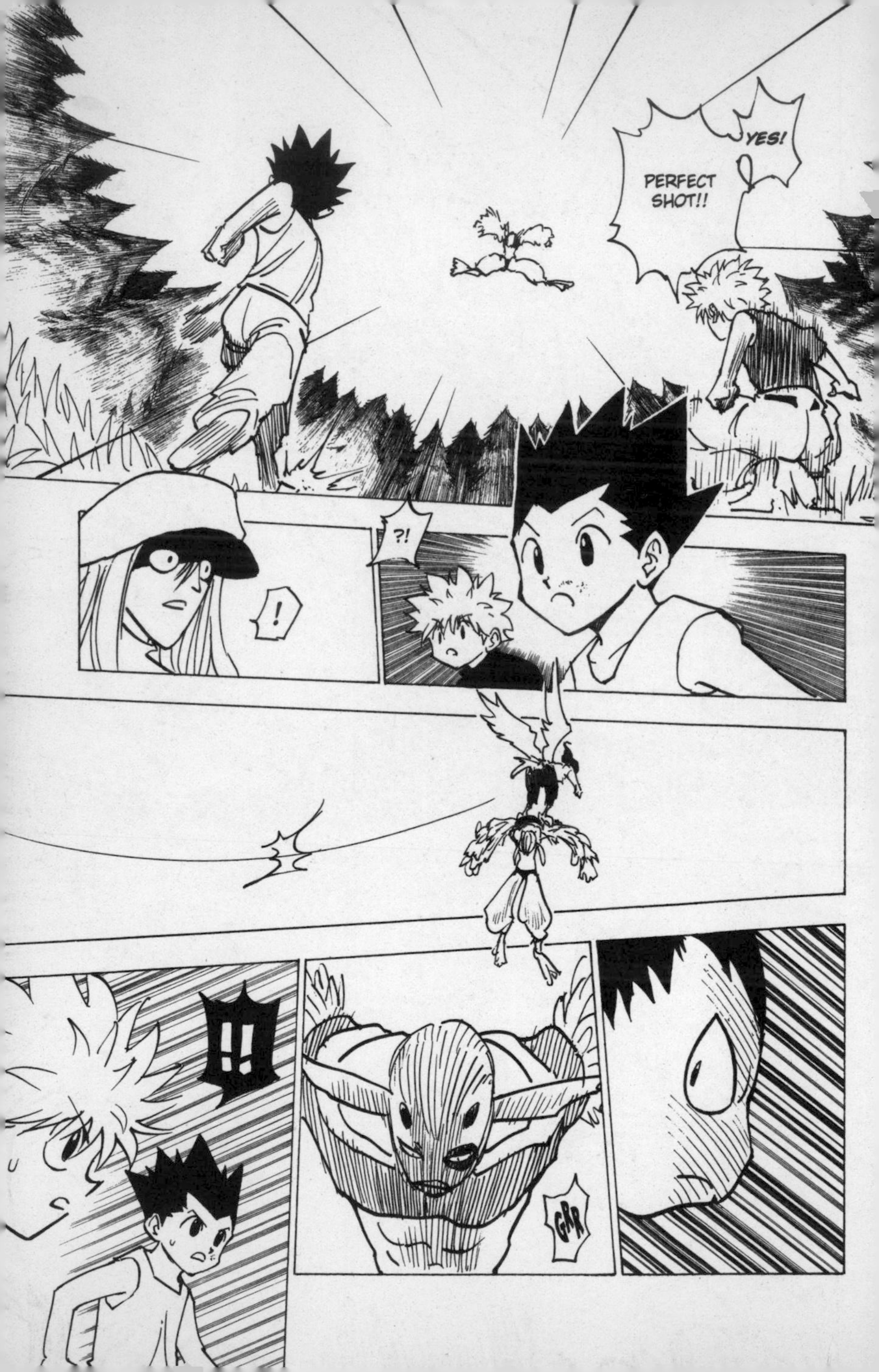
YES!
PERFECT SHOT!!
?!
!
!!
GRR

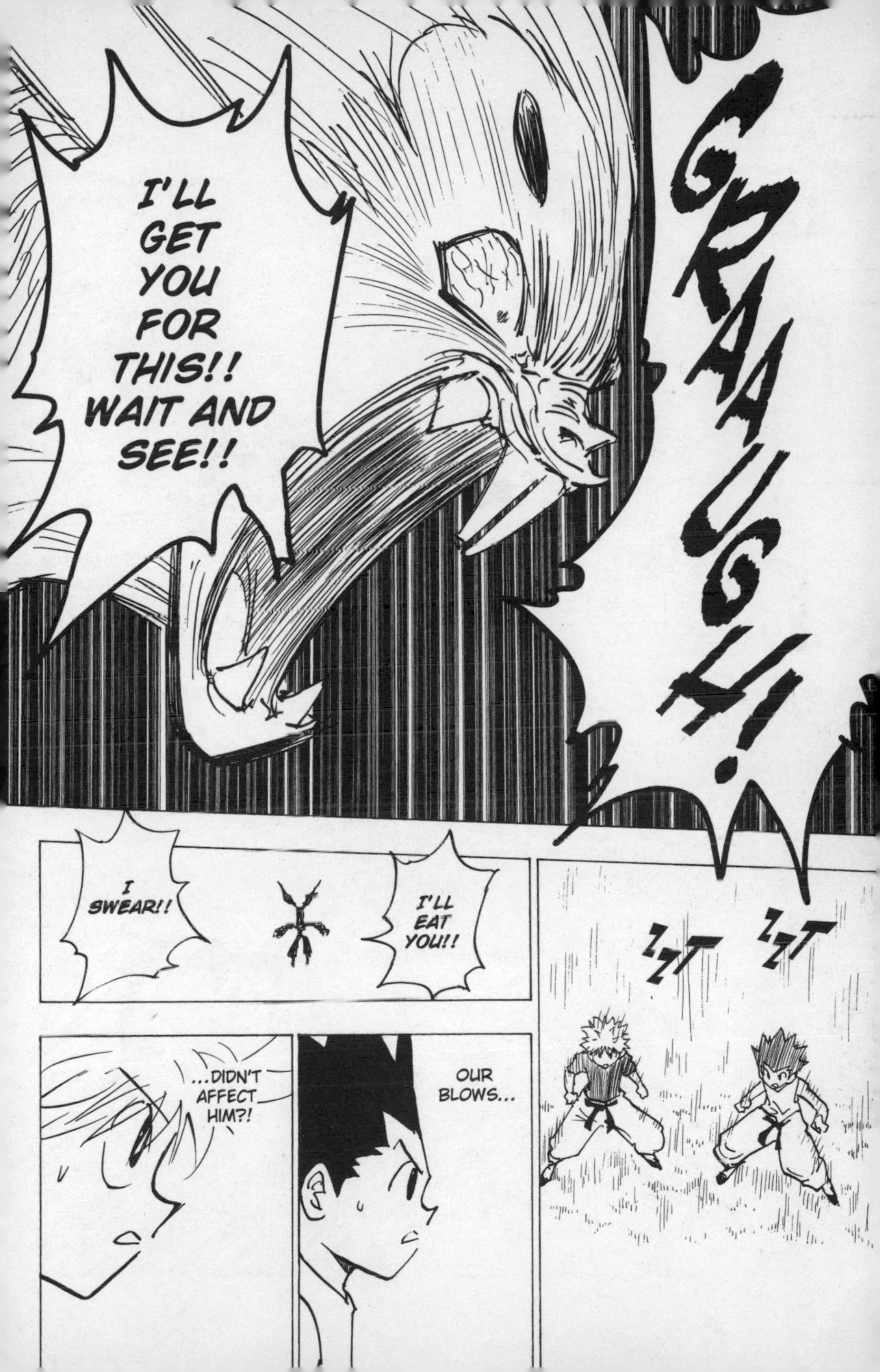
GRAAUGH!
I'LL GET YOU FOR THIS!! WAIT AND SEE!!
ZZT ZZT
I'LL EAT YOU!!
I SWEAR!!
OUR BLOWS...
...DIDN'T AFFECT HIM?!

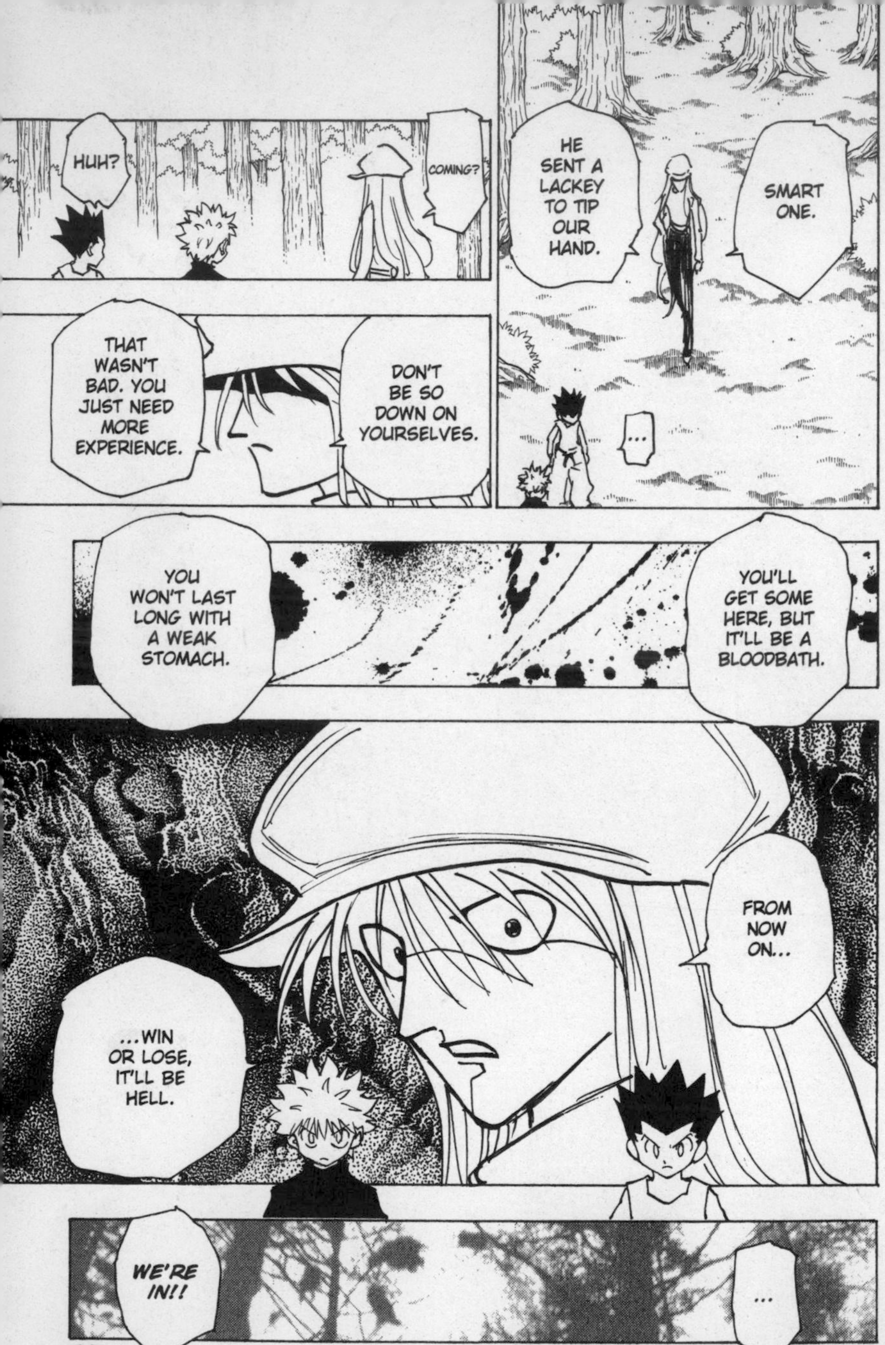
SMART ONE.
HE SENT A LACKEY TO TIP OUR HAND.
...
COMING?
HUH?
DON'T BE SO DOWN ON YOURSELVES.
THAT WASN'T BAD. YOU JUST NEED MORE EXPERIENCE.
YOU'LL GET SOME HERE, BUT IT'LL BE A BLOODBATH.
YOU WON'T LAST LONG WITH A WEAK STOMACH.
FROM NOW ON...
...WIN OR LOSE, IT'LL BE HELL.
...
WE'RE IN!!

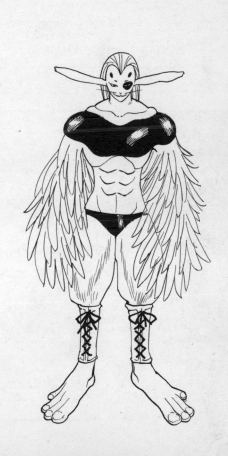

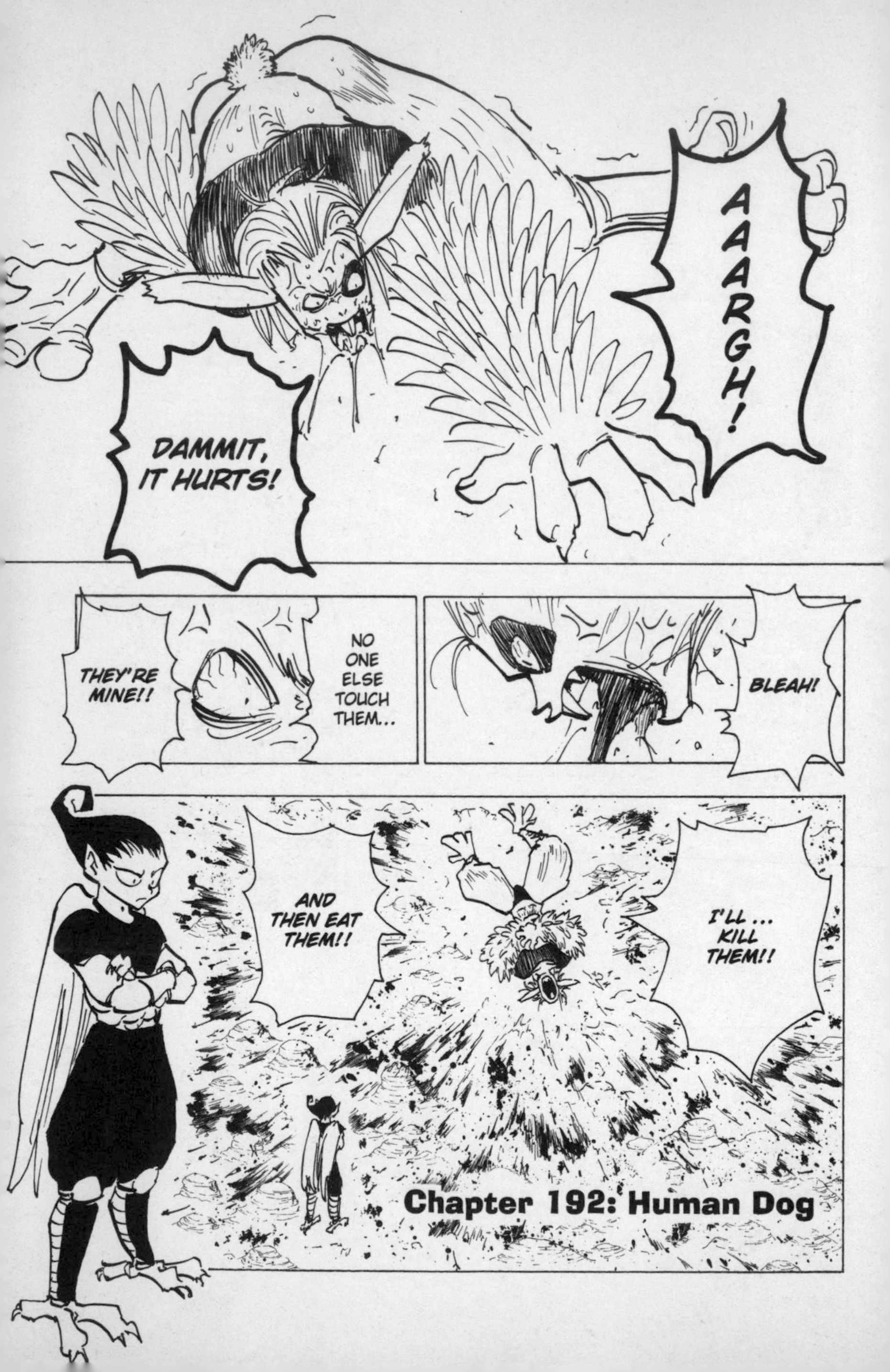
AAARGH!
DAMMIT, IT HURTS!
BLEAH!
NO ONE ELSE TOUCH THEM...
THEY'RE MINE!!
I'LL ... KILL THEM!!
AND THEN EAT THEM!!
Chapter 192: Human Dog

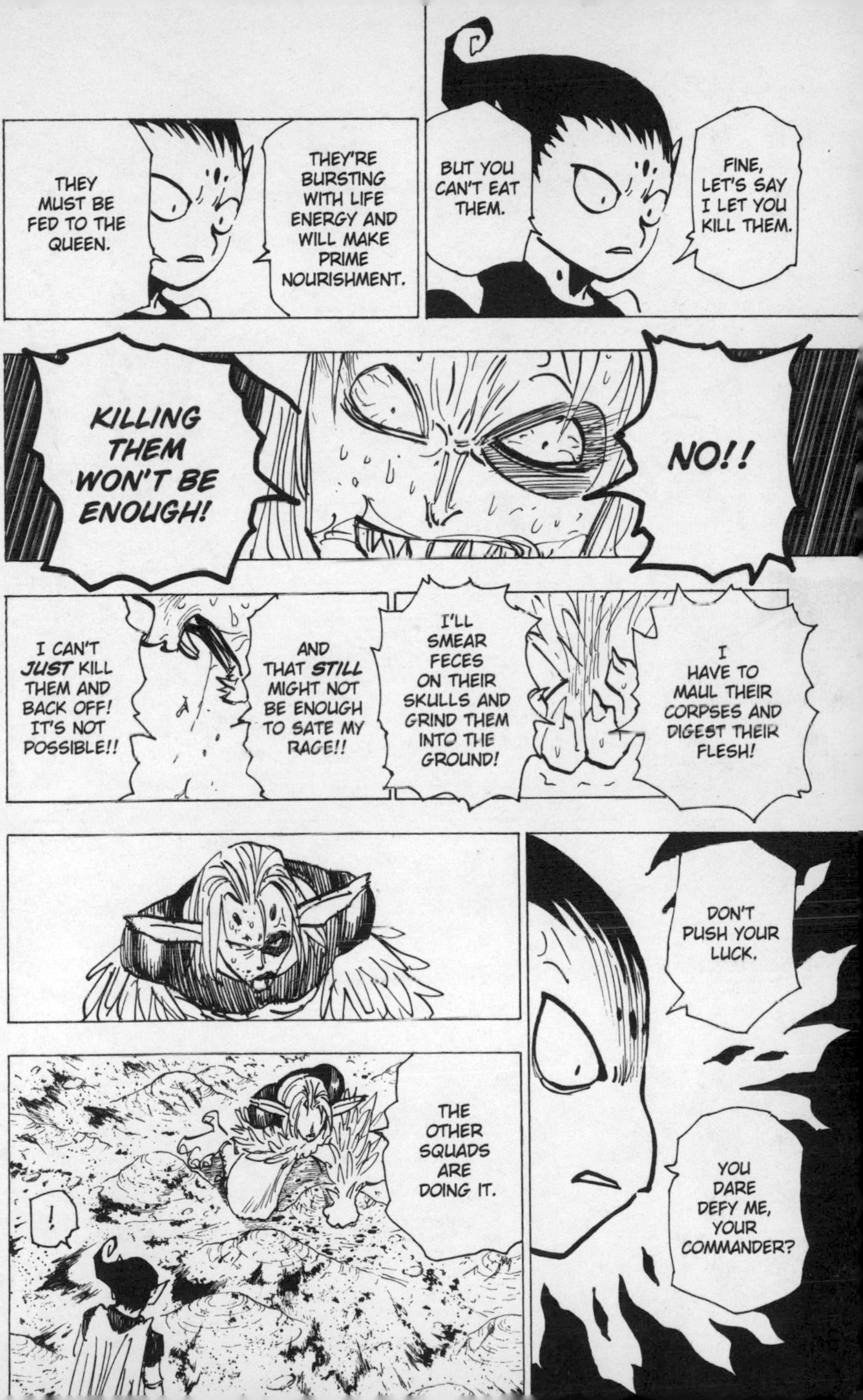
FINE, LET'S SAY I LET YOU KILL THEM.
BUT YOU CAN'T EAT THEM.
THEY'RE BURSTING WITH LIFE ENERGY AND WILL MAKE PRIME NOURISHMENT.
THEY MUST BE FED TO THE QUEEN.
NO!!
KILLING THEM WON'T BE ENOUGH!
I HAVE TO MAUL THEIR CORPSES AND DIGEST THEIR FLESH!
I'LL SMEAR FECES ON THEIR SKULLS AND GRIND THEM INTO THE GROUND!
AND THAT *STILL* MIGHT NOT BE ENOUGH TO SATE MY RAGE!!
I CAN'T *JUST* KILL THEM AND BACK OFF! IT'S NOT POSSIBLE!!
DON'T PUSH YOUR LUCK.
YOU DARE DEFY ME, YOUR COMMANDER?
THE OTHER SQUADS ARE DOING IT.
!

READ THIS WAY

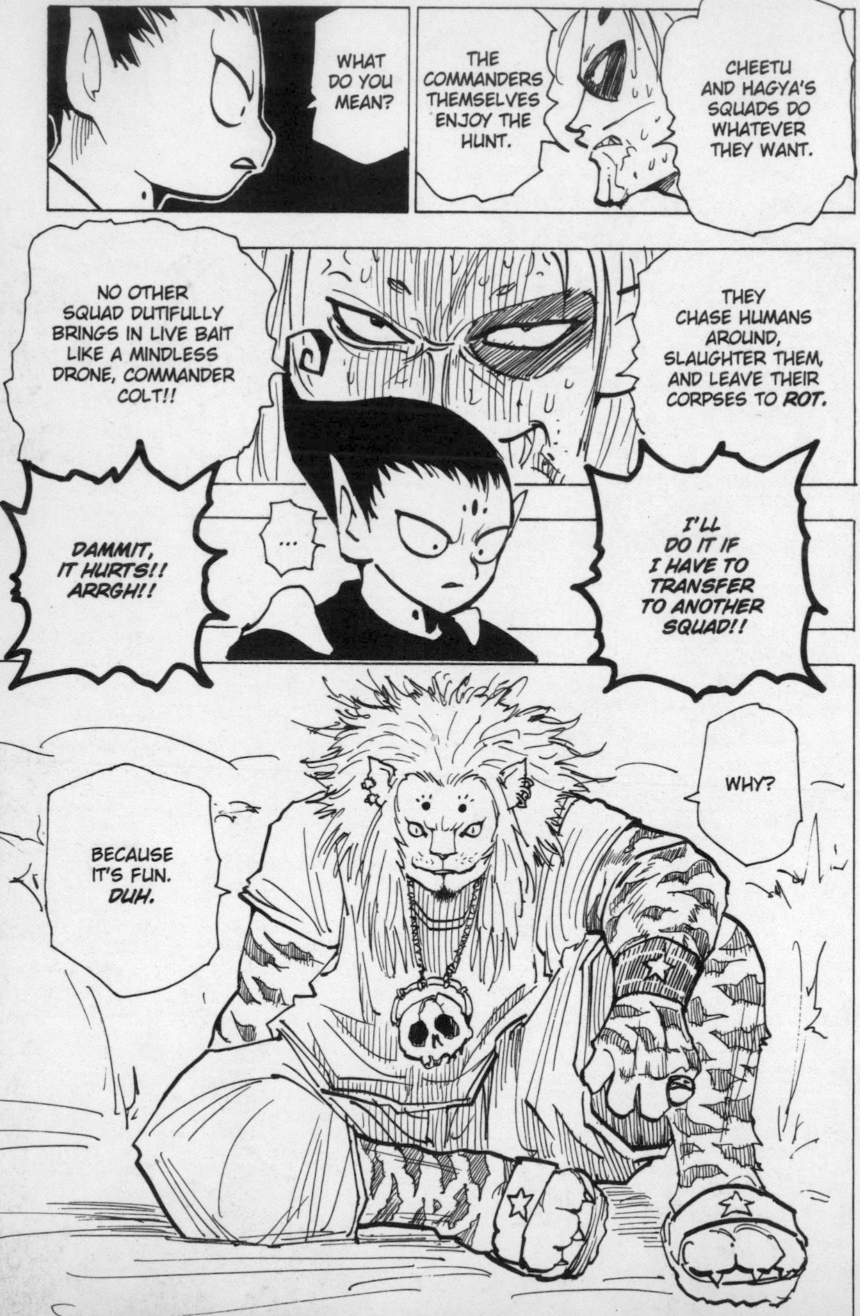

CHEETU AND HAGYA'S SQUADS DO WHATEVER THEY WANT.
THE COMMANDERS THEMSELVES ENJOY THE HUNT.
WHAT DO YOU MEAN?
THEY CHASE HUMANS AROUND, SLAUGHTER THEM, AND LEAVE THEIR CORPSES TO *ROT*.
NO OTHER SQUAD DUTIFULLY BRINGS IN LIVE BAIT LIKE A MINDLESS DRONE, COMMANDER COLT!!
I'LL DO IT IF I HAVE TO TRANSFER TO ANOTHER SQUAD!!
...
DAMMIT, IT HURTS!! ARRGH!!
WHY?
BECAUSE IT'S FUN. *DUH.*

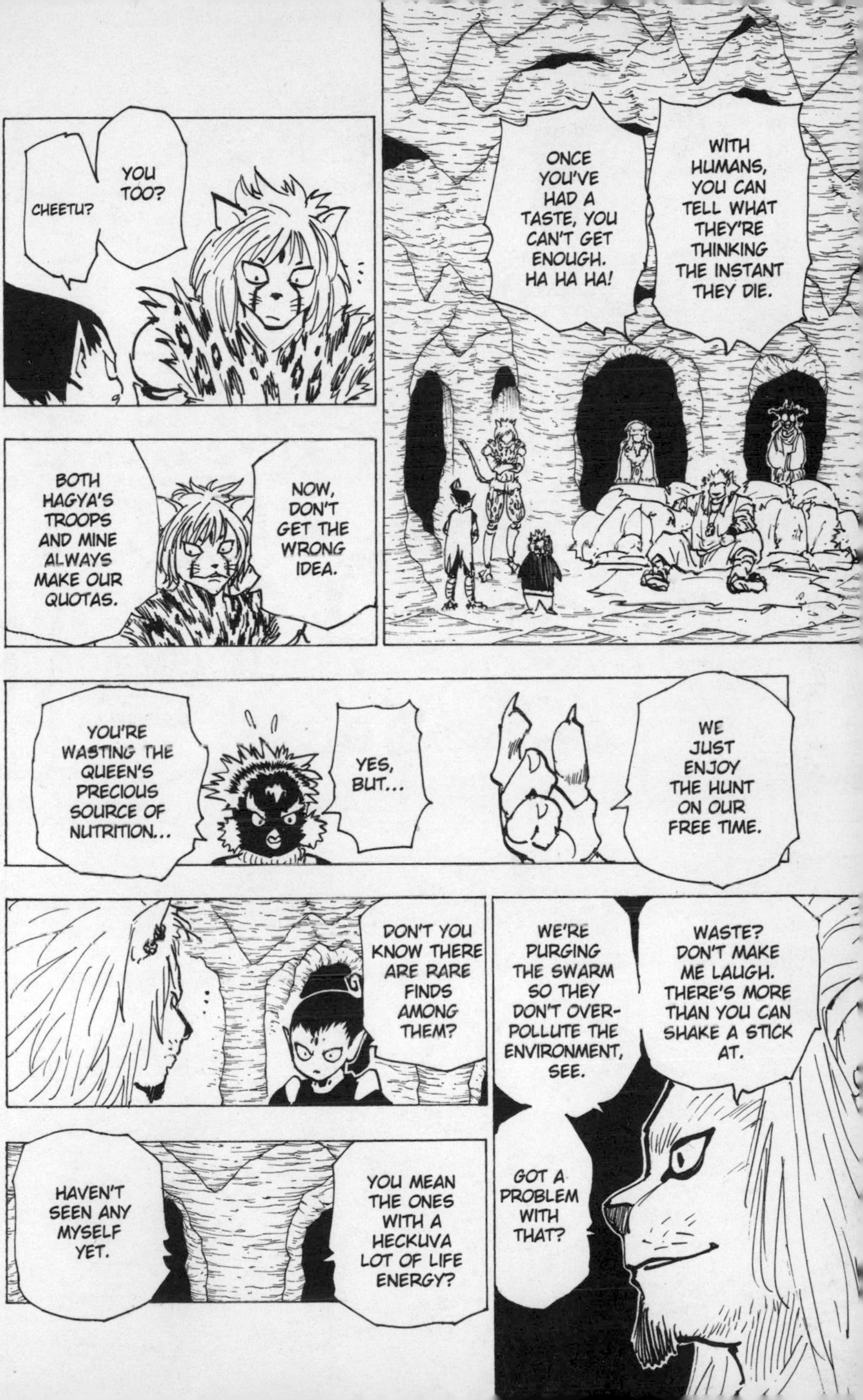
WITH HUMANS, YOU CAN TELL WHAT THEY'RE THINKING THE INSTANT THEY DIE.
ONCE YOU'VE HAD A TASTE, YOU CAN'T GET ENOUGH. HA HA HA!
YOU TOO?
CHEETU?
NOW, DON'T GET THE WRONG IDEA.
BOTH HAGYA'S TROOPS AND MINE ALWAYS MAKE OUR QUOTAS.
WE JUST ENJOY THE HUNT ON OUR FREE TIME.
YES, BUT...
YOU'RE WASTING THE QUEEN'S PRECIOUS SOURCE OF NUTRITION...
WASTE? DON'T MAKE ME LAUGH. THERE'S MORE THAN YOU CAN SHAKE A STICK AT.
WE'RE PURGING THE SWARM SO THEY DON'T OVER-POLLUTE THE ENVIRONMENT, SEE.
GOT A PROBLEM WITH THAT?
DON'T YOU KNOW THERE ARE RARE FINDS AMONG THEM?
YOU MEAN THE ONES WITH A HECKUVA LOT OF LIFE ENERGY?
HAVEN'T SEEN ANY MYSELF YET.

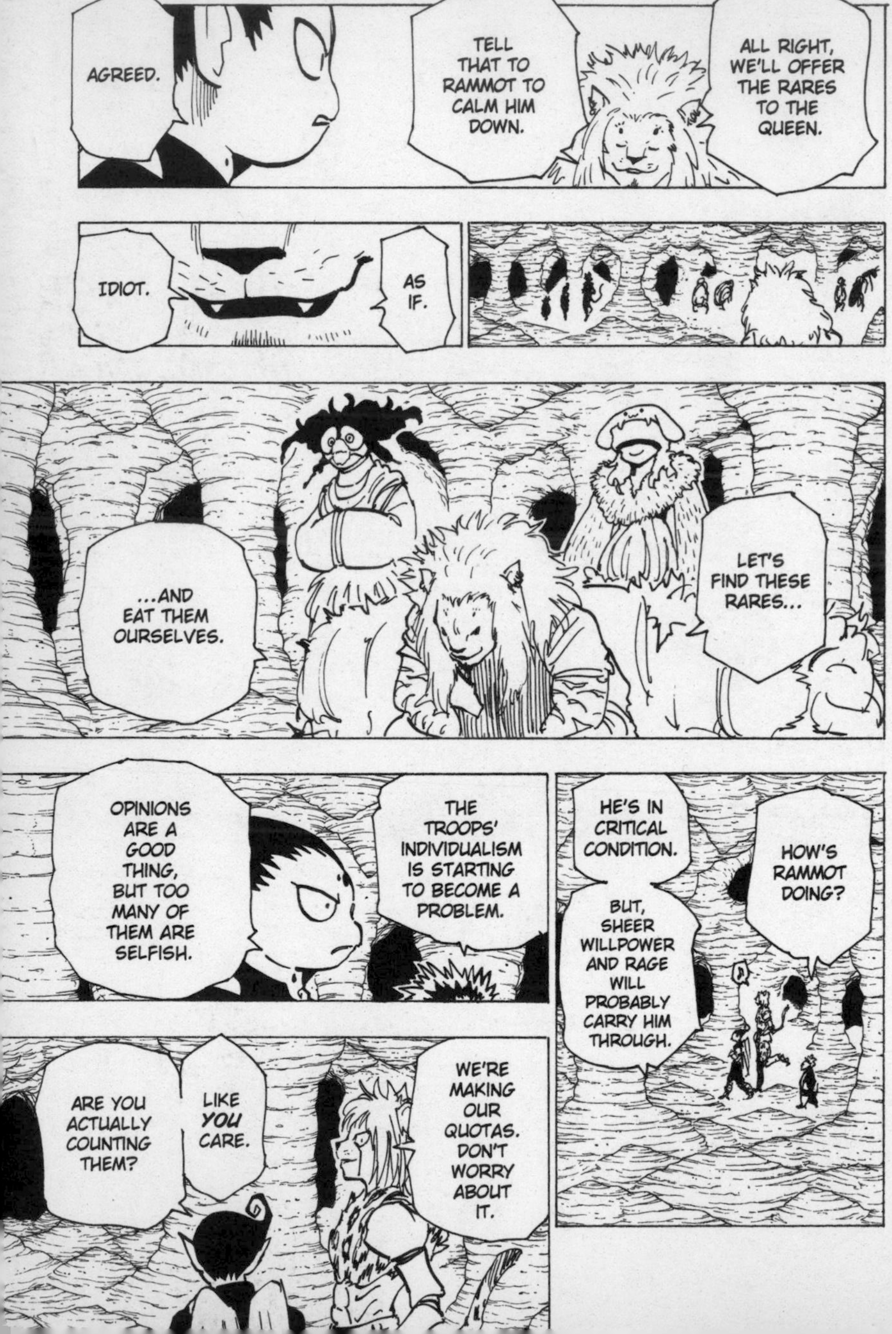
ALL RIGHT, WE'LL OFFER THE RARES TO THE QUEEN.
TELL THAT TO RAMMOT TO CALM HIM DOWN.
AGREED.
AS IF.
IDIOT.
LET'S FIND THESE RARES...
...AND EAT THEM OURSELVES.
HOW'S RAMMOT DOING?
HE'S IN CRITICAL CONDITION.
BUT, SHEER WILLPOWER AND RAGE WILL PROBABLY CARRY HIM THROUGH.
THE TROOPS' INDIVIDUALISM IS STARTING TO BECOME A PROBLEM.
OPINIONS ARE A GOOD THING, BUT TOO MANY OF THEM ARE SELFISH.
WE'RE MAKING OUR QUOTAS. DON'T WORRY ABOUT IT.
LIKE *YOU* CARE.
ARE YOU ACTUALLY COUNTING THEM?

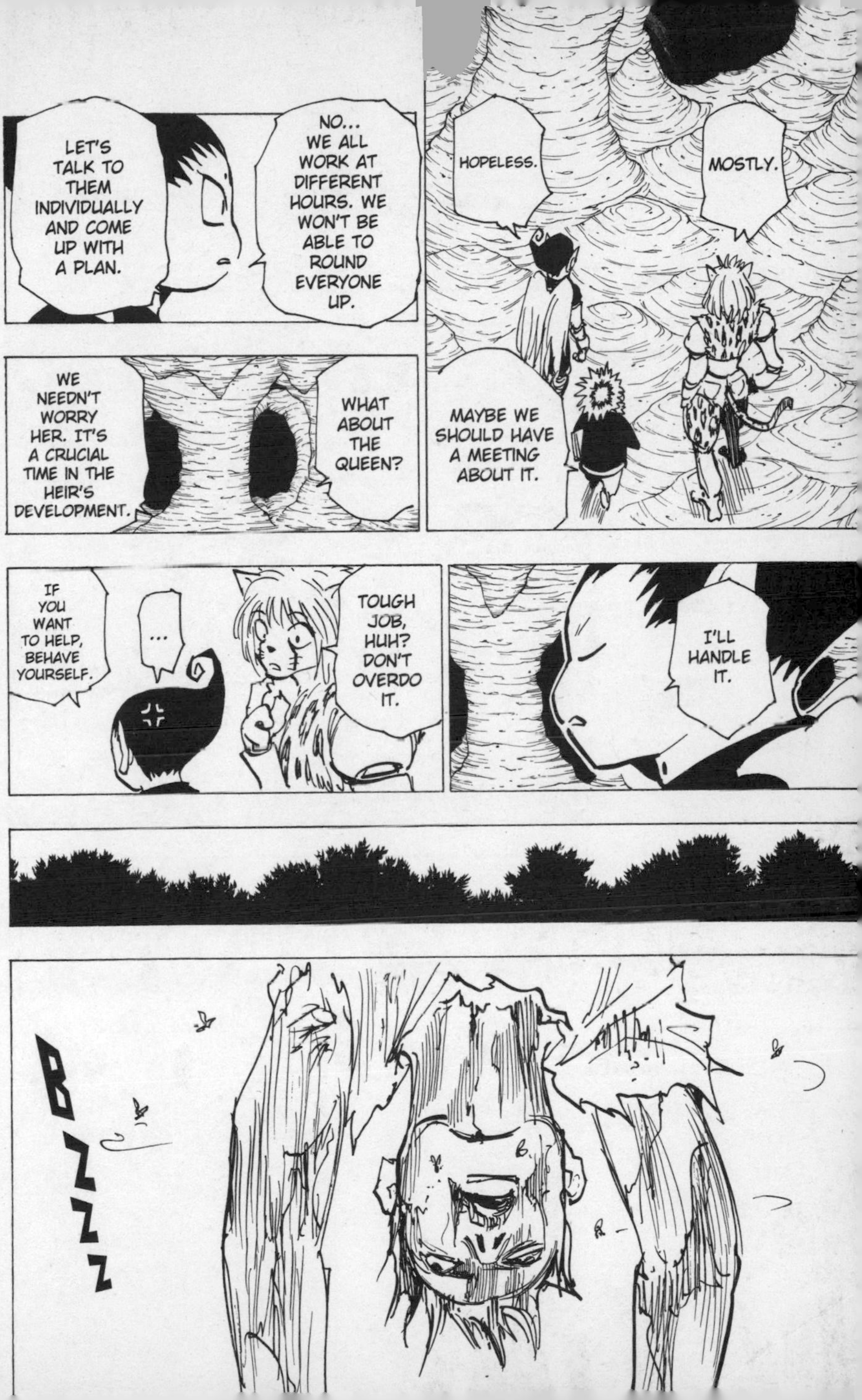
MOSTLY.
HOPELESS.
MAYBE WE SHOULD HAVE A MEETING ABOUT IT.
NO... WE ALL WORK AT DIFFERENT HOURS. WE WON'T BE ABLE TO ROUND EVERYONE UP.
LET'S TALK TO THEM INDIVIDUALLY AND COME UP WITH A PLAN.
WHAT ABOUT THE QUEEN?
WE NEEDN'T WORRY HER. IT'S A CRUCIAL TIME IN THE HEIR'S DEVELOPMENT.
I'LL HANDLE IT.
TOUGH JOB, HUH? DON'T OVERDO IT.
...
IF YOU WANT TO HELP, BEHAVE YOURSELF.
BZZZ

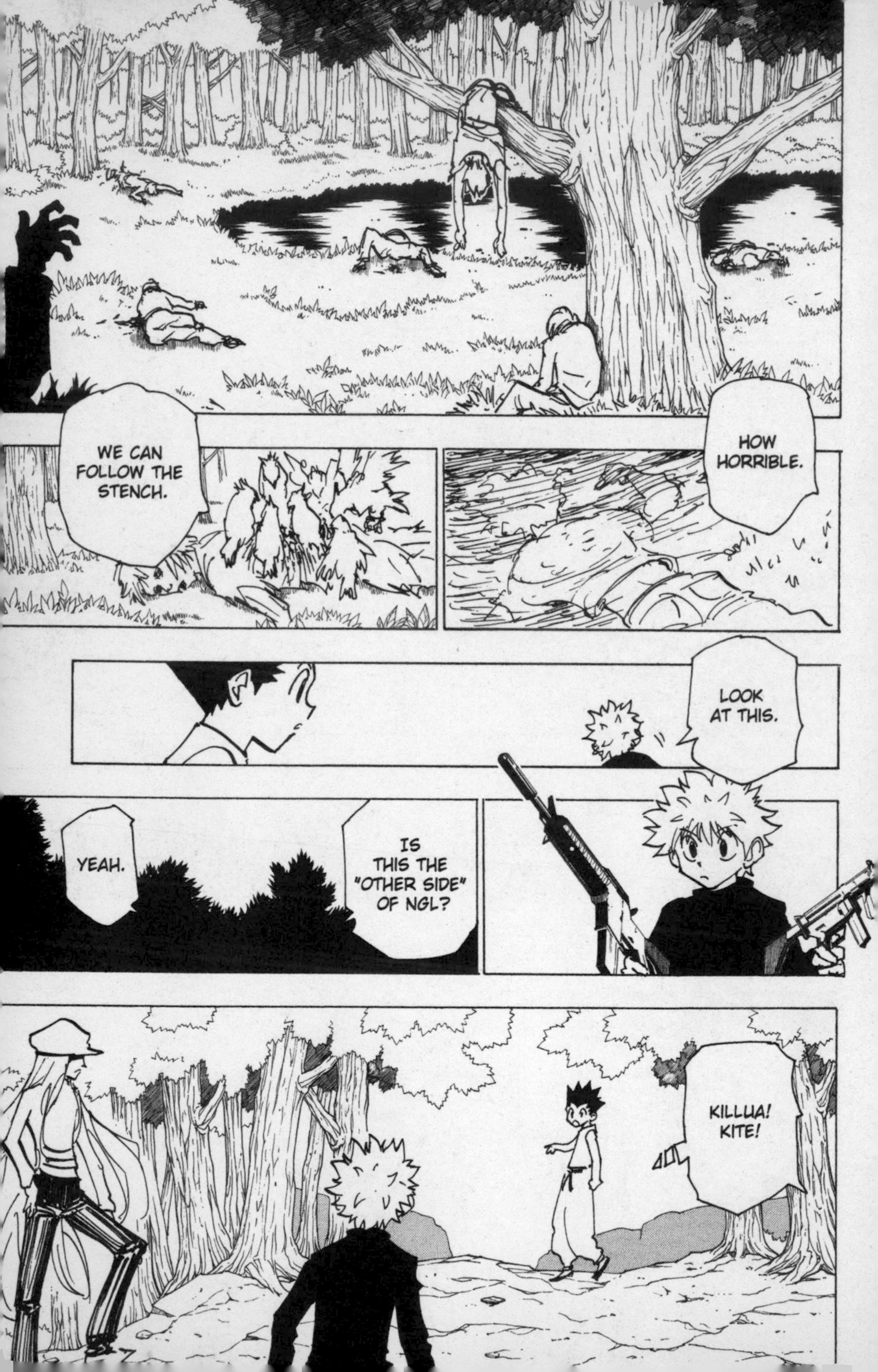
HOW HORRIBLE.
WE CAN FOLLOW THE STENCH.
LOOK AT THIS.
IS THIS THE "OTHER SIDE" OF NGL?
YEAH.
KILLUA! KITE!

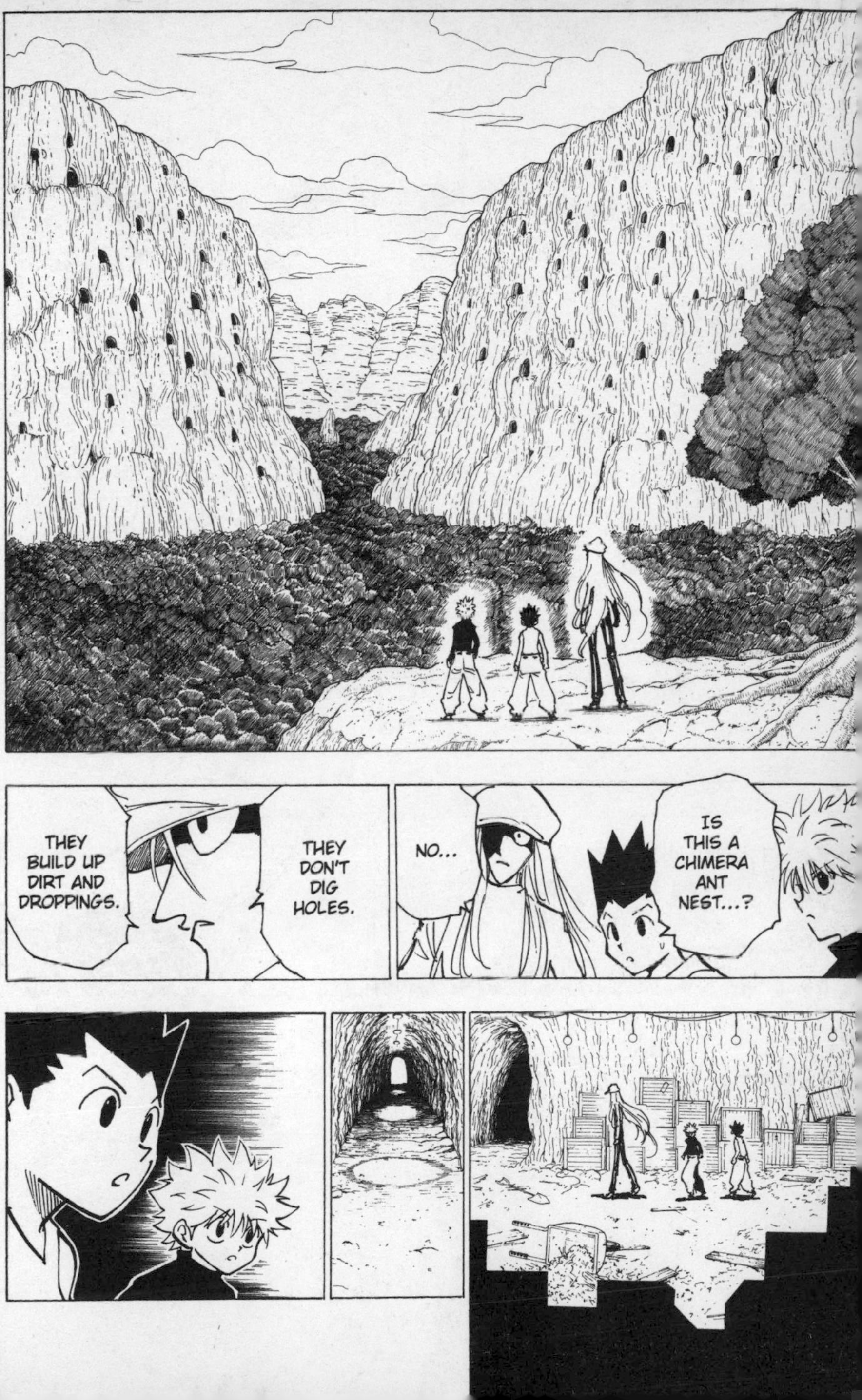
IS THIS A CHIMERA ANT NEST...?
NO...
THEY DON'T DIG HOLES.
THEY BUILD UP DIRT AND DROPPINGS.

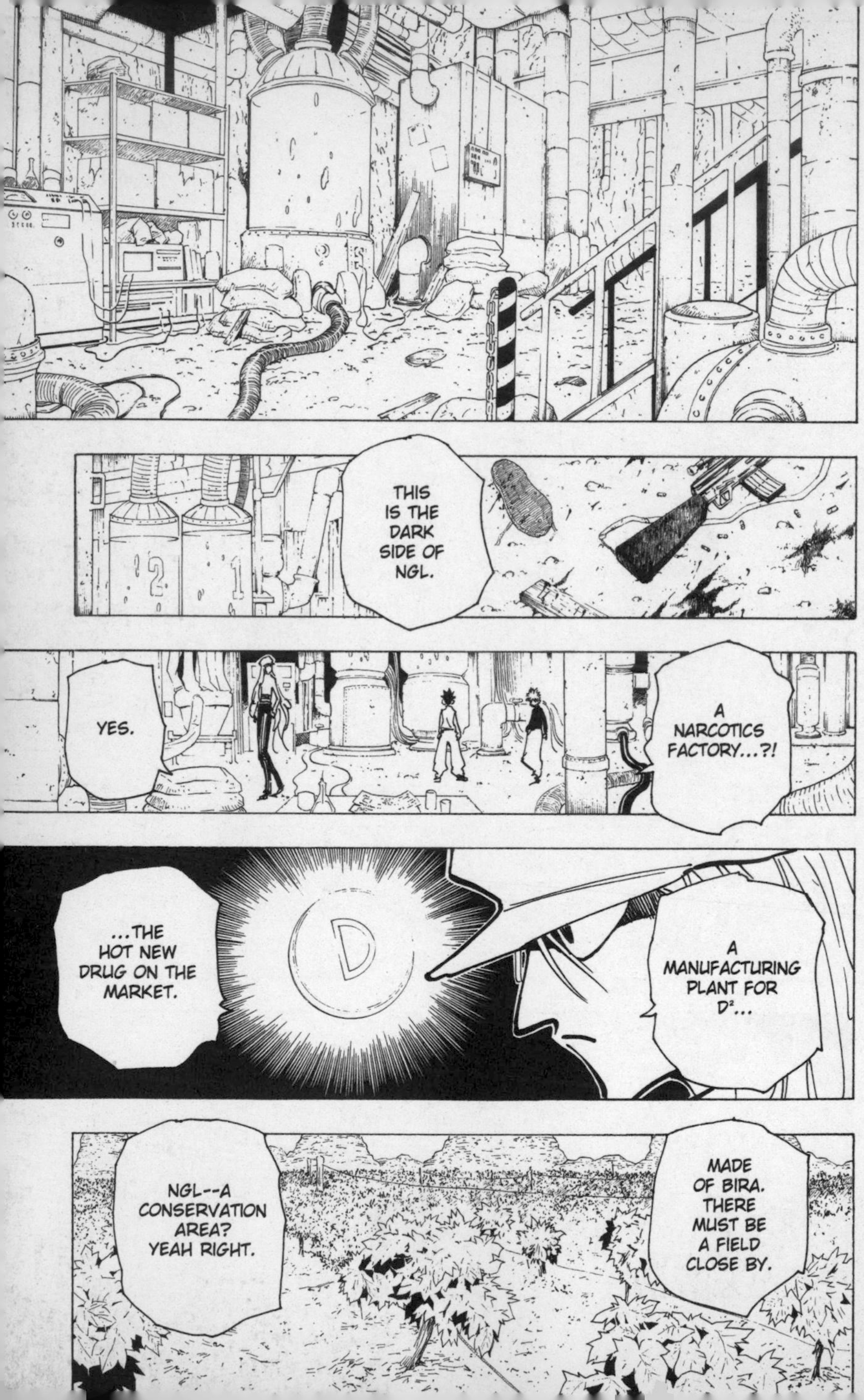
THIS IS THE DARK SIDE OF NGL.
A NARCOTICS FACTORY...?!
YES.
A MANUFACTURING PLANT FOR D^2...
...THE HOT NEW DRUG ON THE MARKET.
MADE OF BIRA. THERE MUST BE A FIELD CLOSE BY.
NGL--A CONSERVATION AREA? YEAH RIGHT.

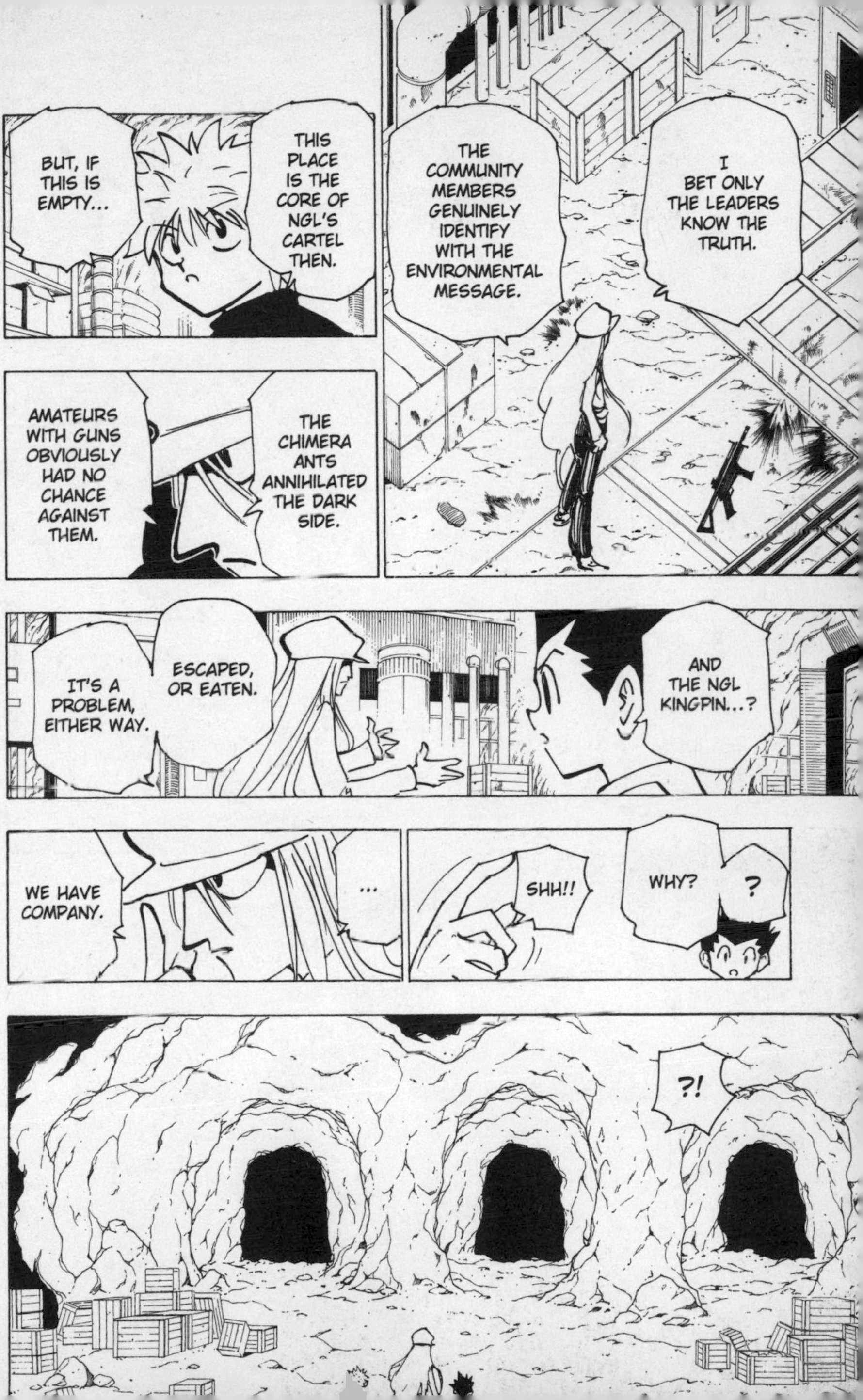
I BET ONLY THE LEADERS KNOW THE TRUTH.
THE COMMUNITY MEMBERS GENUINELY IDENTIFY WITH THE ENVIRONMENTAL MESSAGE.
THIS PLACE IS THE CORE OF NGL'S CARTEL THEN.
BUT, IF THIS IS EMPTY...
THE CHIMERA ANTS ANNIHILATED THE DARK SIDE.
AMATEURS WITH GUNS OBVIOUSLY HAD NO CHANCE AGAINST THEM.
AND THE NGL KINGPIN...?
ESCAPED, OR EATEN.
IT'S A PROBLEM, EITHER WAY.
?
WHY?
SHH!!
...
WE HAVE COMPANY.
?!

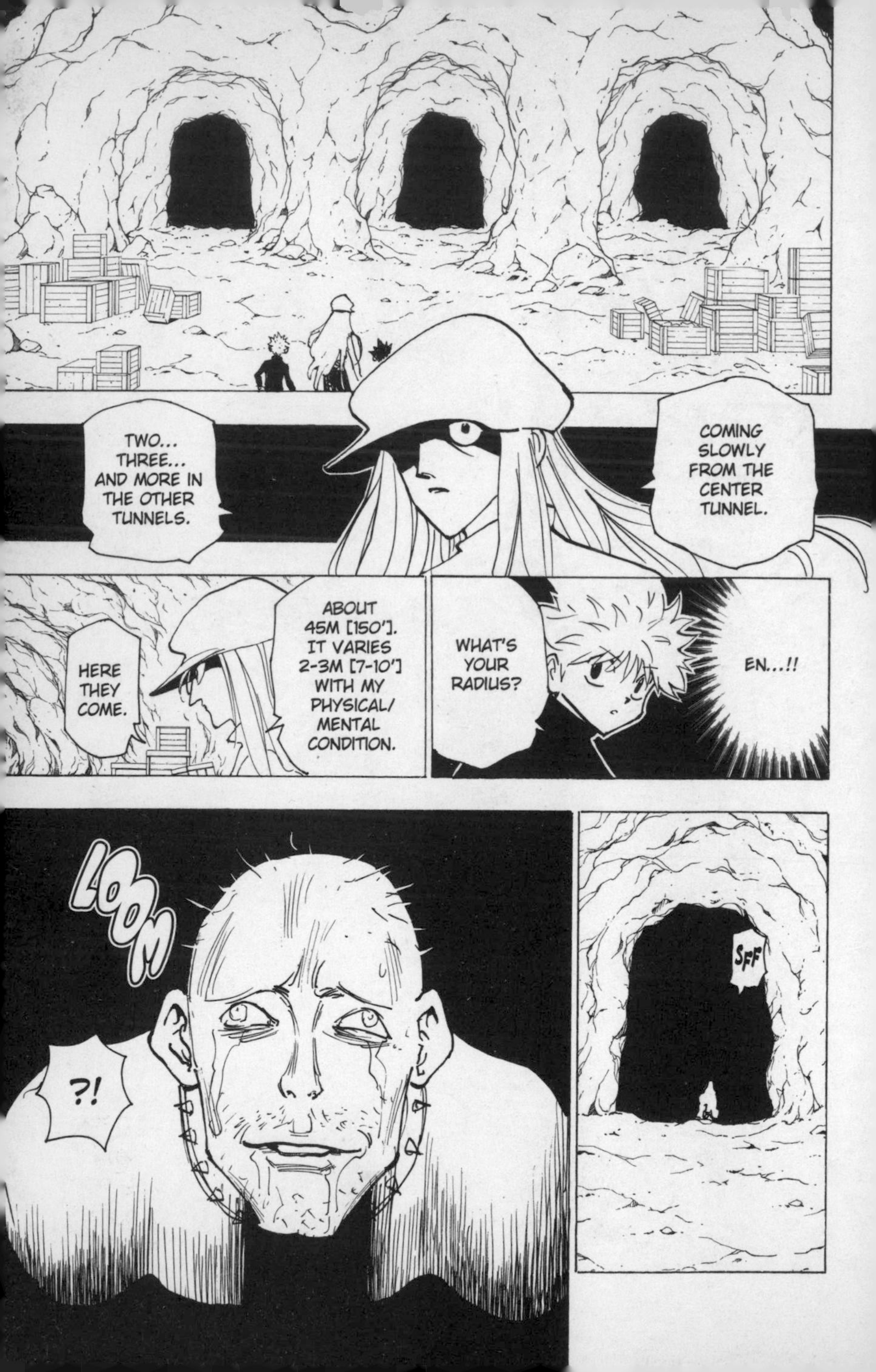
COMING SLOWLY FROM THE CENTER TUNNEL.
TWO... THREE... AND MORE IN THE OTHER TUNNELS.
EN...!!
WHAT'S YOUR RADIUS?
ABOUT 45M [150']. IT VARIES 2-3M [7-10'] WITH MY PHYSICAL/ MENTAL CONDITION.
HERE THEY COME.
SFF
LOOM
?!

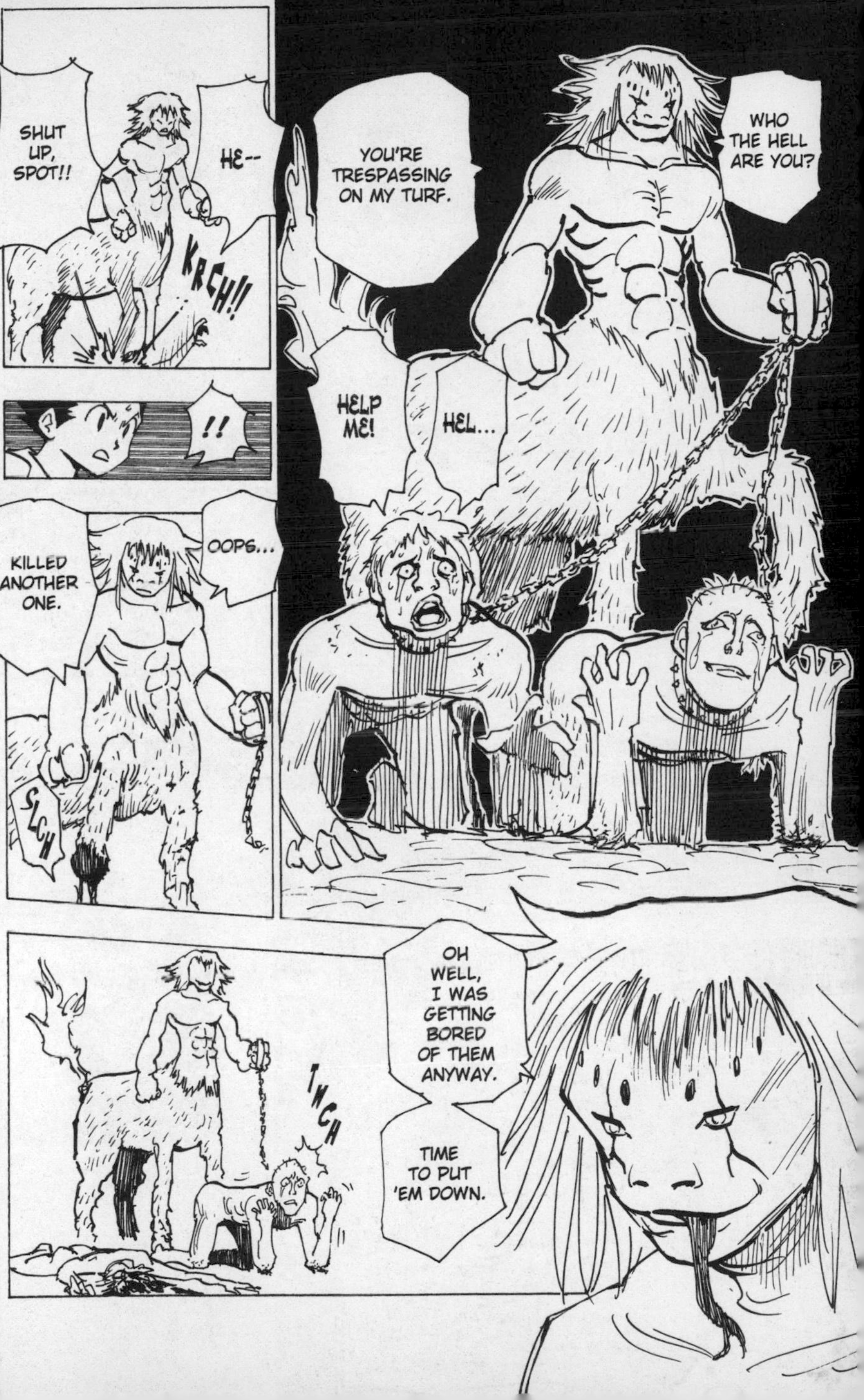
WHO THE HELL ARE YOU?
YOU'RE TRESPASSING ON MY TURF.
HEL...
HELP ME!
HE--
KRCH!!
SHUT UP, SPOT!!
!!
OOPS...
KILLED ANOTHER ONE.
SLCH
OH WELL, I WAS GETTING BORED OF THEM ANYWAY.
TIME TO PUT 'EM DOWN.
TNCH

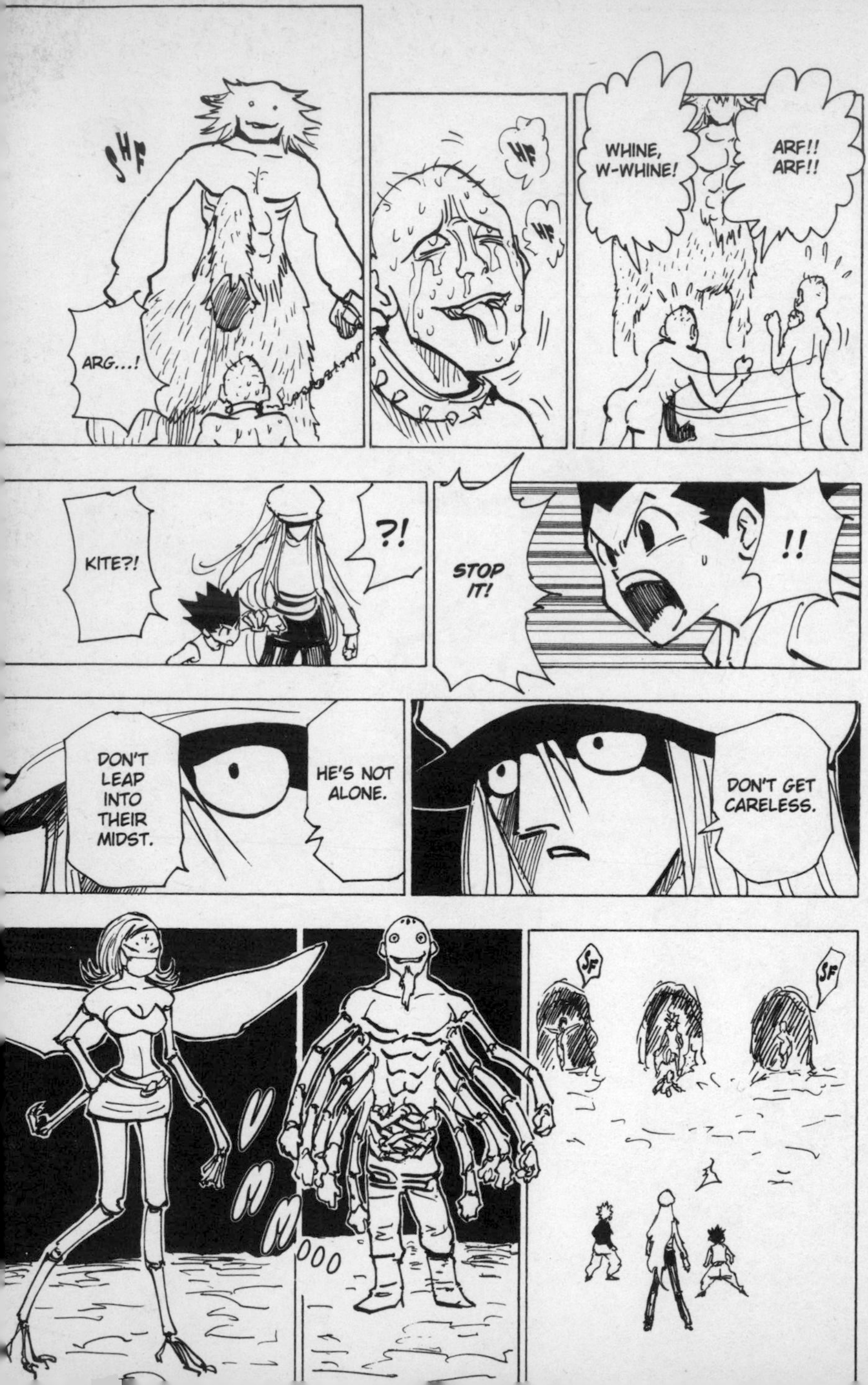
ARF!! ARF!!
WHINE, W-WHINE!
HF
HF
SHF
ARG...!
!!
STOP IT!
?!
KITE?!
DON'T GET CARELESS.
HE'S NOT ALONE.
DON'T LEAP INTO THEIR MIDST.
SF
SF

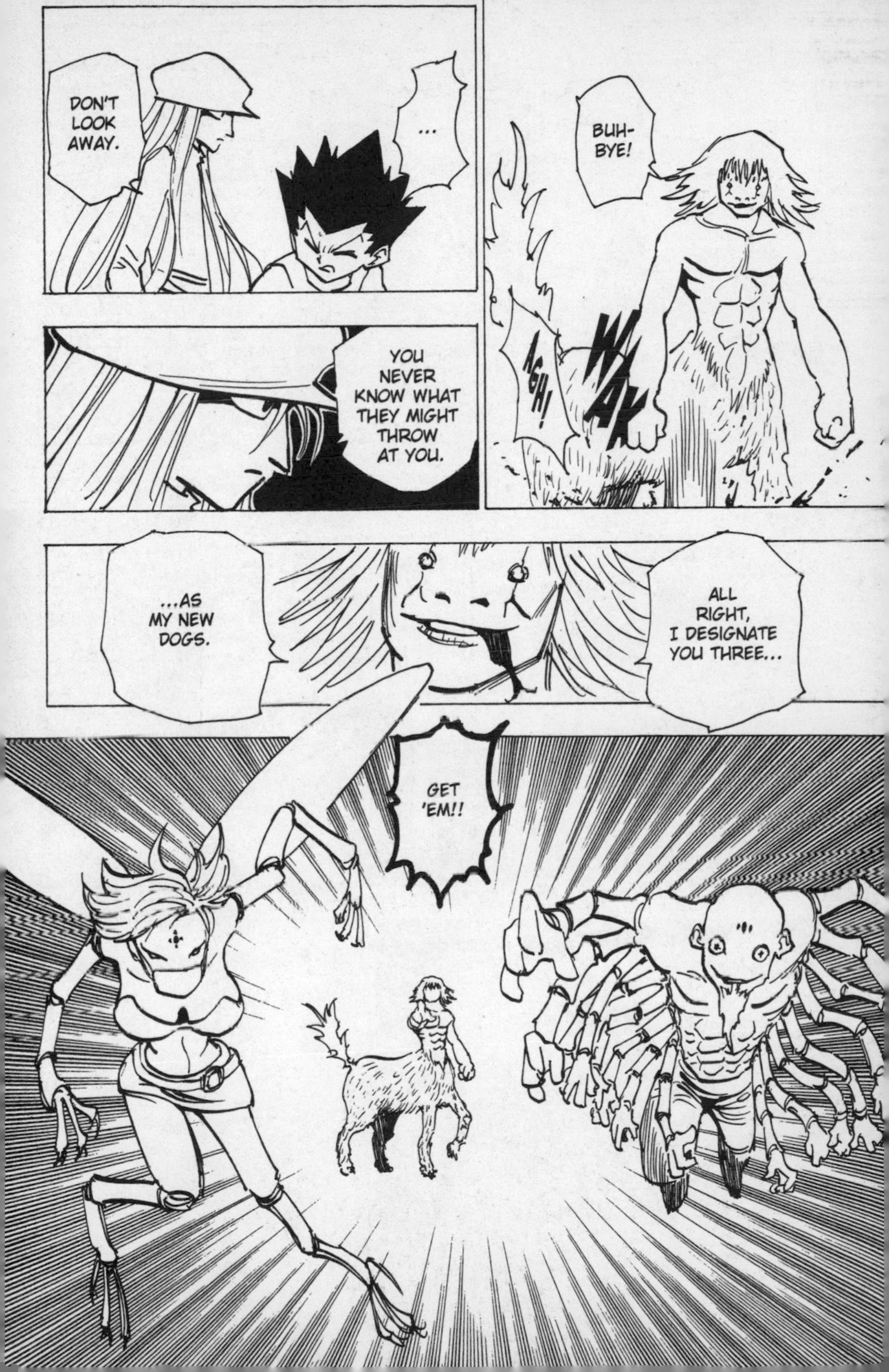
BUH-BYE!
WHAK
AGH!
DON'T LOOK AWAY.
...
YOU NEVER KNOW WHAT THEY MIGHT THROW AT YOU.
ALL RIGHT, I DESIGNATE YOU THREE...
...AS MY NEW DOGS.
GET 'EM!!

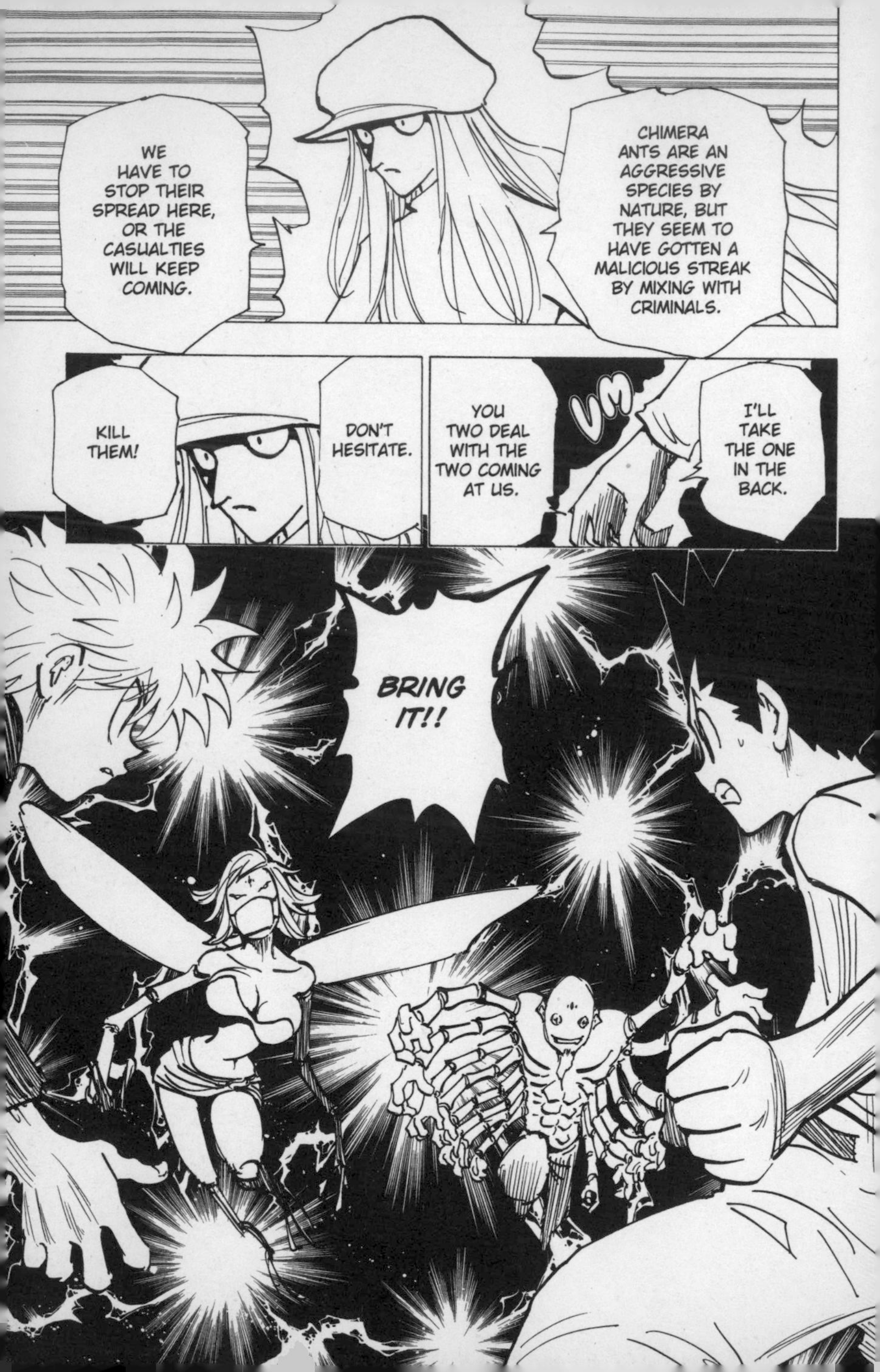
CHIMERA ANTS ARE AN AGGRESSIVE SPECIES BY NATURE, BUT THEY SEEM TO HAVE GOTTEN A MALICIOUS STREAK BY MIXING WITH CRIMINALS.
WE HAVE TO STOP THEIR SPREAD HERE, OR THE CASUALTIES WILL KEEP COMING.
I'LL TAKE THE ONE IN THE BACK.
UM
YOU TWO DEAL WITH THE TWO COMING AT US.
DON'T HESITATE.
KILL THEM!
BRING IT!!

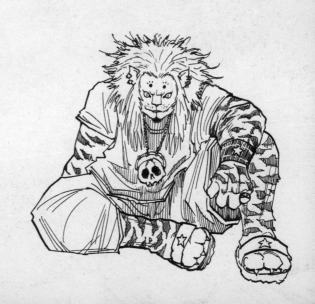

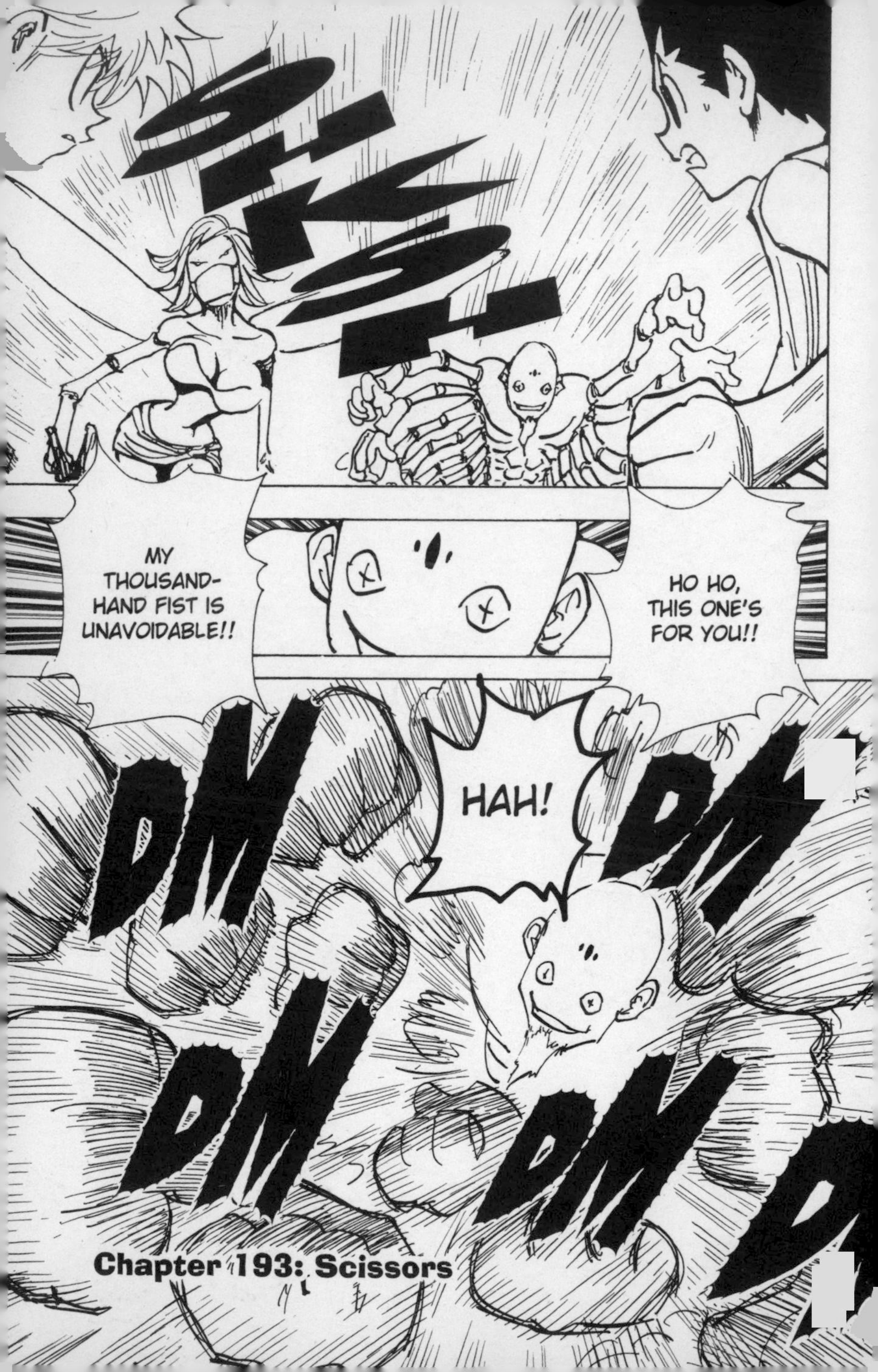
HO HO, THIS ONE'S FOR YOU!!
MY THOUSAND-HAND FIST IS UNAVOIDABLE!!
HAH!

Chapter 193: Scissors

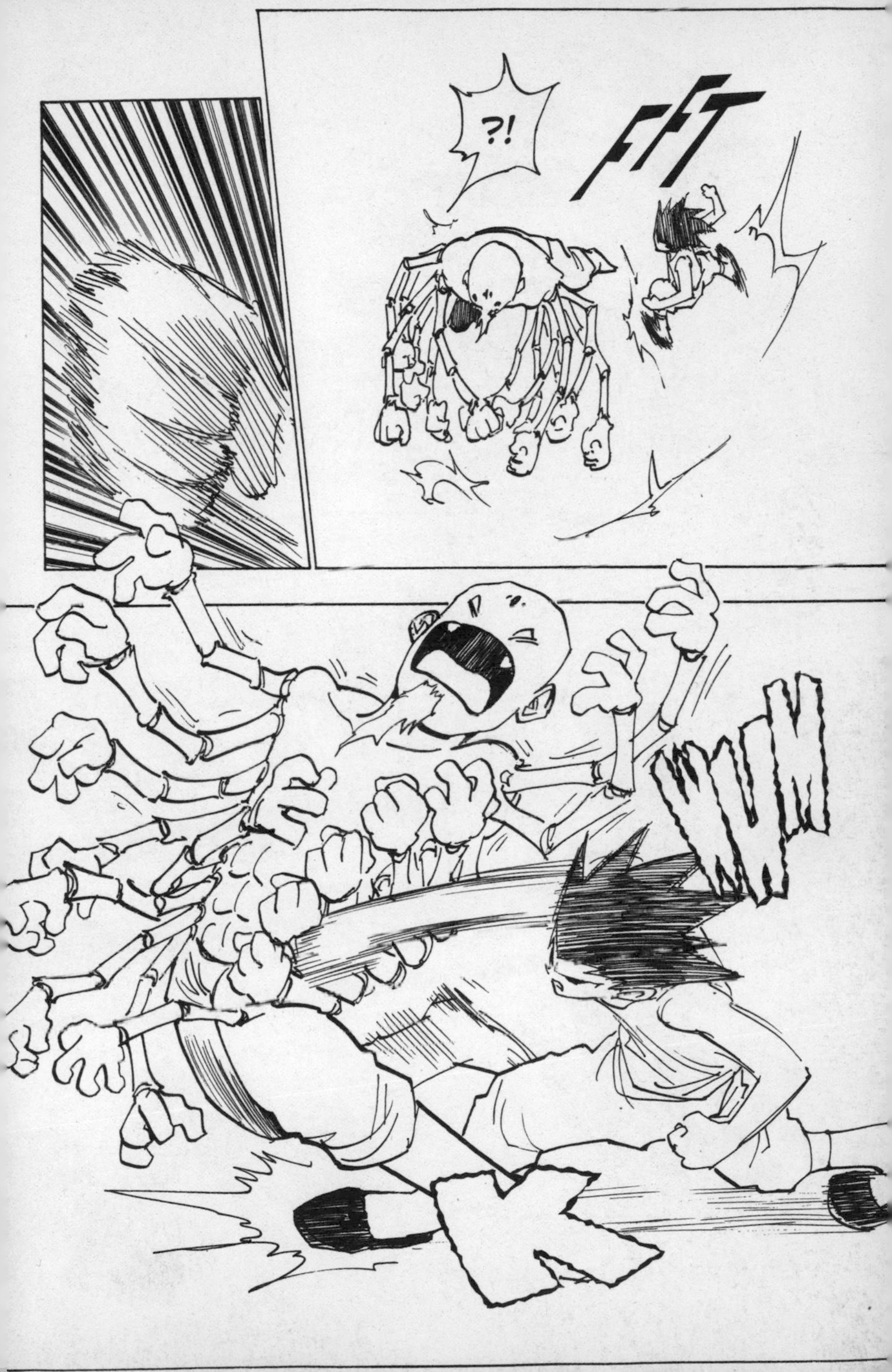
FFT
?!
WHAM

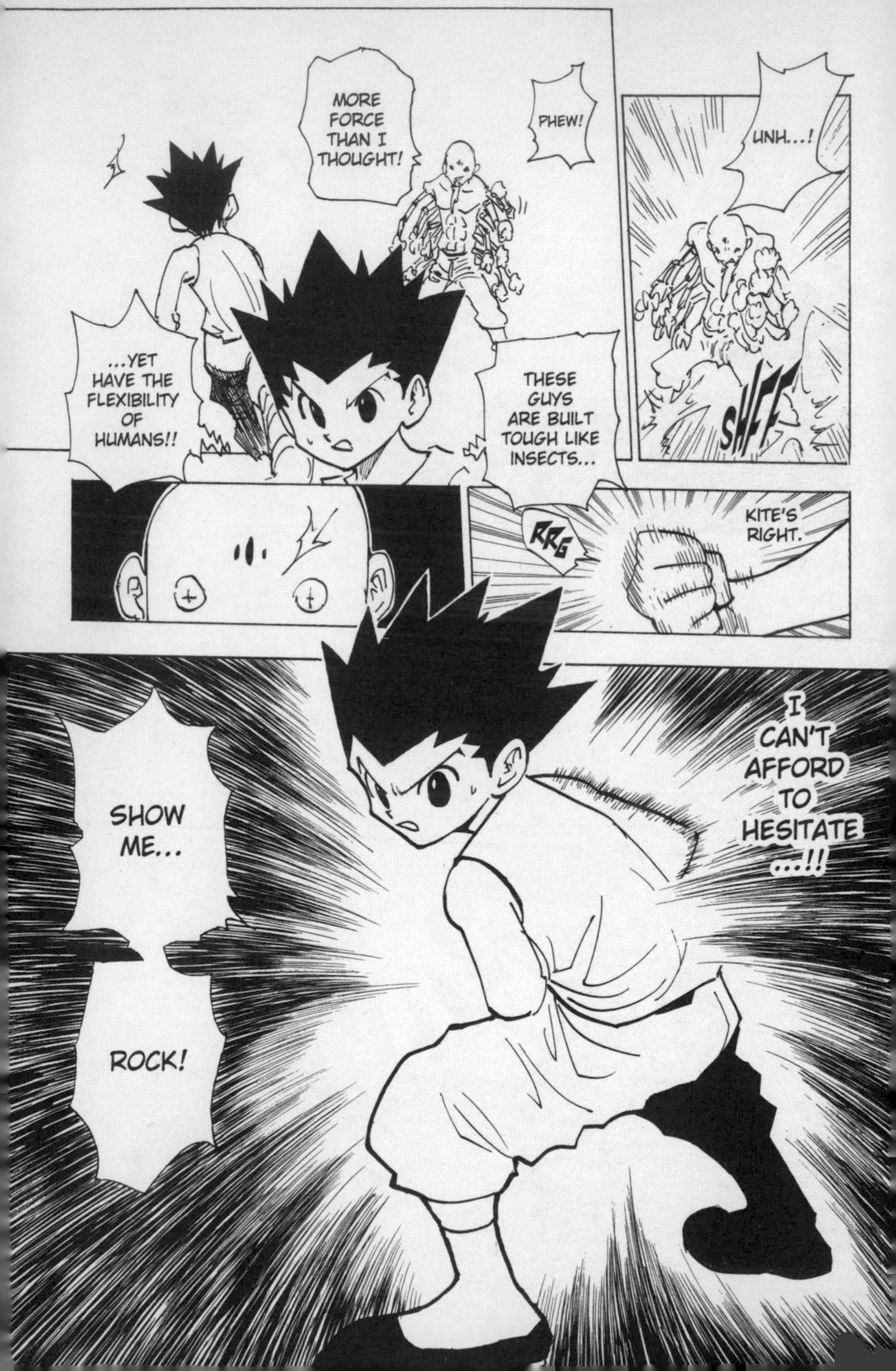
UNH...!
SHFF
PHEW!
MORE FORCE THAN I THOUGHT!
THESE GUYS ARE BUILT TOUGH LIKE INSECTS...
...YET HAVE THE FLEXIBILITY OF HUMANS!!
KITE'S RIGHT.
RRG
I CAN'T AFFORD TO HESITATE ...!!
SHOW ME...
ROCK!

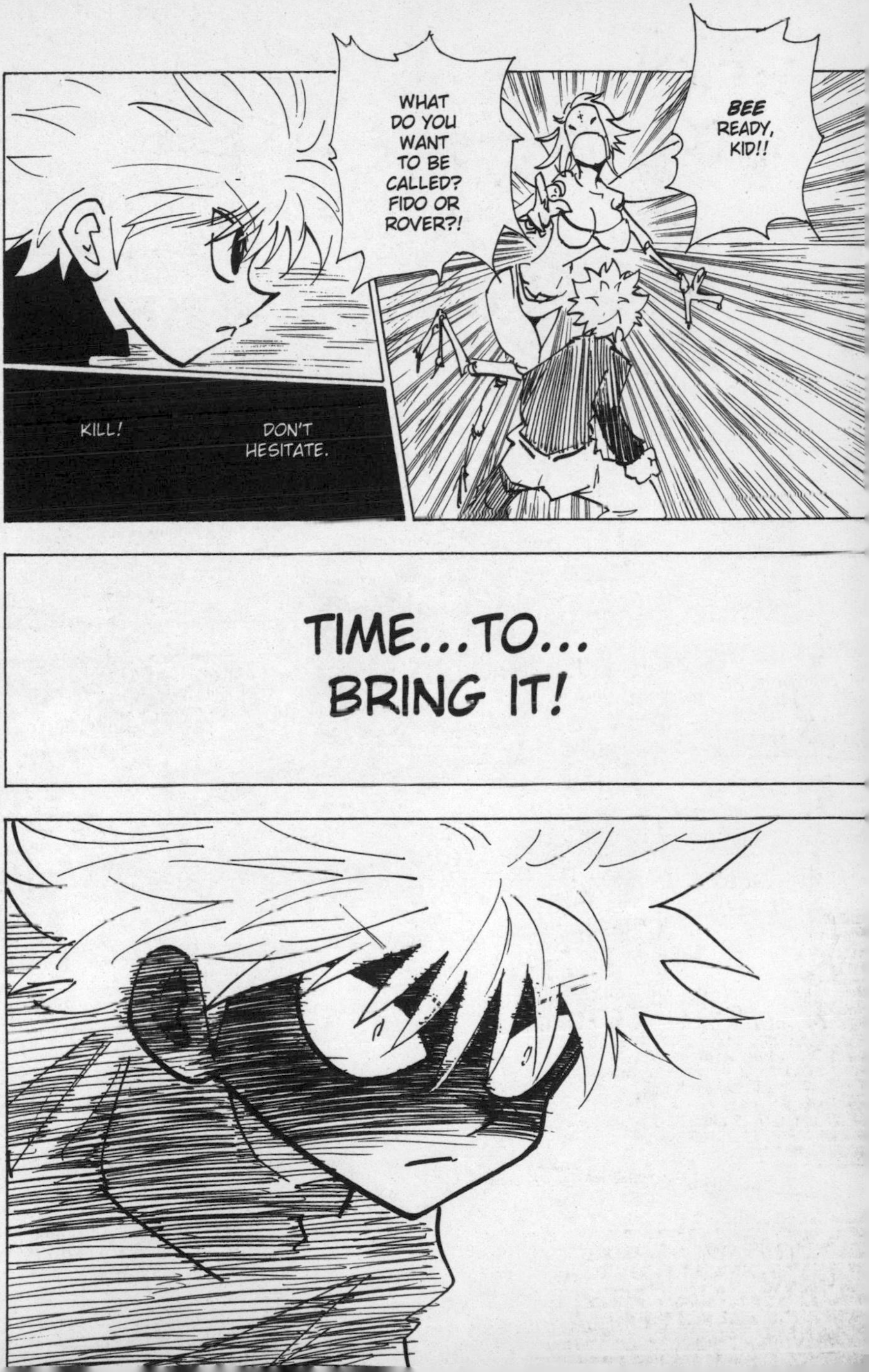
BEE READY, KID!!
WHAT DO YOU WANT TO BE CALLED? FIDO OR ROVER?!
DON'T HESITATE.
KILL!
TIME...TO... BRING IT!

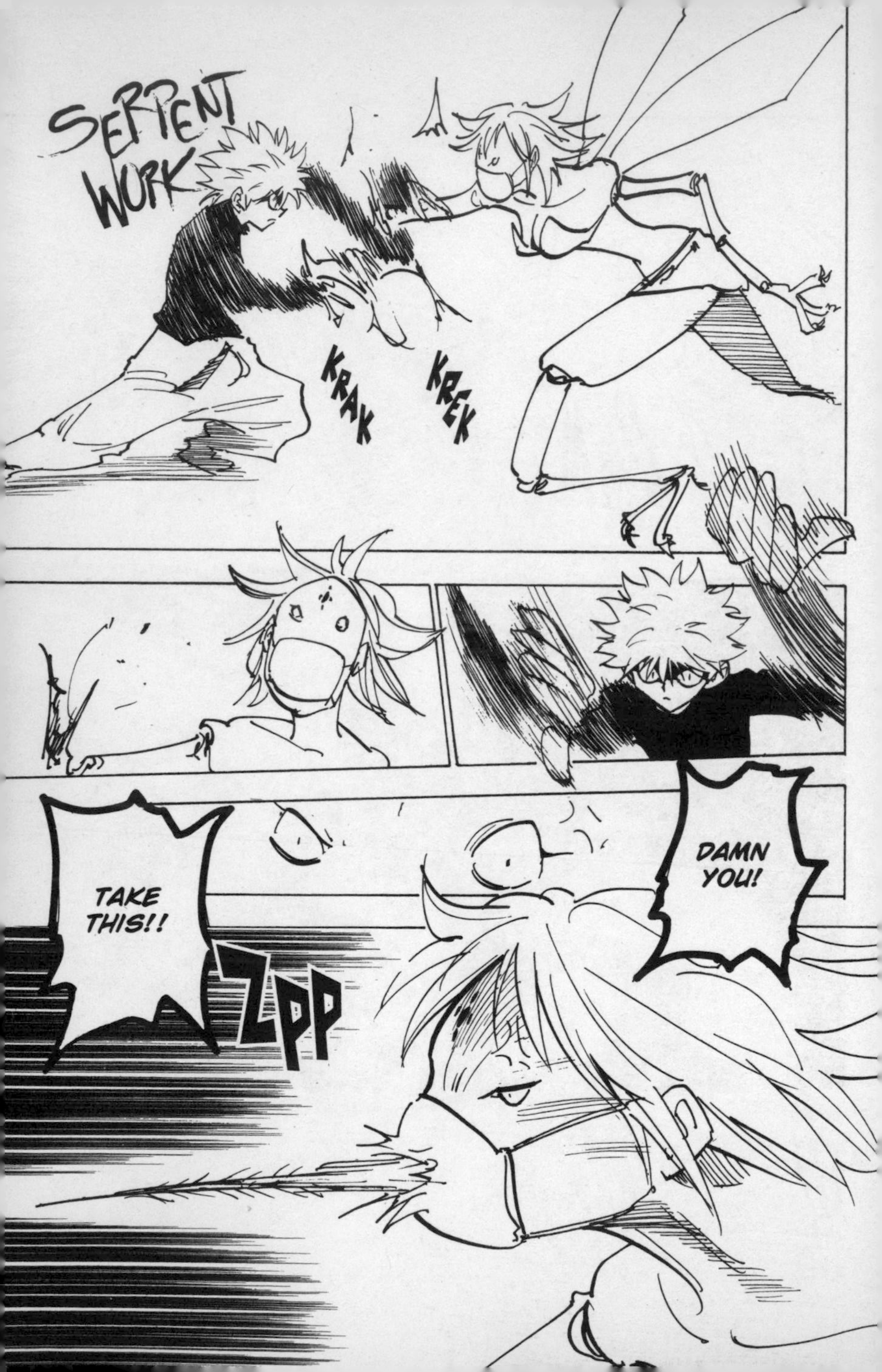
SERPENT WORK
KREK
KRAK
DAMN YOU!
TAKE THIS!!
ZPP

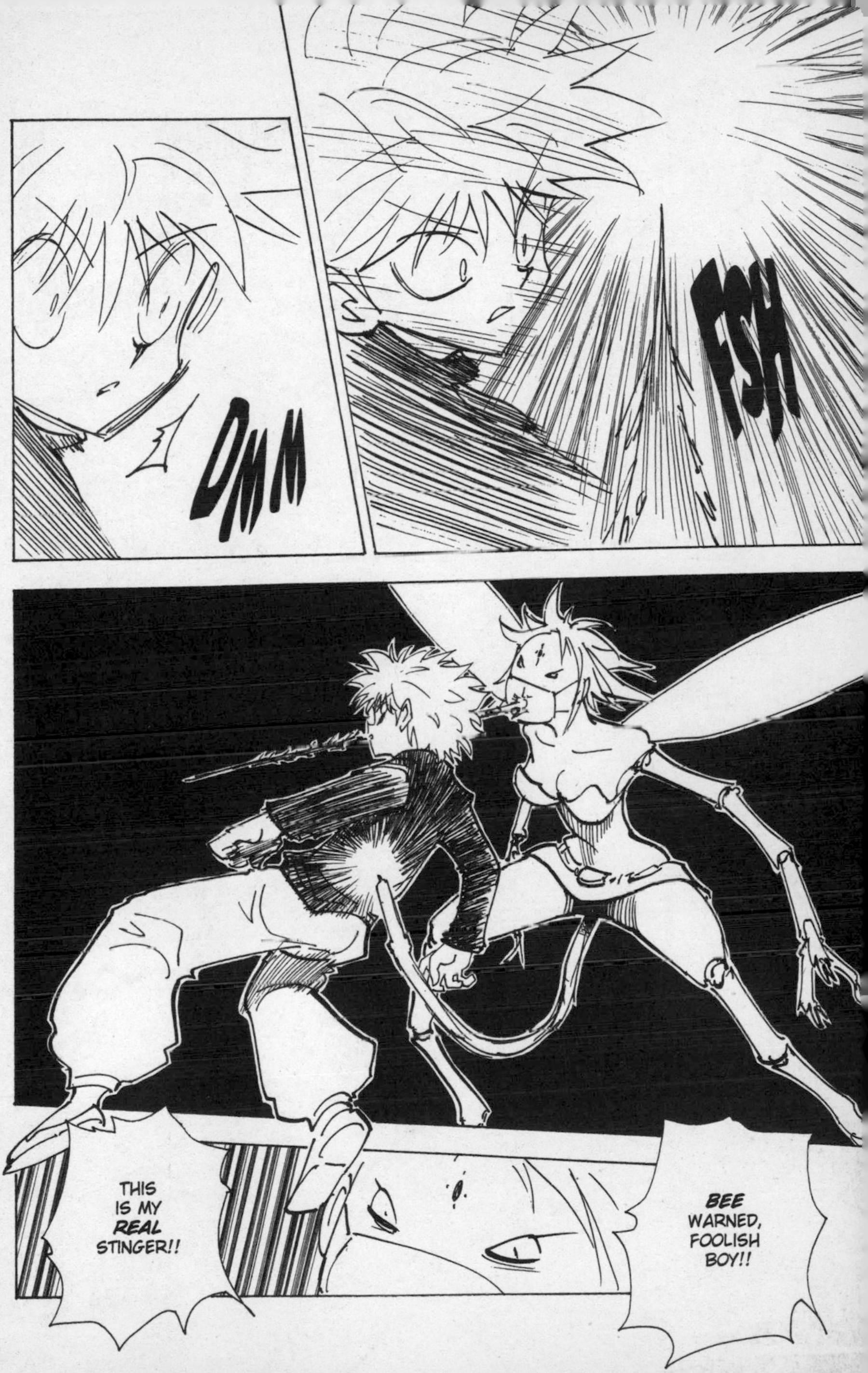
FSH
DMM
BEE WARNED, FOOLISH BOY!!
THIS IS MY *REAL* STINGER!!

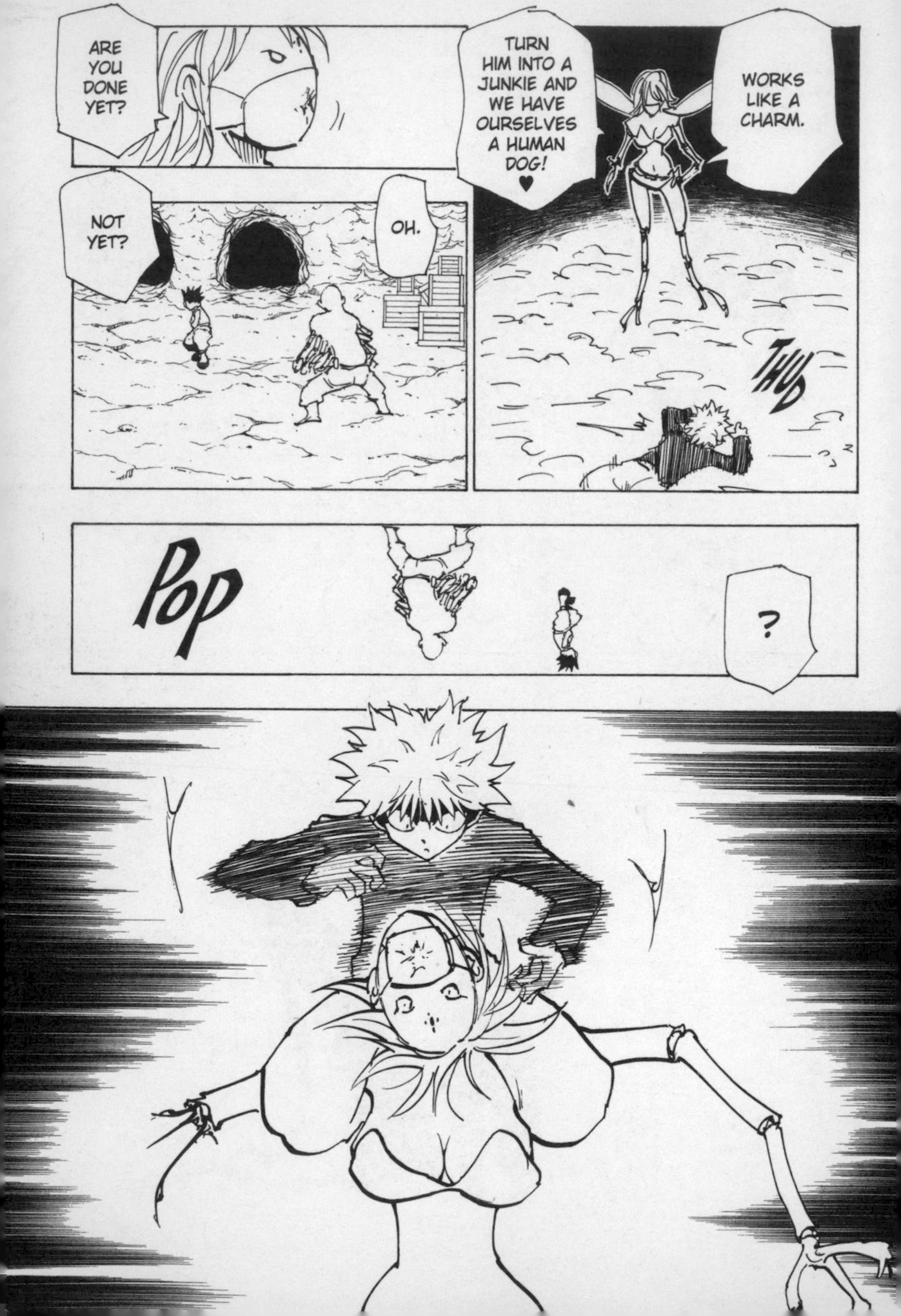
WORKS LIKE A CHARM.
TURN HIM INTO A JUNKIE AND WE HAVE OURSELVES A HUMAN DOG! ♥
THUD
ARE YOU DONE YET?
NOT YET?
OH.
?
Pop

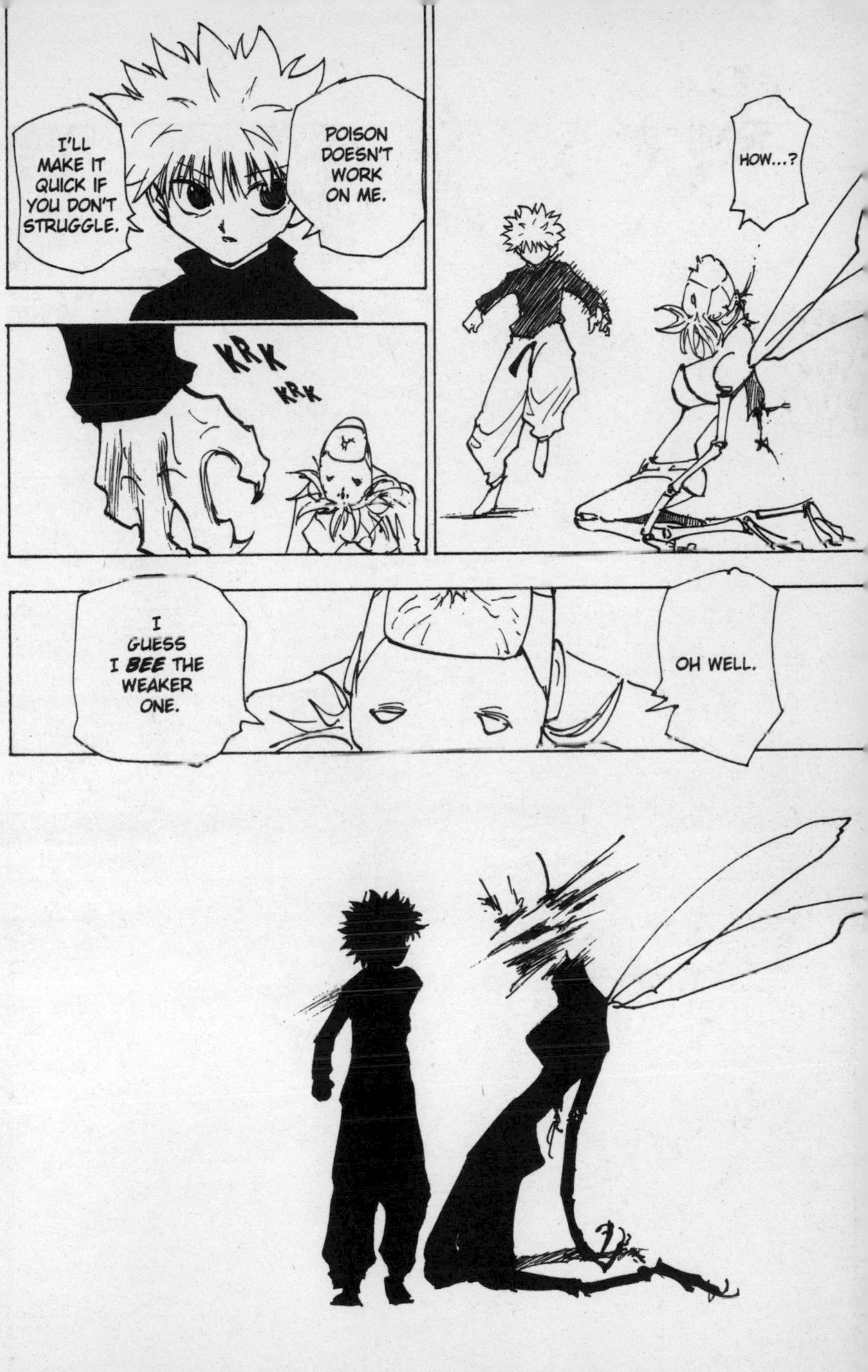
HOW...?
POISON DOESN'T WORK ON ME.
I'LL MAKE IT QUICK IF YOU DON'T STRUGGLE.
KRK
KRK
OH WELL.
I GUESS I BEE THE WEAKER ONE.

READ THIS WAY

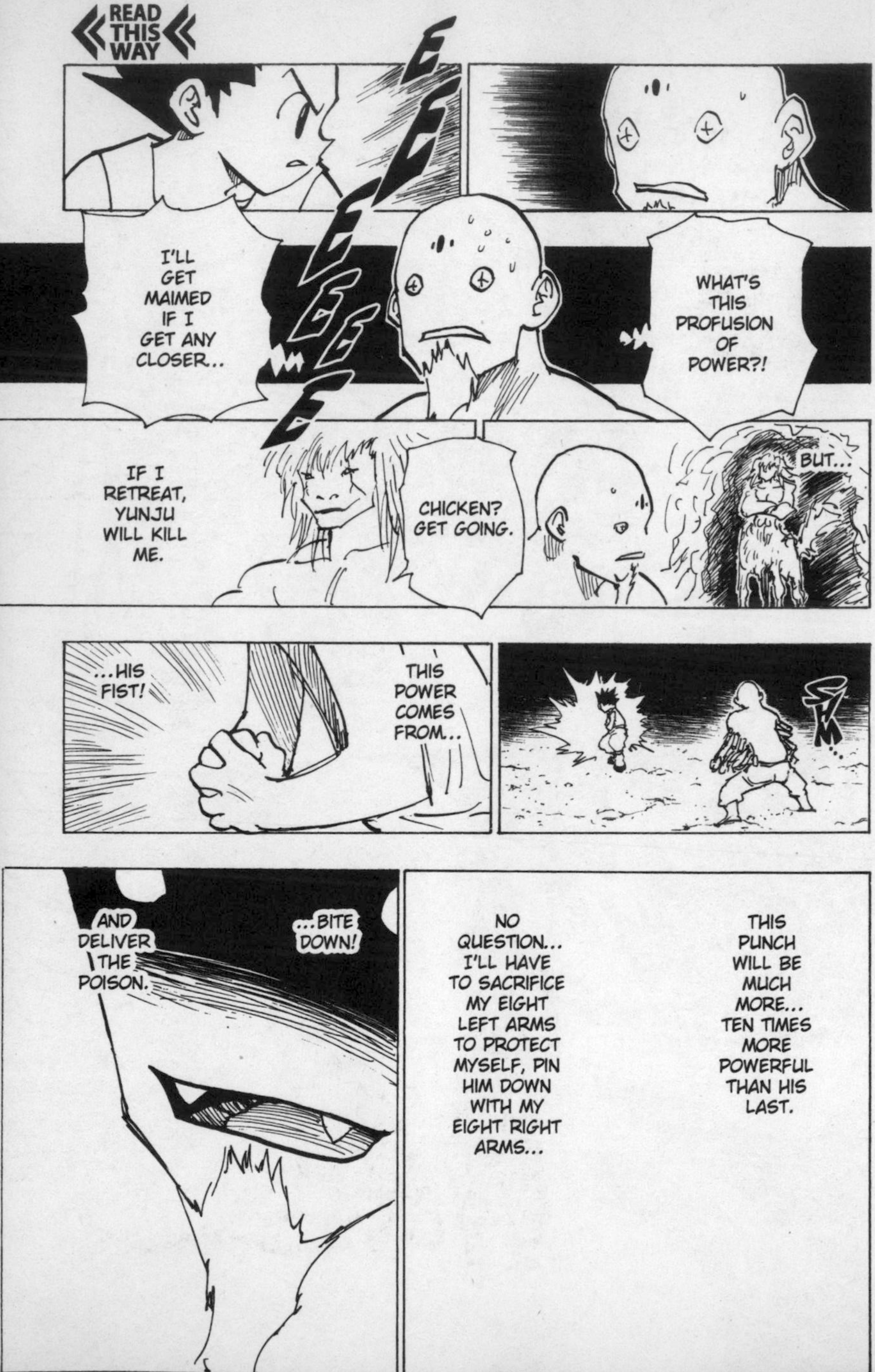
EEEEEEEEE
WHAT'S THIS PROFUSION OF POWER?!
I'LL GET MAIMED IF I GET ANY CLOSER...
BUT...
CHICKEN? GET GOING.
IF I RETREAT, YUNJU WILL KILL ME.
SHM...
THIS POWER COMES FROM...
...HIS FIST!
THIS PUNCH WILL BE MUCH MORE... TEN TIMES MORE POWERFUL THAN HIS LAST.
NO QUESTION... I'LL HAVE TO SACRIFICE MY EIGHT LEFT ARMS TO PROTECT MYSELF, PIN HIM DOWN WITH MY EIGHT RIGHT ARMS...
...BITE DOWN!
AND DELIVER THE POISON.

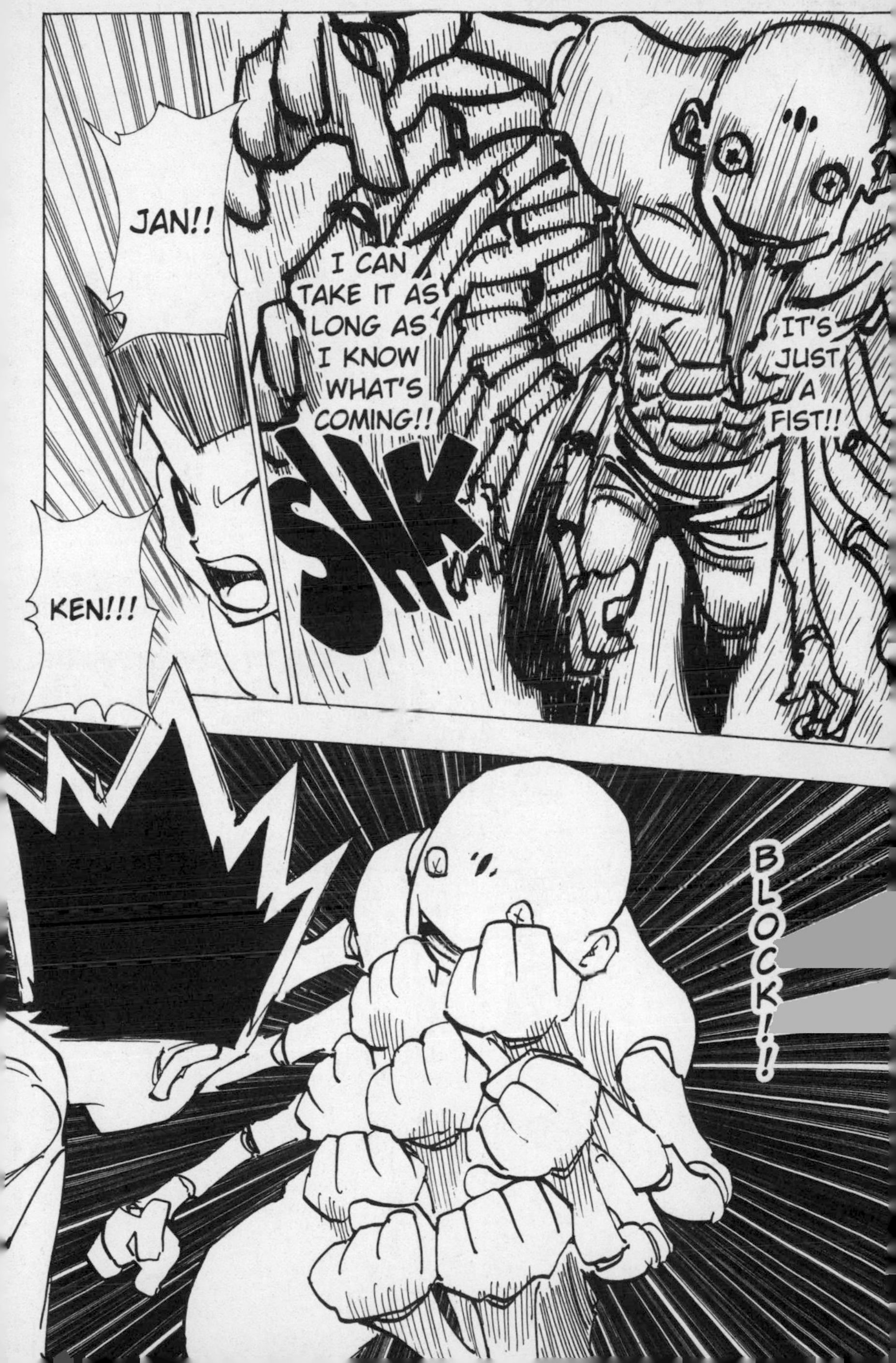
IT'S JUST A FIST!!
I CAN TAKE IT AS LONG AS I KNOW WHAT'S COMING!!
SHK
JAN!!
KEN!!!
BLOCK!!

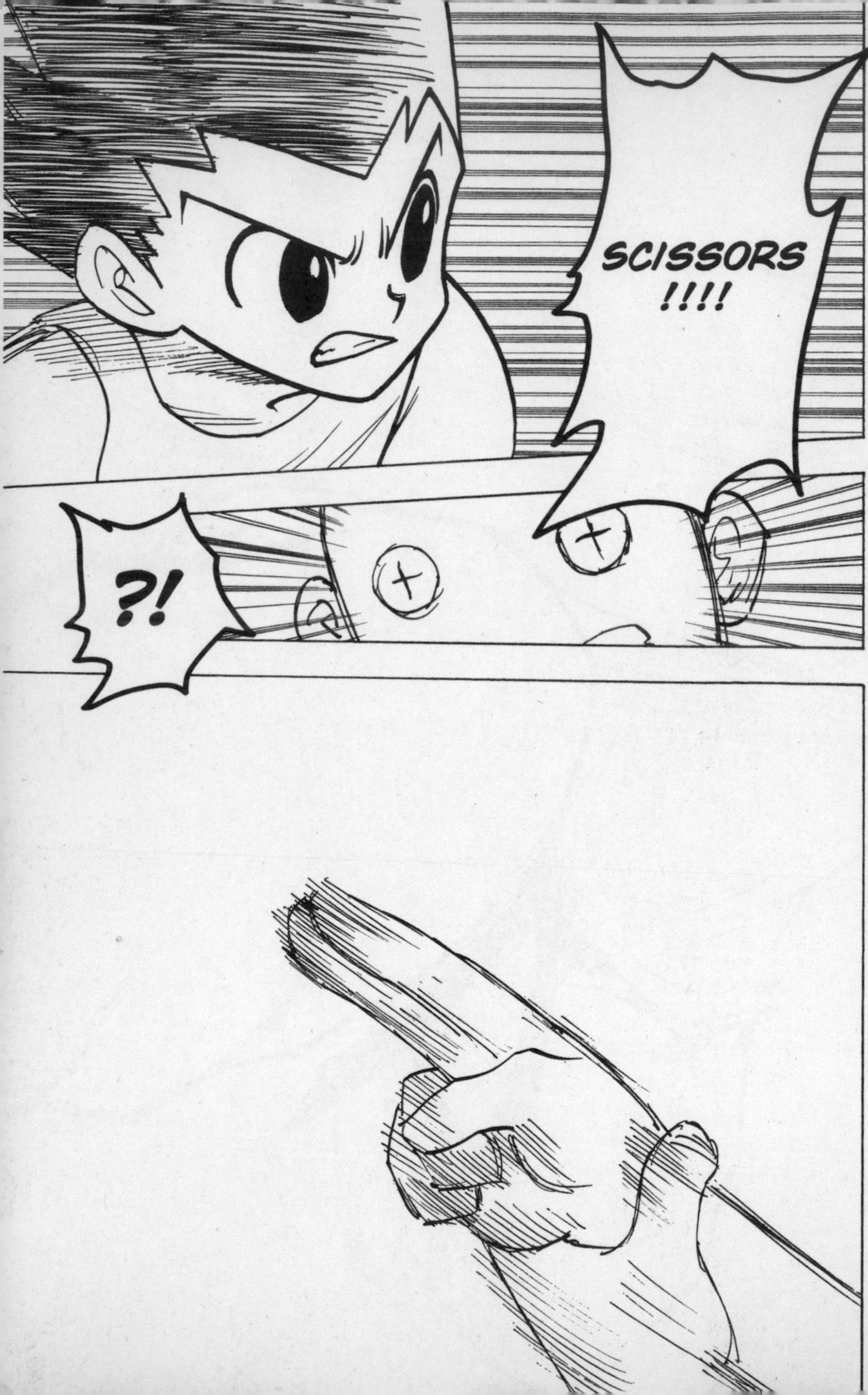
SCISSORS !!!!
?!

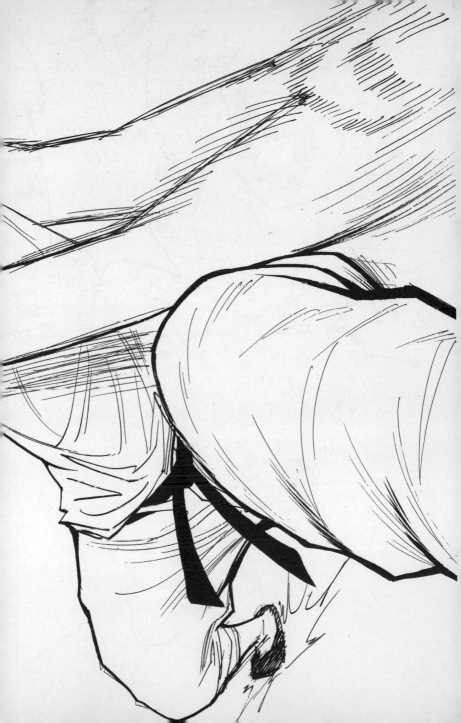

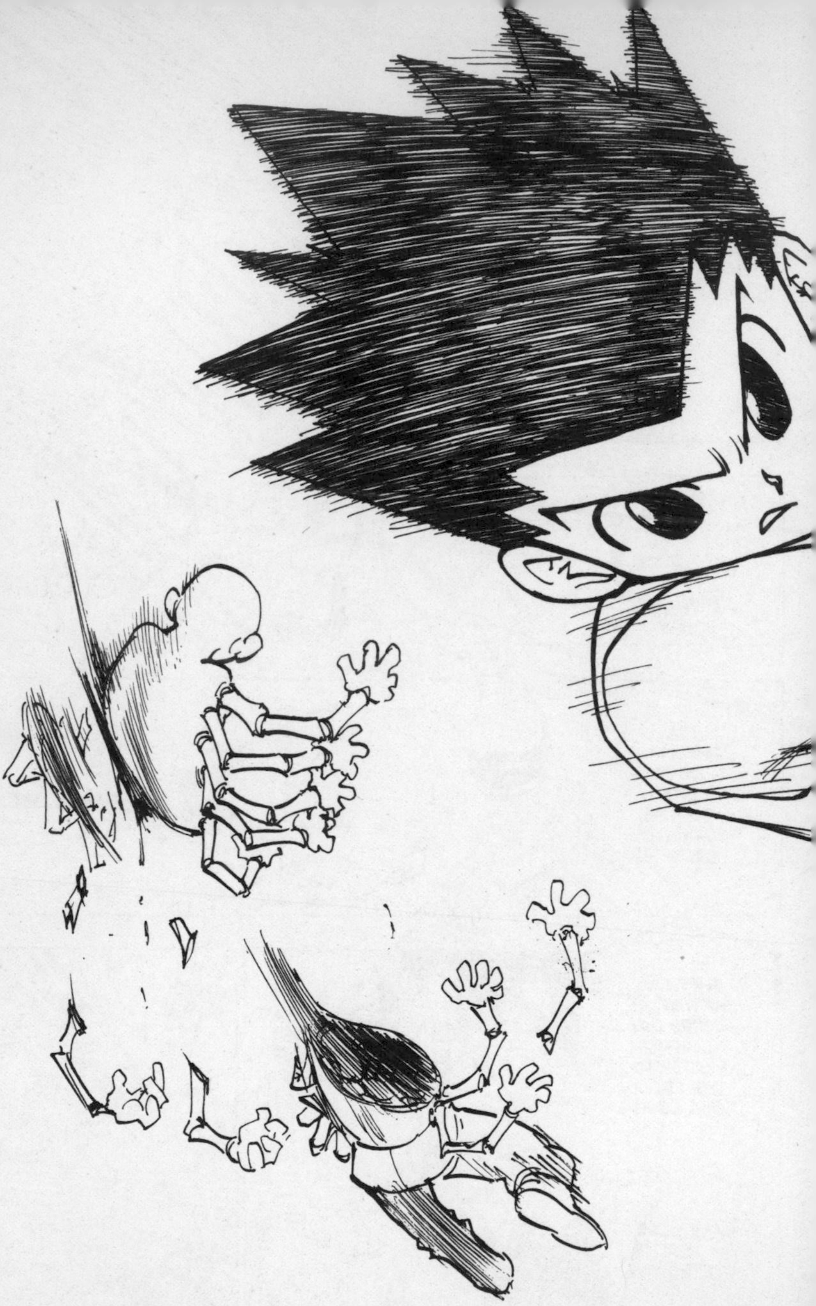

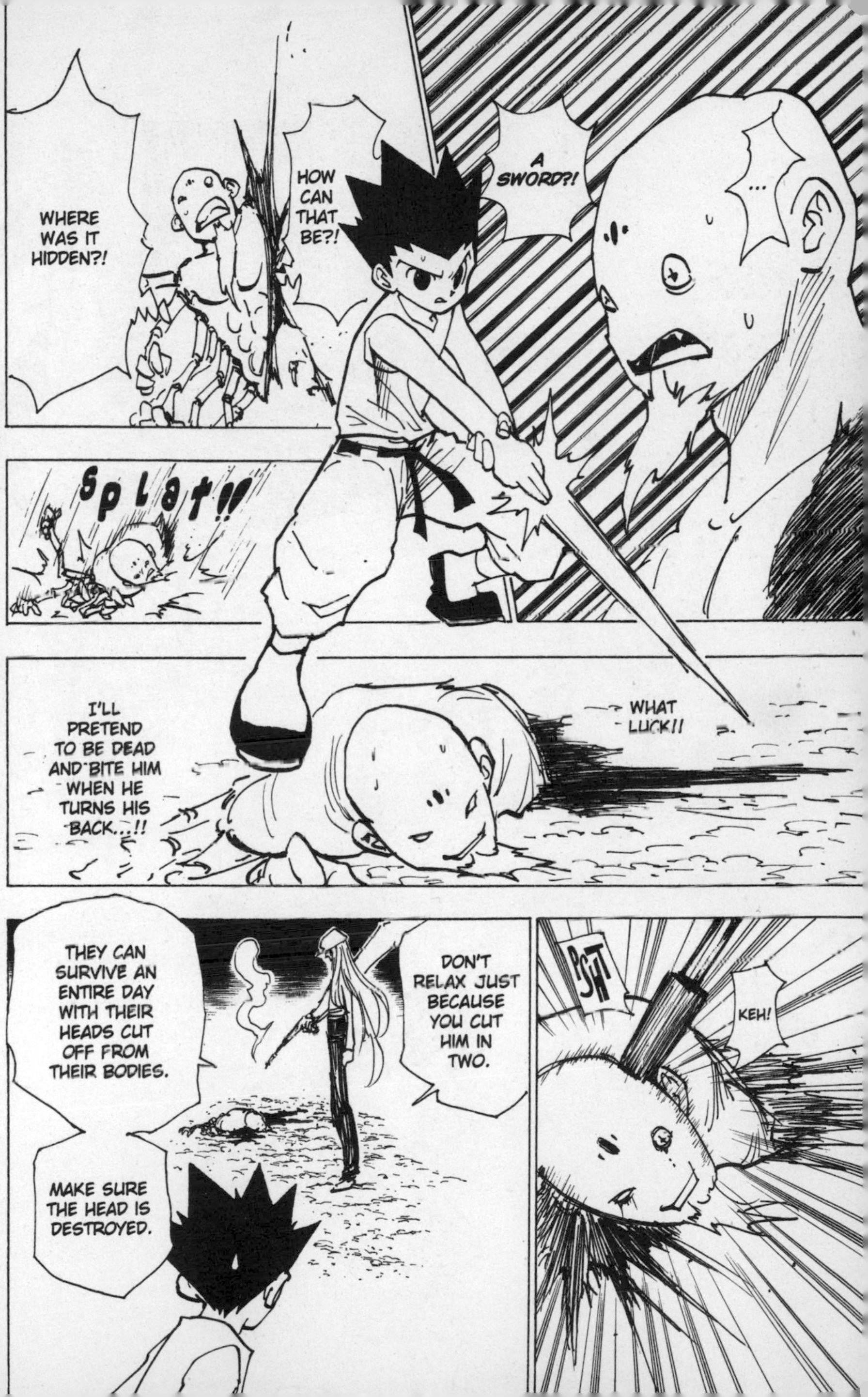
...
A SWORD?!
HOW CAN THAT BE?!
WHERE WAS IT HIDDEN?!
SPLAT!!
WHAT LUCK!!
I'LL PRETEND TO BE DEAD AND BITE HIM WHEN HE TURNS HIS BACK...!!
PSHT
KEH!
DON'T RELAX JUST BECAUSE YOU CUT HIM IN TWO.
THEY CAN SURVIVE AN ENTIRE DAY WITH THEIR HEADS CUT OFF FROM THEIR BODIES.
MAKE SURE THE HEAD IS DESTROYED.

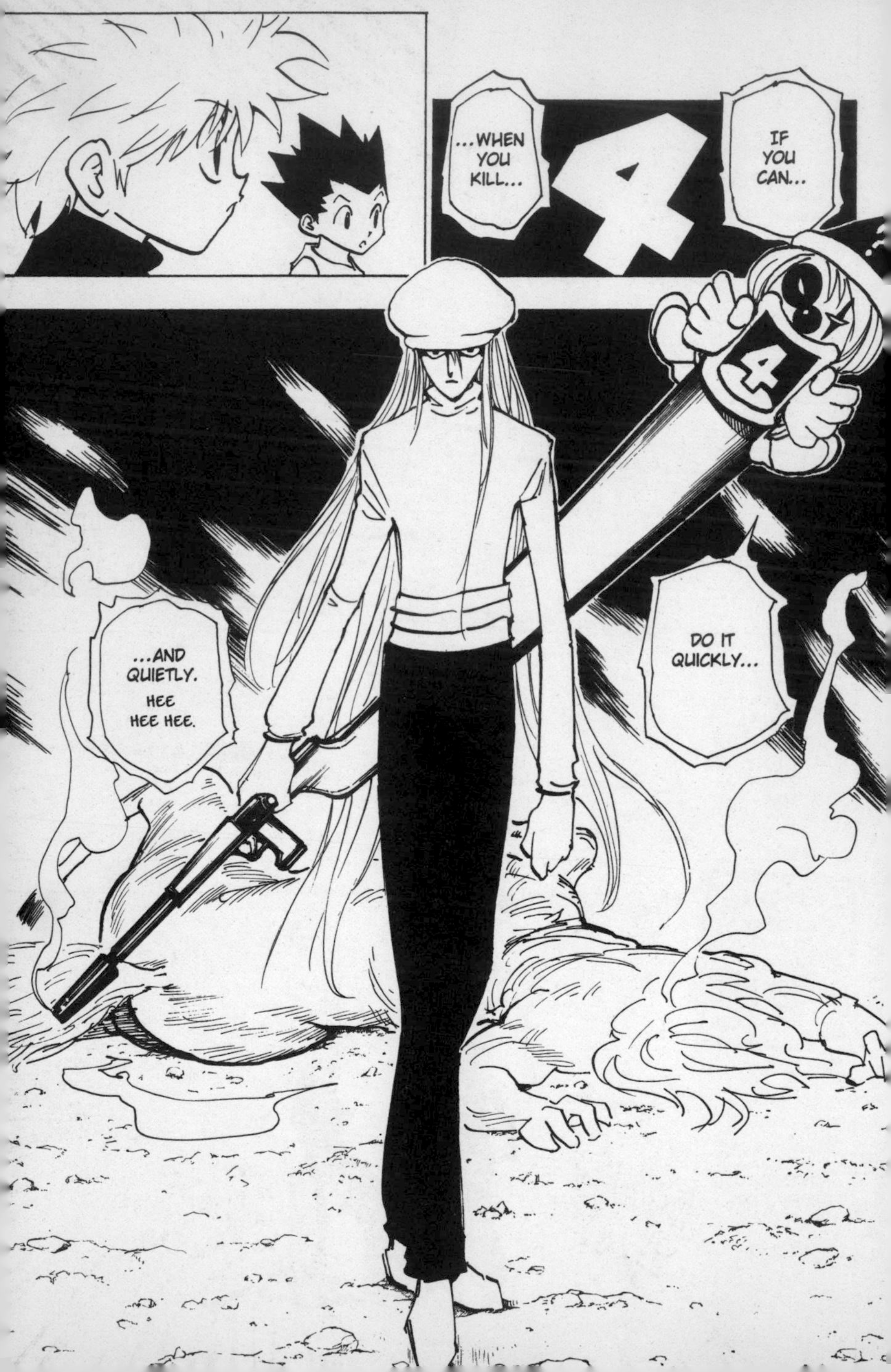
IF YOU CAN...
...WHEN YOU KILL...
DO IT QUICKLY...
...AND QUIETLY.
HEE HEE HEE.

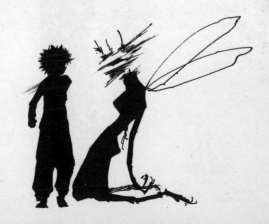

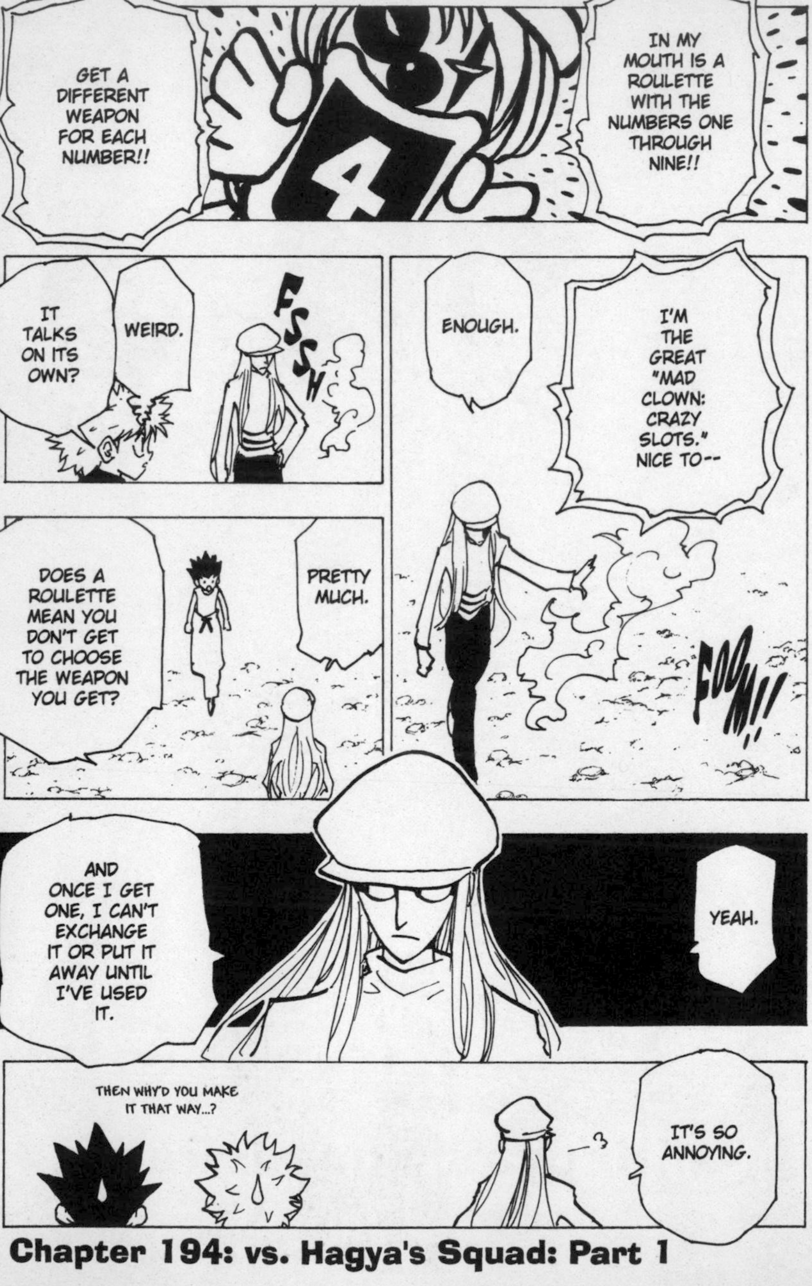
IN MY MOUTH IS A ROULETTE WITH THE NUMBERS ONE THROUGH NINE!!
4
GET A DIFFERENT WEAPON FOR EACH NUMBER!!
I'M THE GREAT "MAD CLOWN: CRAZY SLOTS." NICE TO--
ENOUGH.
FOOM!!
FSSH
WEIRD.
IT TALKS ON ITS OWN?
PRETTY MUCH.
DOES A ROULETTE MEAN YOU DON'T GET TO CHOOSE THE WEAPON YOU GET?
YEAH.
AND ONCE I GET ONE, I CAN'T EXCHANGE IT OR PUT IT AWAY UNTIL I'VE USED IT.
IT'S SO ANNOYING.
THEN WHY'D YOU MAKE IT THAT WAY...?

Chapter 194: vs. Hagya's Squad: Part 1

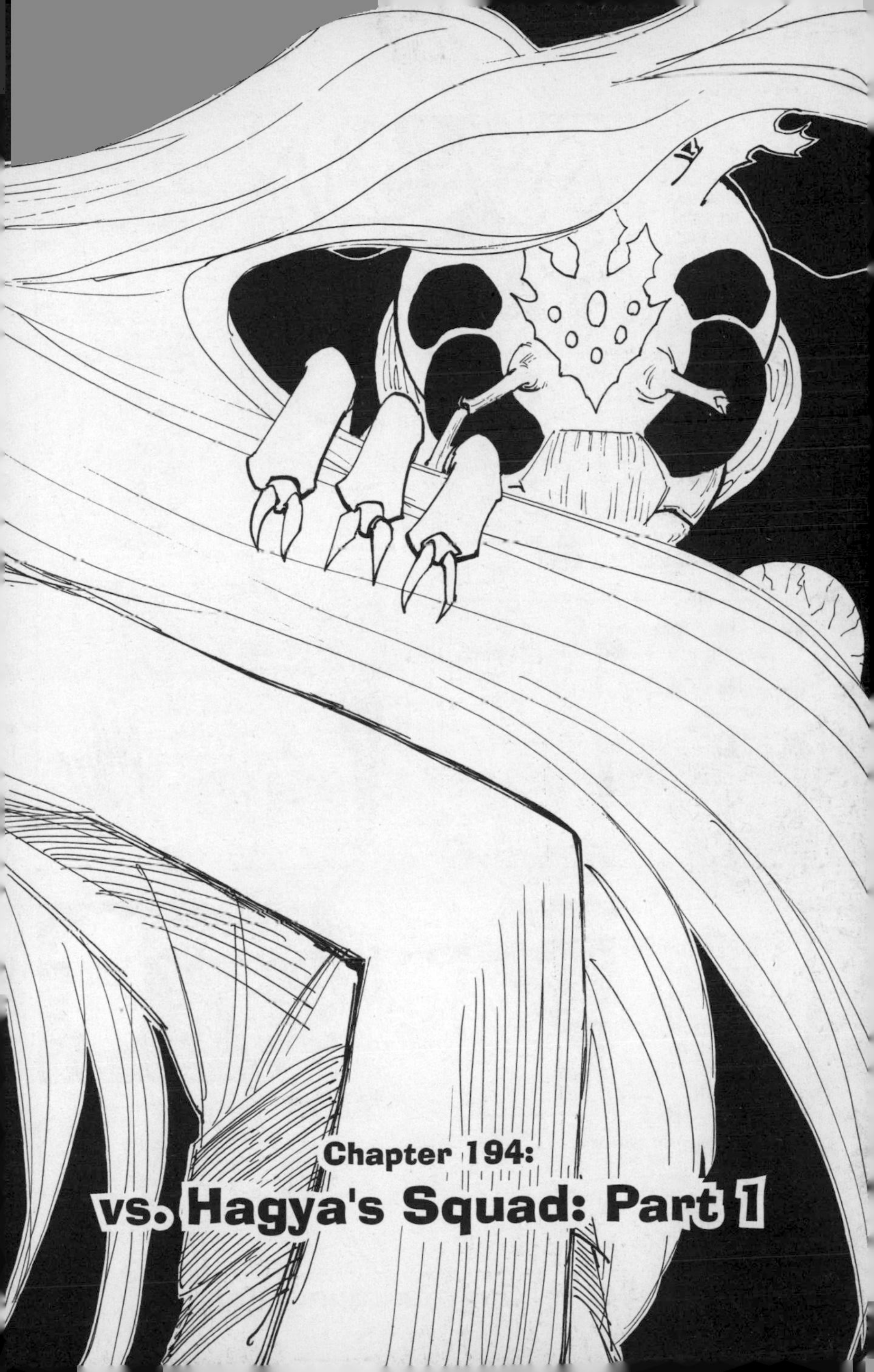
Chapter 194:
vs. Hagya's Squad: Part 1

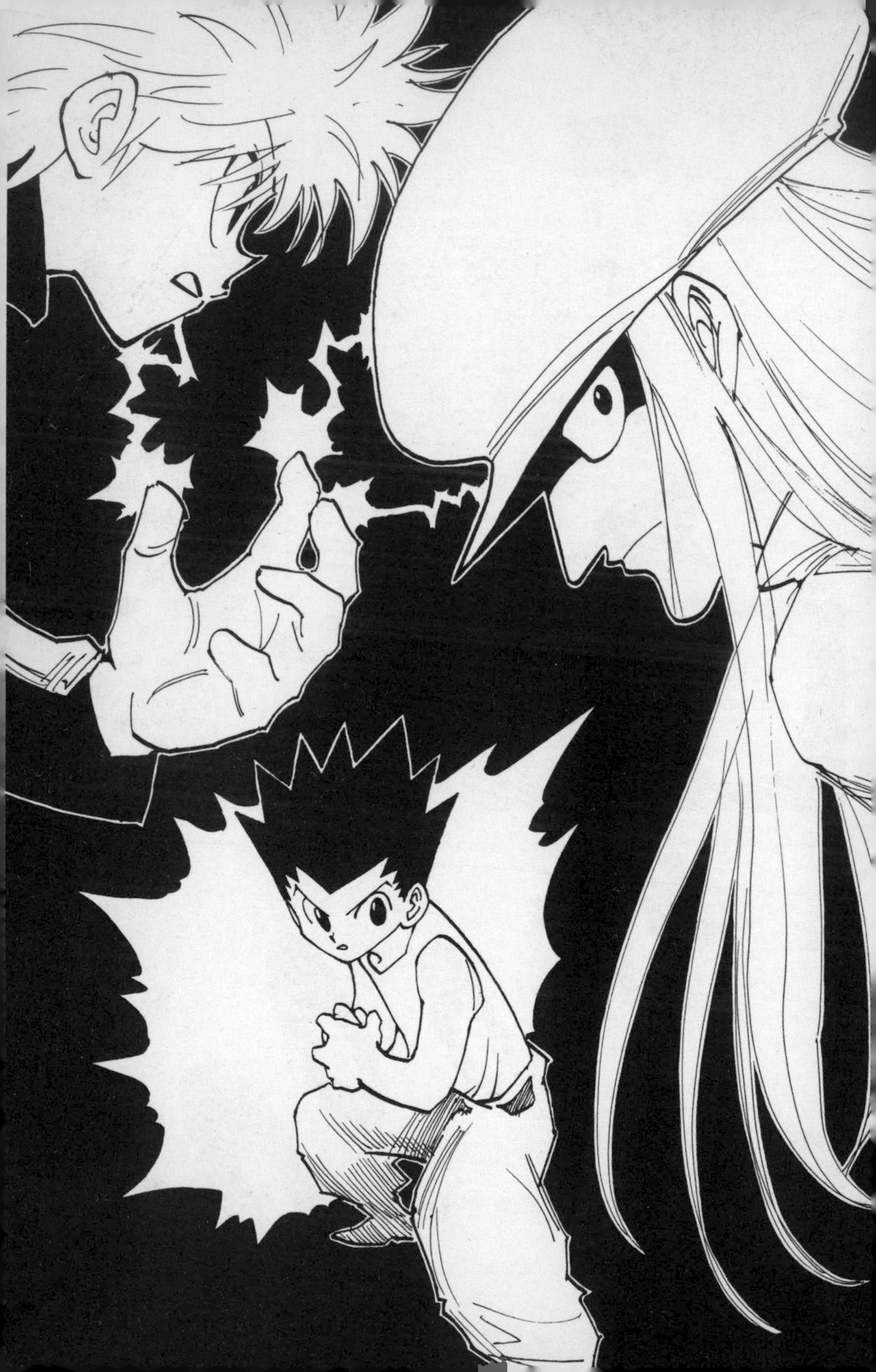

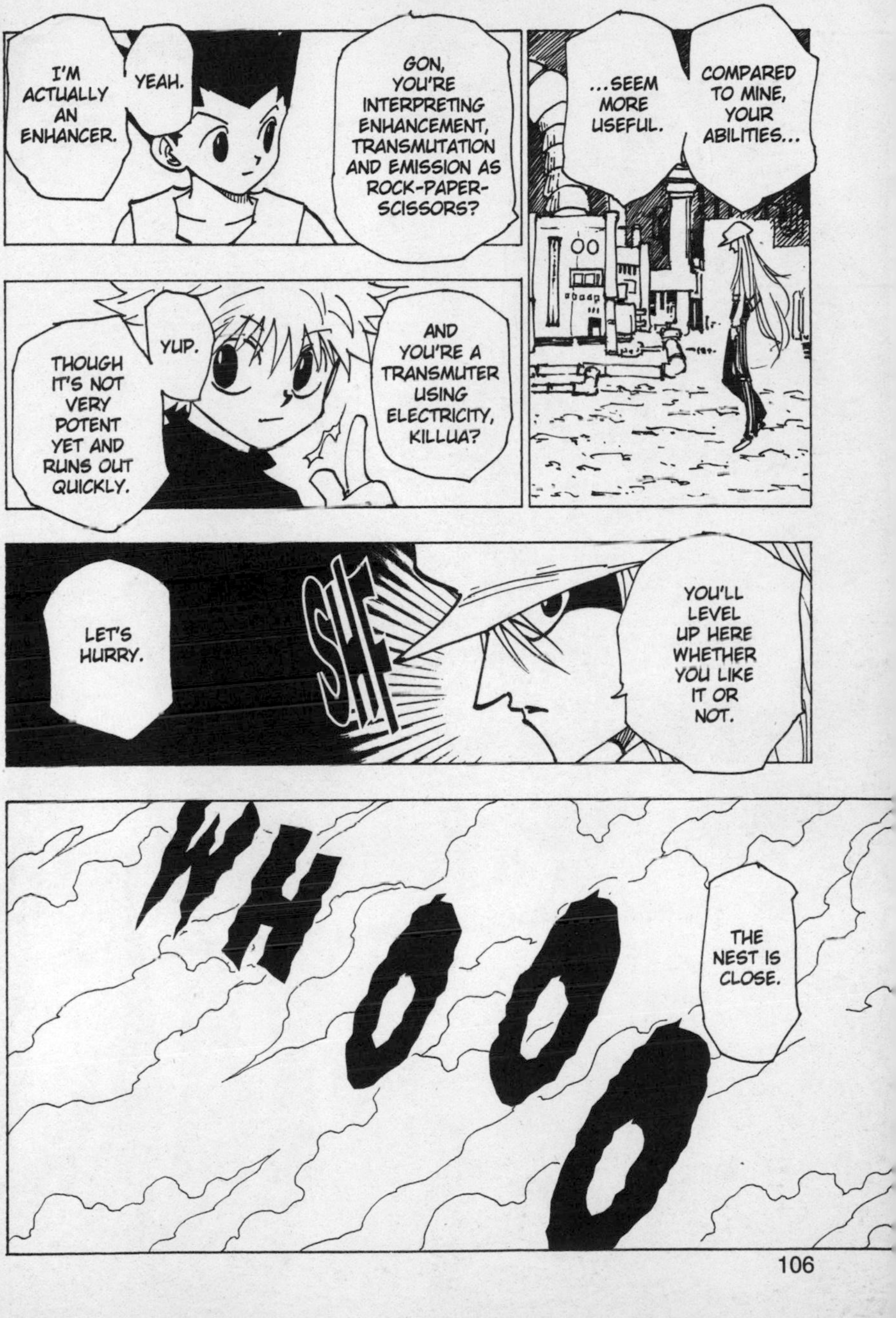
COMPARED TO MINE, YOUR ABILITIES...
...SEEM MORE USEFUL.
GON, YOU'RE INTERPRETING ENHANCEMENT, TRANSMUTATION AND EMISSION AS ROCK-PAPER-SCISSORS?
YEAH.
I'M ACTUALLY AN ENHANCER.
AND YOU'RE A TRANSMUTER USING ELECTRICITY, KILLUA?
YUP.
THOUGH IT'S NOT VERY POTENT YET AND RUNS OUT QUICKLY.
YOU'LL LEVEL UP HERE WHETHER YOU LIKE IT OR NOT.
LET'S HURRY.
THE NEST IS CLOSE.
WHOOOO

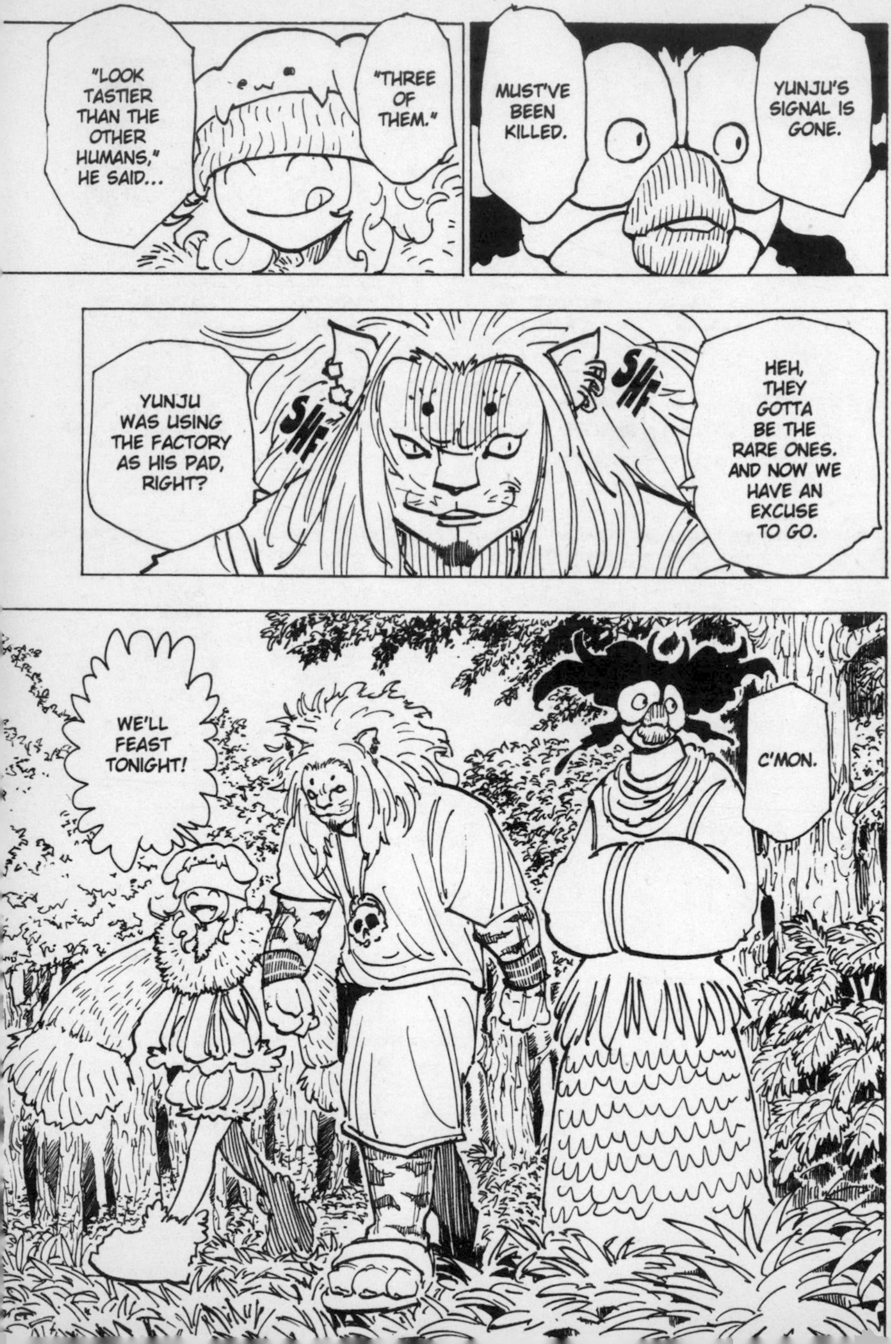
YUNJU'S SIGNAL IS GONE.
MUST'VE BEEN KILLED.
"THREE OF THEM."
"LOOK TASTIER THAN THE OTHER HUMANS," HE SAID...
HEH, THEY GOTTA BE THE RARE ONES. AND NOW WE HAVE AN EXCUSE TO GO.
SHF
SHF
YUNJU WAS USING THE FACTORY AS HIS PAD, RIGHT?
C'MON.
WE'LL FEAST TONIGHT!

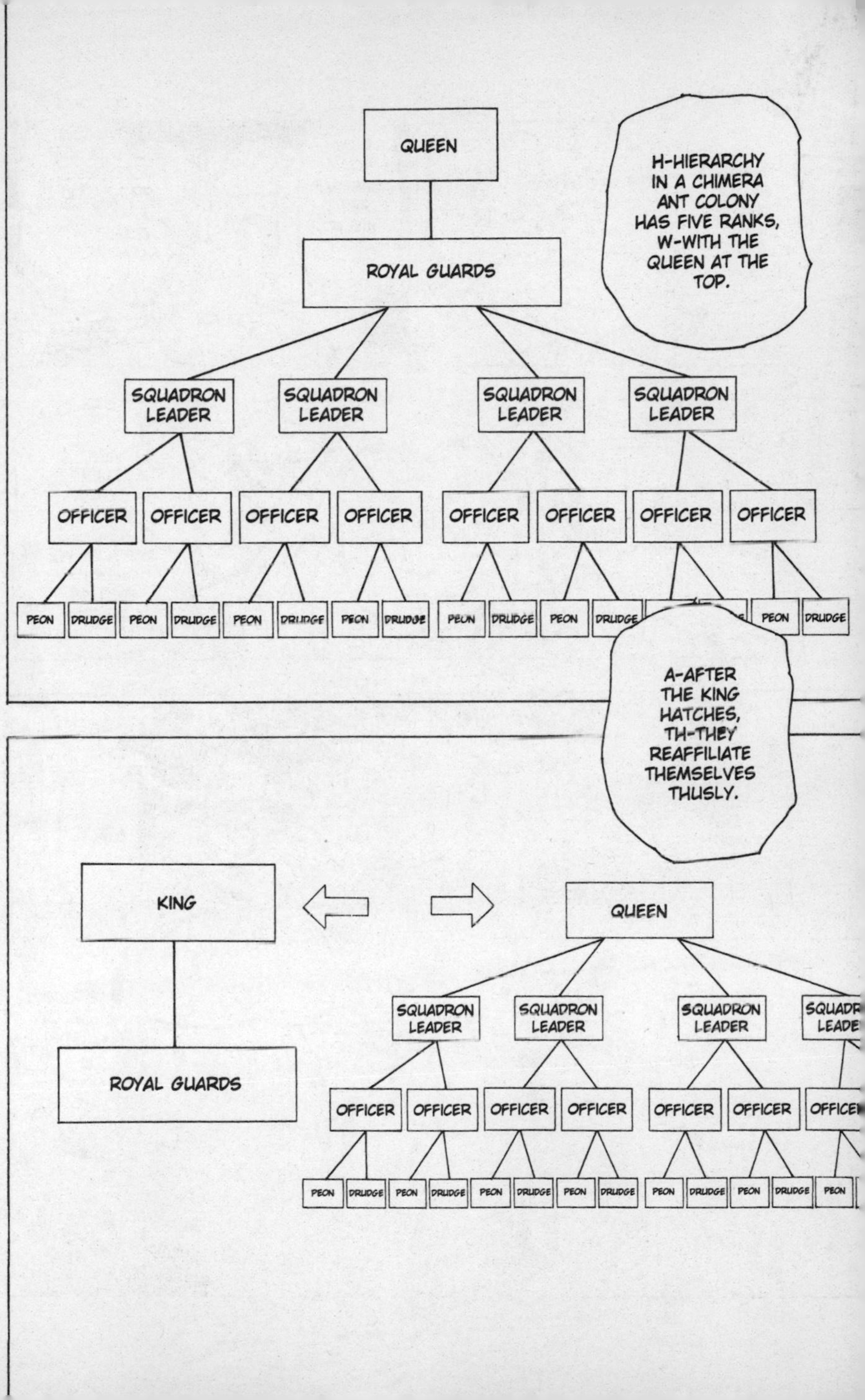
H-HIERARCHY IN A CHIMERA ANT COLONY HAS FIVE RANKS, W-WITH THE QUEEN AT THE TOP.
QUEEN
ROYAL GUARDS
SQUADRON LEADER
SQUADRON LEADER
SQUADRON LEADER
SQUADRON LEADER
OFFICER
OFFICER
OFFICER
OFFICER
OFFICER
OFFICER
OFFICER
OFFICER
PEON
DRUDGE
PEON
DRUDGE
PEON
DRUDGE
PEON
DRUDGE
PEON
DRUDGE
PEON
DRUDGE
PEON
DRUDGE
A-AFTER THE KING HATCHES, TH-THEY REAFFILIATE THEMSELVES THUSLY.
KING
ROYAL GUARDS
QUEEN
SQUADRON LEADER
SQUADRON LEADER
SQUADRON LEADER
OFFICER
OFFICER
OFFICER
OFFICER
OFFICER
OFFICER
PEON
DRUDGE
PEON
DRUDGE
PEON
DRUDGE
PEON
DRUDGE
PEON
DRUDGE
PEON
DRUDGE
PEON

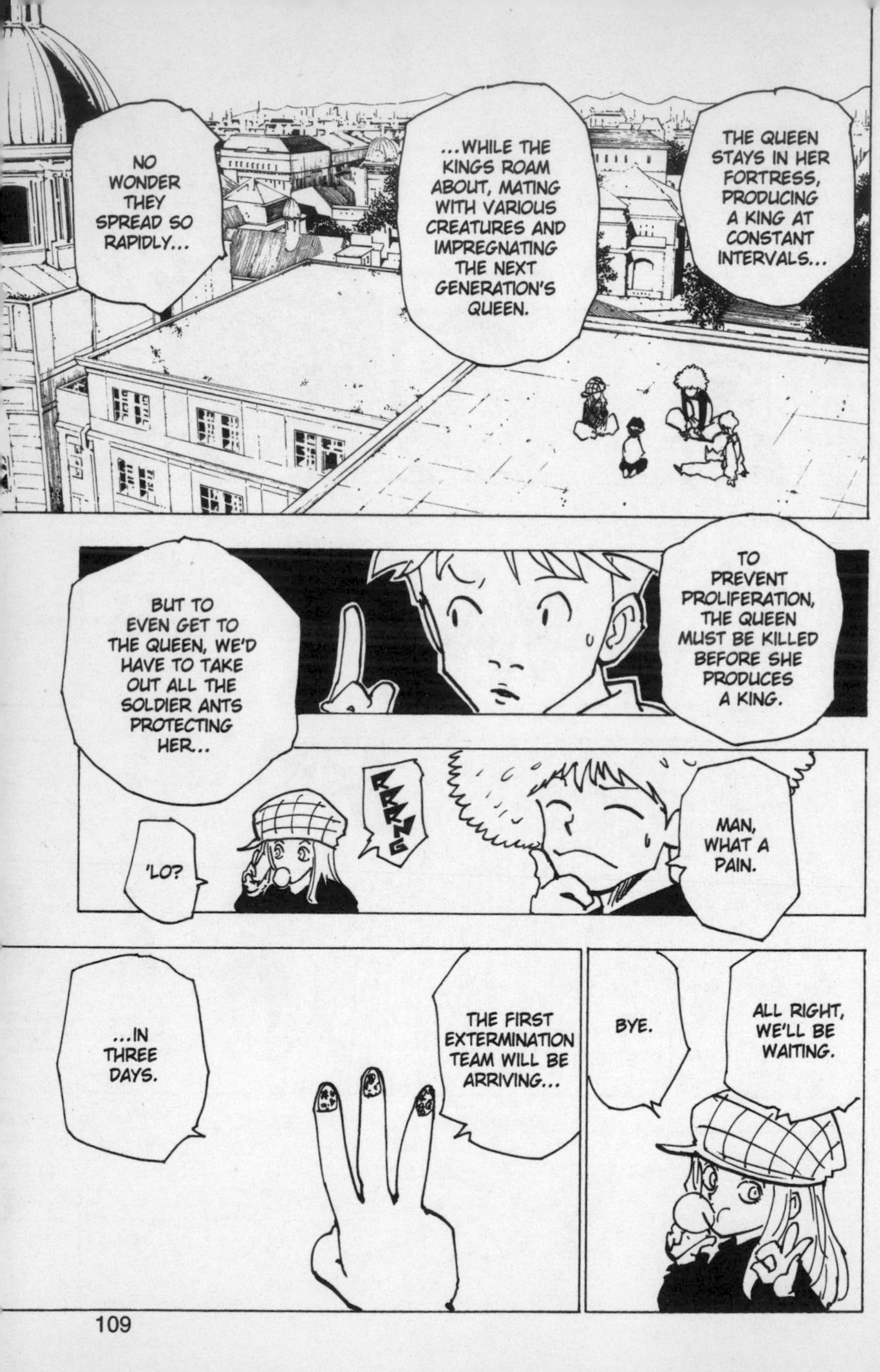
THE QUEEN STAYS IN HER FORTRESS, PRODUCING A KING AT CONSTANT INTERVALS...
...WHILE THE KINGS ROAM ABOUT, MATING WITH VARIOUS CREATURES AND IMPREGNATING THE NEXT GENERATION'S QUEEN.
NO WONDER THEY SPREAD SO RAPIDLY...
TO PREVENT PROLIFERATION, THE QUEEN MUST BE KILLED BEFORE SHE PRODUCES A KING.
BUT TO EVEN GET TO THE QUEEN, WE'D HAVE TO TAKE OUT ALL THE SOLDIER ANTS PROTECTING HER...
MAN, WHAT A PAIN.
RRRNG
'LO?
ALL RIGHT, WE'LL BE WAITING.
BYE.
THE FIRST EXTERMINATION TEAM WILL BE ARRIVING...
...IN THREE DAYS.

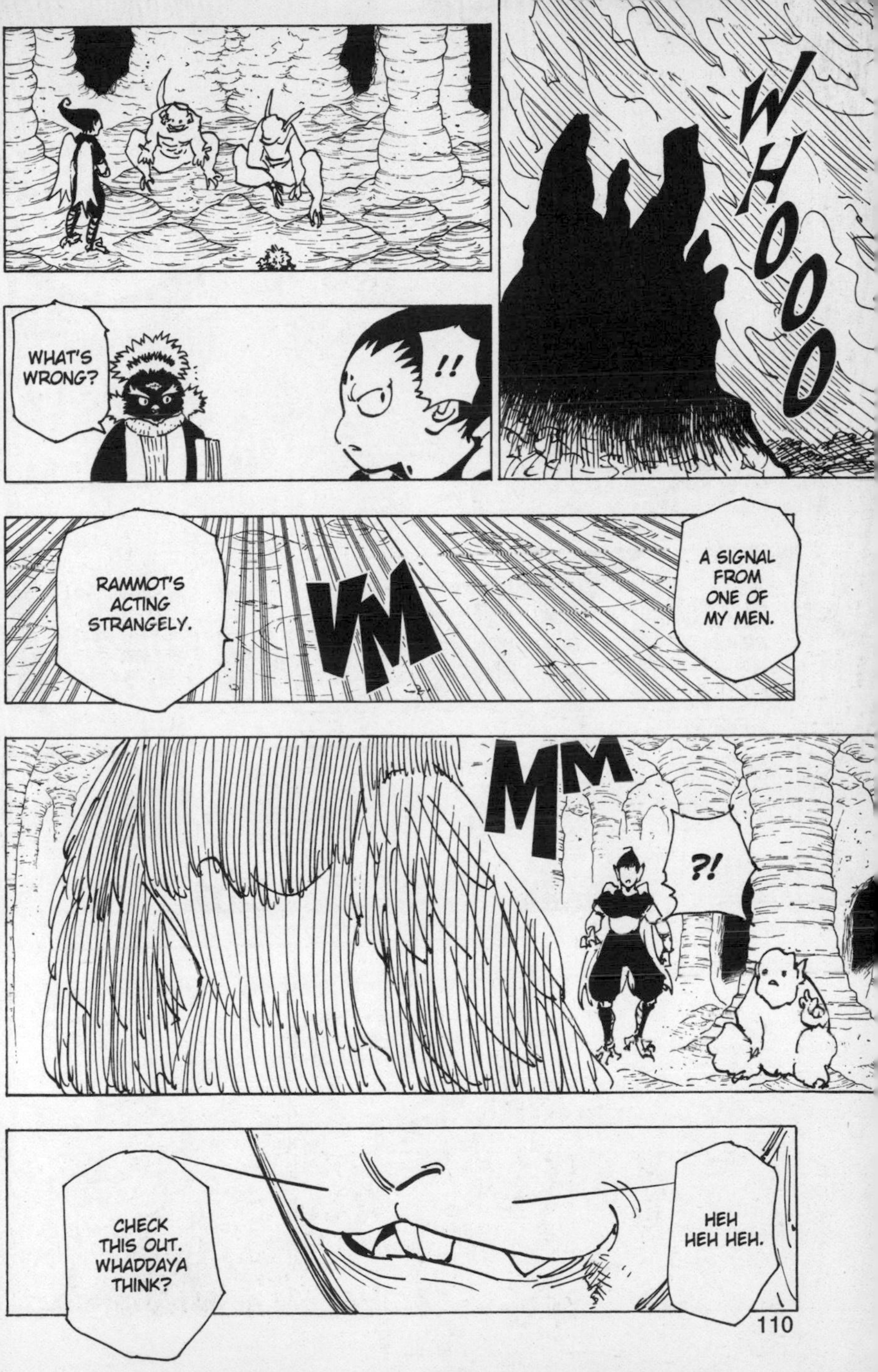
WHOOO
!!
WHAT'S WRONG?
A SIGNAL FROM ONE OF MY MEN.
VVM
RAMMOT'S ACTING STRANGELY.
MM
?!
HEH HEH HEH.
CHECK THIS OUT. WHADDAYA THINK?

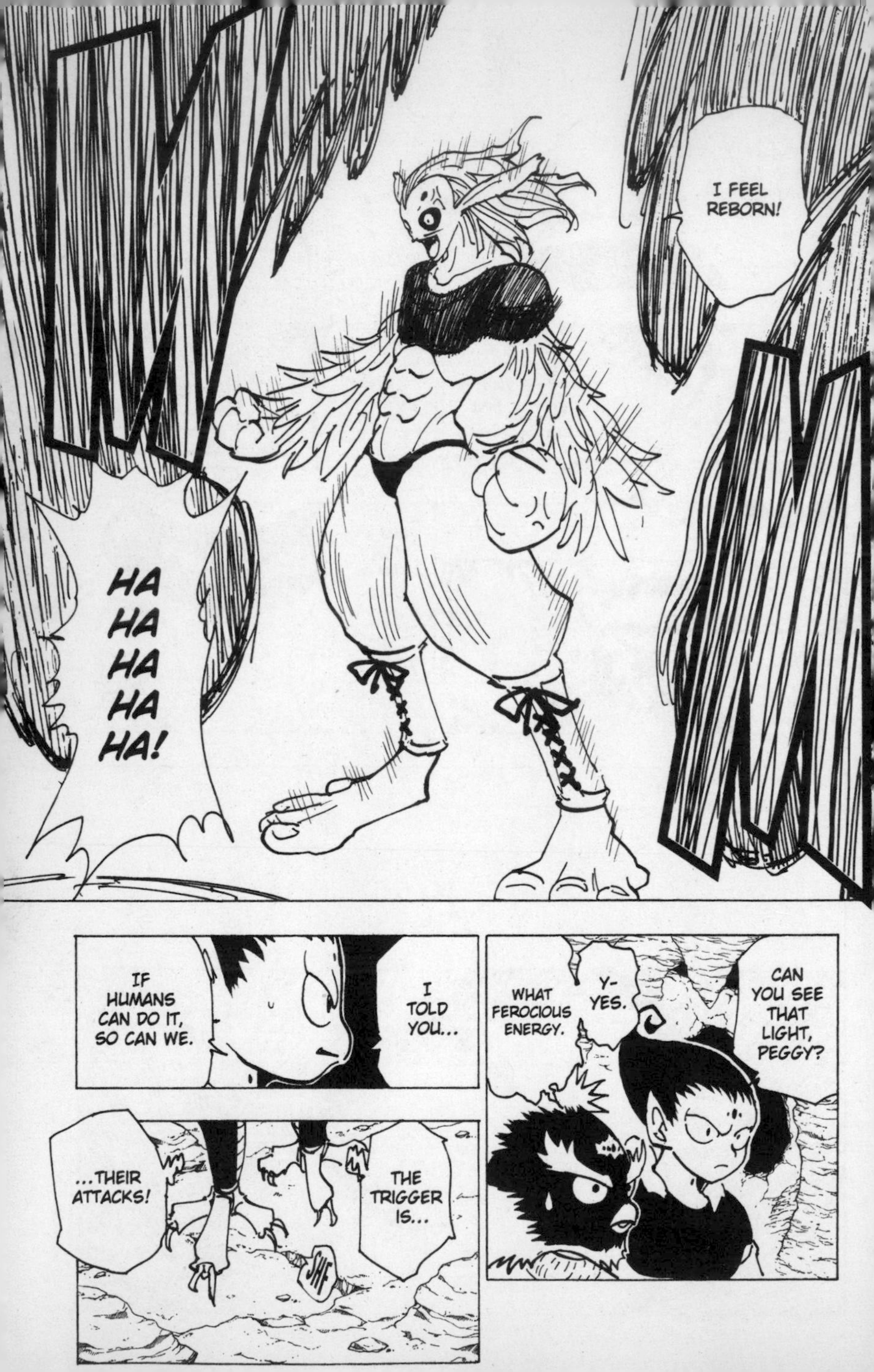
I FEEL REBORN!
HA HA HA HA HA!
CAN YOU SEE THAT LIGHT, PEGGY?
Y-YES.
WHAT FEROCIOUS ENERGY.
I TOLD YOU...
IF HUMANS CAN DO IT, SO CAN WE.
THE TRIGGER IS...
...THEIR ATTACKS!
SHF

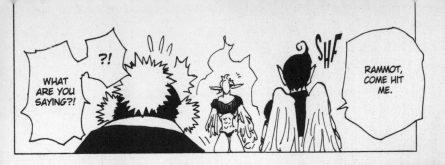

RAMMOT, COME HIT ME.
SHF
?!
WHAT ARE YOU SAYING?!
YOU SURE?
I DON'T PARTICULARLY LIKE YOU.
SO I WON'T HOLD BACK.
THAT'S FINE.
IT PROBABLY NEEDS TO BE HARD ENOUGH TO TAKE EFFECT ANYWAYS.
...

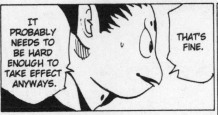

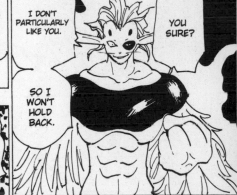

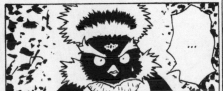

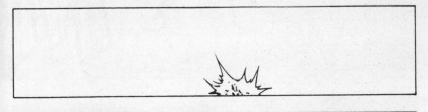

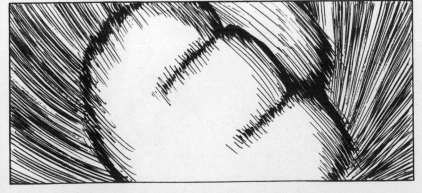

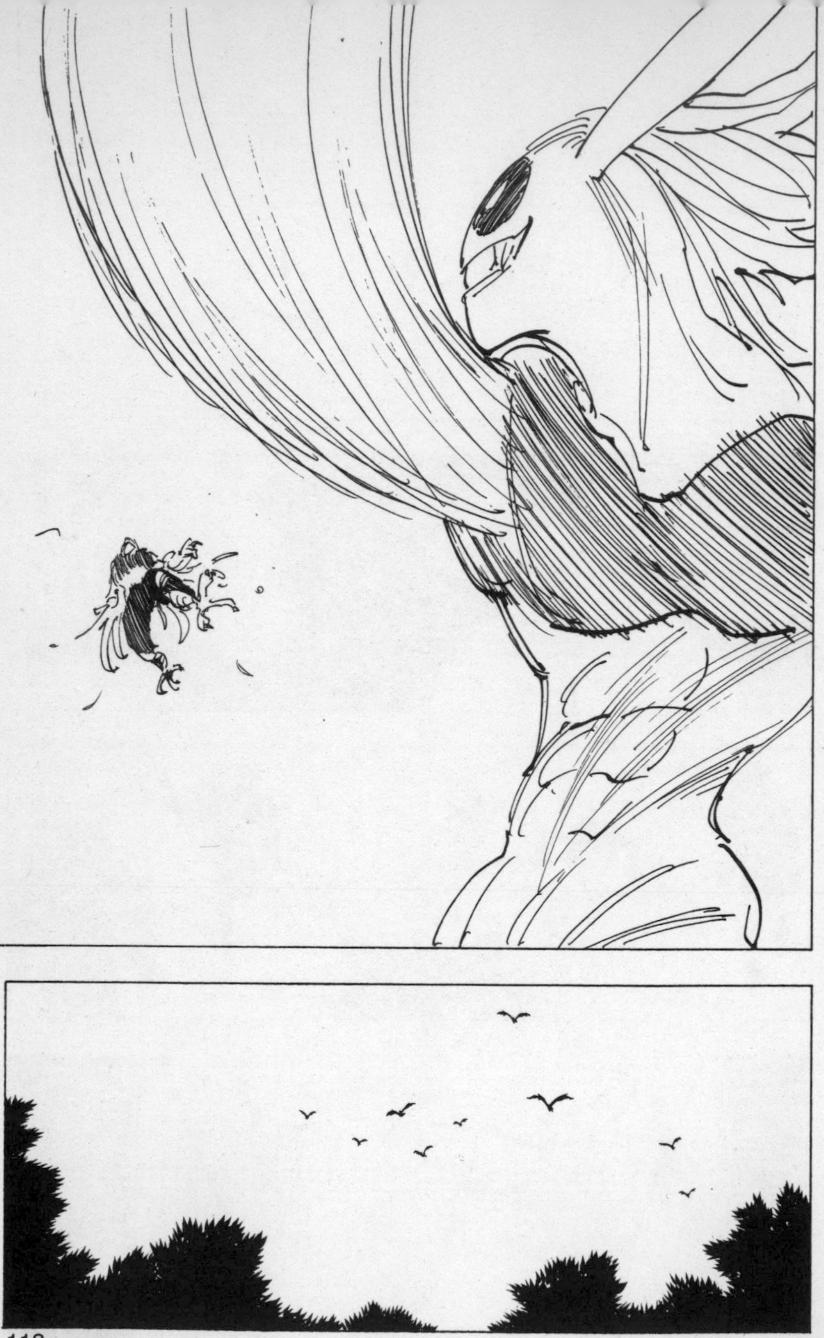

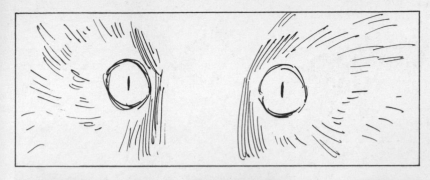

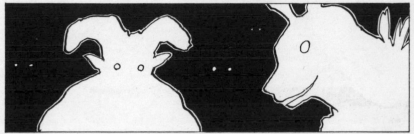

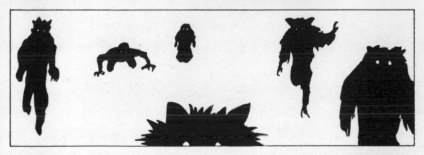

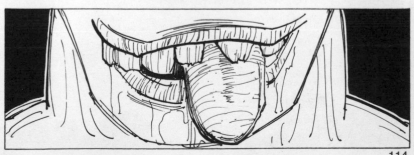

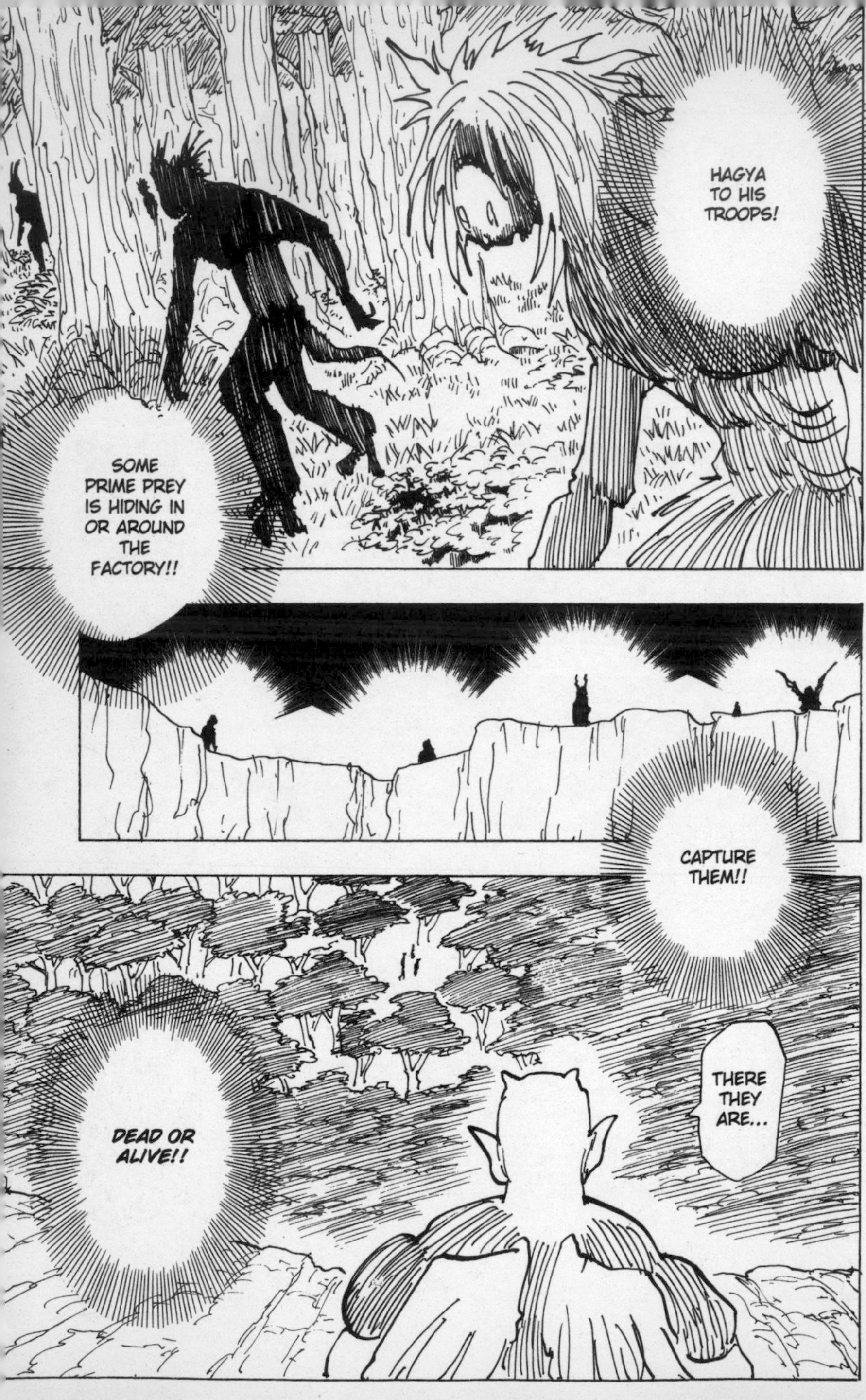
HAGYA TO HIS TROOPS!
SOME PRIME PREY IS HIDING IN OR AROUND THE FACTORY!!
CAPTURE THEM!!
THERE THEY ARE...
DEAD OR ALIVE!!

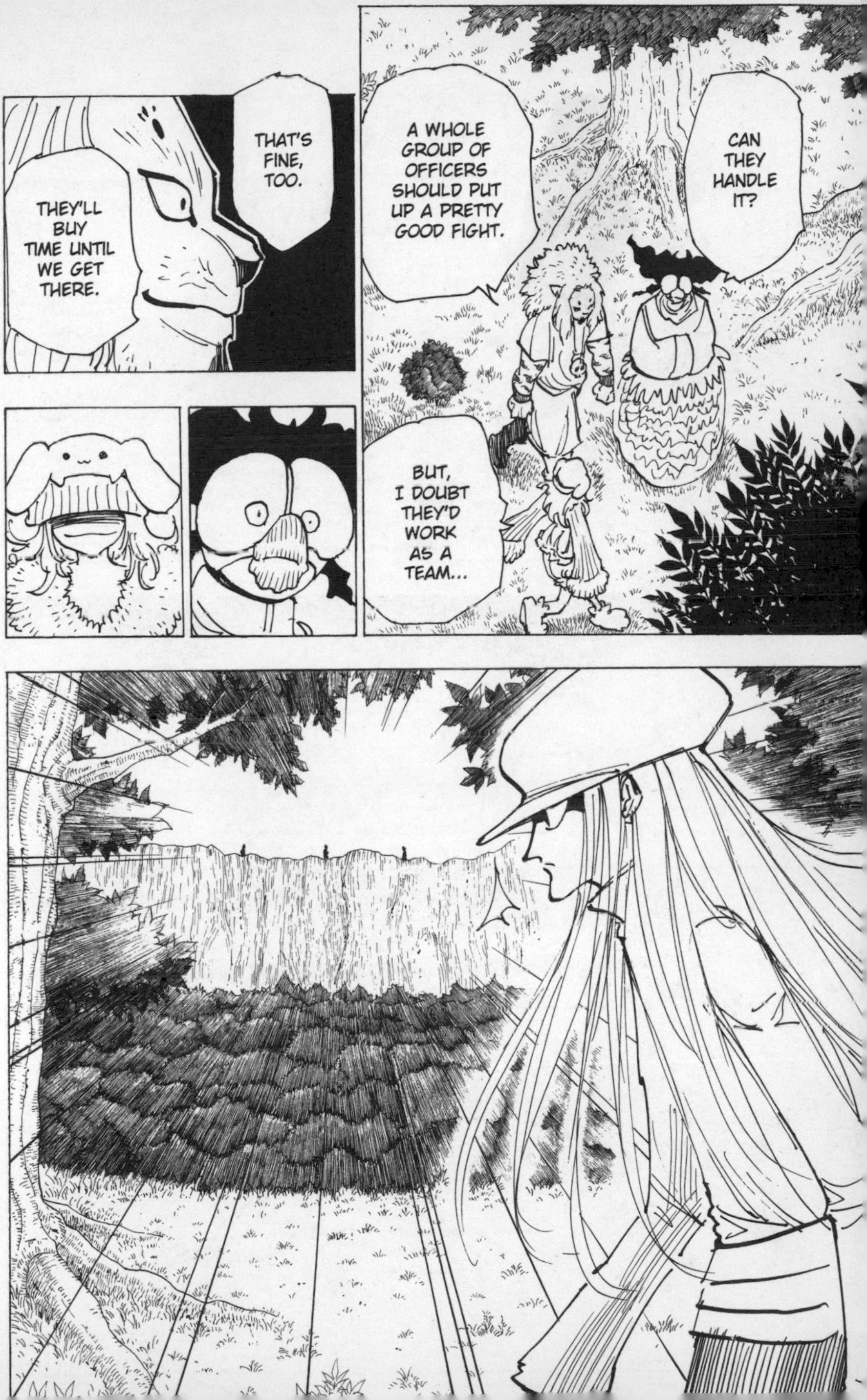
CAN THEY HANDLE IT?
A WHOLE GROUP OF OFFICERS SHOULD PUT UP A PRETTY GOOD FIGHT.
BUT, I DOUBT THEY'D WORK AS A TEAM...
THAT'S FINE, TOO.
THEY'LL BUY TIME UNTIL WE GET THERE.

READ THIS WAY

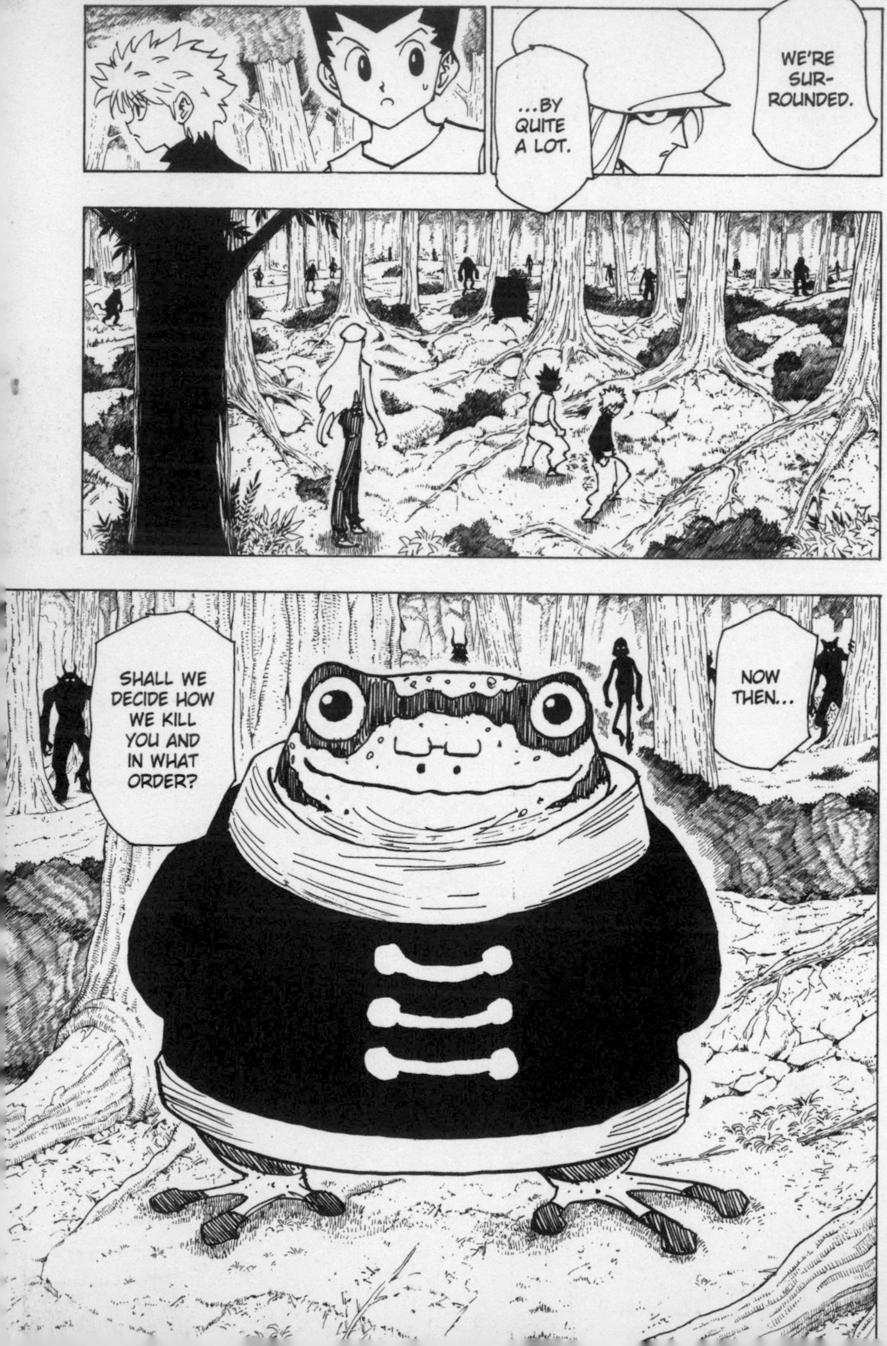
WE'RE SUR-ROUNDED.
...BY QUITE A LOT.
NOW THEN...
SHALL WE DECIDE HOW WE KILL YOU AND IN WHAT ORDER?

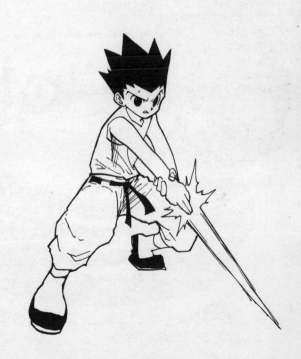

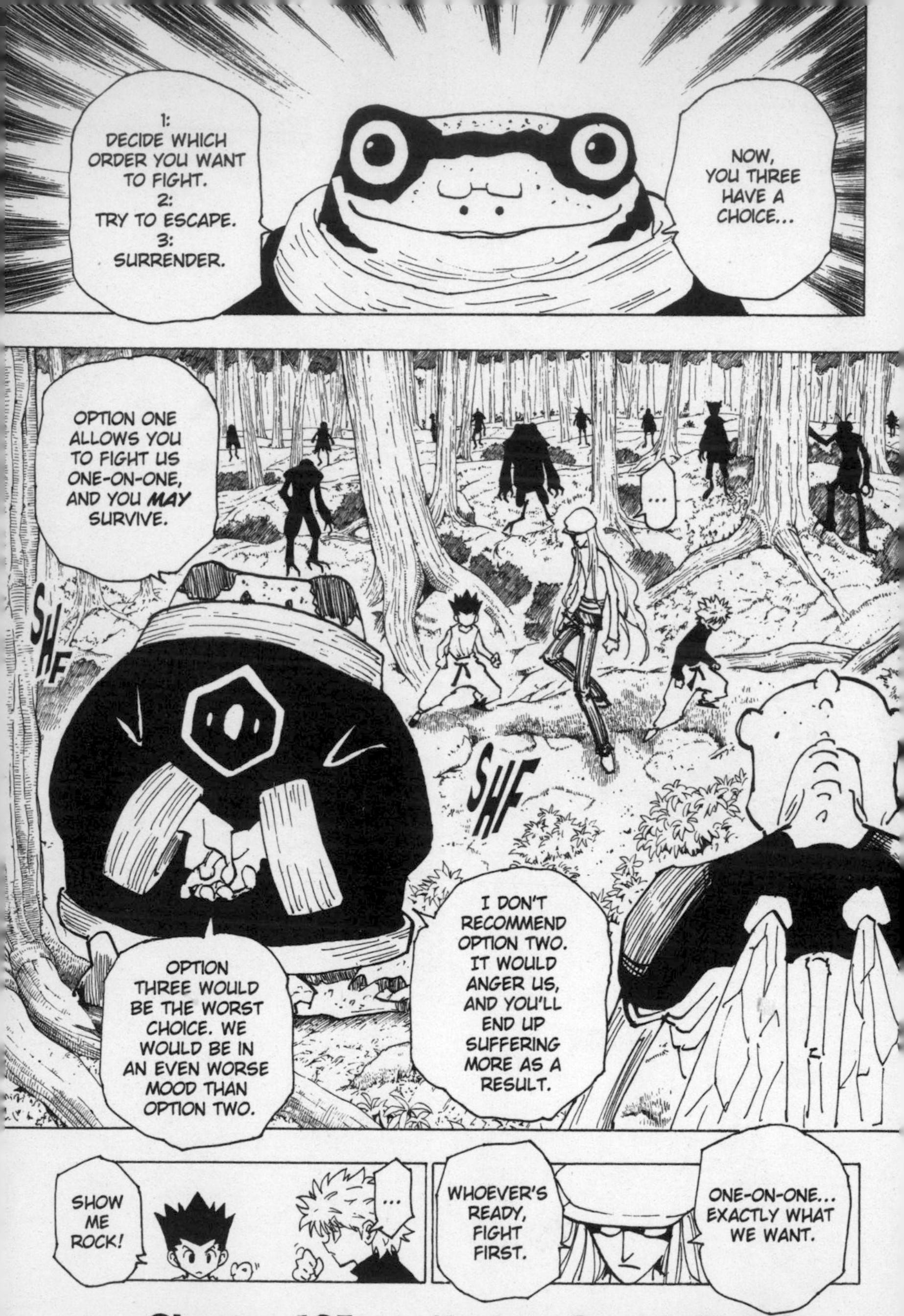
NOW, YOU THREE HAVE A CHOICE...
1: DECIDE WHICH ORDER YOU WANT TO FIGHT. 2: TRY TO ESCAPE. 3: SURRENDER.
OPTION ONE ALLOWS YOU TO FIGHT US ONE-ON-ONE, AND YOU *MAY* SURVIVE.
...
SHF
SHF
I DON'T RECOMMEND OPTION TWO. IT WOULD ANGER US, AND YOU'LL END UP SUFFERING MORE AS A RESULT.
OPTION THREE WOULD BE THE WORST CHOICE. WE WOULD BE IN AN EVEN WORSE MOOD THAN OPTION TWO.
ONE-ON-ONE... EXACTLY WHAT WE WANT.
WHOEVER'S READY, FIGHT FIRST.
...
SHOW ME ROCK!

Chapter 195: vs. Hagya's Squad: Part 2

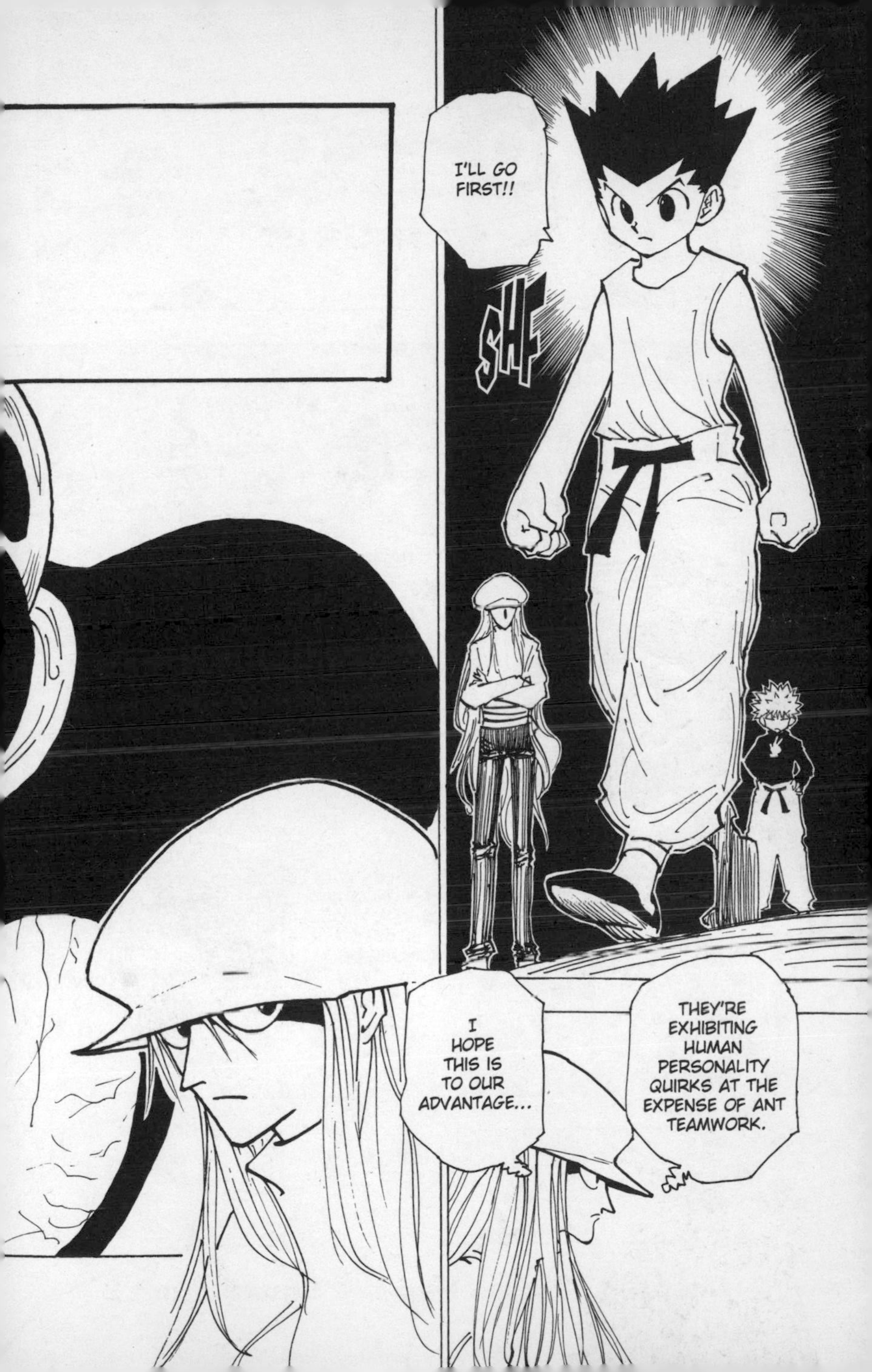
I'LL GO FIRST!!
SHF
THEY'RE EXHIBITING HUMAN PERSONALITY QUIRKS AT THE EXPENSE OF ANT TEAMWORK.
I HOPE THIS IS TO OUR ADVANTAGE...

Chapter 195:

vs. Hagya's Squad: Part 2

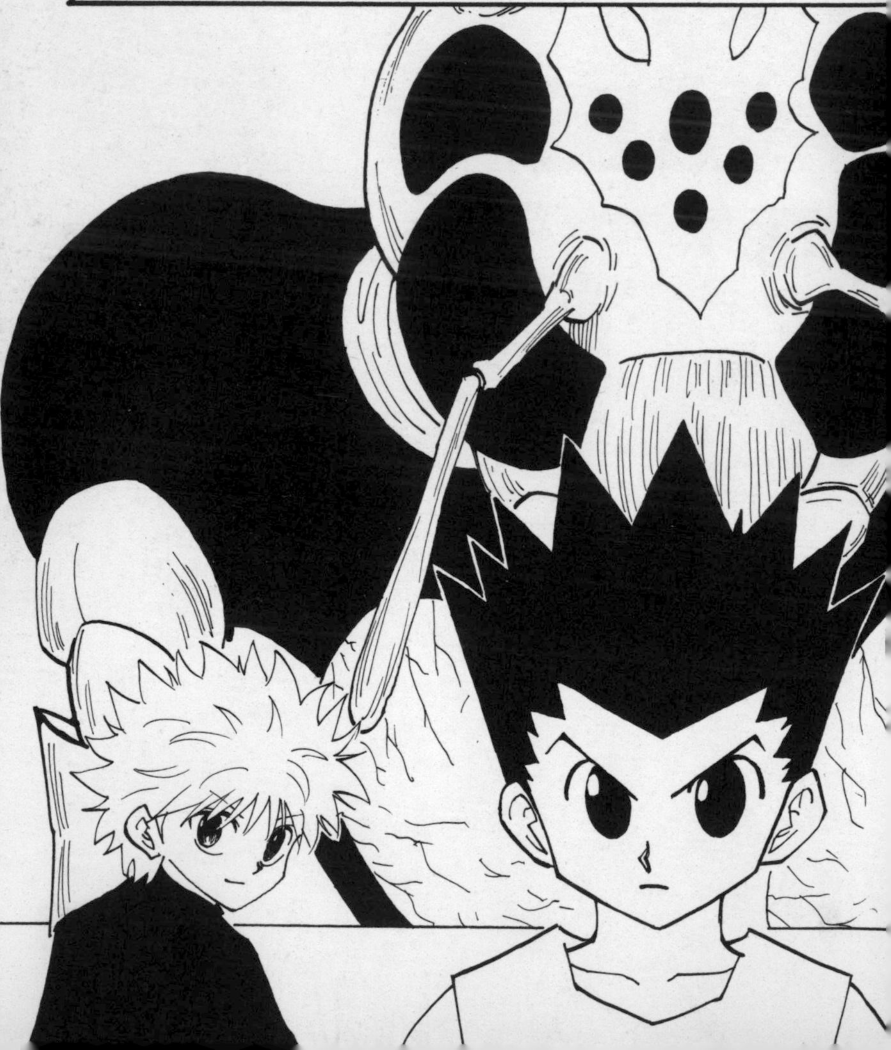

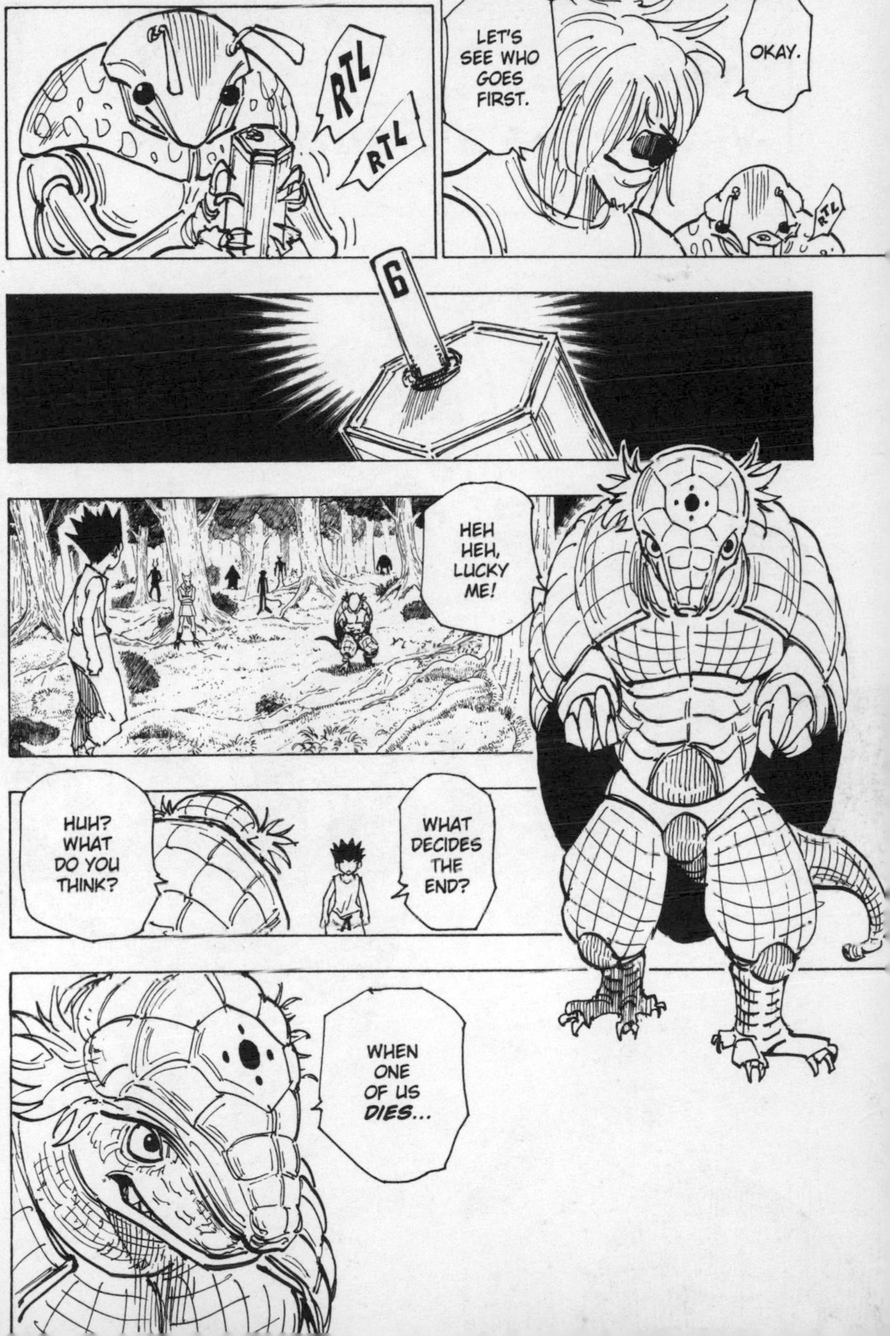
OKAY.
LET'S SEE WHO GOES FIRST.
RTL
RTL
RTL
6
HEH HEH, LUCKY ME!
WHAT DECIDES THE END?
HUH? WHAT DO YOU THINK?
WHEN ONE OF US DIES...

READ THIS WAY

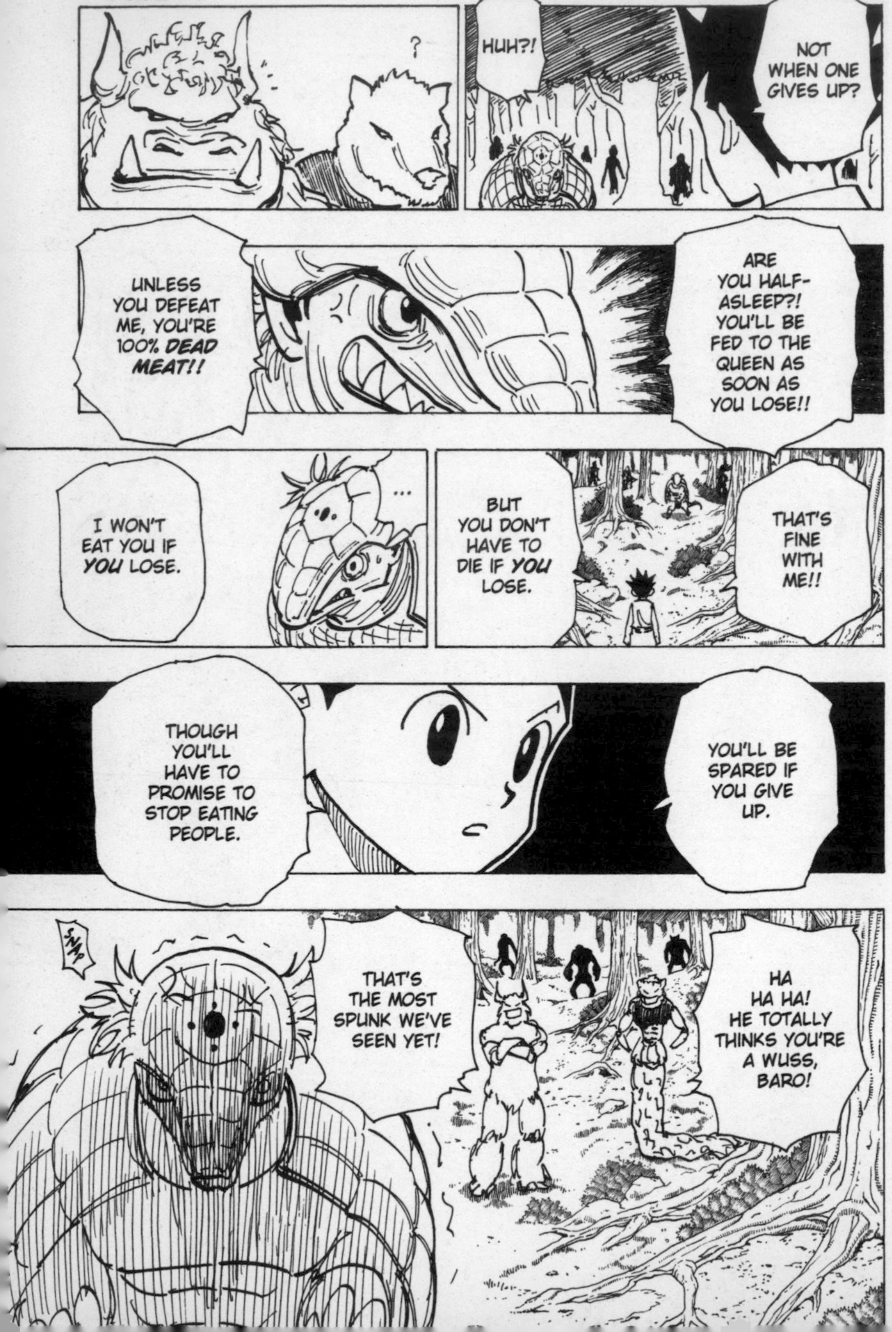
NOT WHEN ONE GIVES UP?
HUH?!
ARE YOU HALF-ASLEEP?! YOU'LL BE FED TO THE QUEEN AS SOON AS YOU LOSE!!
UNLESS YOU DEFEAT ME, YOU'RE 100% DEAD MEAT!!
THAT'S FINE WITH ME!!
BUT YOU DON'T HAVE TO DIE IF YOU LOSE.
...
I WON'T EAT YOU IF YOU LOSE.
YOU'LL BE SPARED IF YOU GIVE UP.
THOUGH YOU'LL HAVE TO PROMISE TO STOP EATING PEOPLE.
HA HA HA! HE TOTALLY THINKS YOU'RE A WUSS, BARO!
THAT'S THE MOST SPUNK WE'VE SEEN YET!
SNAP

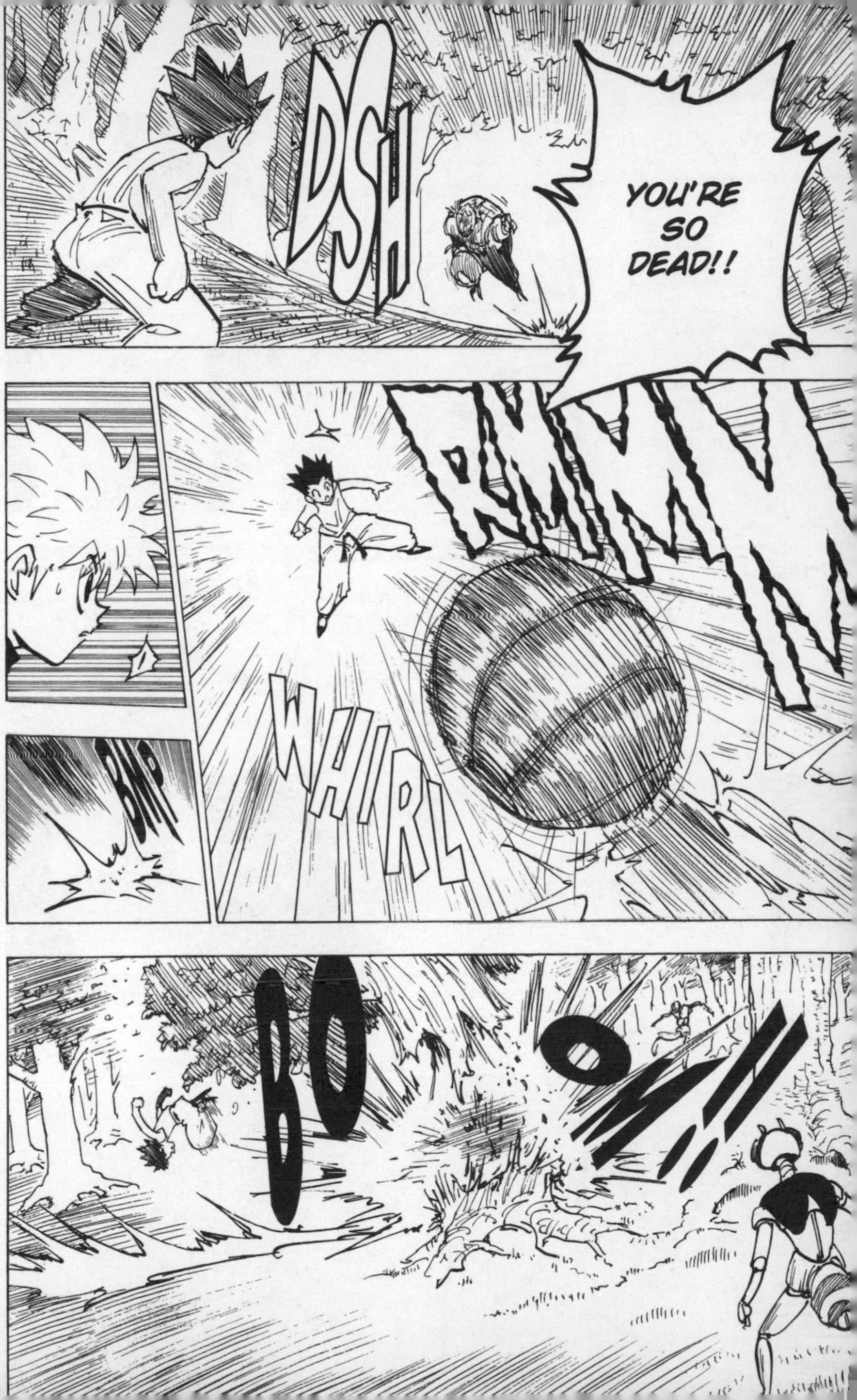
YOU'RE SO DEAD!!
DSH
WHIRL
BMP
BOOM!!

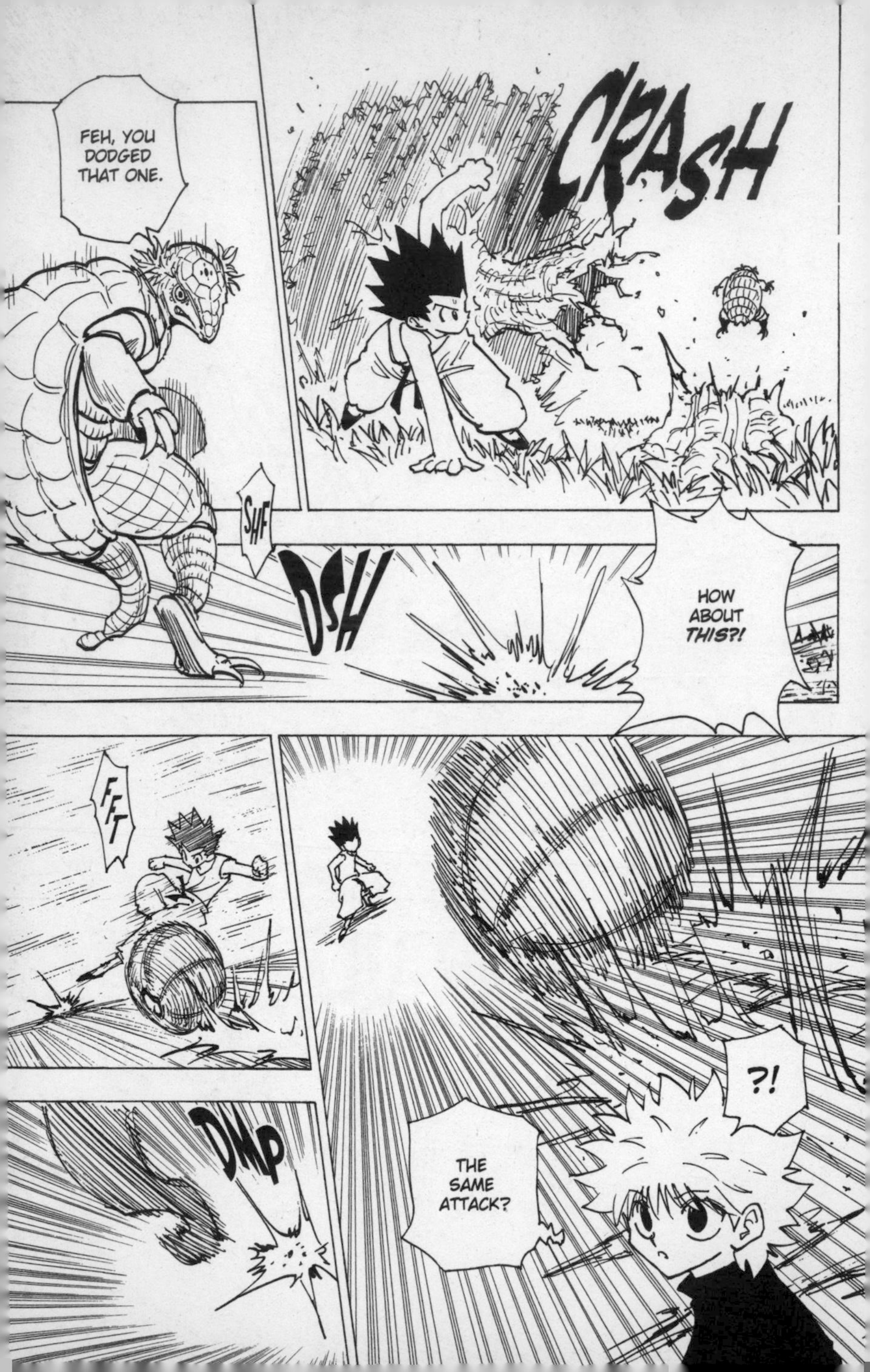
CRASH
FEH, YOU DODGED THAT ONE.
SHF
DSH
HOW ABOUT *THIS?!*
?!
THE SAME ATTACK?
FFFT
DMP

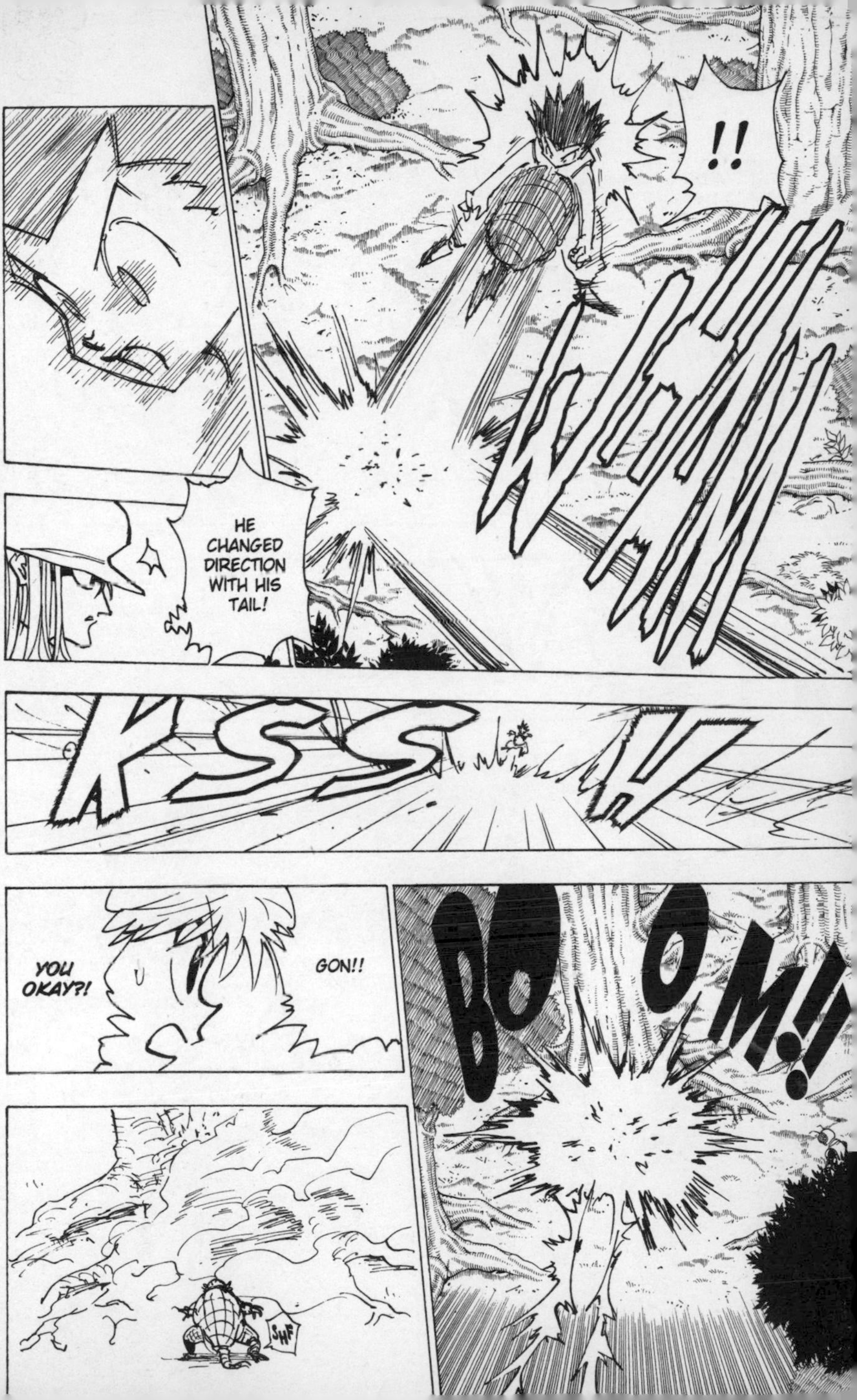
!!
WHAM
HE CHANGED DIRECTION WITH HIS TAIL!
KSSH!
BOOM!!
GON!!
YOU OKAY?!
SHF

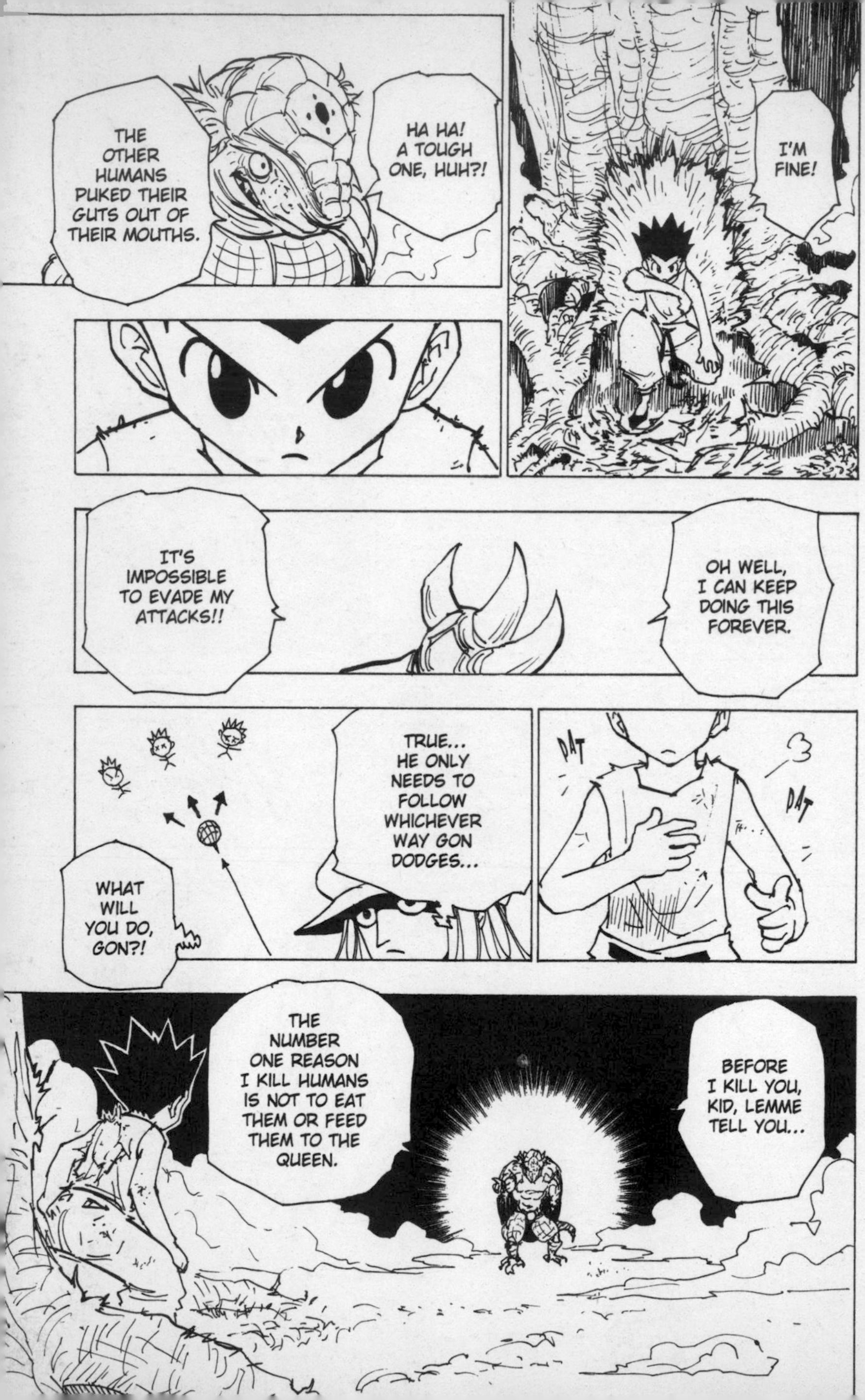
I'M FINE!
HA HA! A TOUGH ONE, HUH?!
THE OTHER HUMANS PUKED THEIR GUTS OUT OF THEIR MOUTHS.
OH WELL, I CAN KEEP DOING THIS FOREVER.
IT'S IMPOSSIBLE TO EVADE MY ATTACKS!!
PAT
PAT
TRUE... HE ONLY NEEDS TO FOLLOW WHICHEVER WAY GON DODGES...
WHAT WILL YOU DO, GON?!
BEFORE I KILL YOU, KID, LEMME TELL YOU...
THE NUMBER ONE REASON I KILL HUMANS IS NOT TO EAT THEM OR FEED THEM TO THE QUEEN.

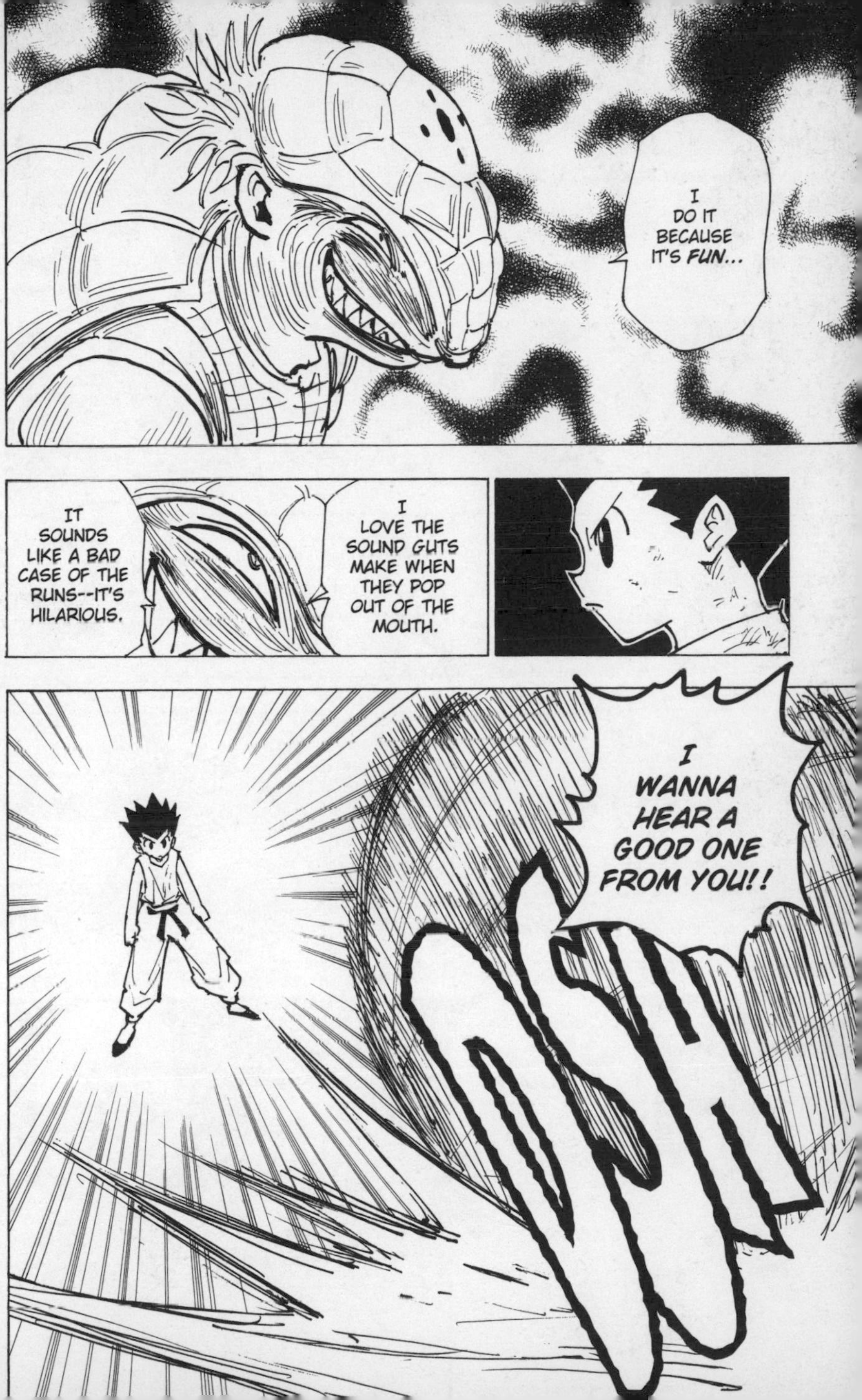
I DO IT BECAUSE IT'S *FUN*...
I LOVE THE SOUND GUTS MAKE WHEN THEY POP OUT OF THE MOUTH.
IT SOUNDS LIKE A BAD CASE OF THE RUNS--IT'S HILARIOUS.
I WANNA HEAR A GOOD ONE FROM YOU!!

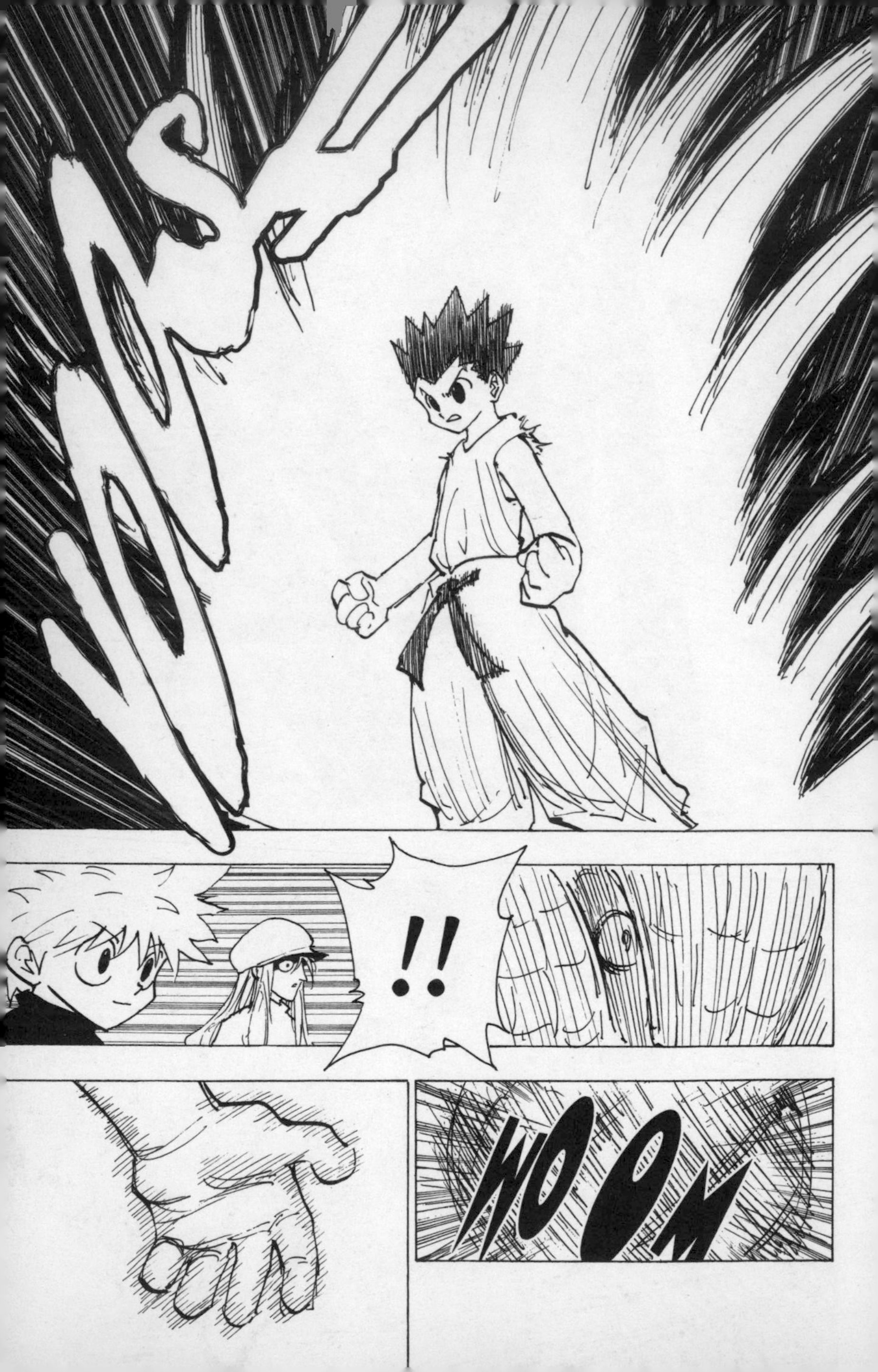
!!
WOOM

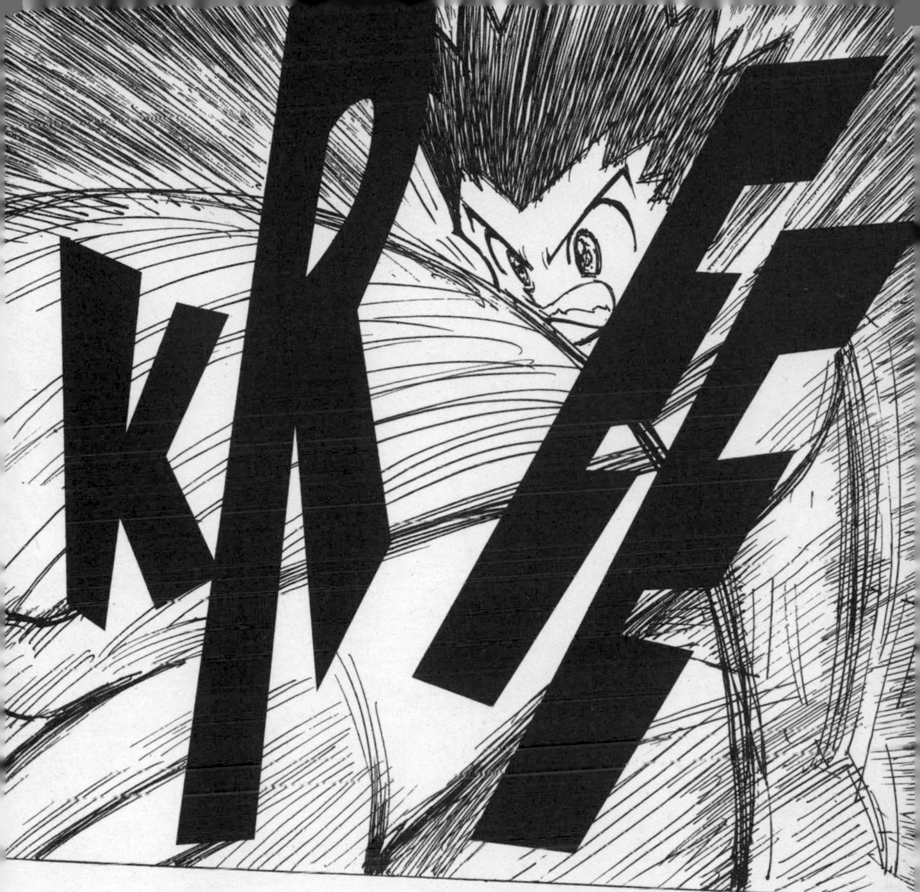
KREE

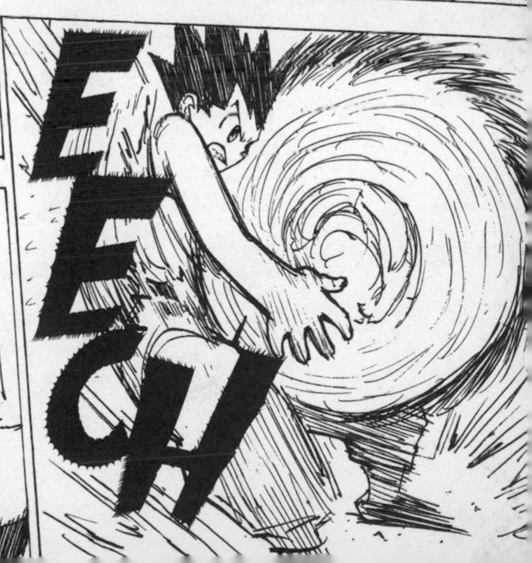
EEECH

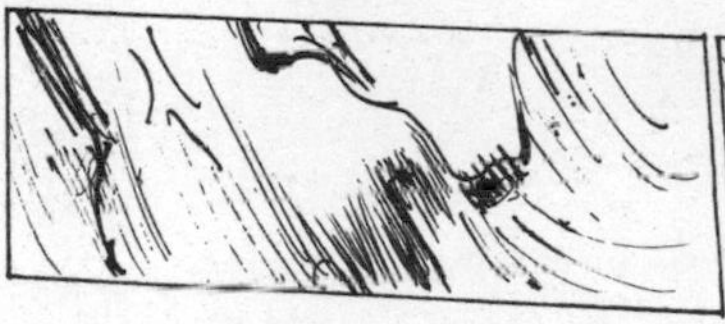

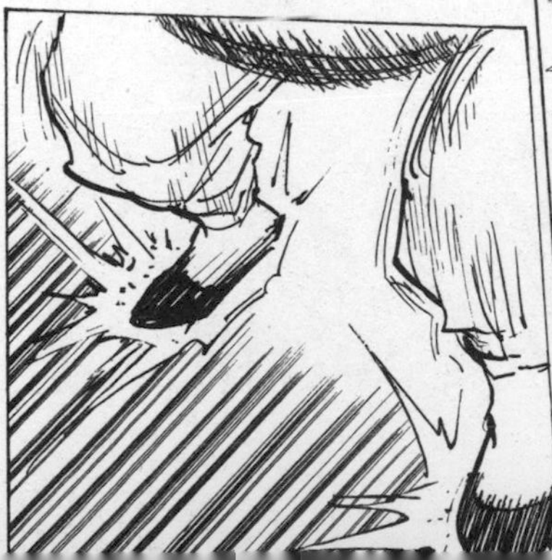

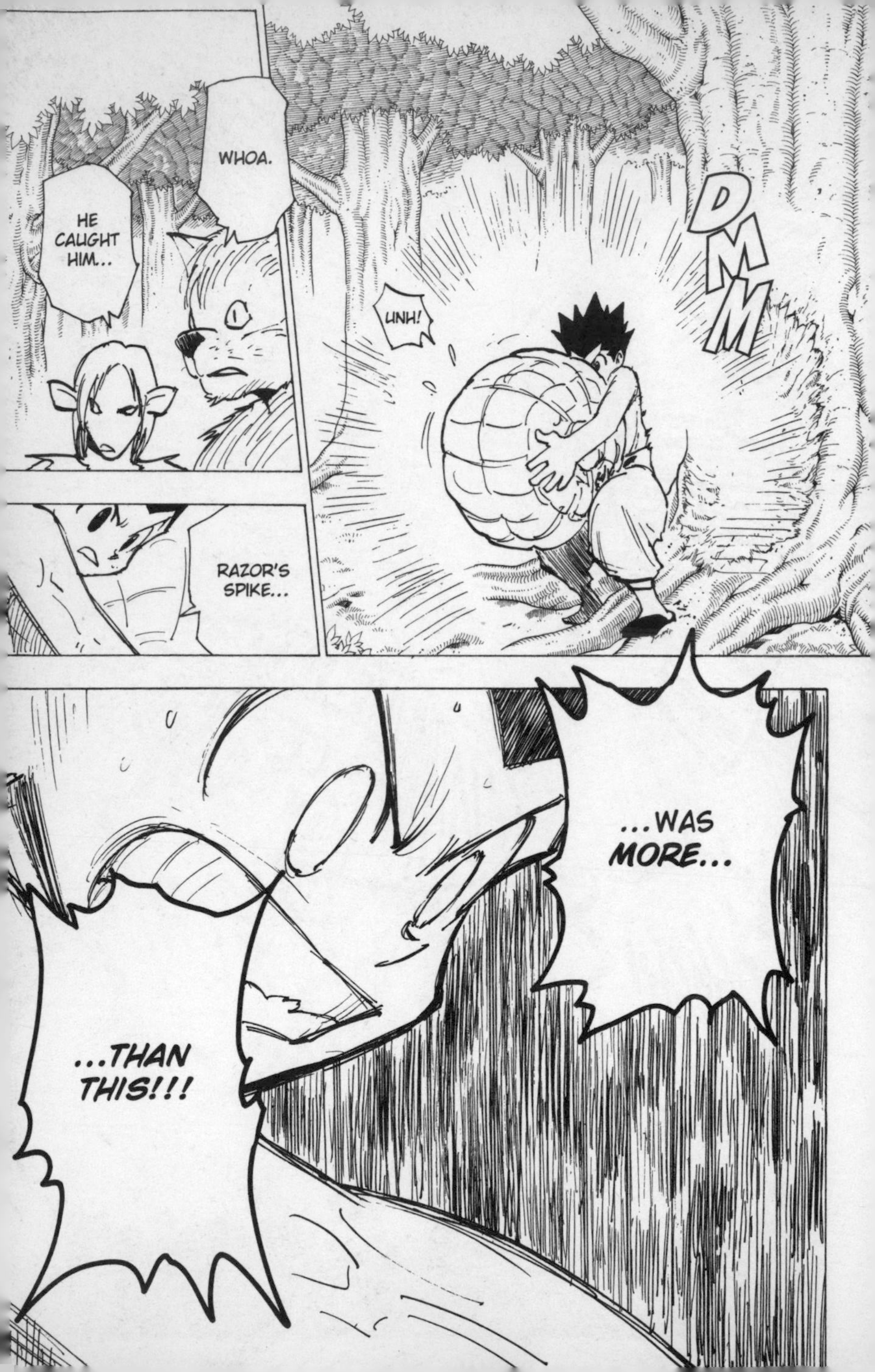
DMM
UNH!
WHOA.
HE CAUGHT HIM...
RAZOR'S SPIKE...
...WAS MORE...
...THAN THIS!!!

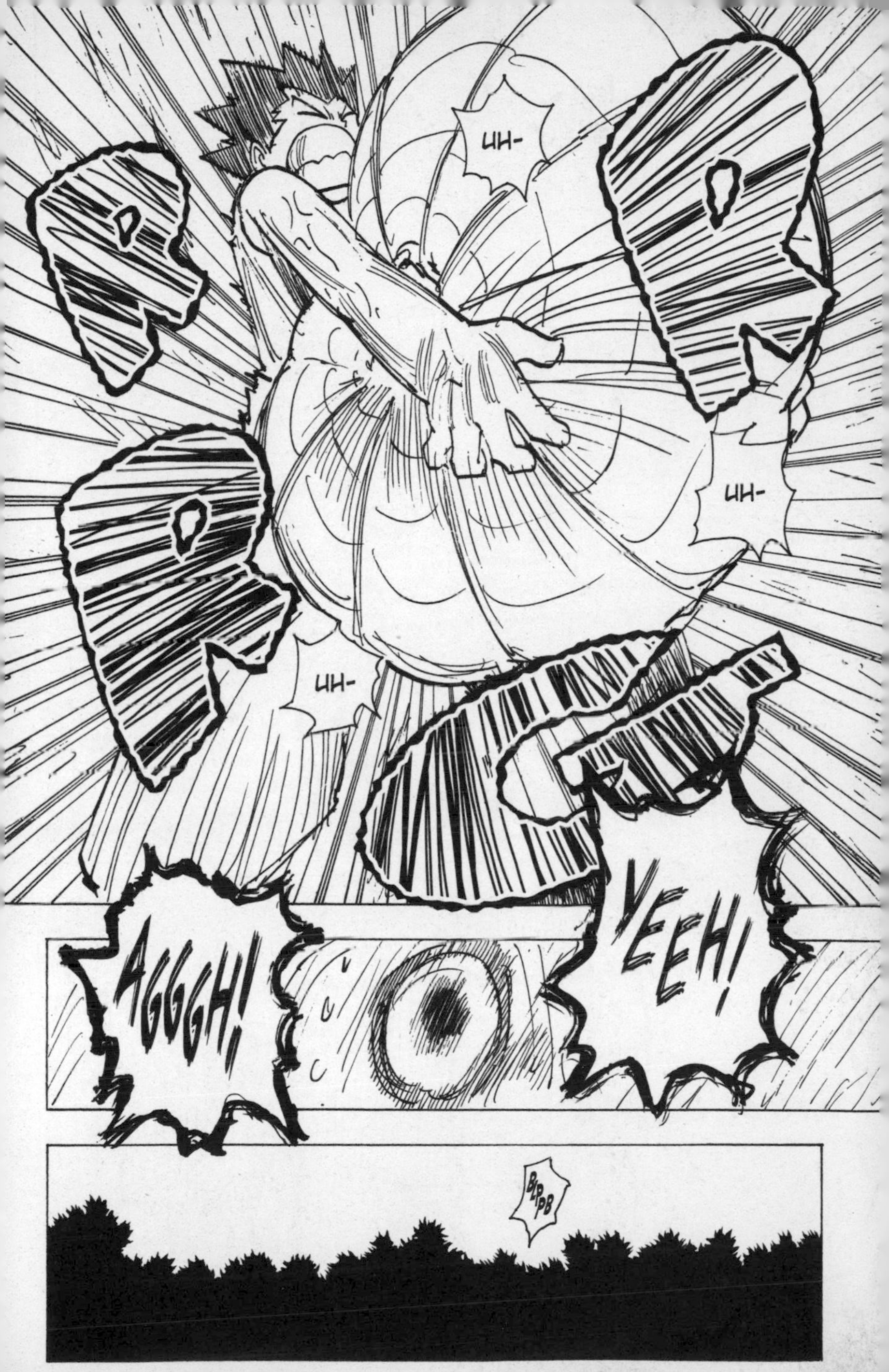
UH-
UH-
UH-
VEEH!
AGGGH!
BLPPB

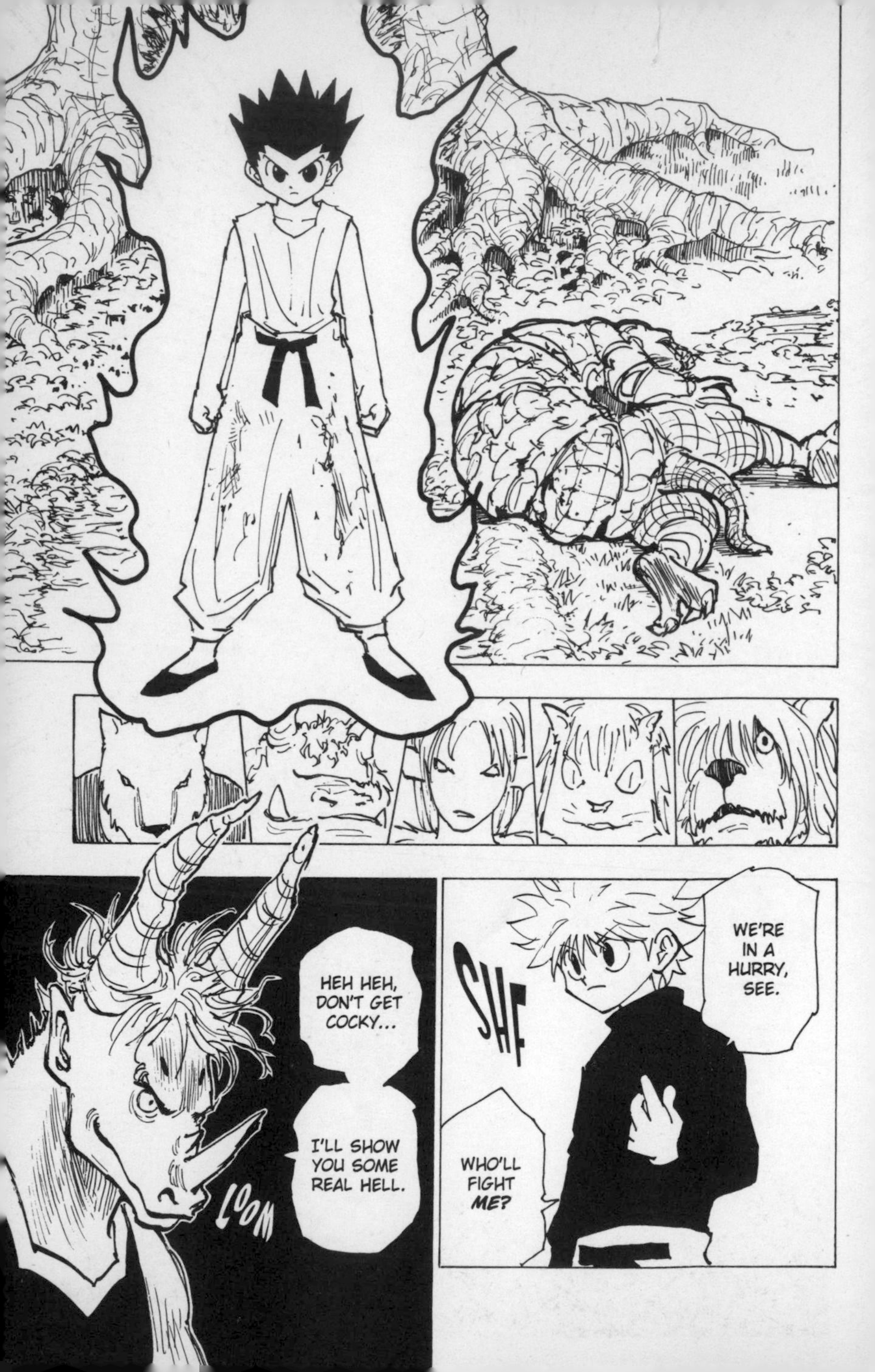
WE'RE IN A HURRY, SEE.
SHF
WHO'LL FIGHT *ME?*
HEH HEH, DON'T GET COCKY...
I'LL SHOW YOU SOME REAL HELL.
LOOM

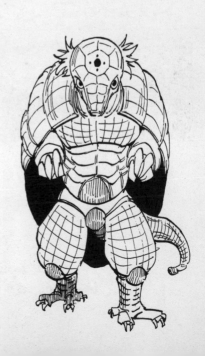

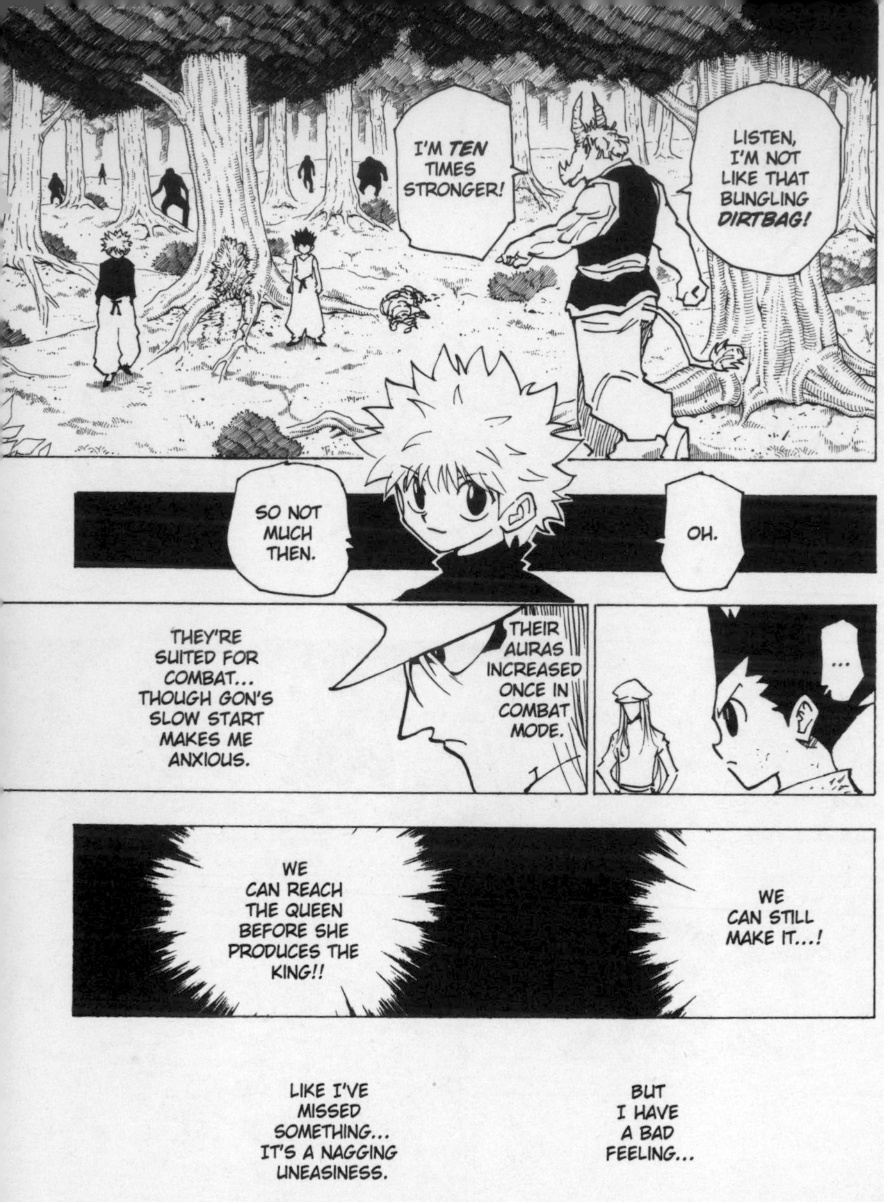
LISTEN, I'M NOT LIKE THAT BUNGLING *DIRTBAG!*
I'M *TEN* TIMES STRONGER!
OH.
SO NOT MUCH THEN.
...
THEIR AURAS INCREASED ONCE IN COMBAT MODE.
THEY'RE SUITED FOR COMBAT... THOUGH GON'S SLOW START MAKES ME ANXIOUS.
WE CAN STILL MAKE IT...!
WE CAN REACH THE QUEEN BEFORE SHE PRODUCES THE KING!!
BUT I HAVE A BAD FEELING...
LIKE I'VE MISSED SOMETHING... IT'S A NAGGING UNEASINESS.

Chapter 196:
vs. Hagya's Squad: Part 3

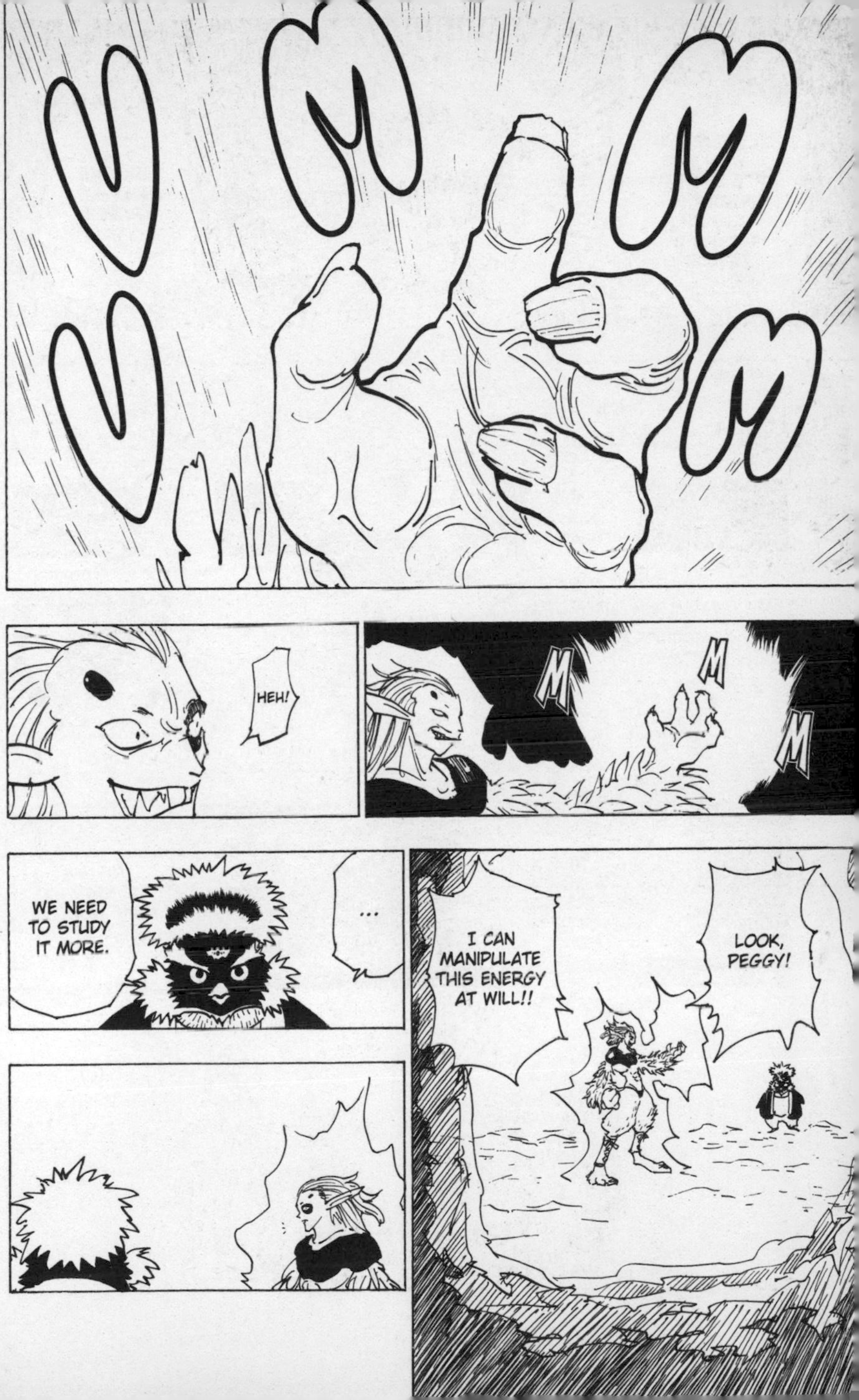
M
M
M
HEH!
LOOK, PEGGY!
I CAN MANIPULATE THIS ENERGY AT WILL!!
...
WE NEED TO STUDY IT MORE.

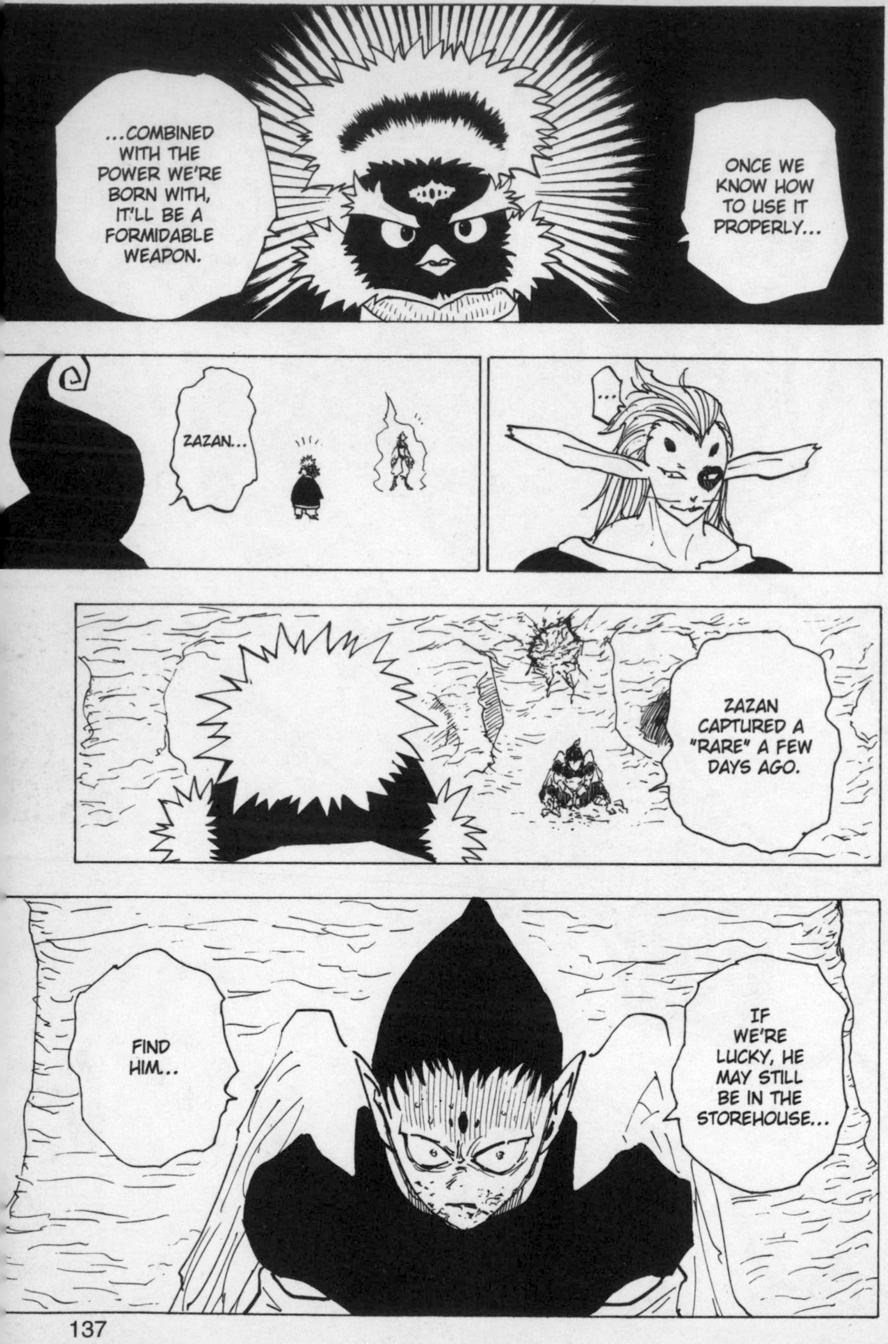
ONCE WE KNOW HOW TO USE IT PROPERLY...
...COMBINED WITH THE POWER WE'RE BORN WITH, IT'LL BE A FORMIDABLE WEAPON.
...
ZAZAN...
ZAZAN CAPTURED A "RARE" A FEW DAYS AGO.
IF WE'RE LUCKY, HE MAY STILL BE IN THE STOREHOUSE...
FIND HIM...

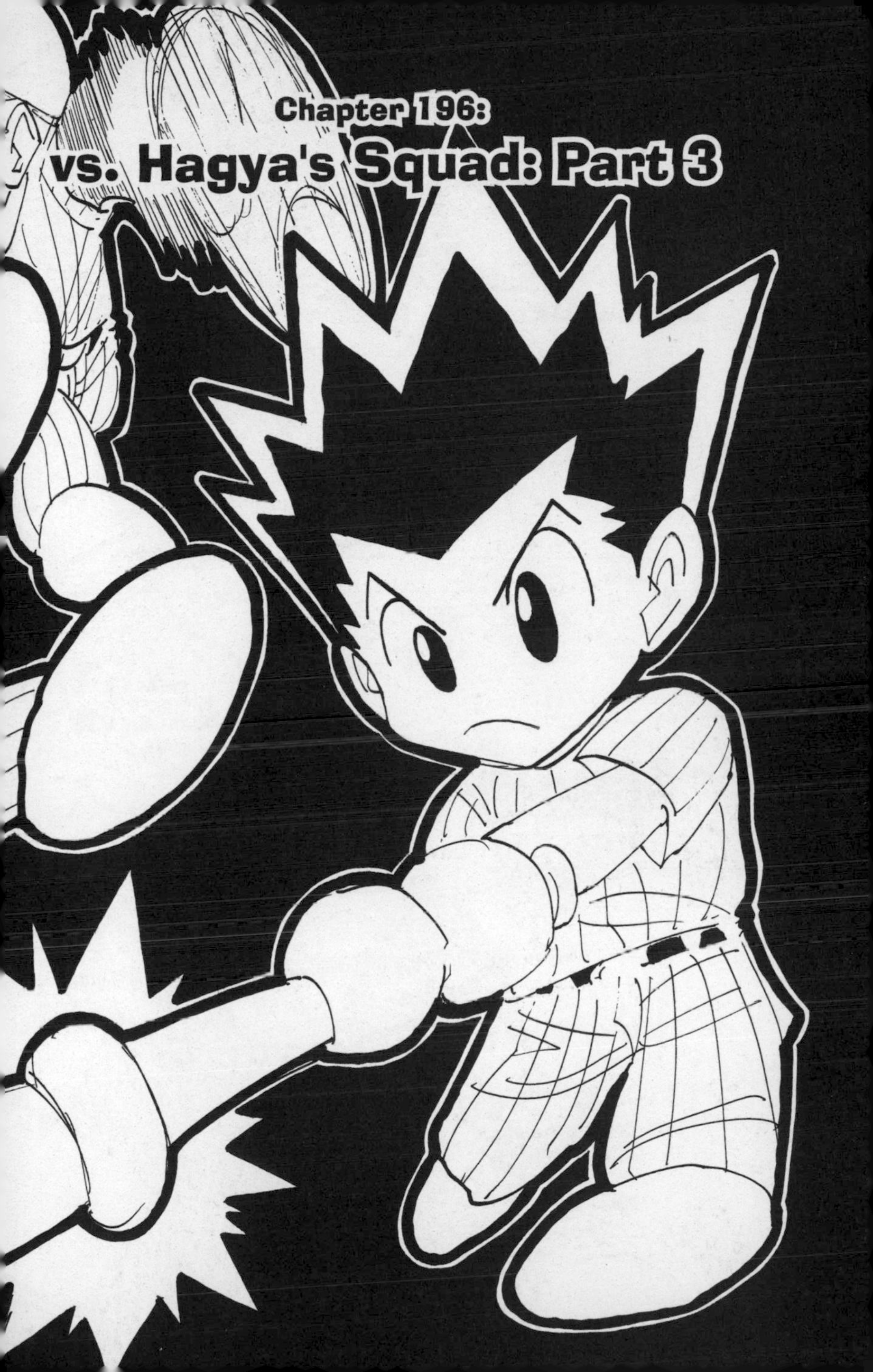
Chapter 196:
vs. Hagya's Squad: Part 3

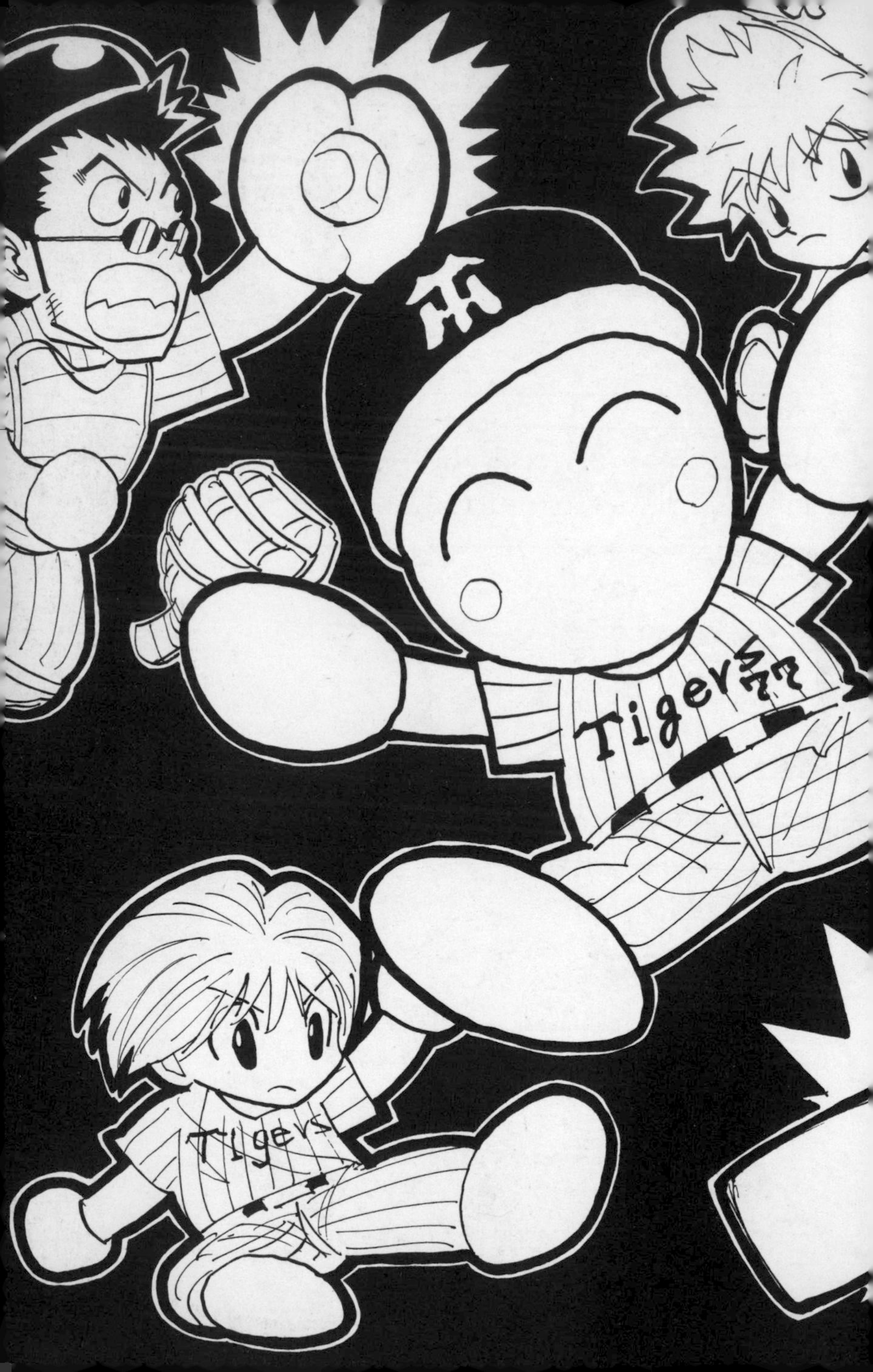
Tigers
Tigers

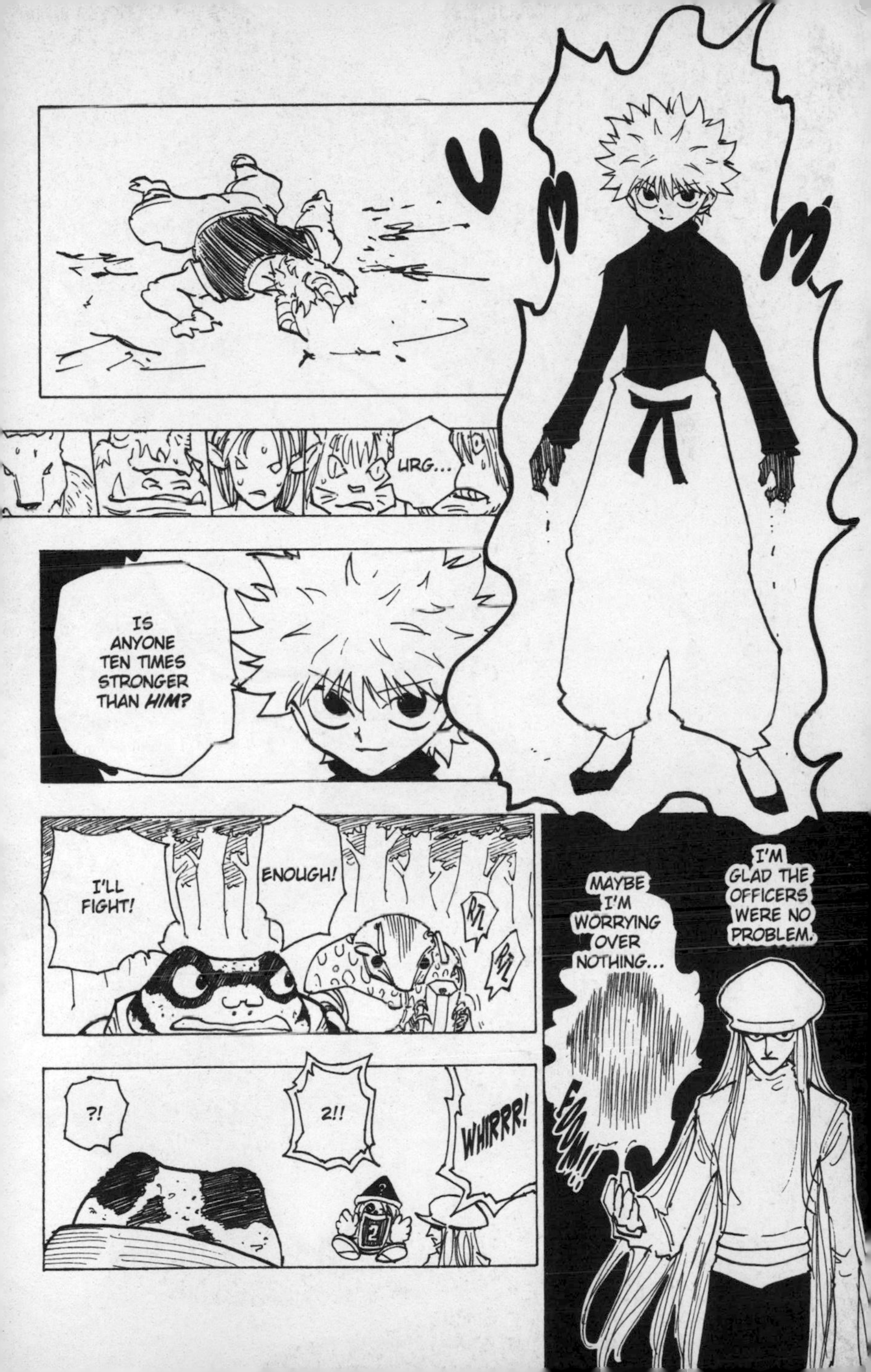
URG...
IS ANYONE TEN TIMES STRONGER THAN *HIM*?
I'M GLAD THE OFFICERS WERE NO PROBLEM.
MAYBE I'M WORRYING OVER NOTHING...
FOOM!!
ENOUGH!
I'LL FIGHT!
RTL
RTL
WHIRRR!
2!!
?!

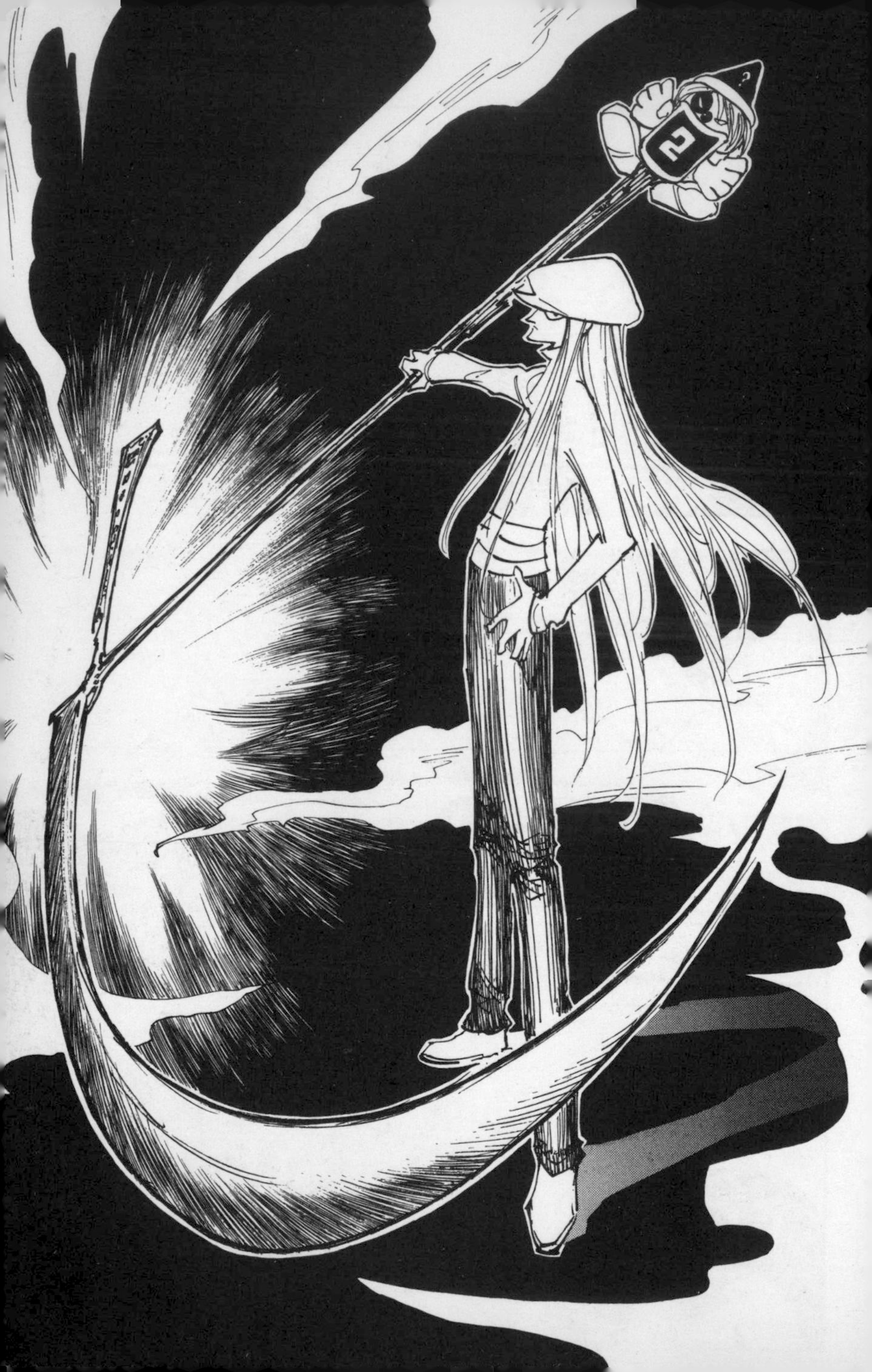

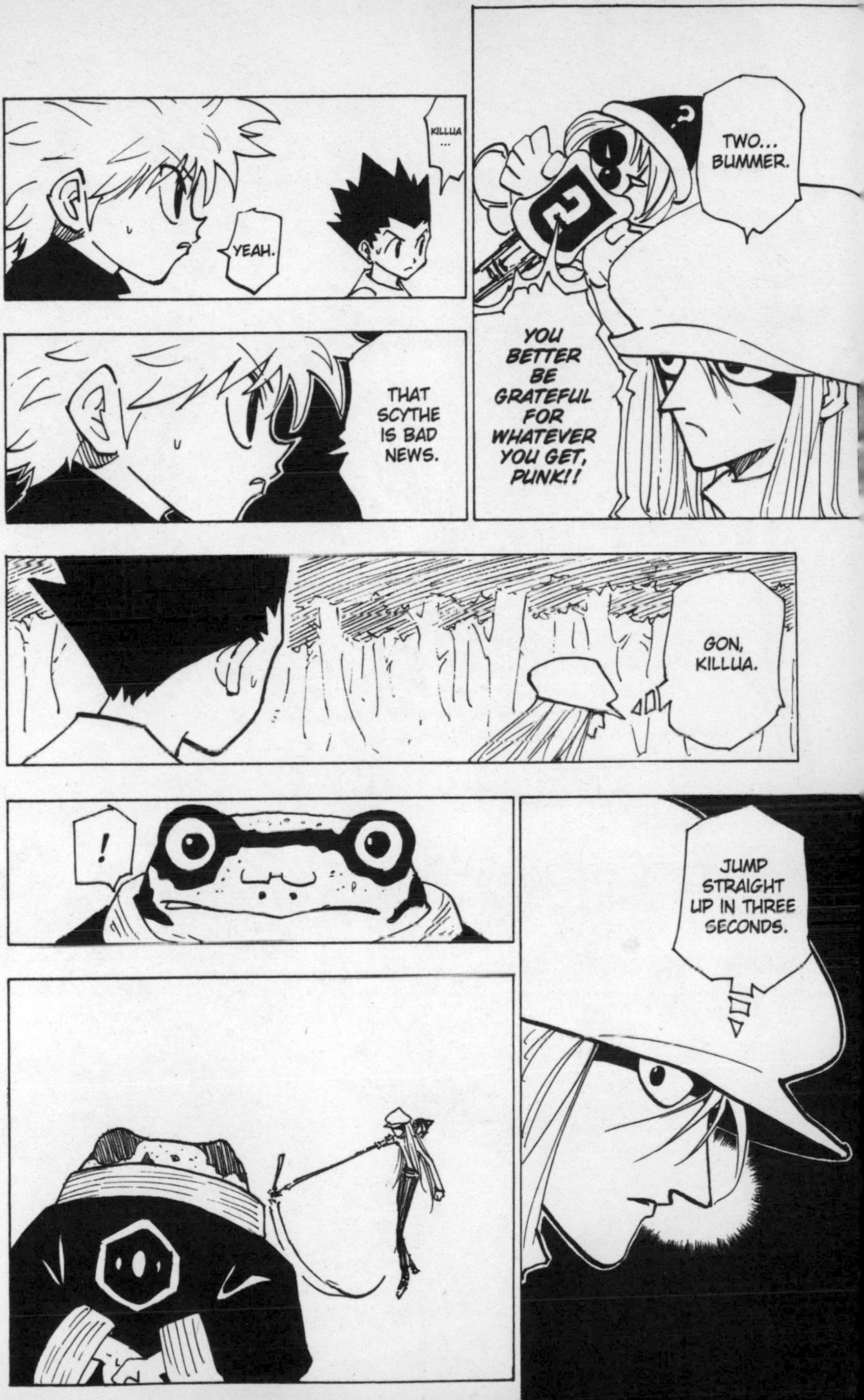
TWO... BUMMER.
YOU BETTER BE GRATEFUL FOR WHATEVER YOU GET, PUNK!!
KILLUA ...
YEAH.
THAT SCYTHE IS BAD NEWS.
GON, KILLUA.
JUMP STRAIGHT UP IN THREE SECONDS.
!

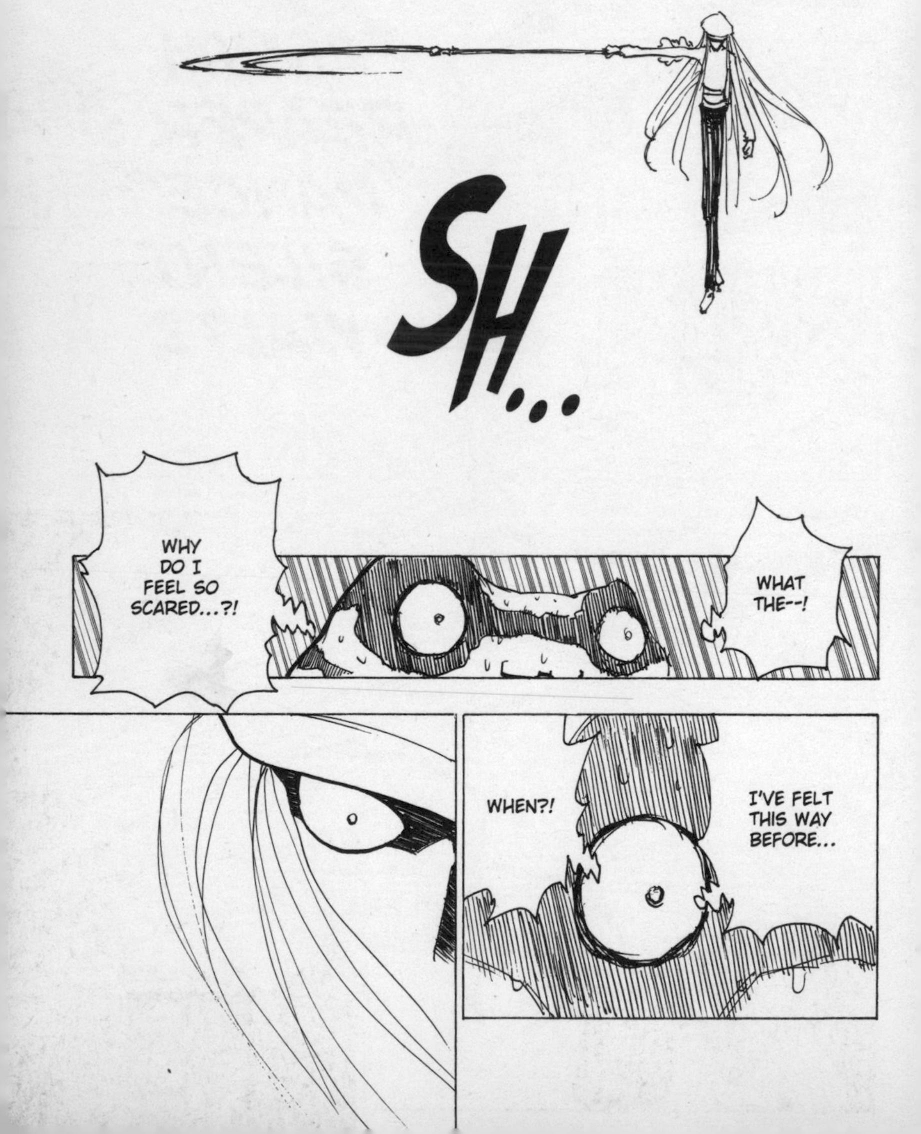
SH...
WHAT THE--!
WHY DO I FEEL SO SCARED...?!
I'VE FELT THIS WAY BEFORE...
WHEN?!

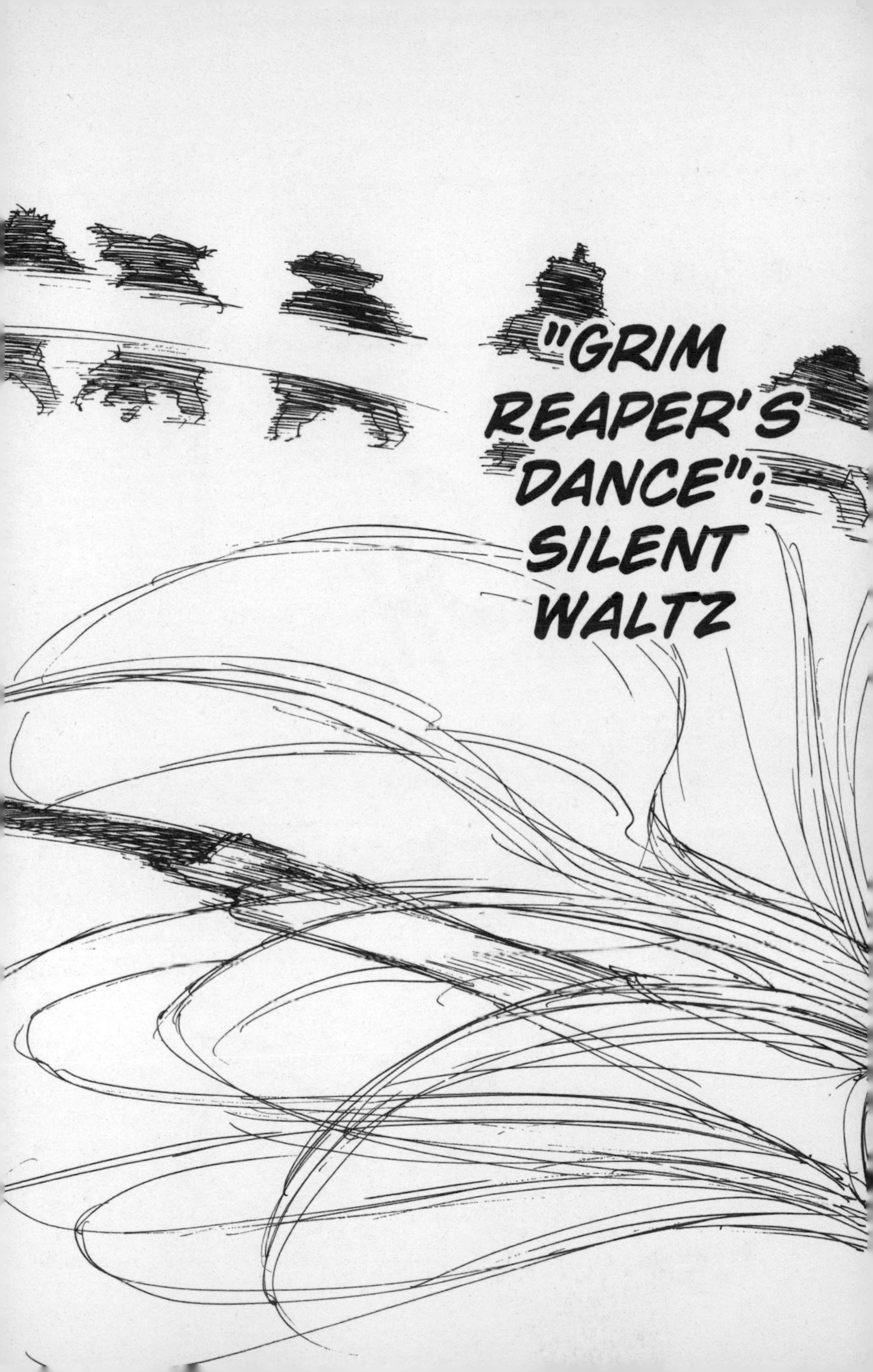
"GRIM REAPER'S DANCE": SILENT WALTZ

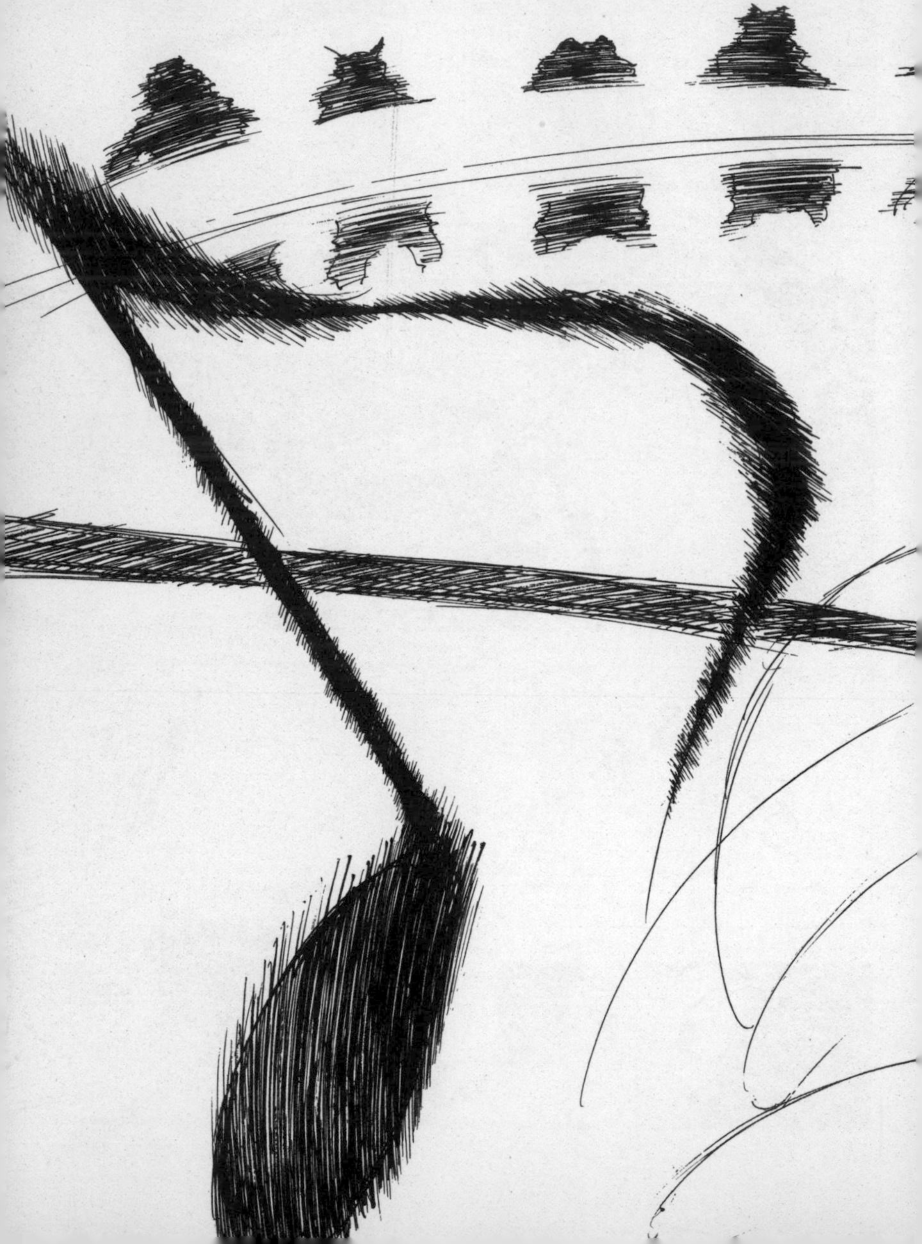

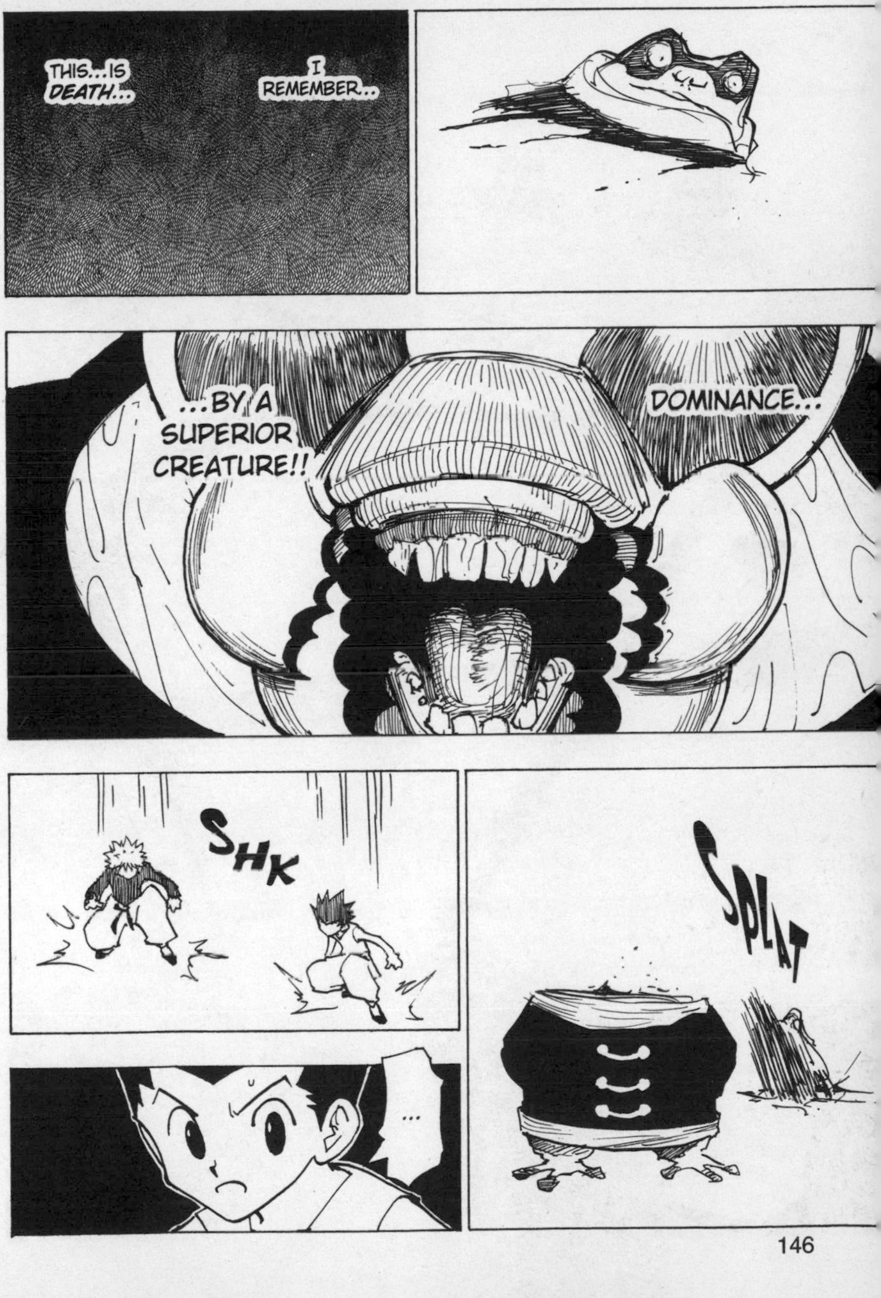
I REMEMBER...
THIS...IS DEATH...
DOMINANCE...
...BY A SUPERIOR CREATURE!!
SPLAT
SHK
...

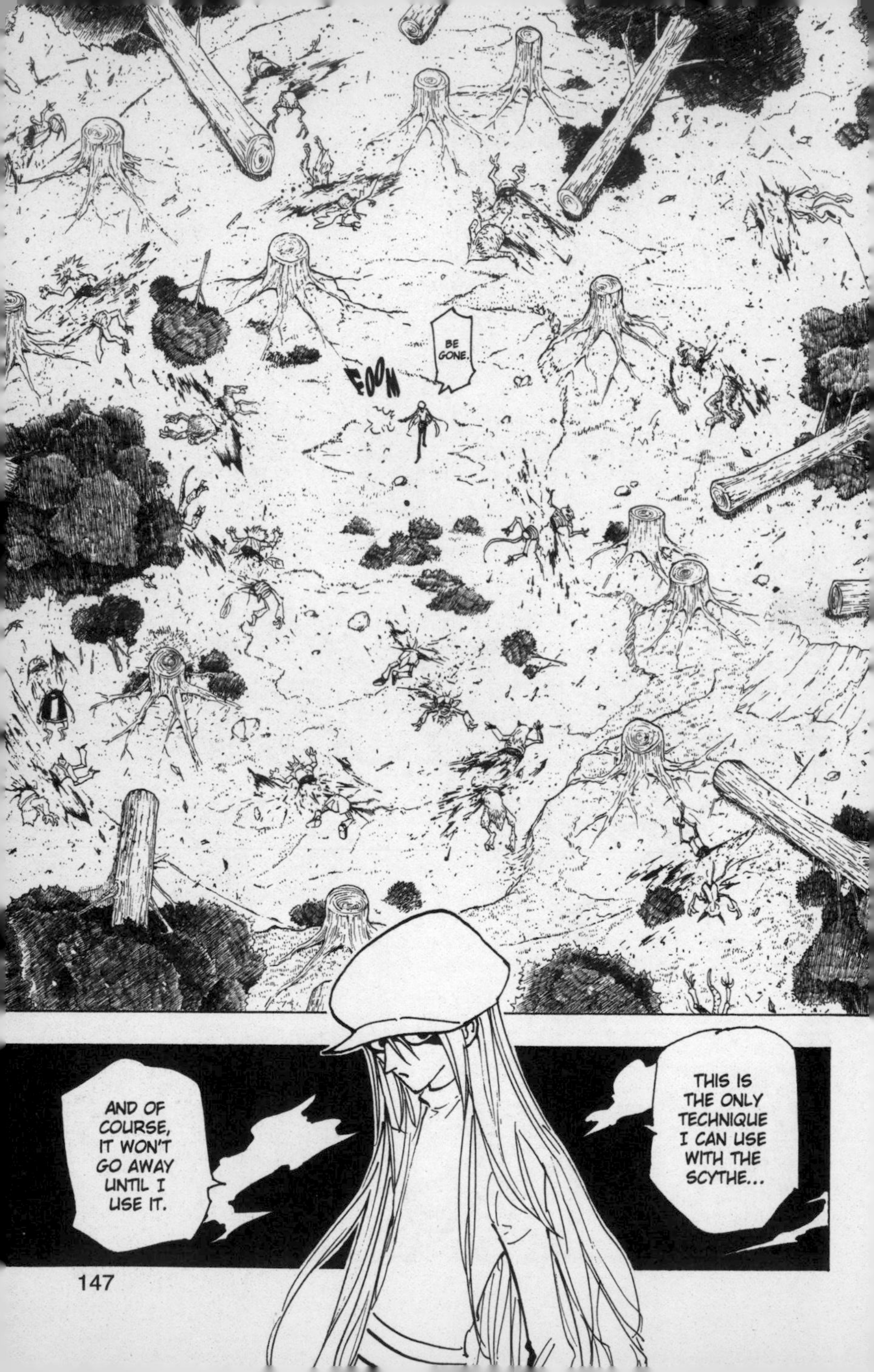
BE GONE.
FOOM
THIS IS THE ONLY TECHNIQUE I CAN USE WITH THE SCYTHE...
AND OF COURSE, IT WON'T GO AWAY UNTIL I USE IT.

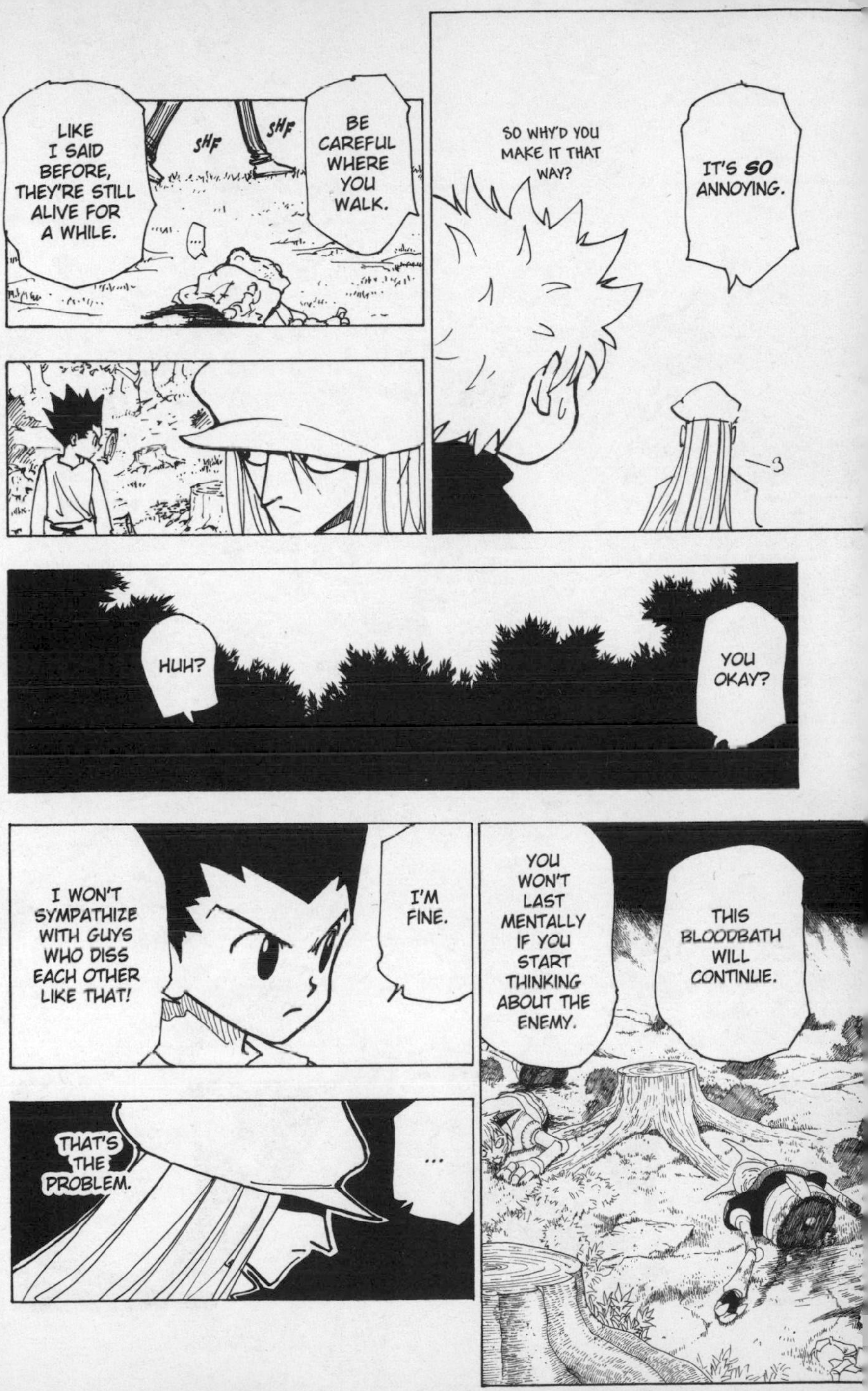
IT'S SO ANNOYING.
SO WHY'D YOU MAKE IT THAT WAY?
BE CAREFUL WHERE YOU WALK.
SHF
SHF
...
LIKE I SAID BEFORE, THEY'RE STILL ALIVE FOR A WHILE.
YOU OKAY?
HUH?
THIS BLOODBATH WILL CONTINUE.
YOU WON'T LAST MENTALLY IF YOU START THINKING ABOUT THE ENEMY.
I'M FINE.
I WON'T SYMPATHIZE WITH GUYS WHO DISS EACH OTHER LIKE THAT!
...
THAT'S THE PROBLEM.

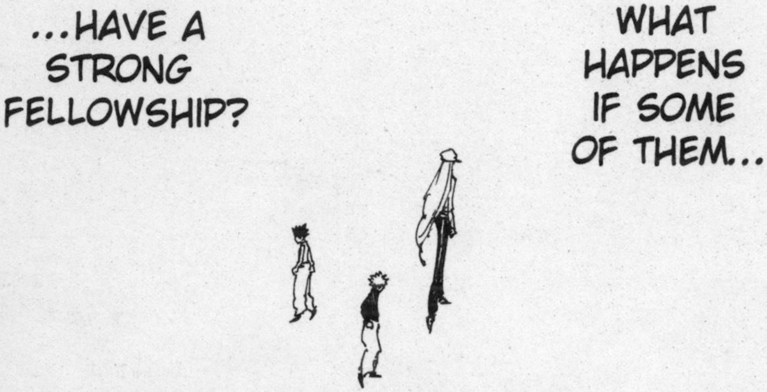
WHAT HAPPENS IF SOME OF THEM...
...HAVE A STRONG FELLOWSHIP?

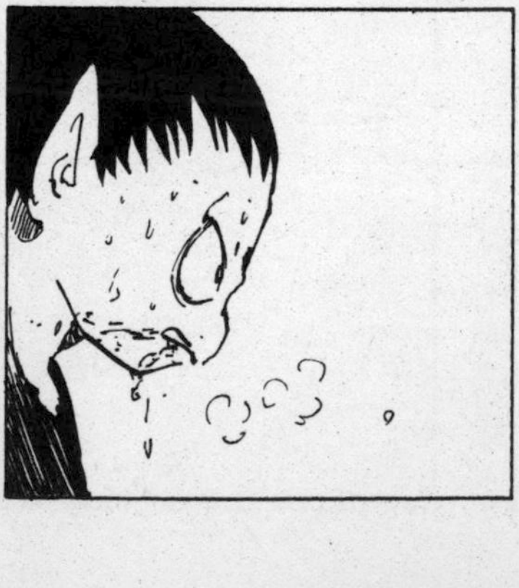

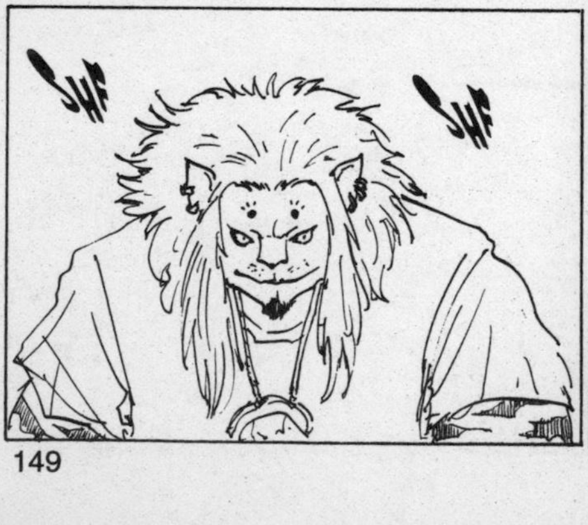
SHF
SHF

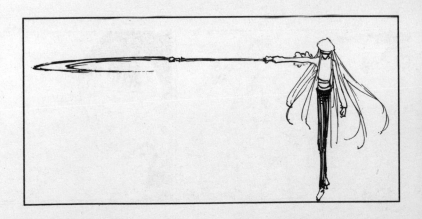

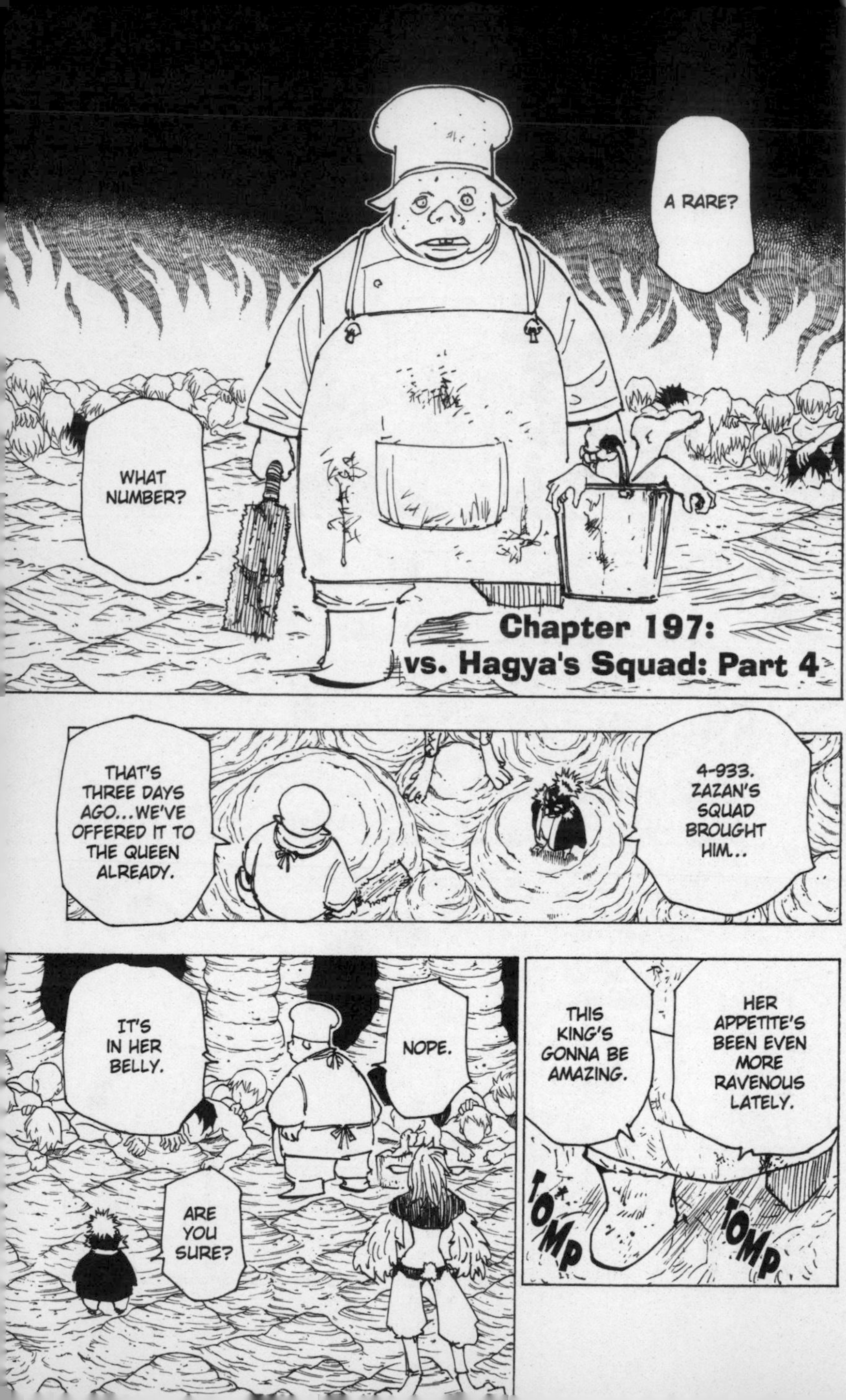
A RARE?
WHAT NUMBER?
Chapter 197:
vs. Hagya's Squad: Part 4
4-933. ZAZAN'S SQUAD BROUGHT HIM...
THAT'S THREE DAYS AGO...WE'VE OFFERED IT TO THE QUEEN ALREADY.
HER APPETITE'S BEEN EVEN MORE RAVENOUS LATELY.
THIS KING'S GONNA BE AMAZING.
TOMP
TOMP
NOPE.
IT'S IN HER BELLY.
ARE YOU SURE?

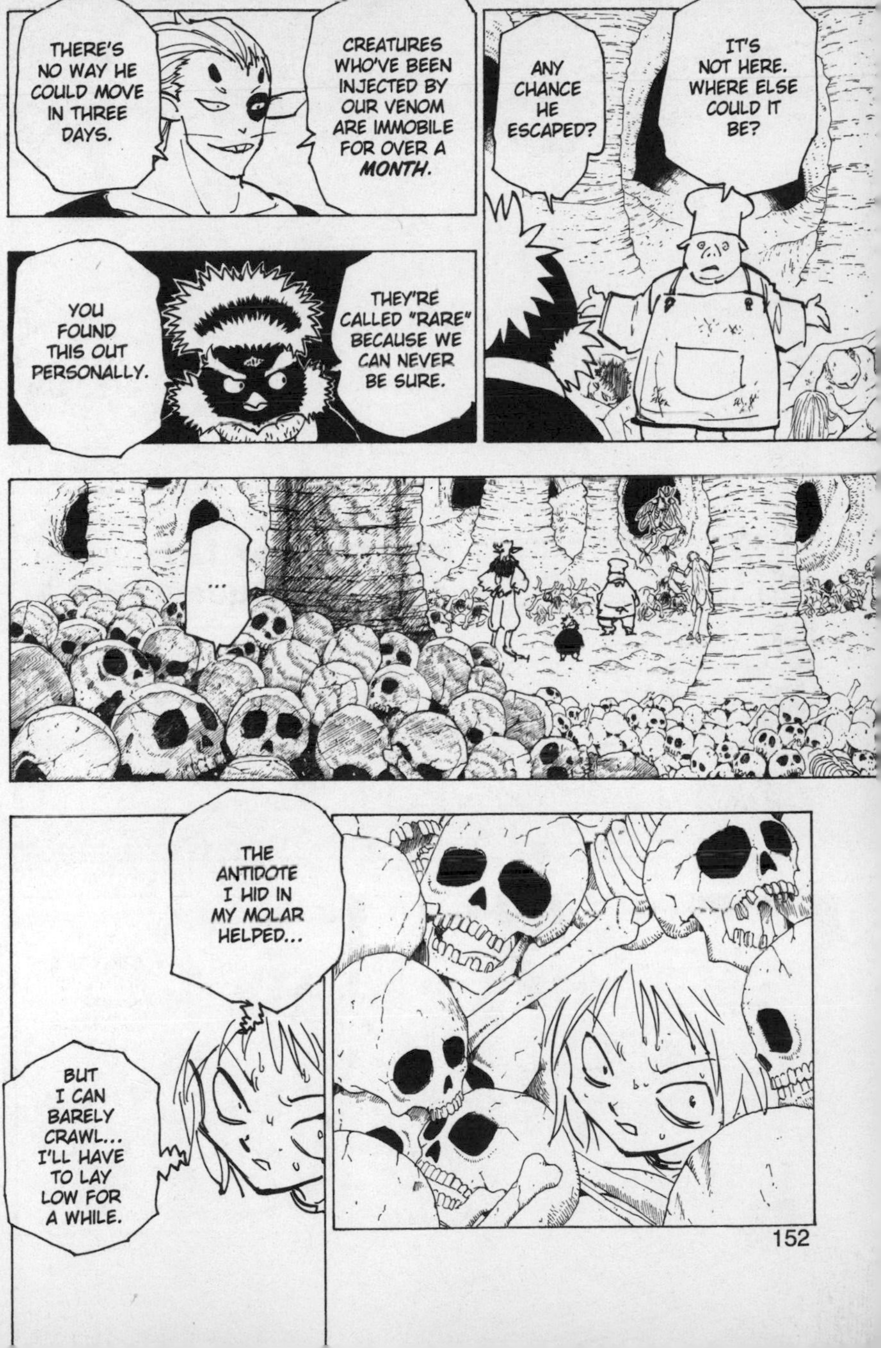
IT'S NOT HERE. WHERE ELSE COULD IT BE?
ANY CHANCE HE ESCAPED?
CREATURES WHO'VE BEEN INJECTED BY OUR VENOM ARE IMMOBILE FOR OVER A *MONTH*.
THERE'S NO WAY HE COULD MOVE IN THREE DAYS.
THEY'RE CALLED "RARE" BECAUSE WE CAN NEVER BE SURE.
YOU FOUND THIS OUT PERSONALLY.
...
THE ANTIDOTE I HID IN MY MOLAR HELPED...
BUT I CAN BARELY CRAWL... I'LL HAVE TO LAY LOW FOR A WHILE.

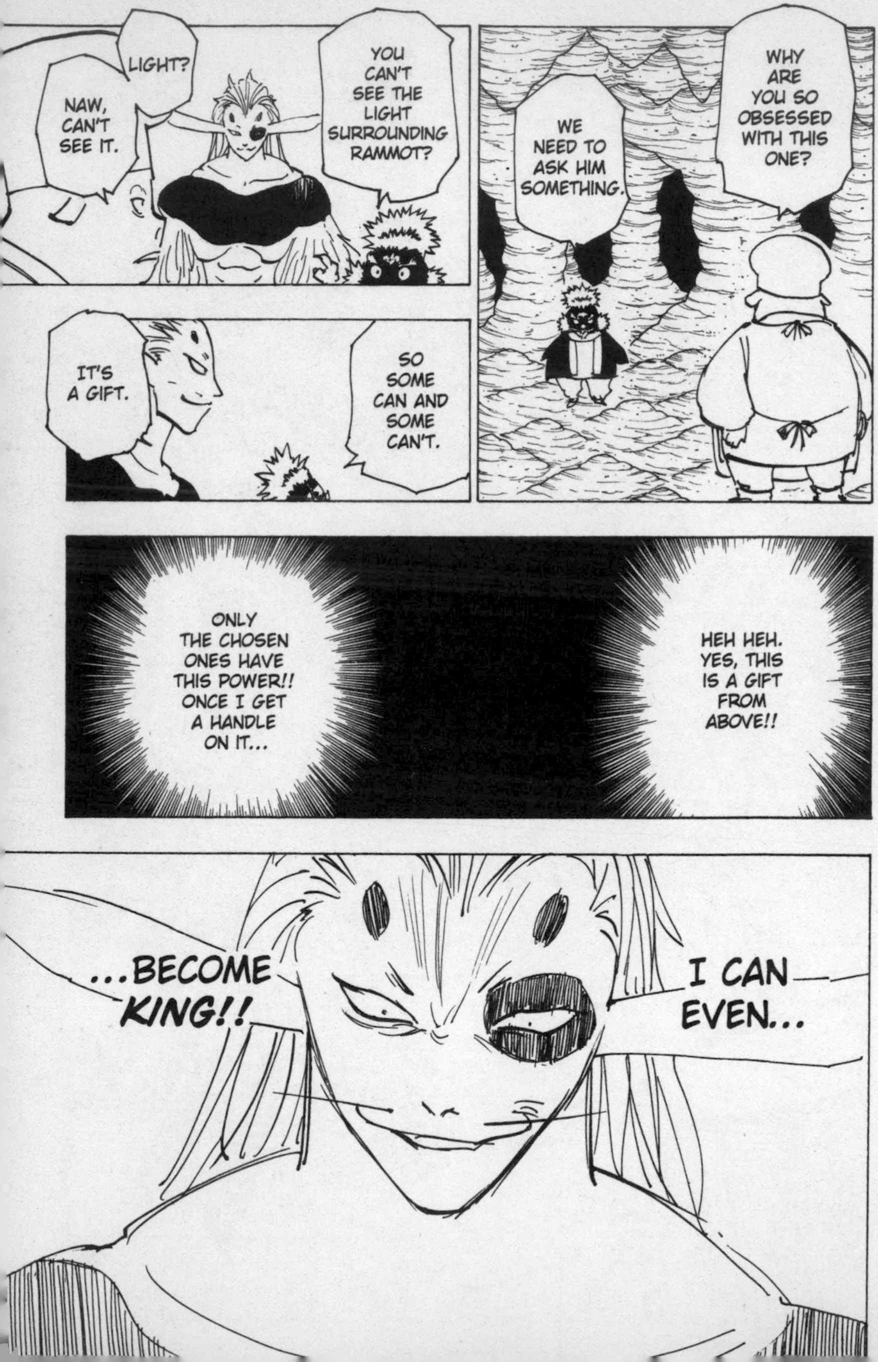
WHY ARE YOU SO OBSESSED WITH THIS ONE?
WE NEED TO ASK HIM SOMETHING.
YOU CAN'T SEE THE LIGHT SURROUNDING RAMMOT?
LIGHT?
NAW, CAN'T SEE IT.
SO SOME CAN AND SOME CAN'T.
IT'S A GIFT.
HEH HEH. YES, THIS IS A GIFT FROM ABOVE!!
ONLY THE CHOSEN ONES HAVE THIS POWER!! ONCE I GET A HANDLE ON IT...
I CAN EVEN...
...BECOME KING!!

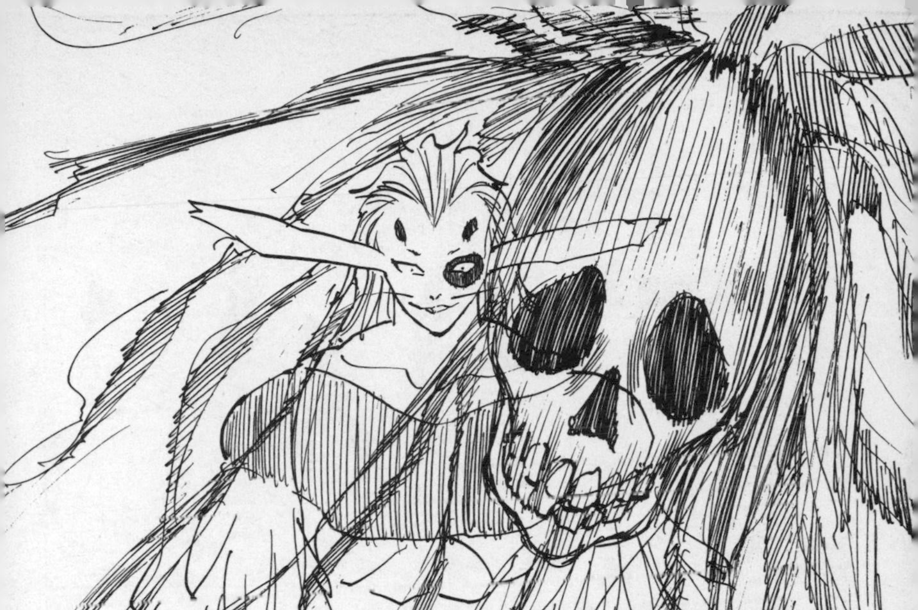

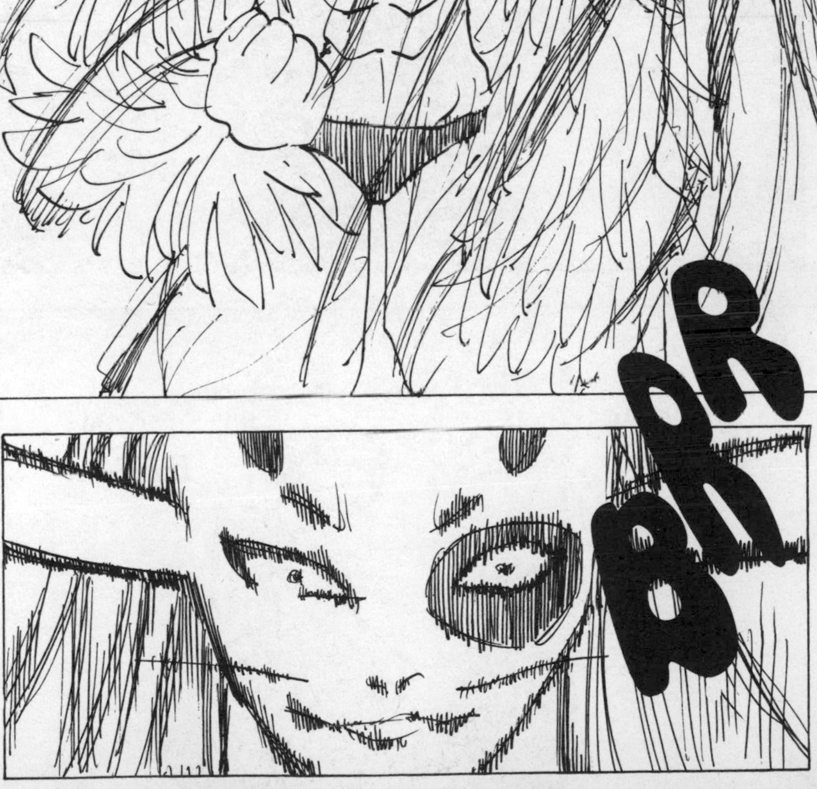
BRR

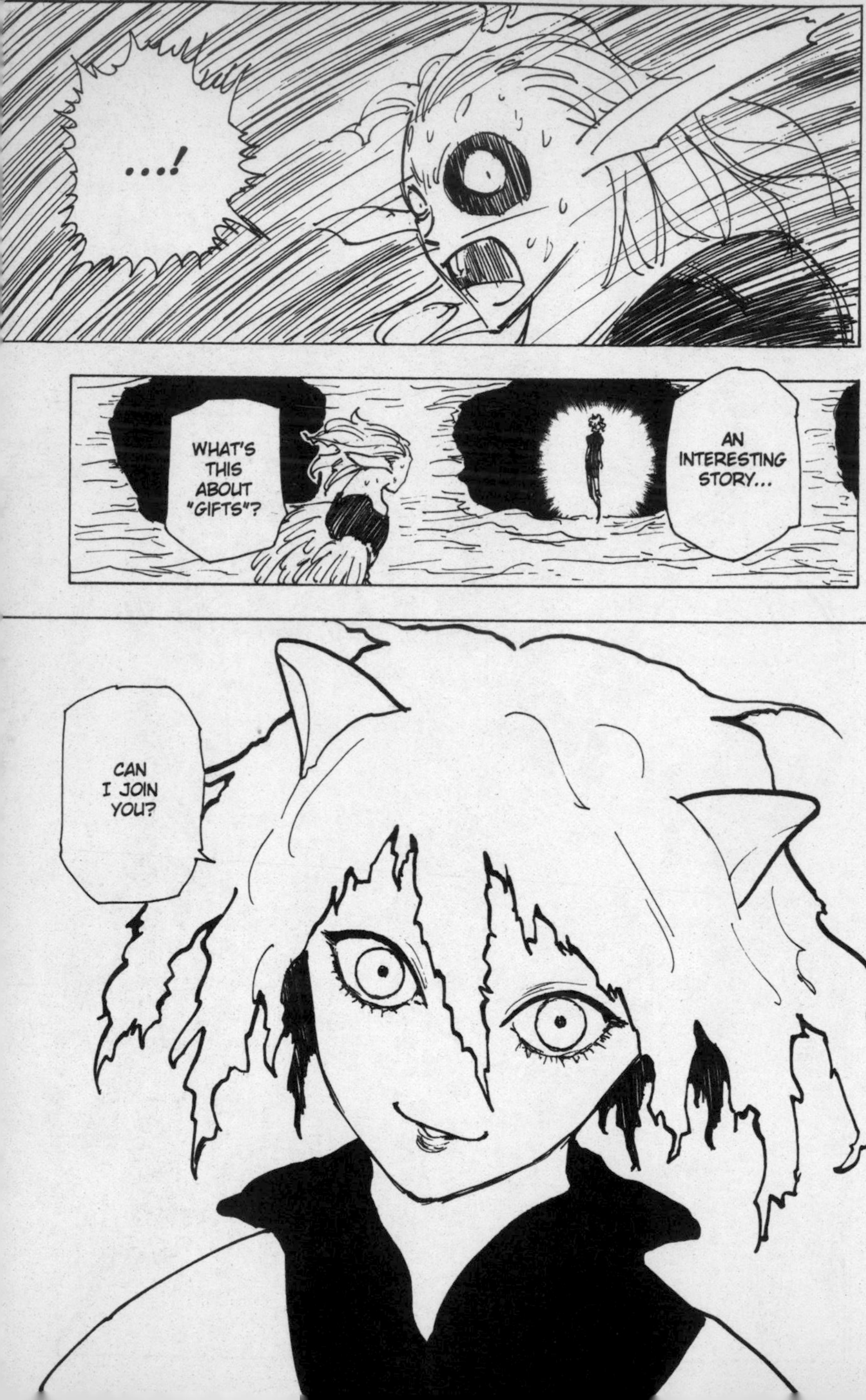
...!
AN INTERESTING STORY...
WHAT'S THIS ABOUT "GIFTS"?
CAN I JOIN YOU?

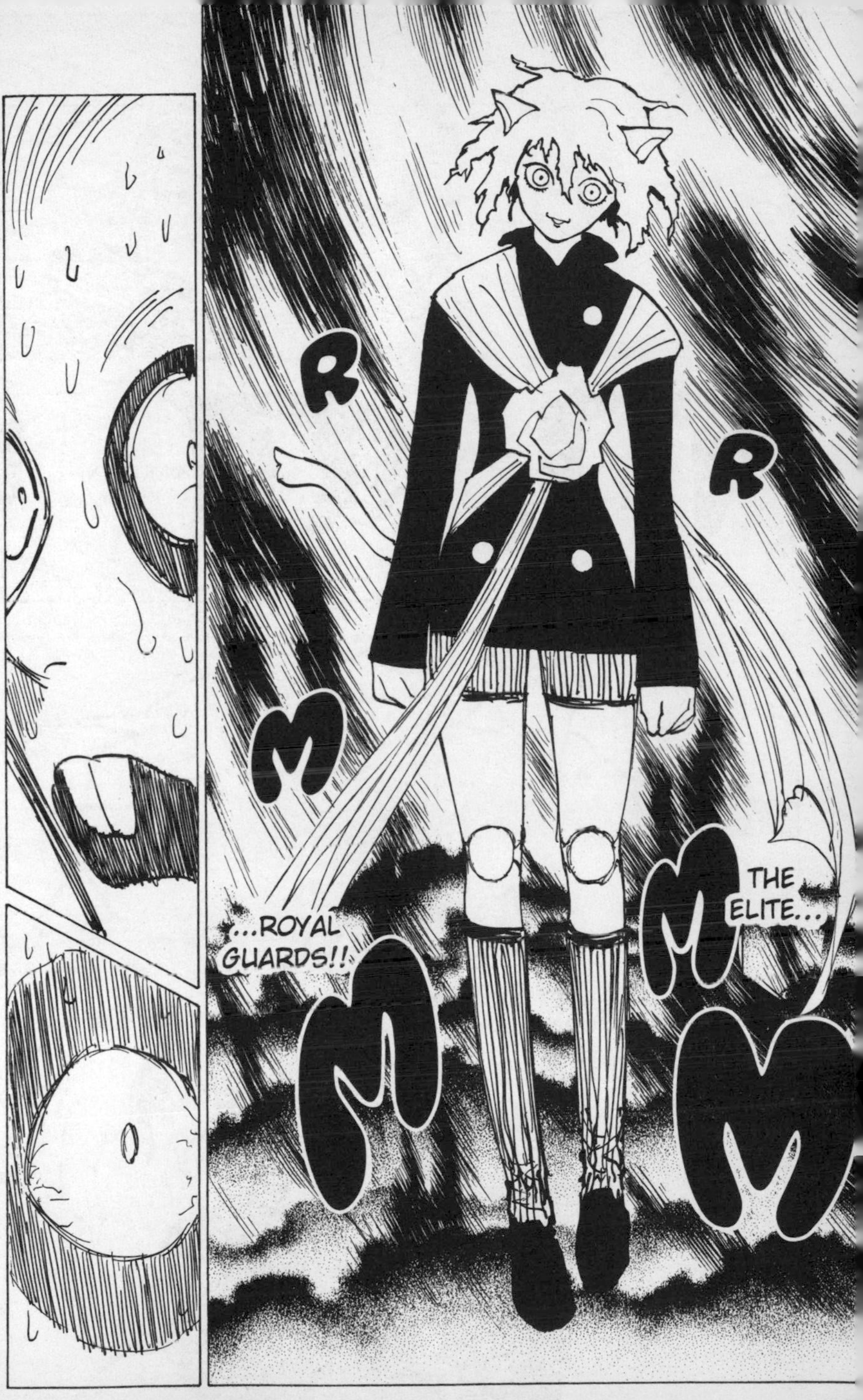
THE ELITE...
...ROYAL GUARDS!!
RRMMMM

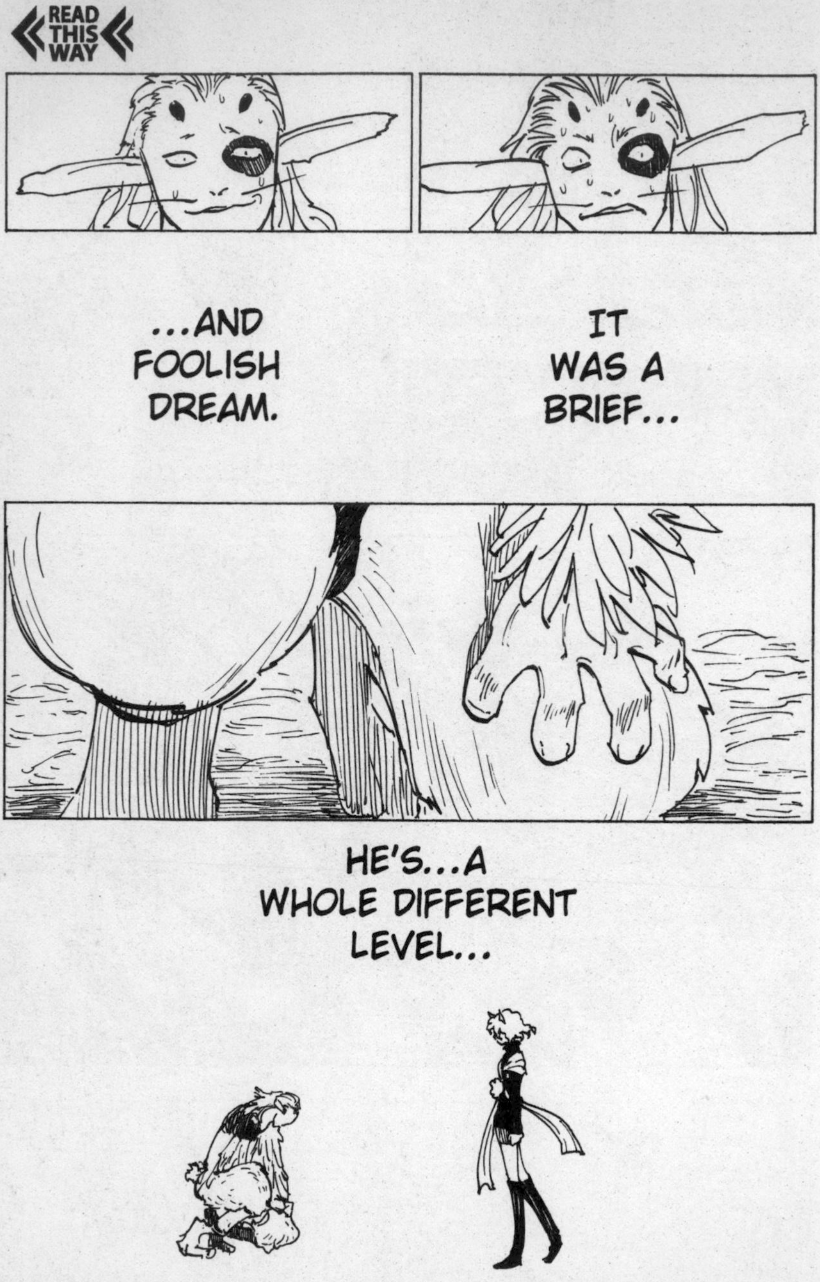
READ THIS WAY
IT WAS A BRIEF...
...AND FOOLISH DREAM.
HE'S...A WHOLE DIFFERENT LEVEL...

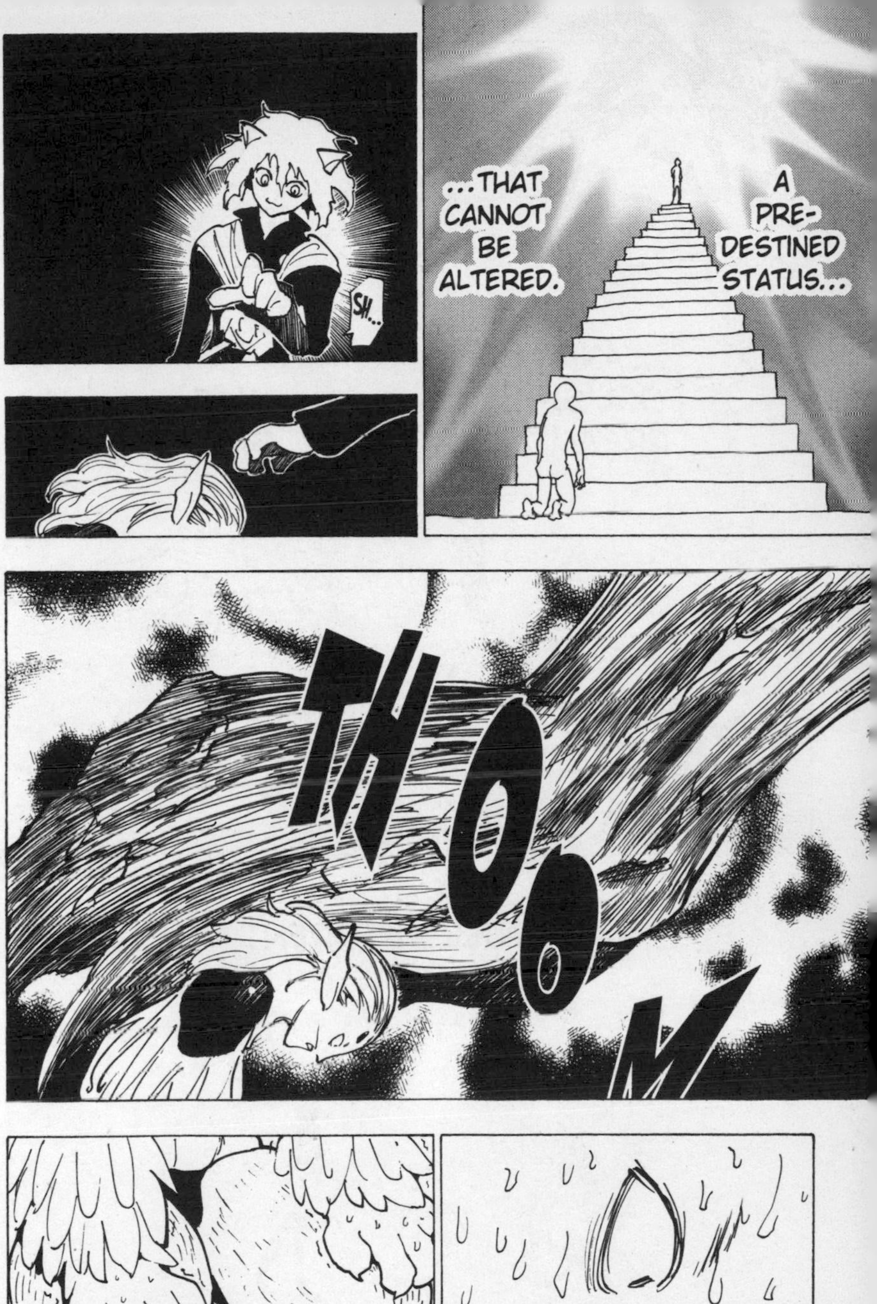
A PRE-DESTINED STATUS...
...THAT CANNOT BE ALTERED.
SH...
THOOOM

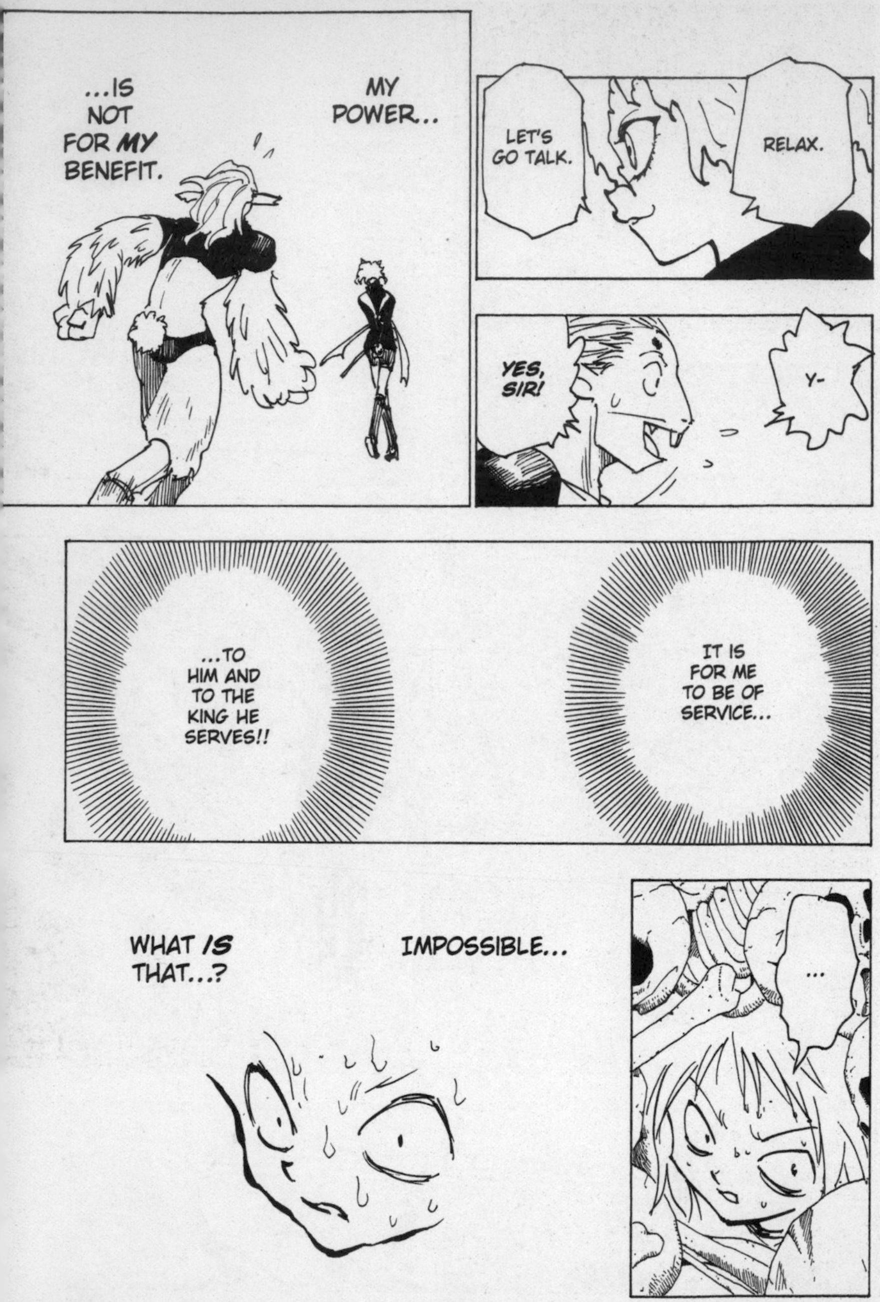
RELAX.
LET'S GO TALK.
Y-
YES, SIR!
MY POWER...
...IS NOT FOR MY BENEFIT.
IT IS FOR ME TO BE OF SERVICE...
...TO HIM AND TO THE KING HE SERVES!!
...
IMPOSSIBLE...
WHAT IS THAT...?

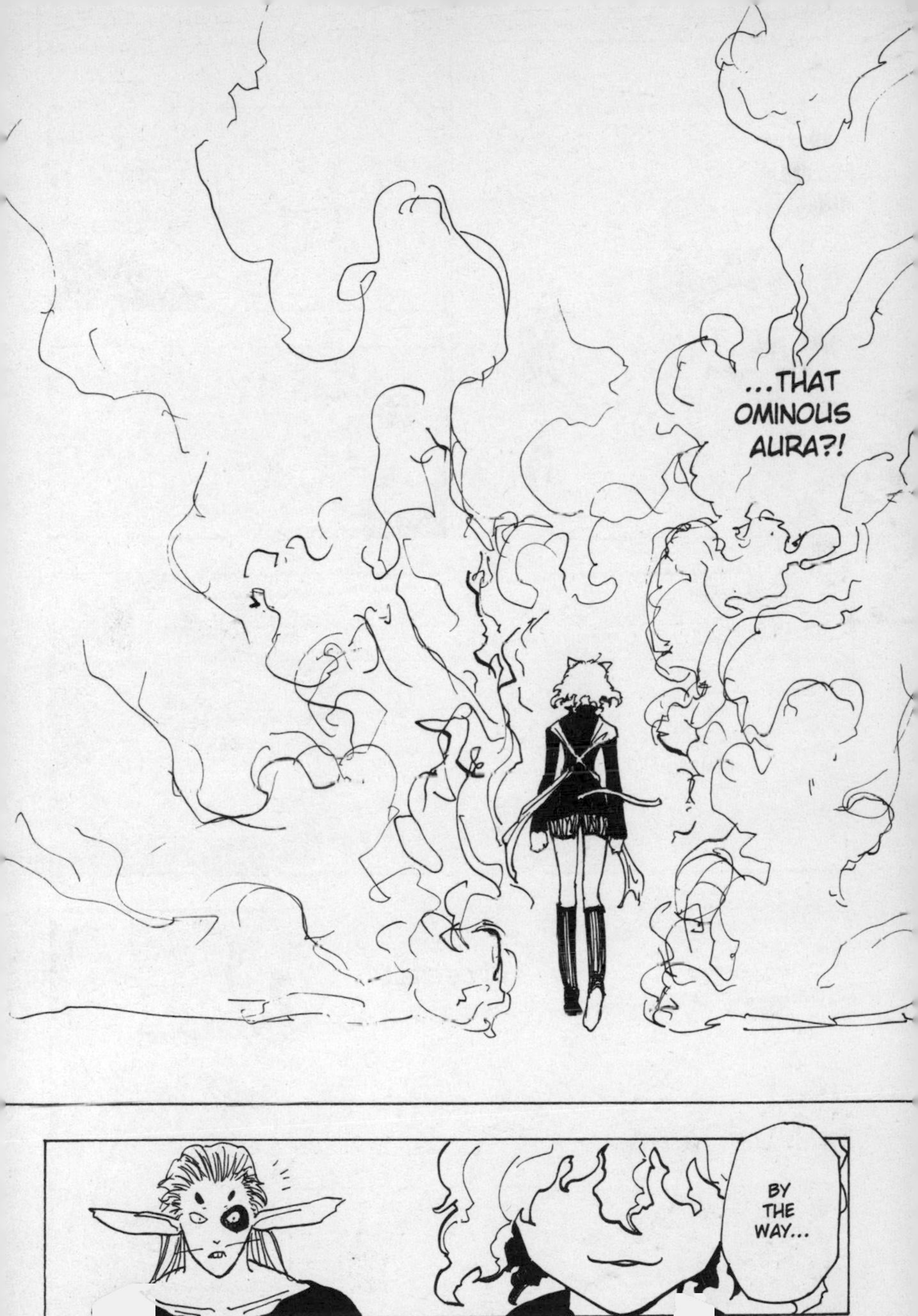
...THAT OMINOUS AURA?!
BY THE WAY...

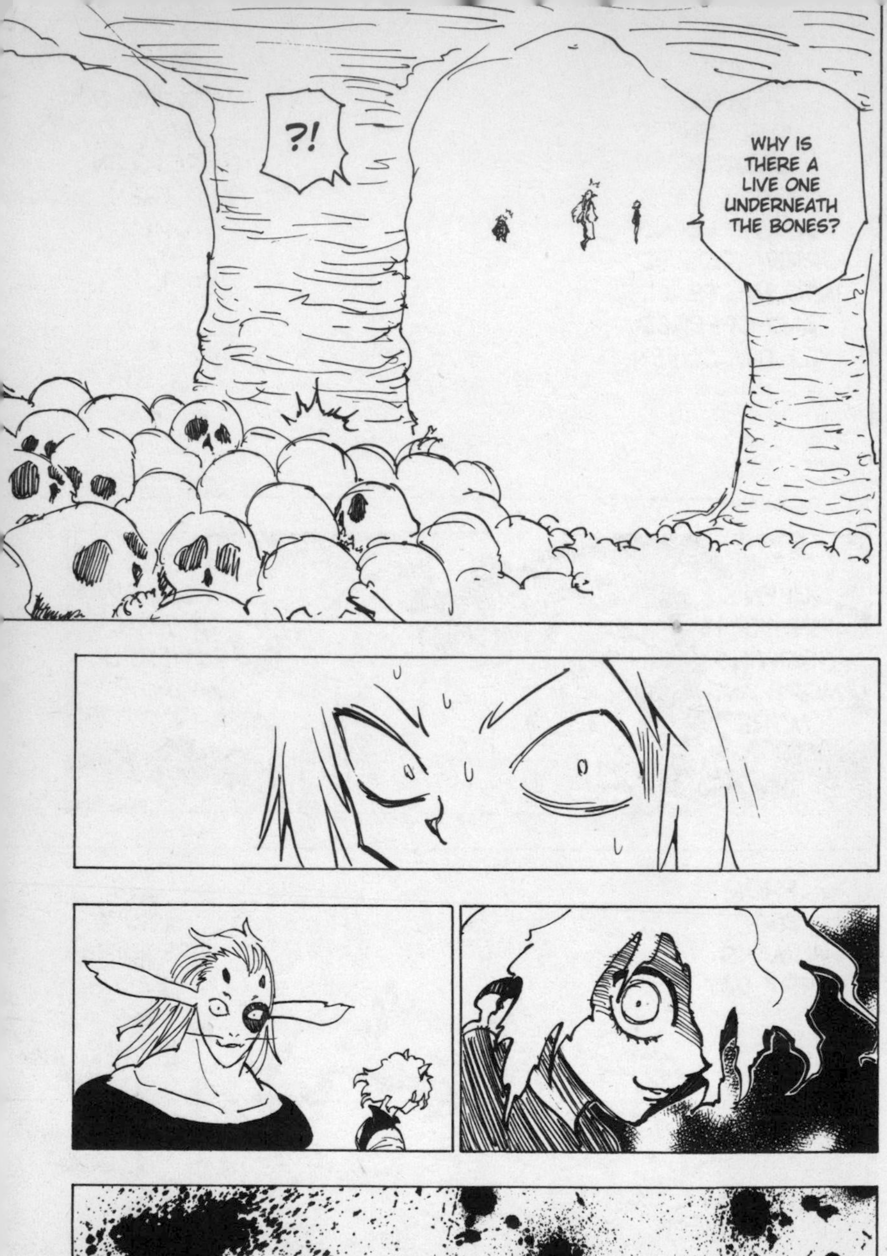
WHY IS THERE A LIVE ONE UNDERNEATH THE BONES?
?!

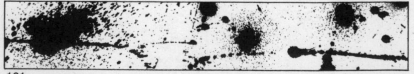

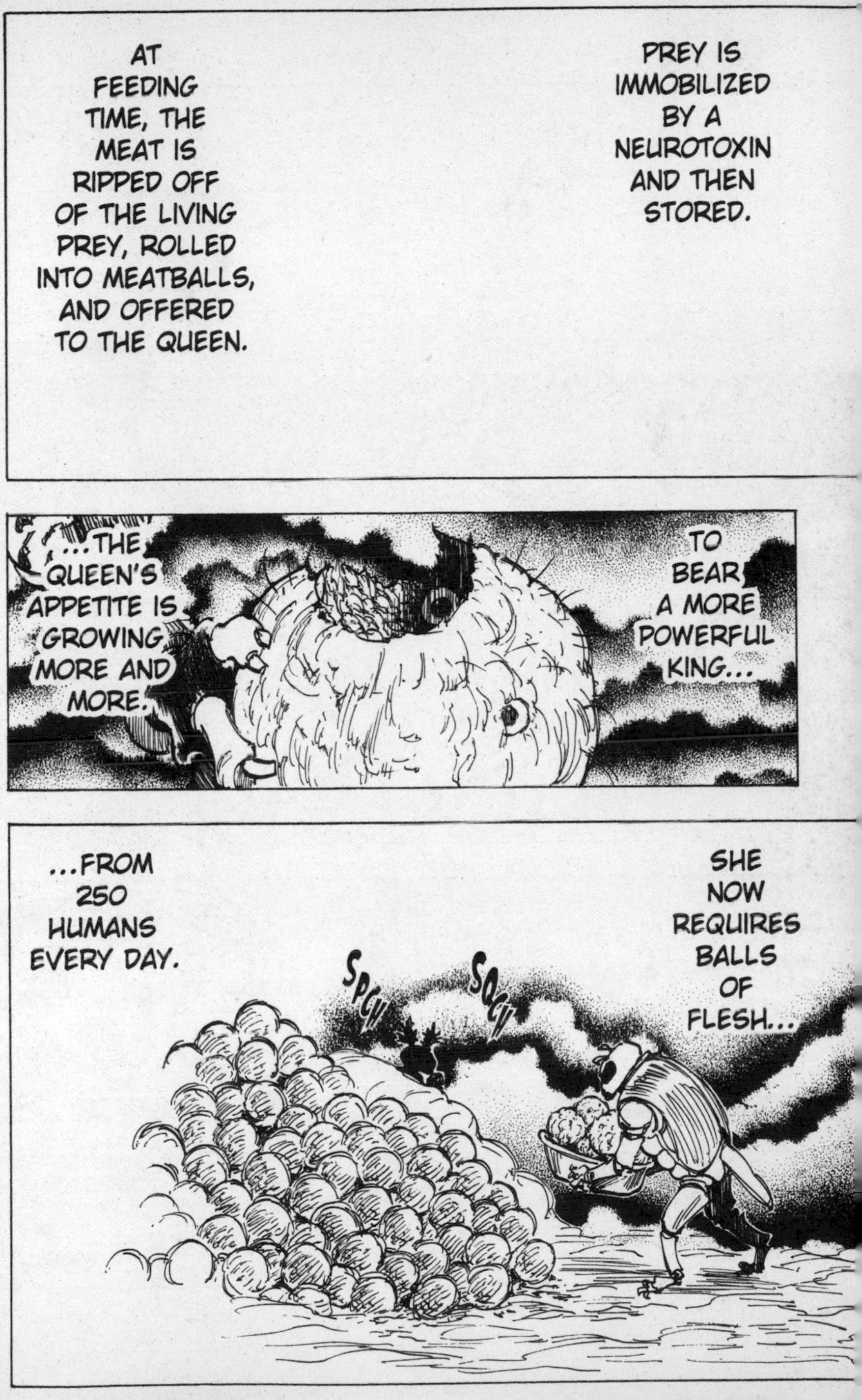
PREY IS IMMOBILIZED BY A NEUROTOXIN AND THEN STORED.
AT FEEDING TIME, THE MEAT IS RIPPED OFF OF THE LIVING PREY, ROLLED INTO MEATBALLS, AND OFFERED TO THE QUEEN.
TO BEAR A MORE POWERFUL KING...
...THE QUEEN'S APPETITE IS GROWING MORE AND MORE.
SHE NOW REQUIRES BALLS OF FLESH...
SQCH
SPCH
...FROM 250 HUMANS EVERY DAY.

READ THIS WAY

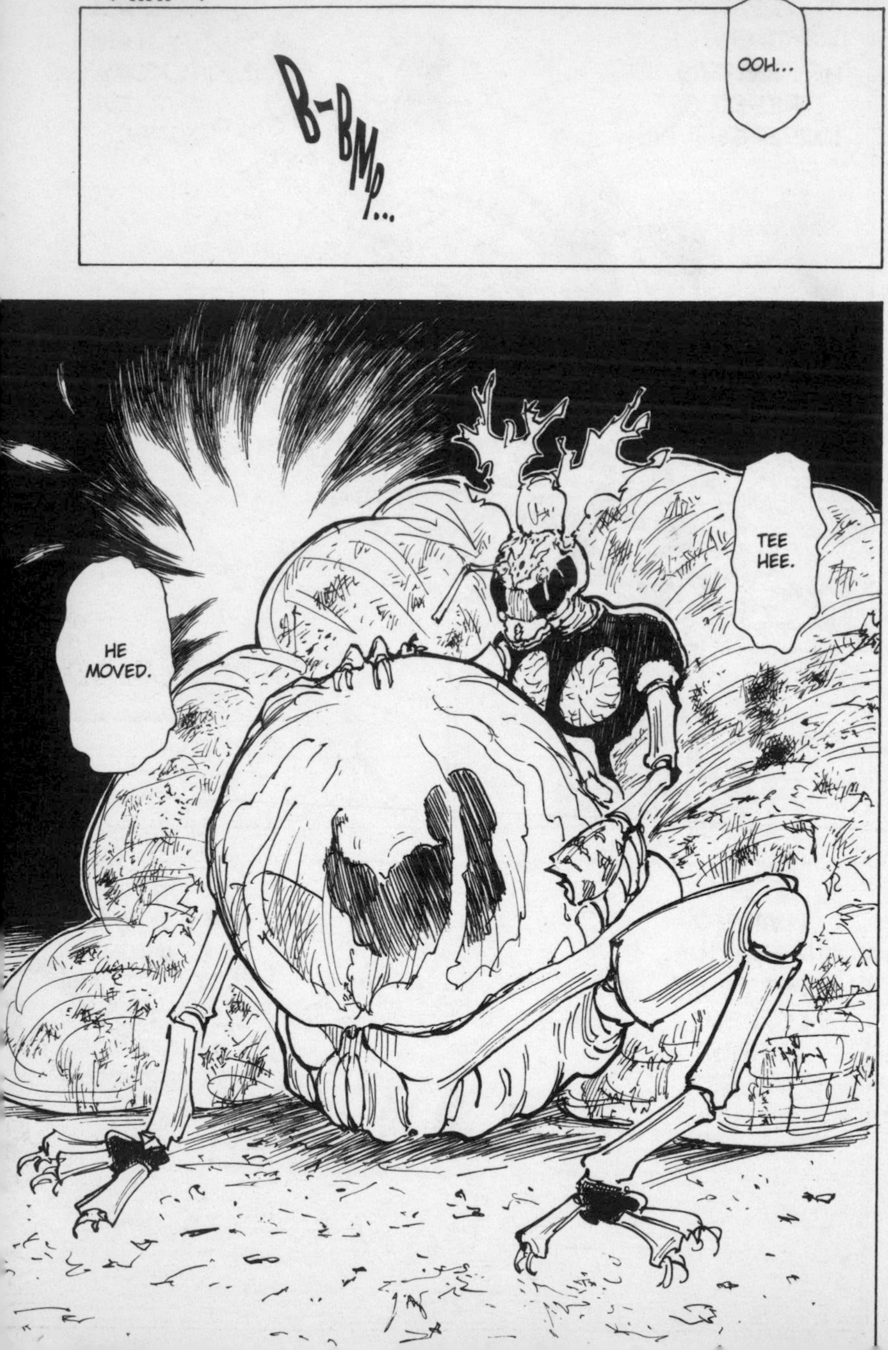
OOH...
B-BMP...
TEE HEE.
HE MOVED.

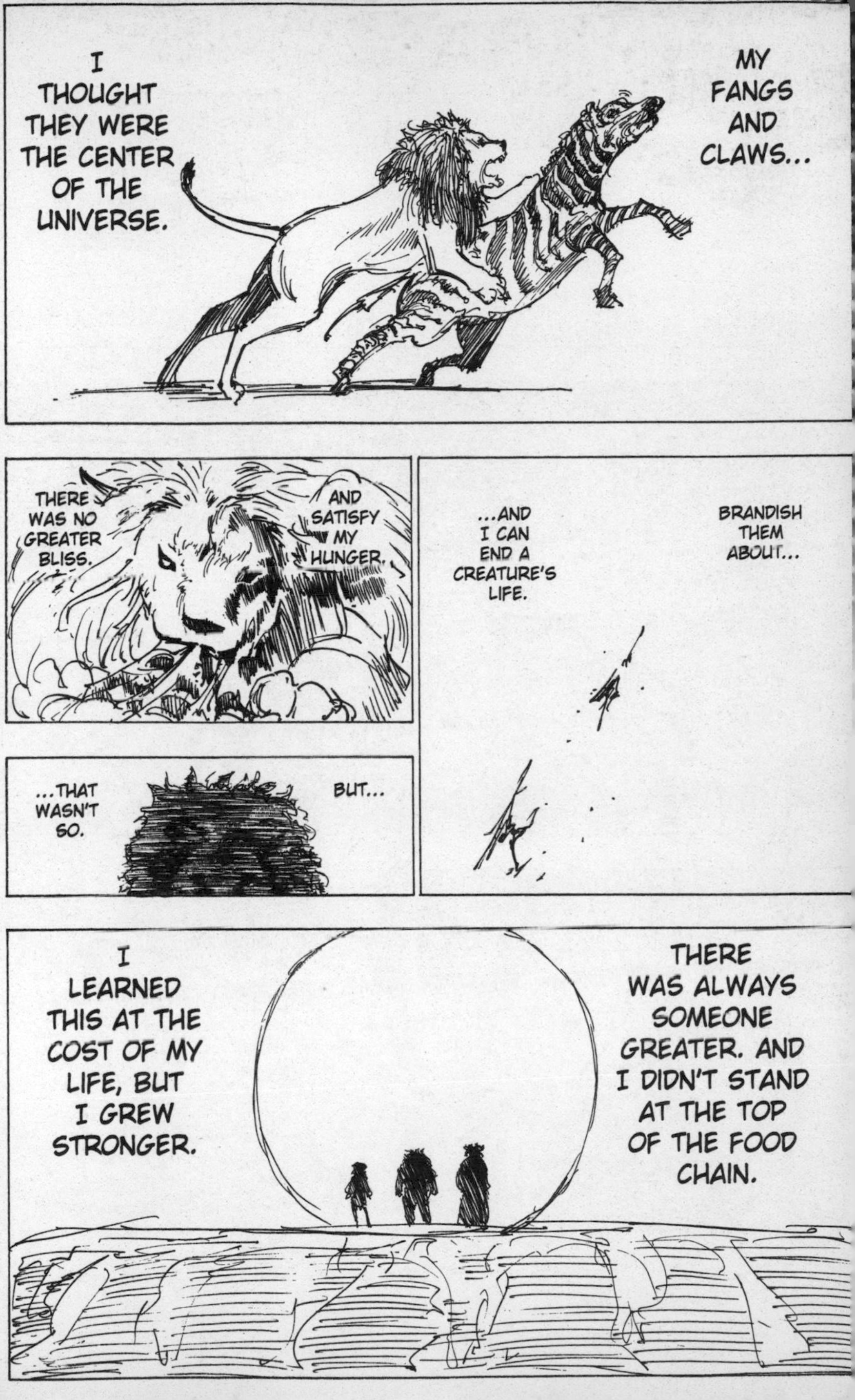
MY FANGS AND CLAWS...
I THOUGHT THEY WERE THE CENTER OF THE UNIVERSE.
BRANDISH THEM ABOUT...
...AND I CAN END A CREATURE'S LIFE.
AND SATISFY MY HUNGER.
THERE WAS NO GREATER BLISS.
BUT...
...THAT WASN'T SO.
THERE WAS ALWAYS SOMEONE GREATER. AND I DIDN'T STAND AT THE TOP OF THE FOOD CHAIN.
I LEARNED THIS AT THE COST OF MY LIFE, BUT I GREW STRONGER.

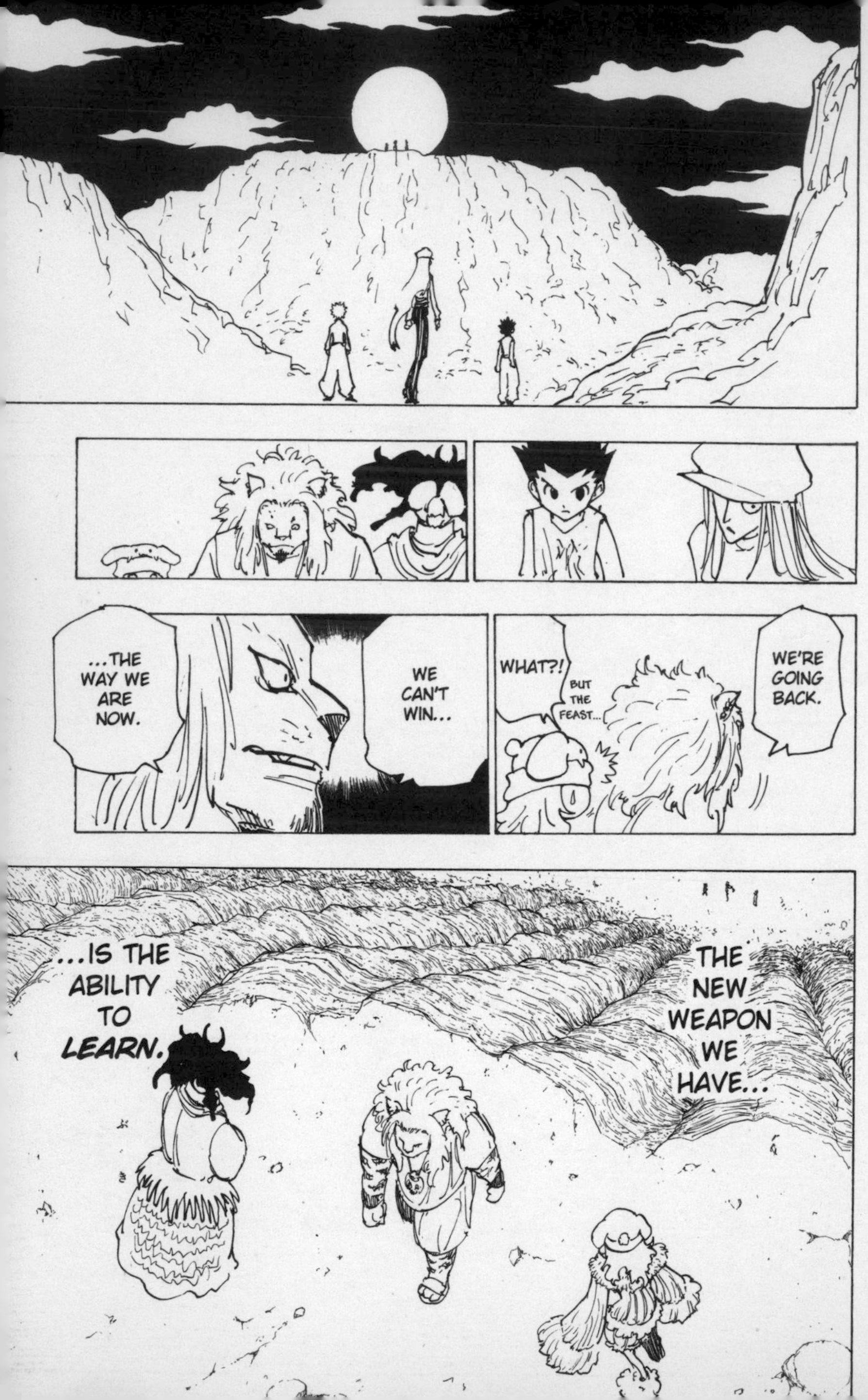
WE'RE GOING BACK.
WHAT?!
BUT THE FEAST...
WE CAN'T WIN...
...THE WAY WE ARE NOW.
THE NEW WEAPON WE HAVE...
...IS THE ABILITY TO *LEARN.*

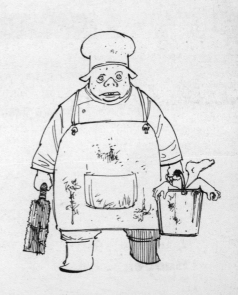

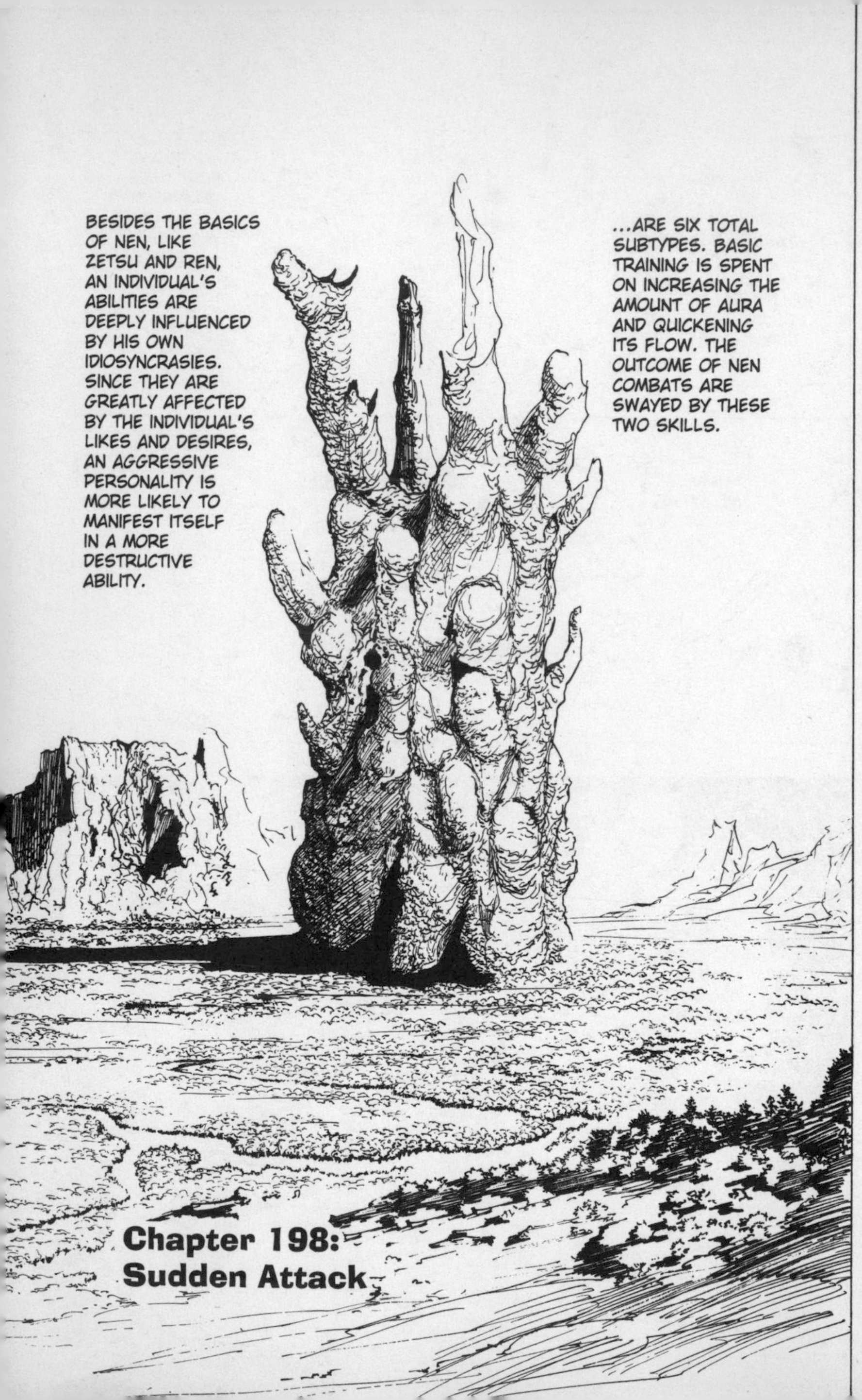
...ARE SIX TOTAL SUBTYPES. BASIC TRAINING IS SPENT ON INCREASING THE AMOUNT OF AURA AND QUICKENING ITS FLOW. THE OUTCOME OF NEN COMBATS ARE SWAYED BY THESE TWO SKILLS.
BESIDES THE BASICS OF NEN, LIKE ZETSU AND REN, AN INDIVIDUAL'S ABILITIES ARE DEEPLY INFLUENCED BY HIS OWN IDIOSYNCRASIES. SINCE THEY ARE GREATLY AFFECTED BY THE INDIVIDUAL'S LIKES AND DESIRES, AN AGGRESSIVE PERSONALITY IS MORE LIKELY TO MANIFEST ITSELF IN A MORE DESTRUCTIVE ABILITY.

Chapter 198: Sudden Attack

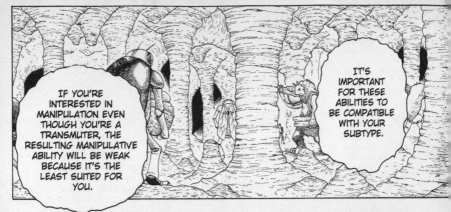

IT'S IMPORTANT FOR THESE ABILITIES TO BE COMPATIBLE WITH YOUR SUBTYPE.
IF YOU'RE INTERESTED IN MANIPULATION EVEN THOUGH YOU'RE A TRANSMUTER, THE RESULTING MANIPULATIVE ABILITY WILL BE WEAK BECAUSE IT'S THE LEAST SUITED FOR YOU.
IF YOUR SUBTYPE AND PREFERENCE ARE LUCKILY THE SAME, YOUR ABILITY MAY BE MORE POWERFUL...
HMM, MEOWKAY.
QCH
HOW DO YOU FIND OUT YOUR SUBTYPE?
SKWICH
AH!
A-A COMMON AND SIMPLE M-METHOD IS WATER DIVINATION...
AH!
AH!
AH!
AH!

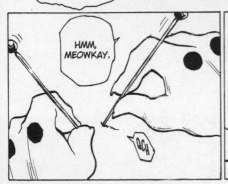

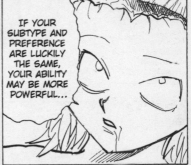

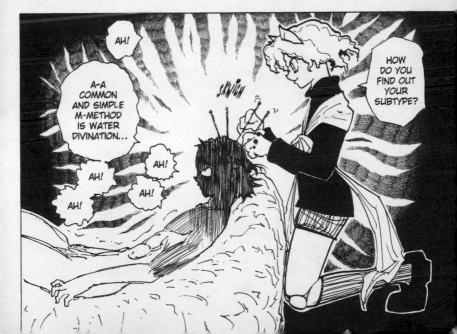

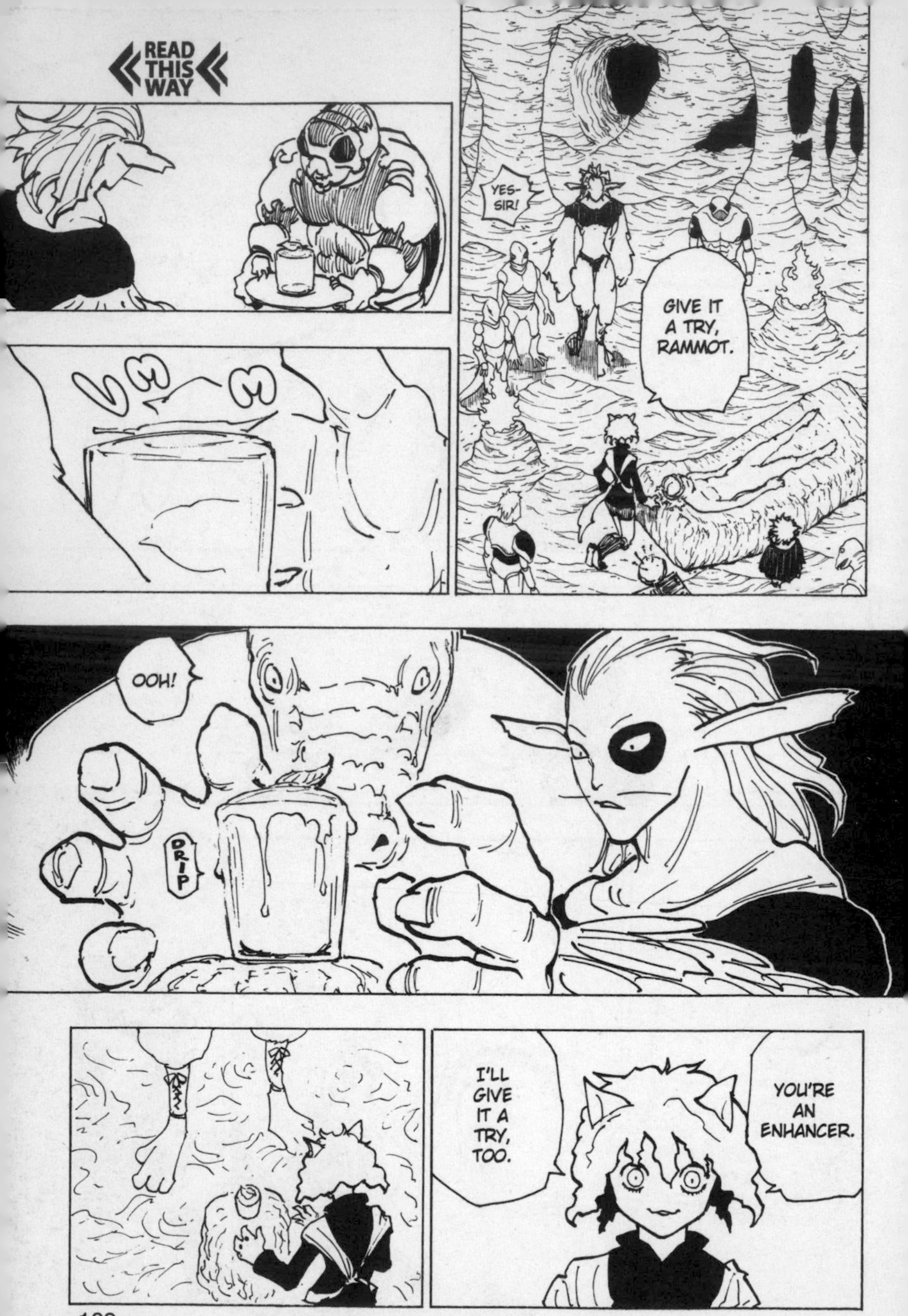
READ THIS WAY
YES-SIR!
GIVE IT A TRY, RAMMOT.
OOH!
DRIP
YOU'RE AN ENHANCER.
I'LL GIVE IT A TRY, TOO.

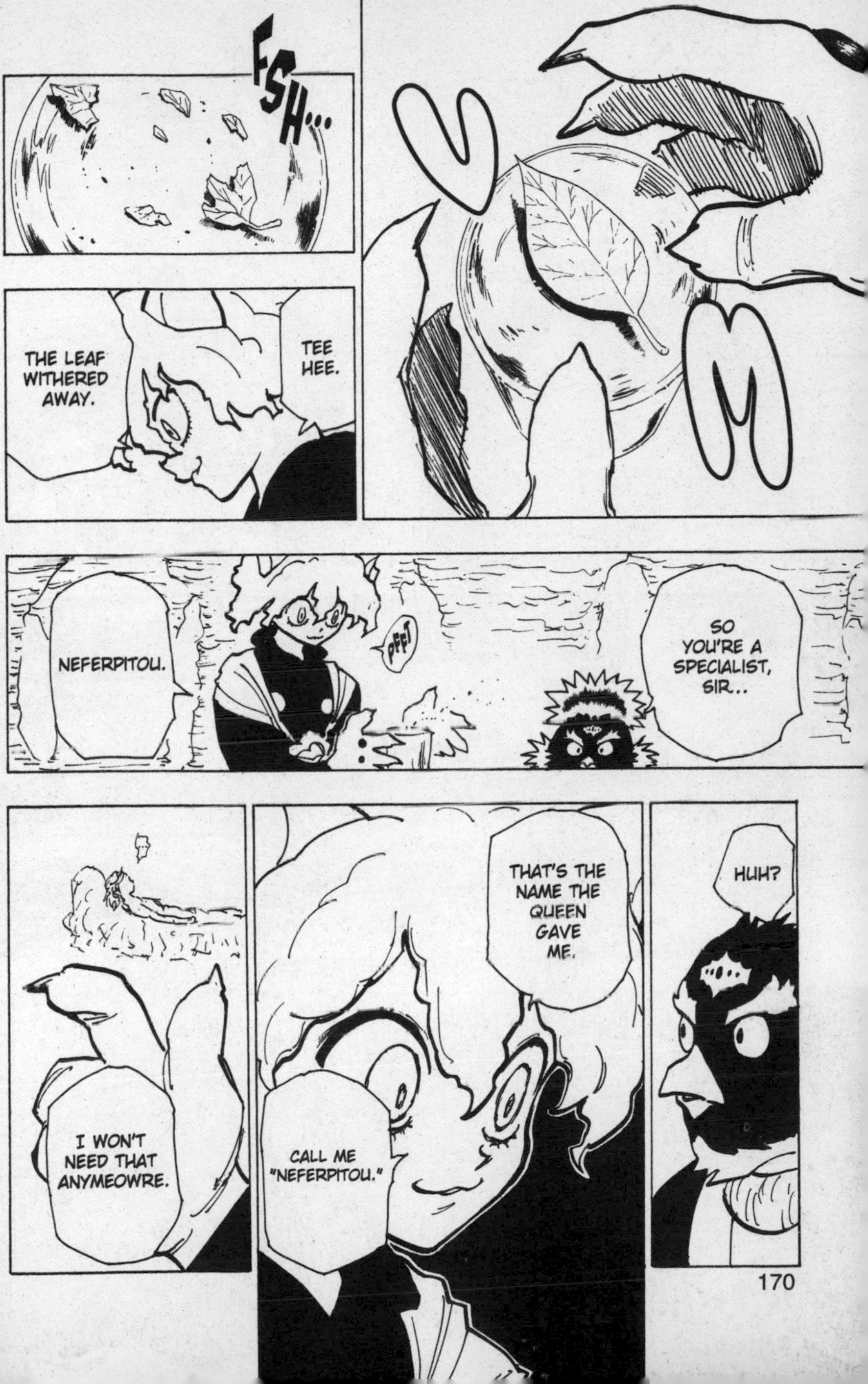
FSH...
TEE HEE.
THE LEAF WITHERED AWAY.
SO YOU'RE A SPECIALIST, SIR...
PFFT
NEFERPITOU.
HUH?
THAT'S THE NAME THE QUEEN GAVE ME.
CALL ME "NEFERPITOU."
I WON'T NEED THAT ANYMEOWRE.

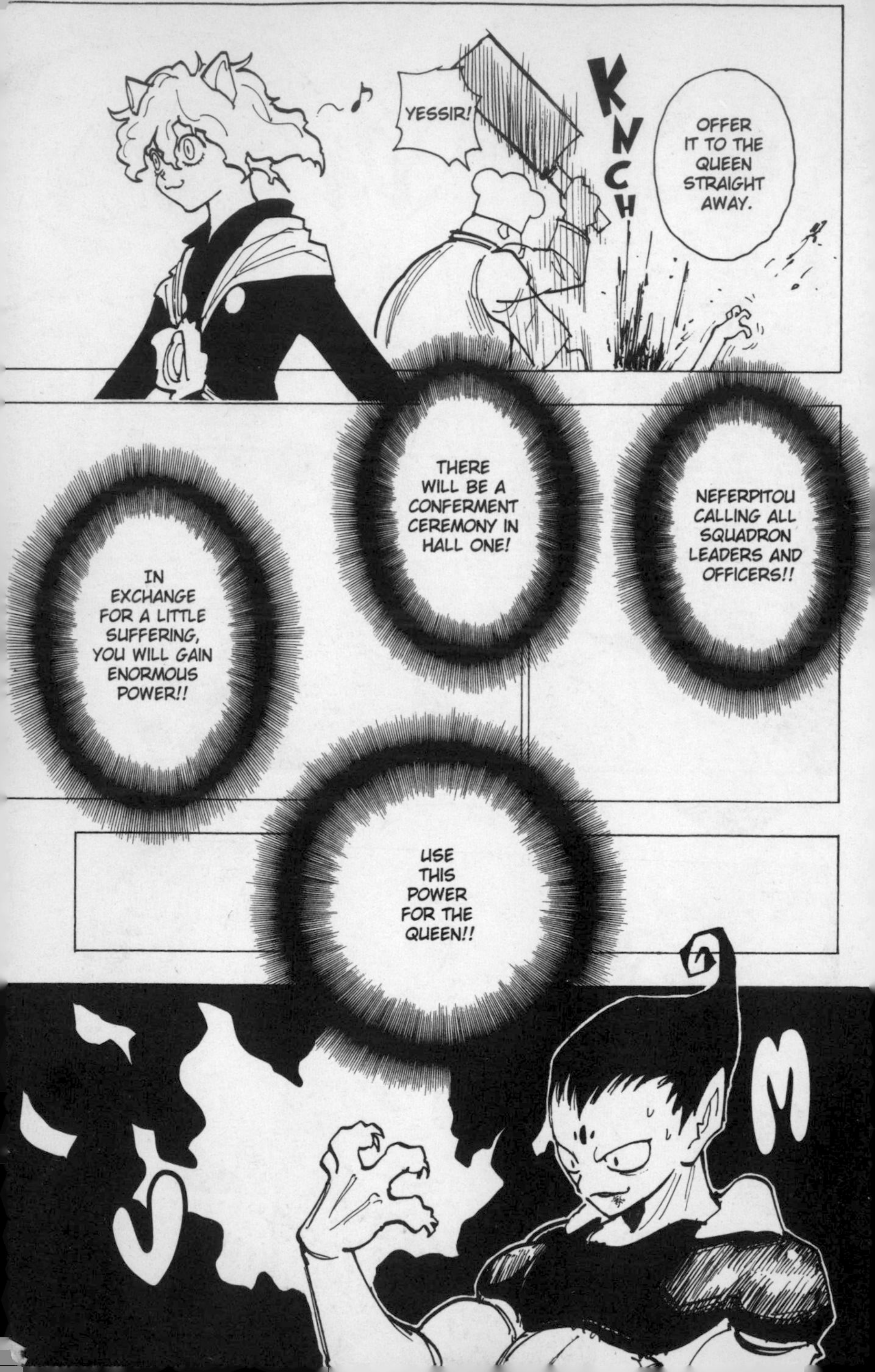
OFFER IT TO THE QUEEN STRAIGHT AWAY.
KNCH
YESSIR!
NEFERPITOU CALLING ALL SQUADRON LEADERS AND OFFICERS!!
THERE WILL BE A CONFERMENT CEREMONY IN HALL ONE!
IN EXCHANGE FOR A LITTLE SUFFERING, YOU WILL GAIN ENORMOUS POWER!!
USE THIS POWER FOR THE QUEEN!!

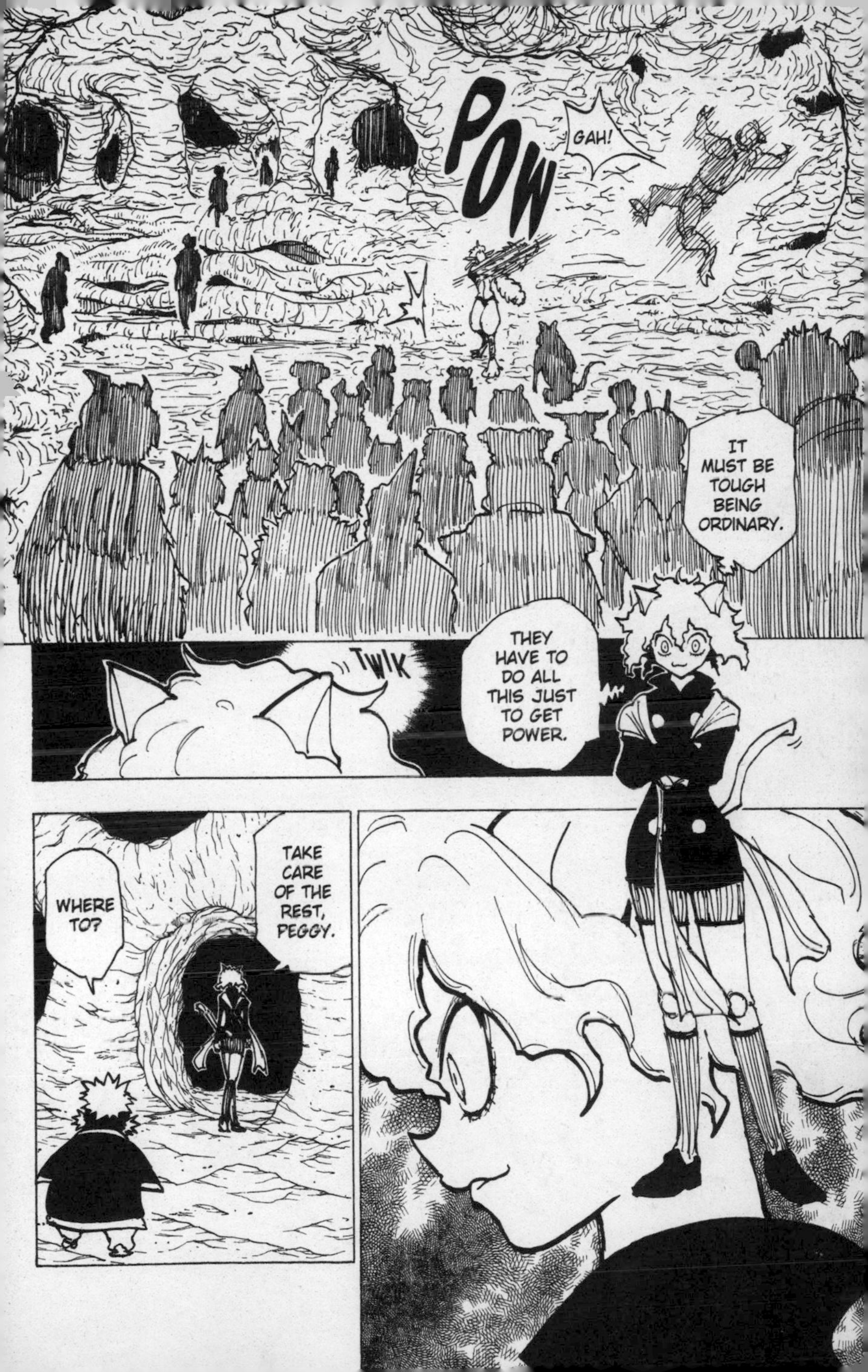
GAH!
POW
IT MUST BE TOUGH BEING ORDINARY.
THEY HAVE TO DO ALL THIS JUST TO GET POWER.
TWIK
TAKE CARE OF THE REST, PEGGY.
WHERE TO?

READ THIS WAY

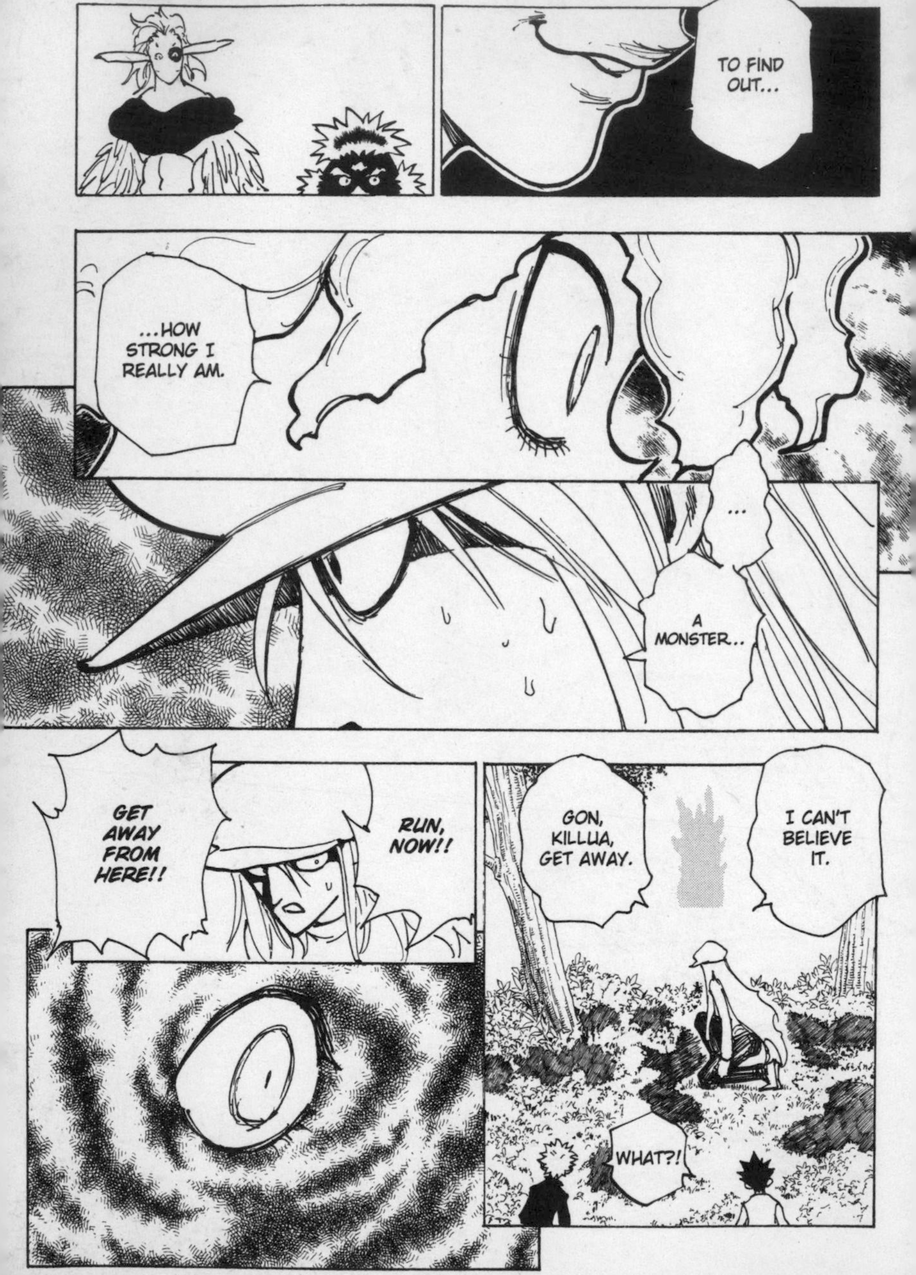

TO FIND OUT...
...HOW STRONG I REALLY AM.
...
A MONSTER...
I CAN'T BELIEVE IT.
GON, KILLUA, GET AWAY.
WHAT?!
RUN, NOW!!
GET AWAY FROM HERE!!

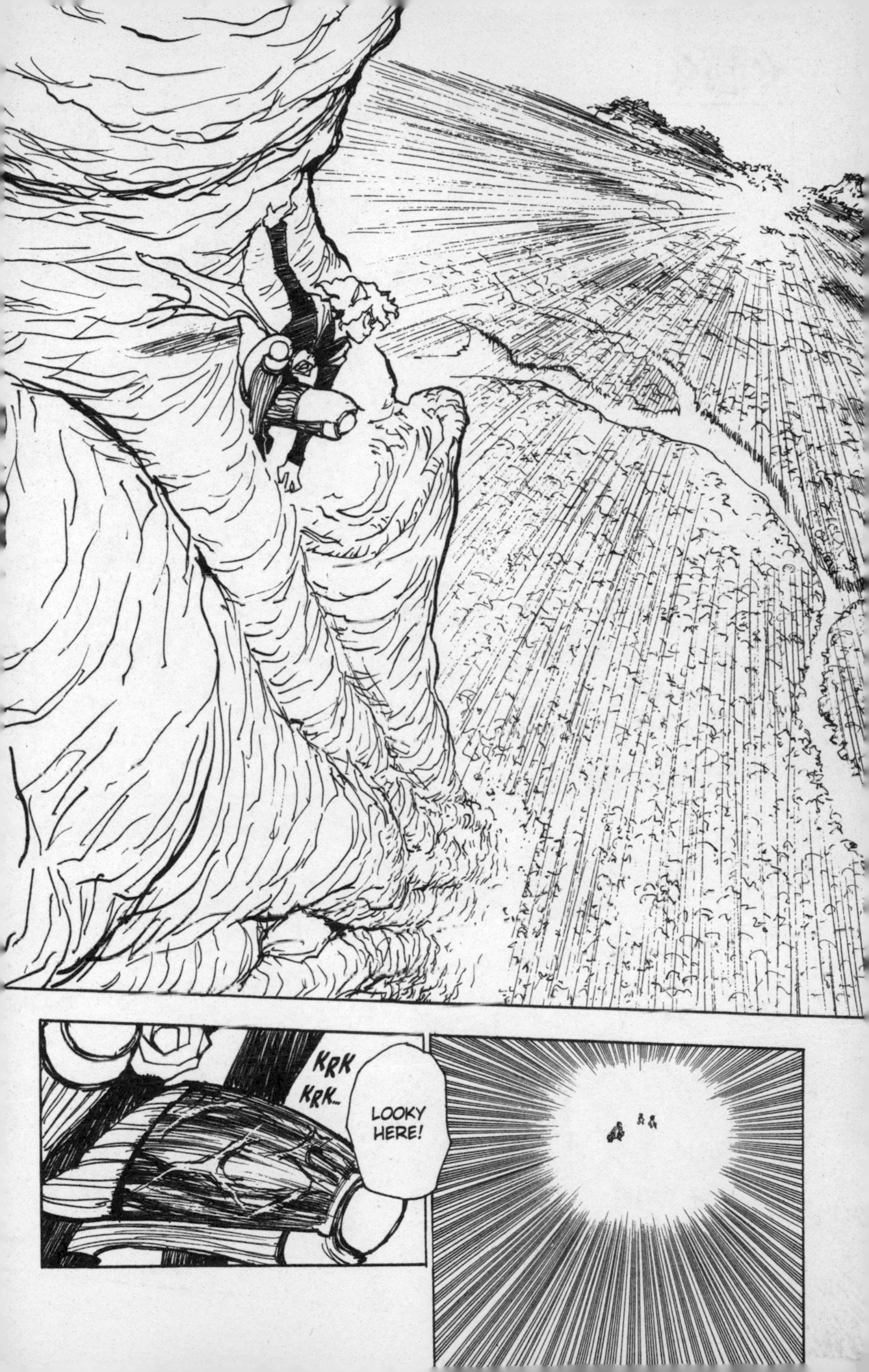
KRK
KRK..
LOOKY HERE!

READ THIS WAY

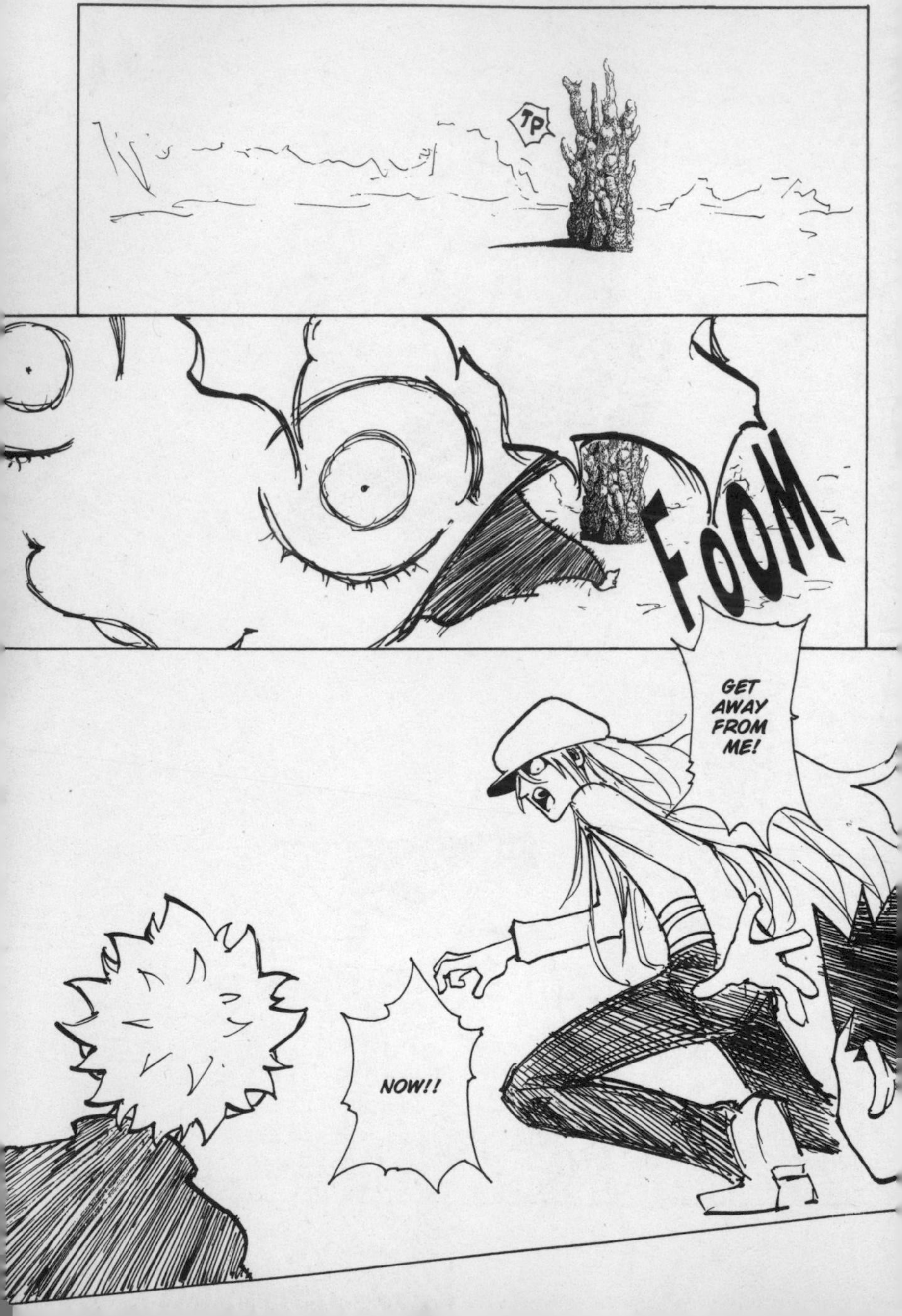
TP
FOOM
GET AWAY FROM ME!
NOW!!

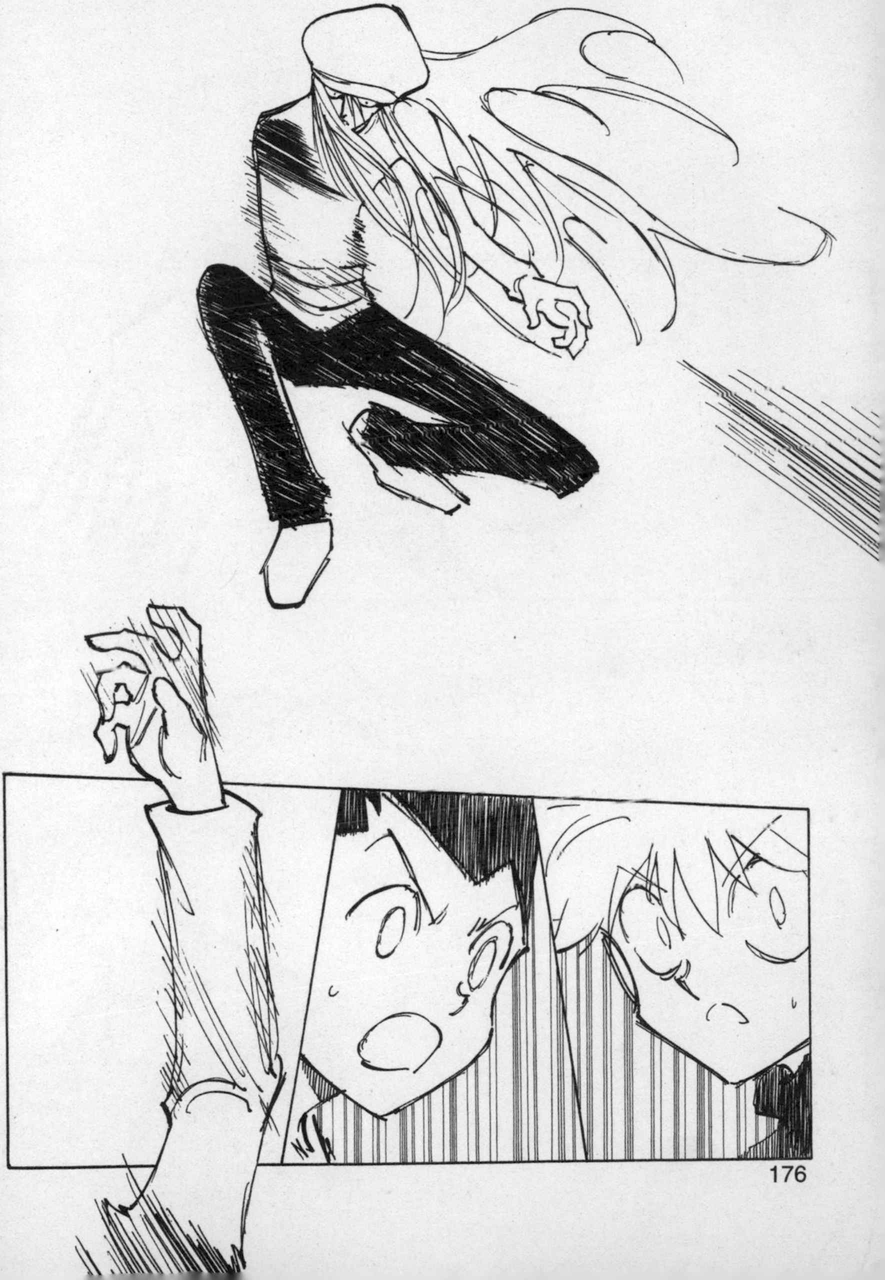

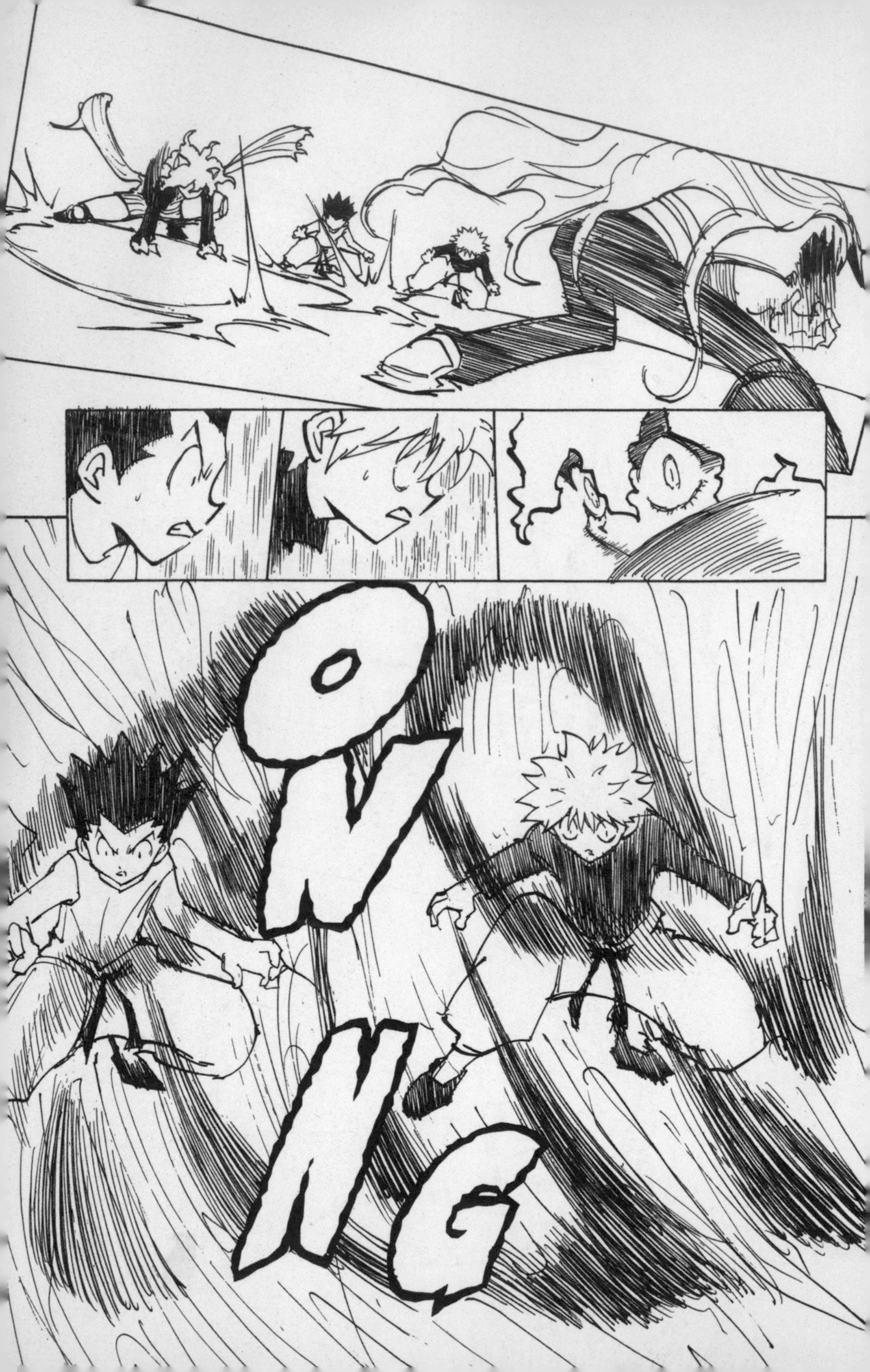
OWNG

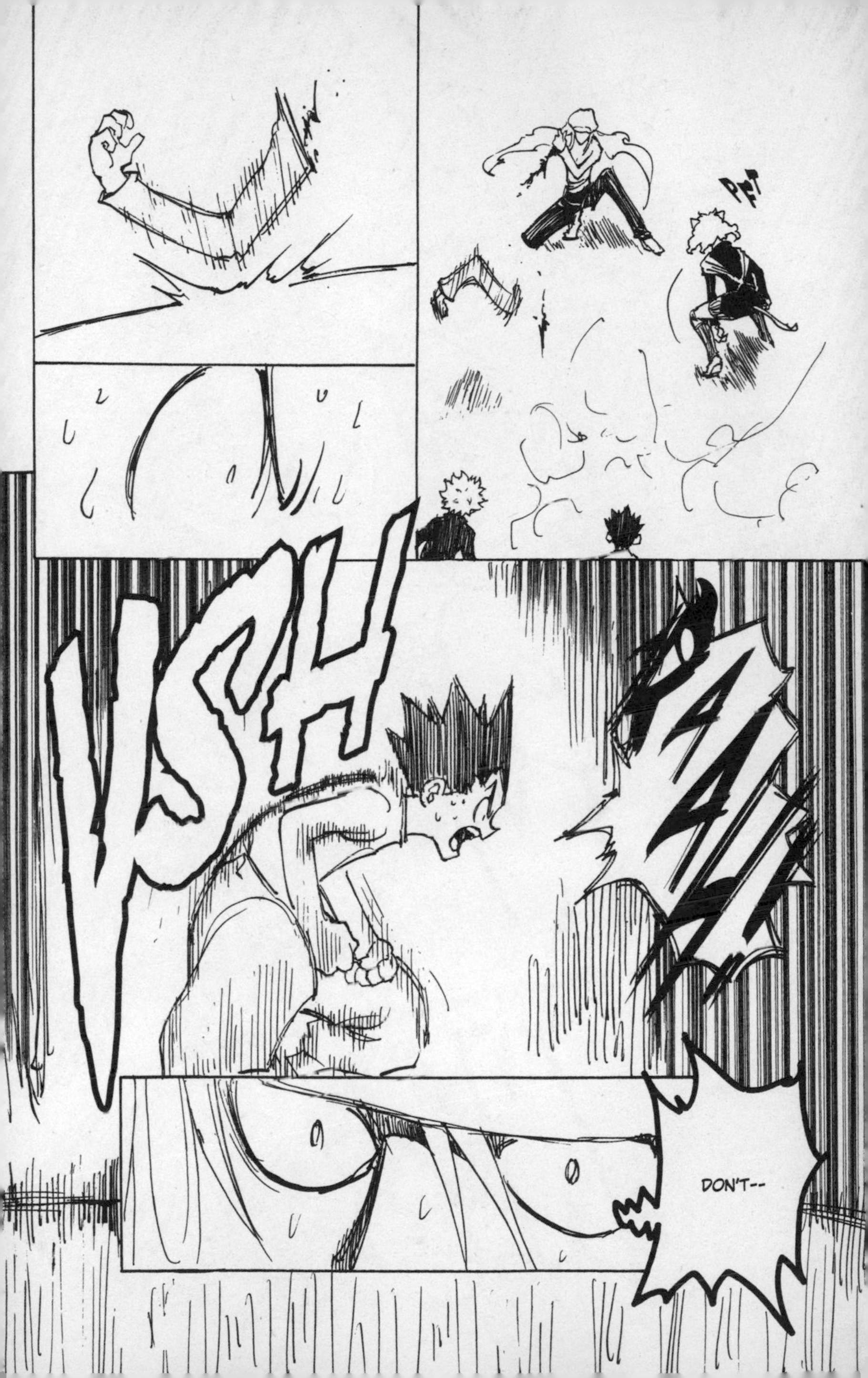
PFT
DON'T--

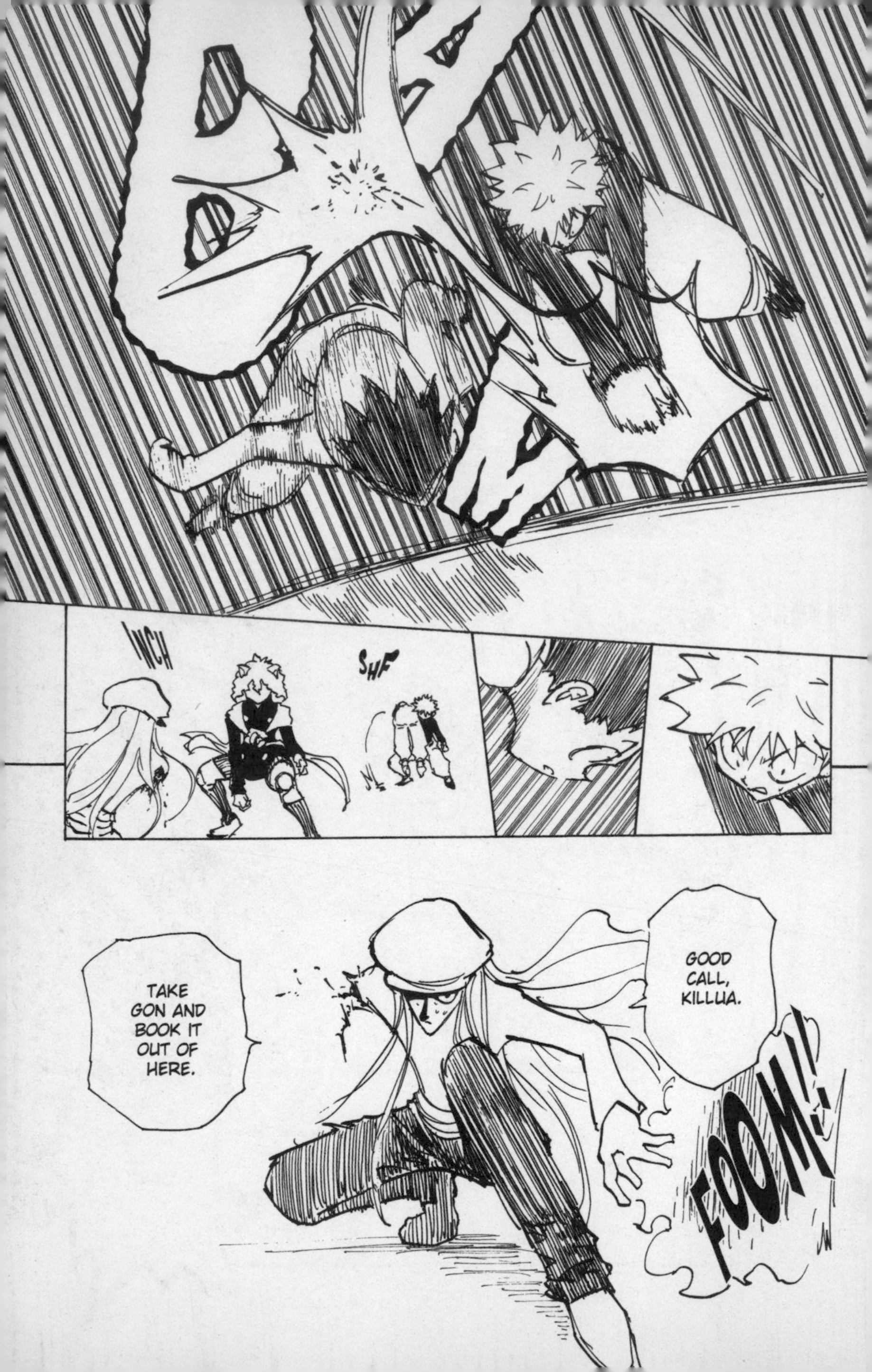
SHF
INCH
GOOD CALL, KILLUA.
FOOM!!
TAKE GON AND BOOK IT OUT OF HERE.

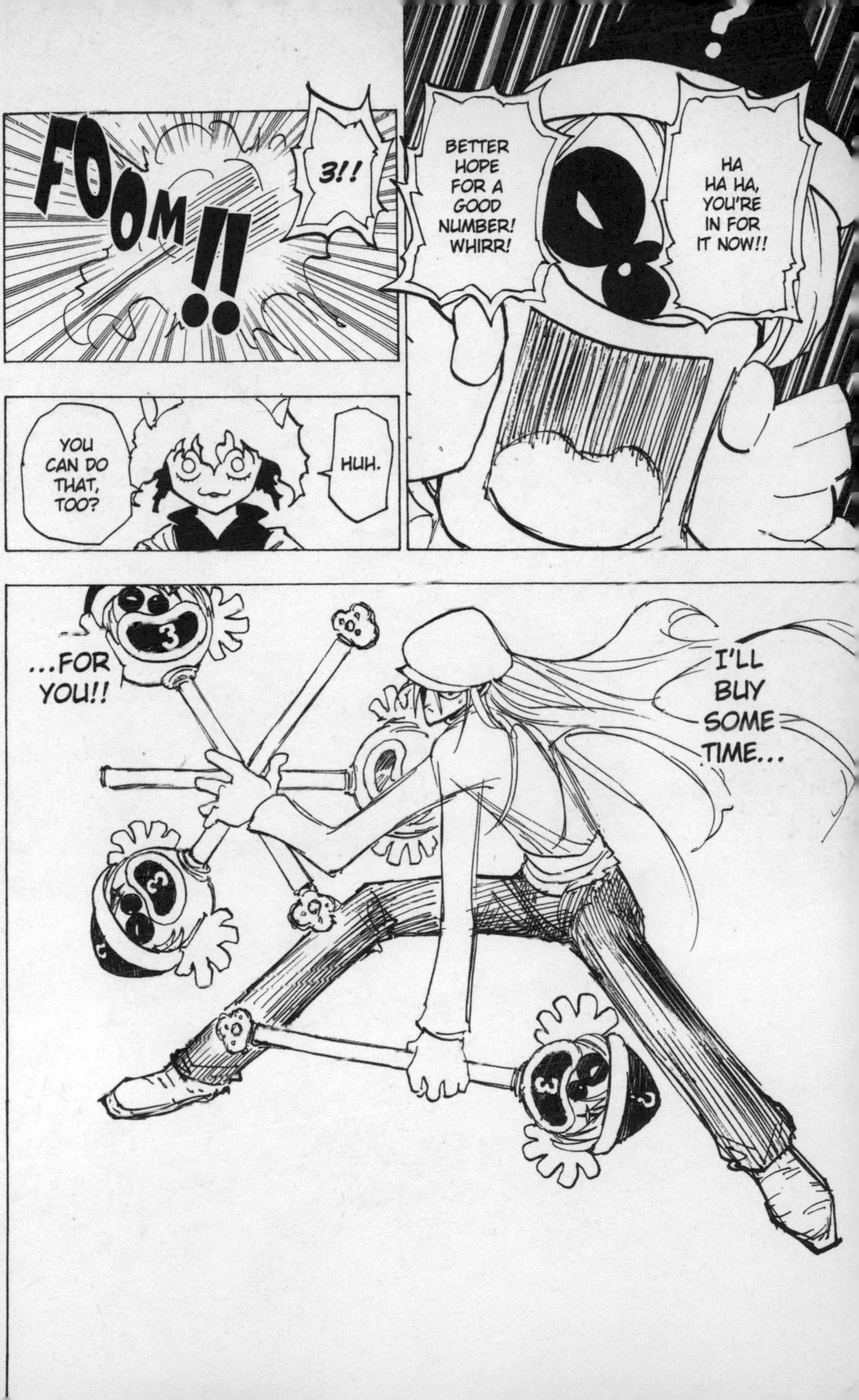
HA HA HA, YOU'RE IN FOR IT NOW!!
BETTER HOPE FOR A GOOD NUMBER! WHIRR!
3!!
FOOM!!
HUH.
YOU CAN DO THAT, TOO?
I'LL BUY SOME TIME...
...FOR YOU!!

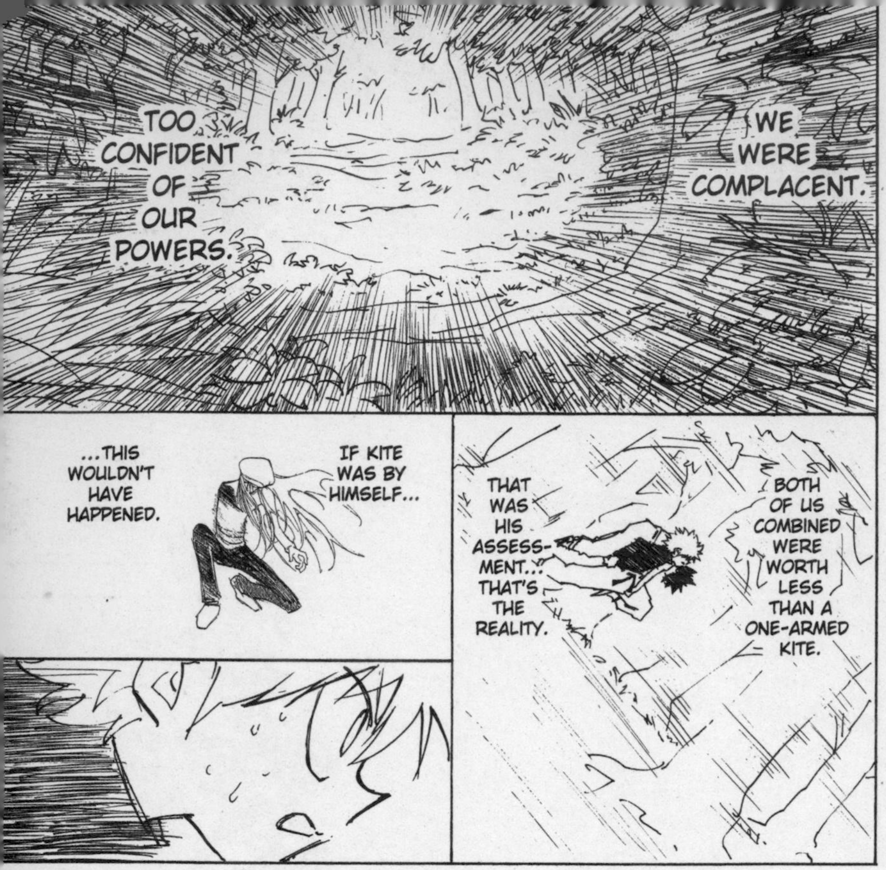
WE WERE COMPLACENT.
TOO CONFIDENT OF OUR POWERS.
BOTH OF US COMBINED WERE WORTH LESS THAN A ONE-ARMED KITE.
THAT WAS HIS ASSESSMENT... THAT'S THE REALITY.
IF KITE WAS BY HIMSELF...
...THIS WOULDN'T HAVE HAPPENED.

WE WERE FOOLS.

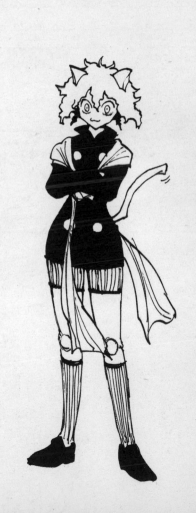

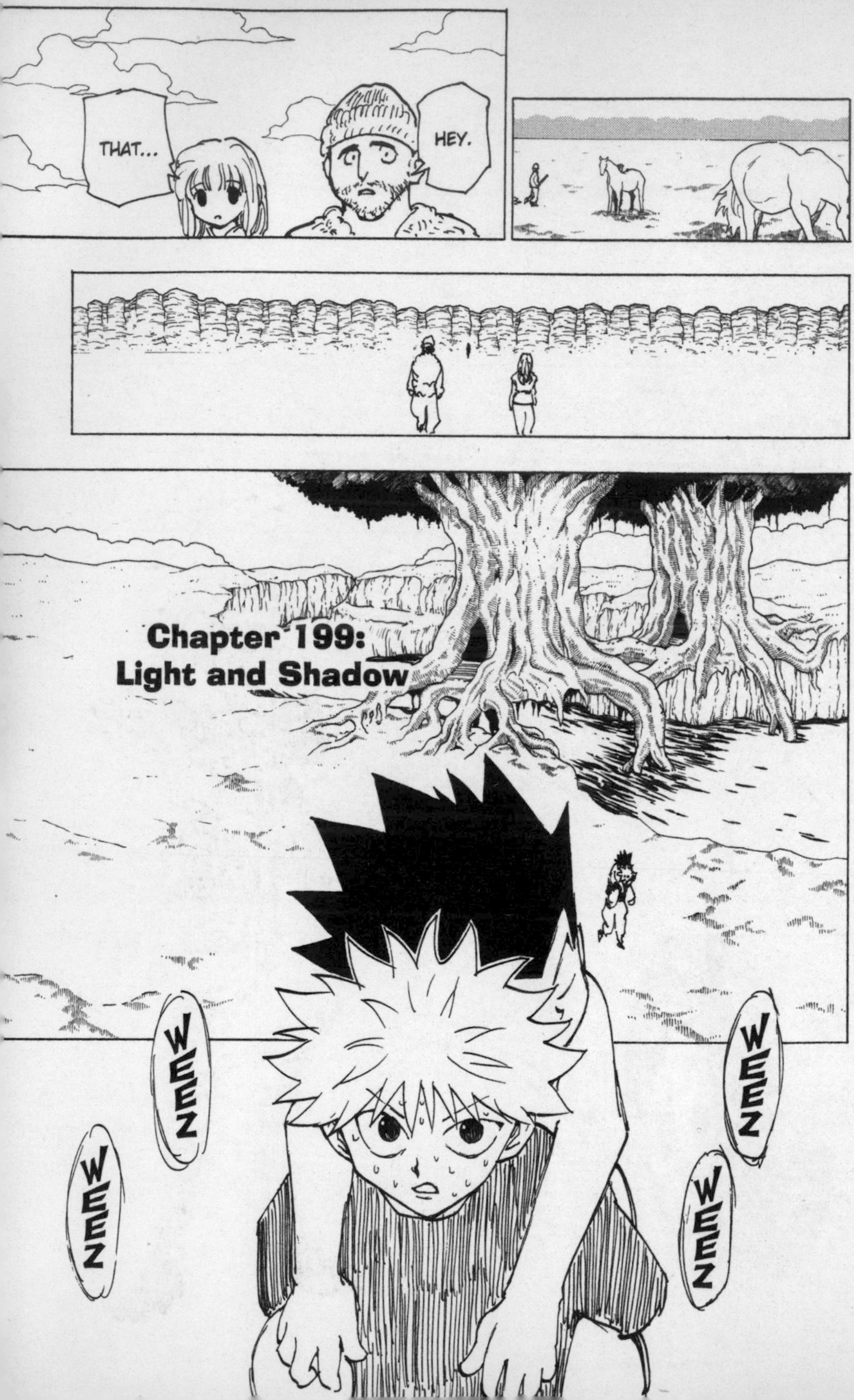
HEY.
THAT...
Chapter 199:
Light and Shadow
WEEZ
WEEZ
WEEZ
WEEZ

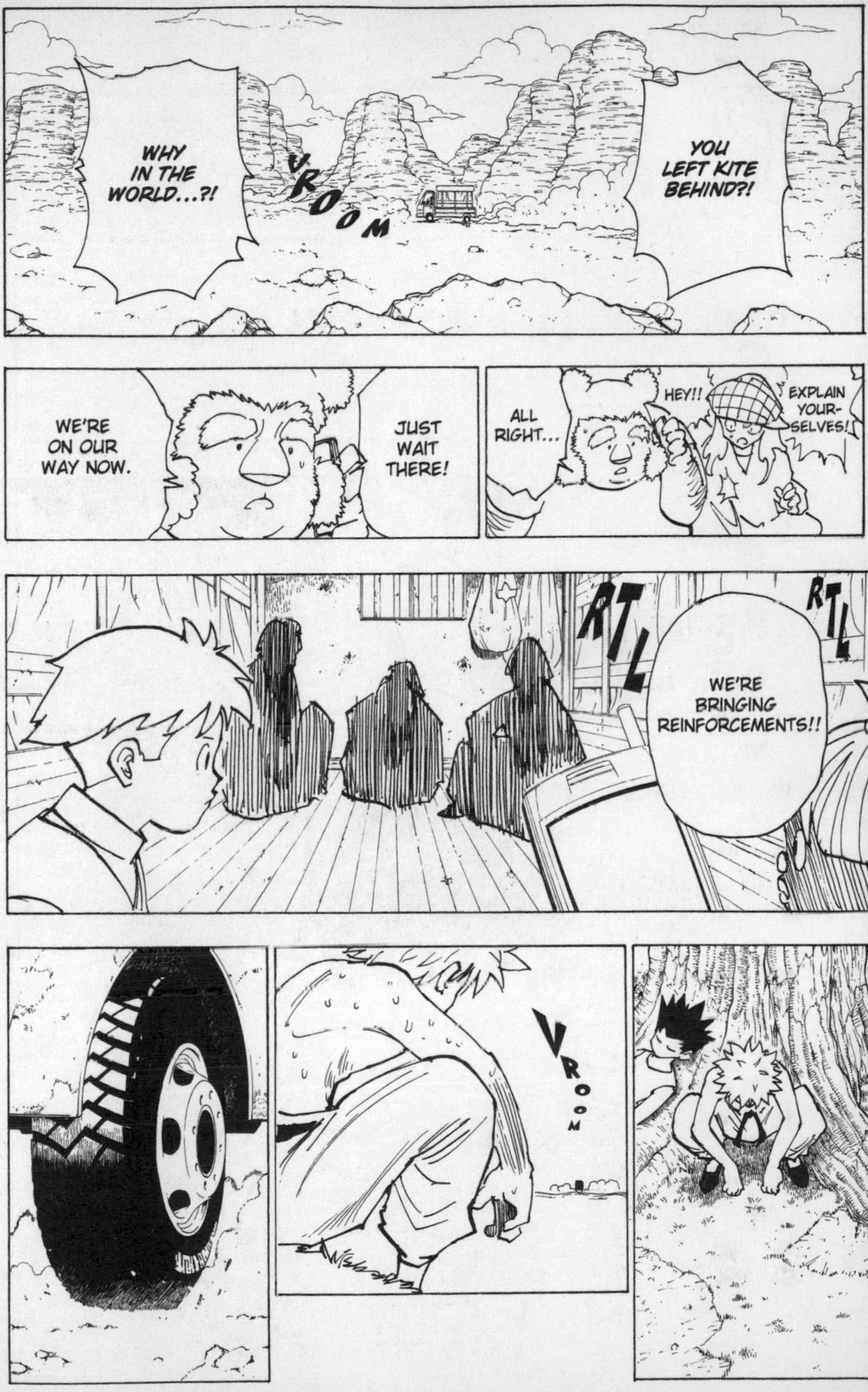
WHY IN THE WORLD...?!
VROOM
YOU LEFT KITE BEHIND?!
HEY!!
EXPLAIN YOUR-SELVES!
ALL RIGHT...
JUST WAIT THERE!
WE'RE ON OUR WAY NOW.
RTL
WE'RE BRINGING REINFORCEMENTS!!
RTL
VROOM

READ THIS WAY

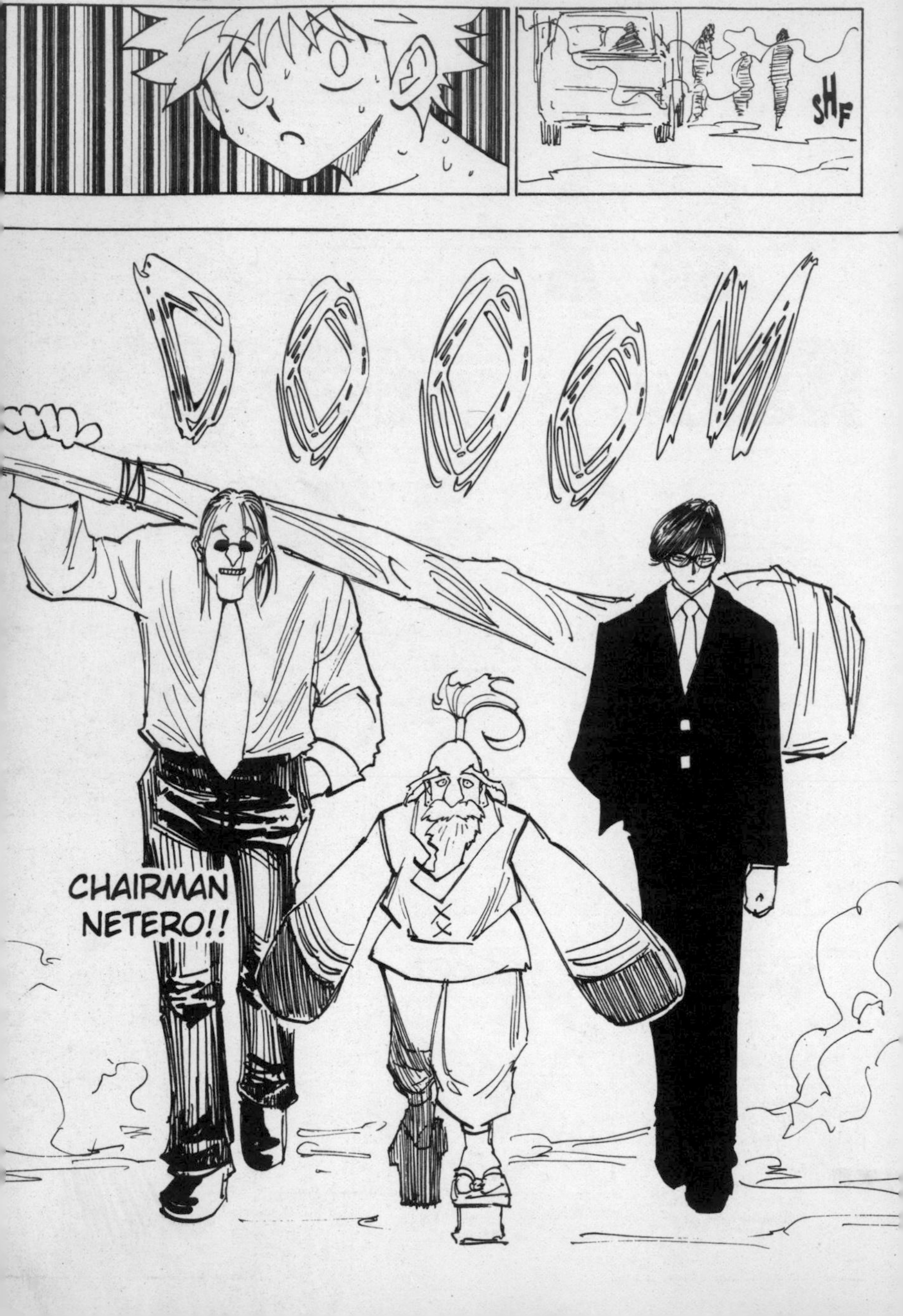
SHF
DOOOM
CHAIRMAN NETERO!!

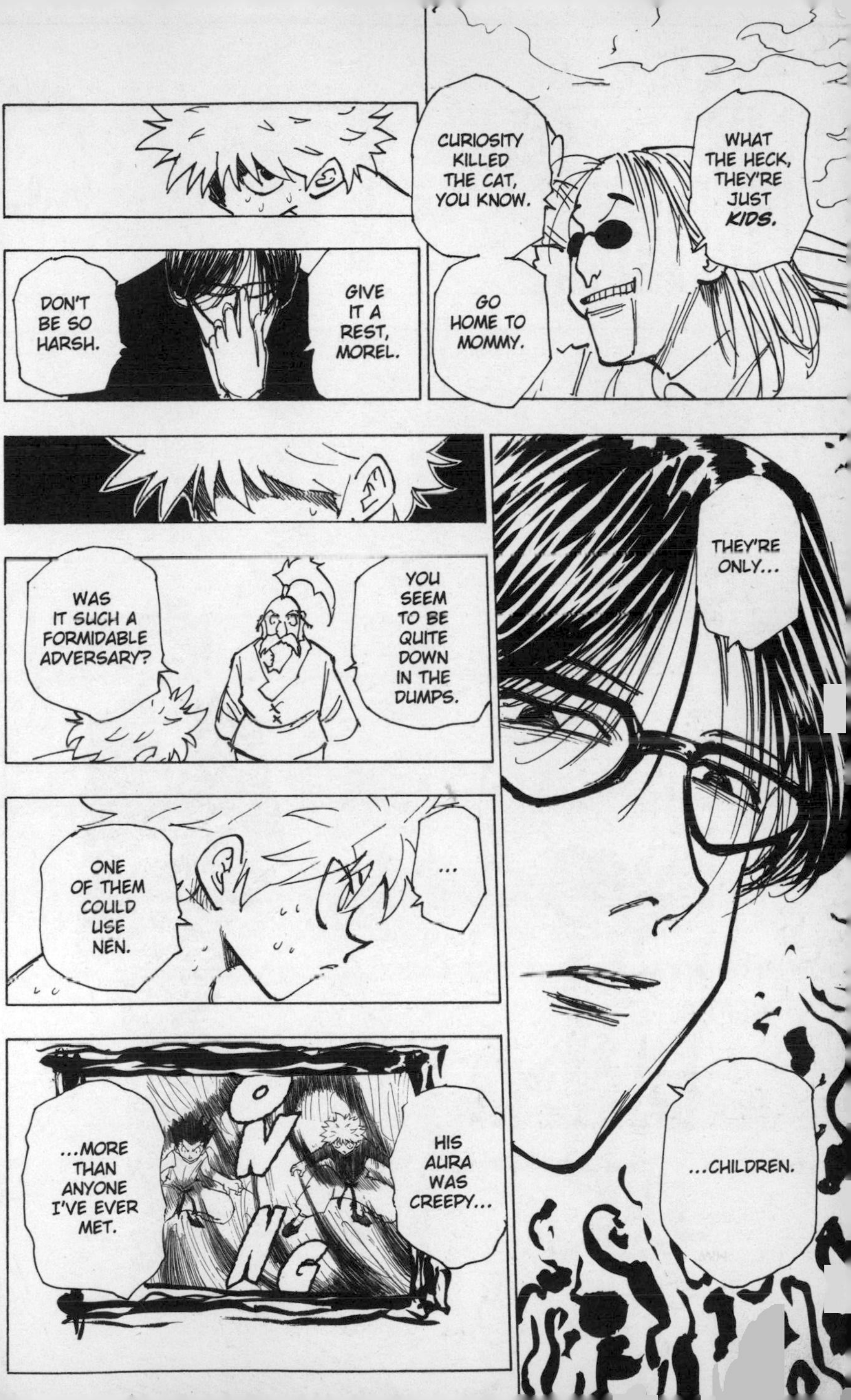
WHAT THE HECK, THEY'RE JUST *KIDS.*
CURIOSITY KILLED THE CAT, YOU KNOW.
GO HOME TO MOMMY.
GIVE IT A REST, MOREL.
DON'T BE SO HARSH.
THEY'RE ONLY...
...CHILDREN.
YOU SEEM TO BE QUITE DOWN IN THE DUMPS.
WAS IT SUCH A FORMIDABLE ADVERSARY?
...
ONE OF THEM COULD USE NEN.
HIS AURA WAS CREEPY...
...MORE THAN ANYONE I'VE EVER MET.

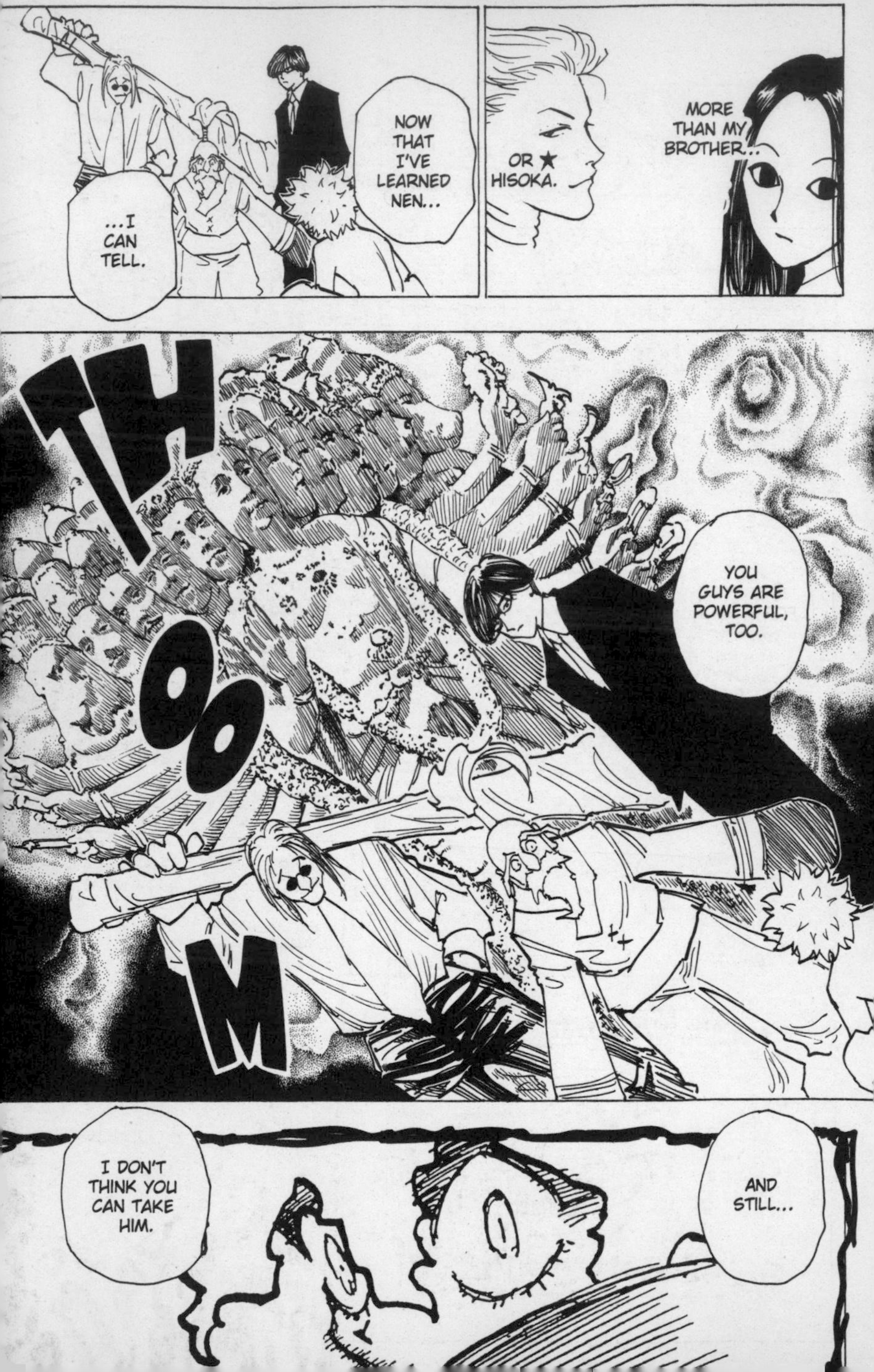
MORE THAN MY BROTHER...
OR ★ HISOKA.
NOW THAT I'VE LEARNED NEN...
...I CAN TELL.
YOU GUYS ARE POWERFUL, TOO.
THOOM
AND STILL...
I DON'T THINK YOU CAN TAKE HIM.

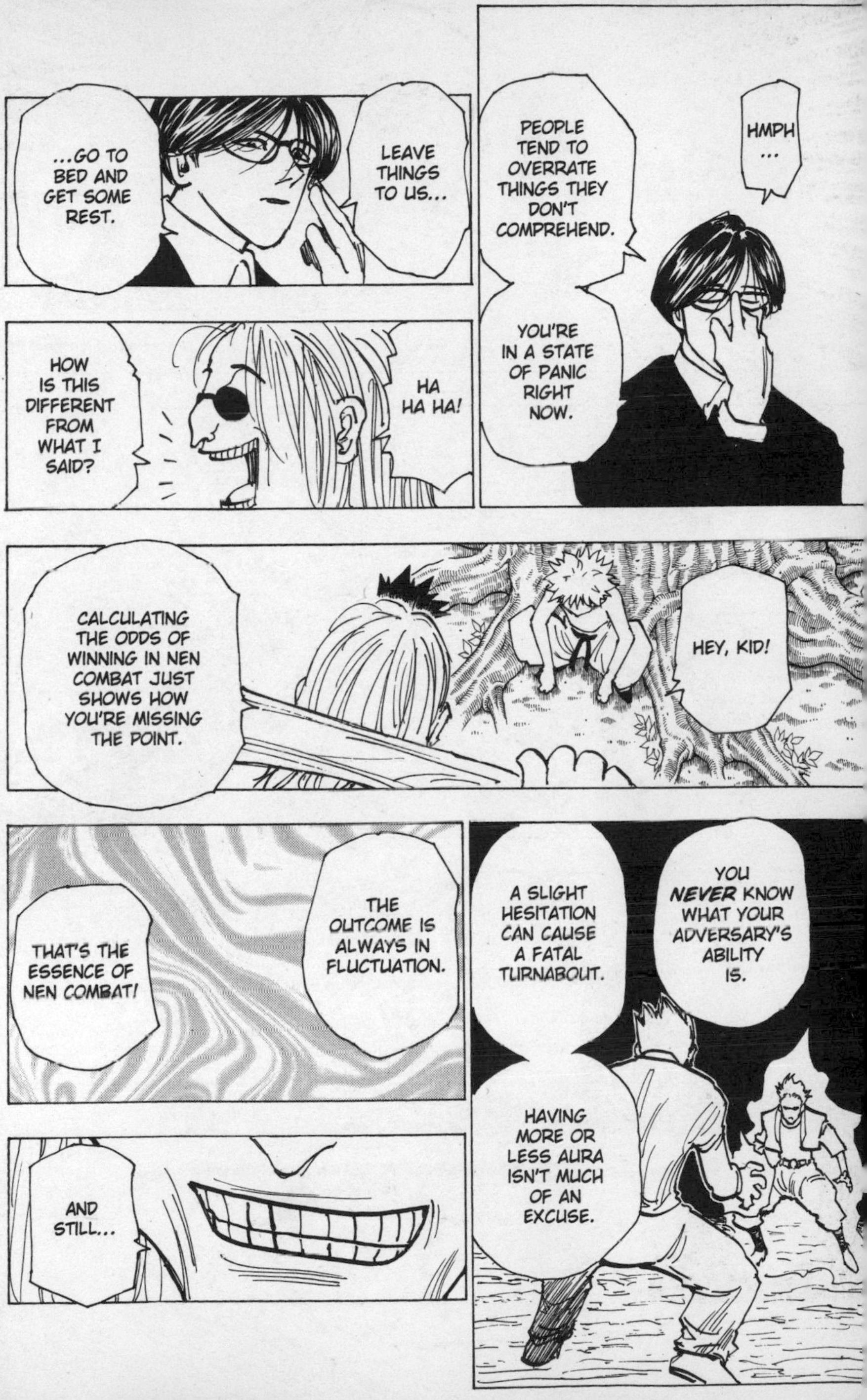
HMPH ...
PEOPLE TEND TO OVERRATE THINGS THEY DON'T COMPREHEND.
YOU'RE IN A STATE OF PANIC RIGHT NOW.
LEAVE THINGS TO US...
...GO TO BED AND GET SOME REST.
HA HA HA!
HOW IS THIS DIFFERENT FROM WHAT I SAID?
HEY, KID!
CALCULATING THE ODDS OF WINNING IN NEN COMBAT JUST SHOWS HOW YOU'RE MISSING THE POINT.
YOU **NEVER** KNOW WHAT YOUR ADVERSARY'S ABILITY IS.
A SLIGHT HESITATION CAN CAUSE A FATAL TURNABOUT.
HAVING MORE OR LESS AURA ISN'T MUCH OF AN EXCUSE.
THE OUTCOME IS ALWAYS IN FLUCTUATION.
THAT'S THE ESSENCE OF NEN COMBAT!
AND STILL...

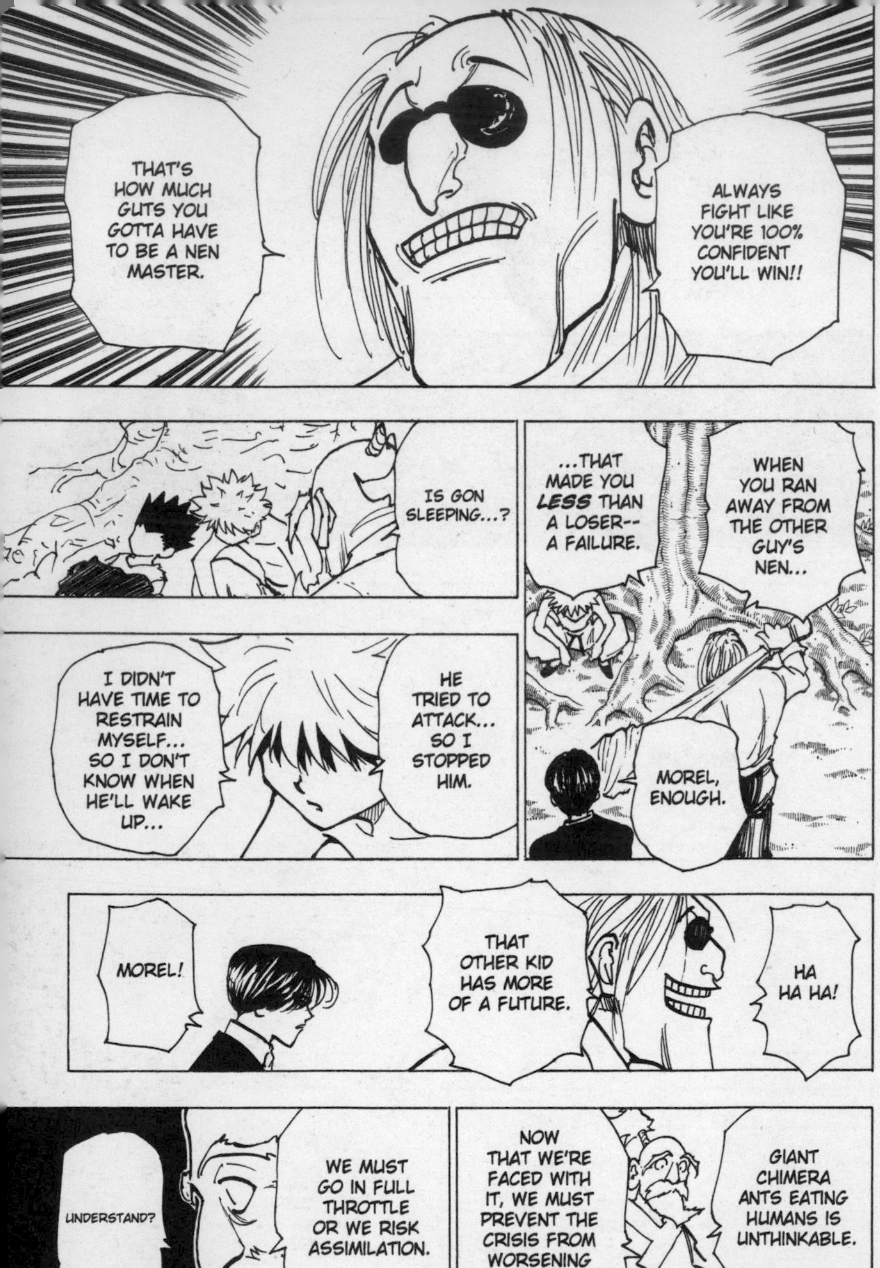
ALWAYS FIGHT LIKE YOU'RE 100% CONFIDENT YOU'LL WIN!!
THAT'S HOW MUCH GUTS YOU GOTTA HAVE TO BE A NEN MASTER.
WHEN YOU RAN AWAY FROM THE OTHER GUY'S NEN...
...THAT MADE YOU *LESS* THAN A LOSER-- A FAILURE.
MOREL, ENOUGH.
IS GON SLEEPING...?
HE TRIED TO ATTACK... SO I STOPPED HIM.
I DIDN'T HAVE TIME TO RESTRAIN MYSELF... SO I DON'T KNOW WHEN HE'LL WAKE UP...
HA HA HA!
THAT OTHER KID HAS MORE OF A FUTURE.
MOREL!
GIANT CHIMERA ANTS EATING HUMANS IS UNTHINKABLE.
NOW THAT WE'RE FACED WITH IT, WE MUST PREVENT THE CRISIS FROM WORSENING AT ALL COSTS.
WE MUST GO IN FULL THROTTLE OR WE RISK ASSIMILATION.
UNDERSTAND?

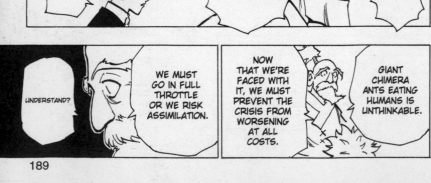

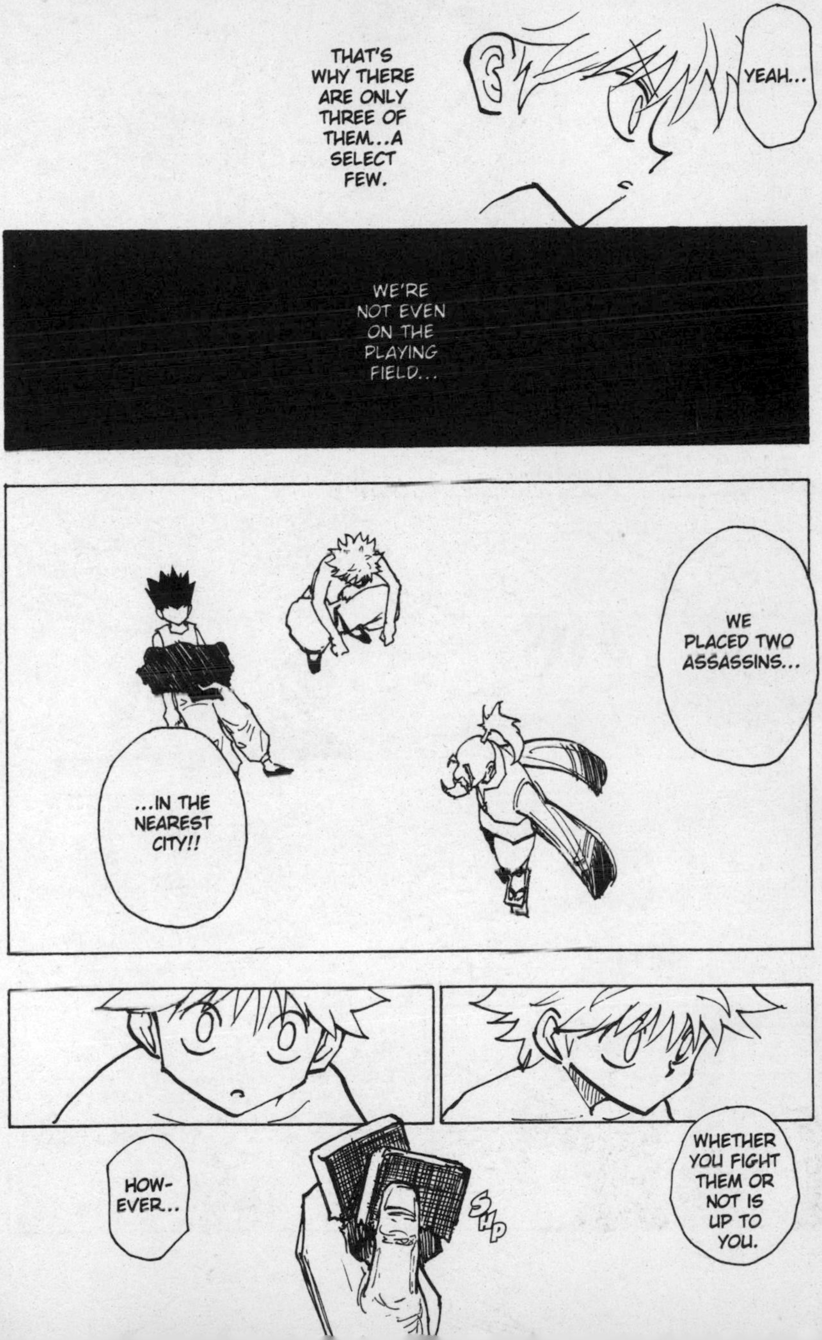
YEAH...
THAT'S WHY THERE ARE ONLY THREE OF THEM...A SELECT FEW.
WE'RE NOT EVEN ON THE PLAYING FIELD...
WE PLACED TWO ASSASSINS...
...IN THE NEAREST CITY!!
WHETHER YOU FIGHT THEM OR NOT IS UP TO YOU.
SHP
HOW-EVER...

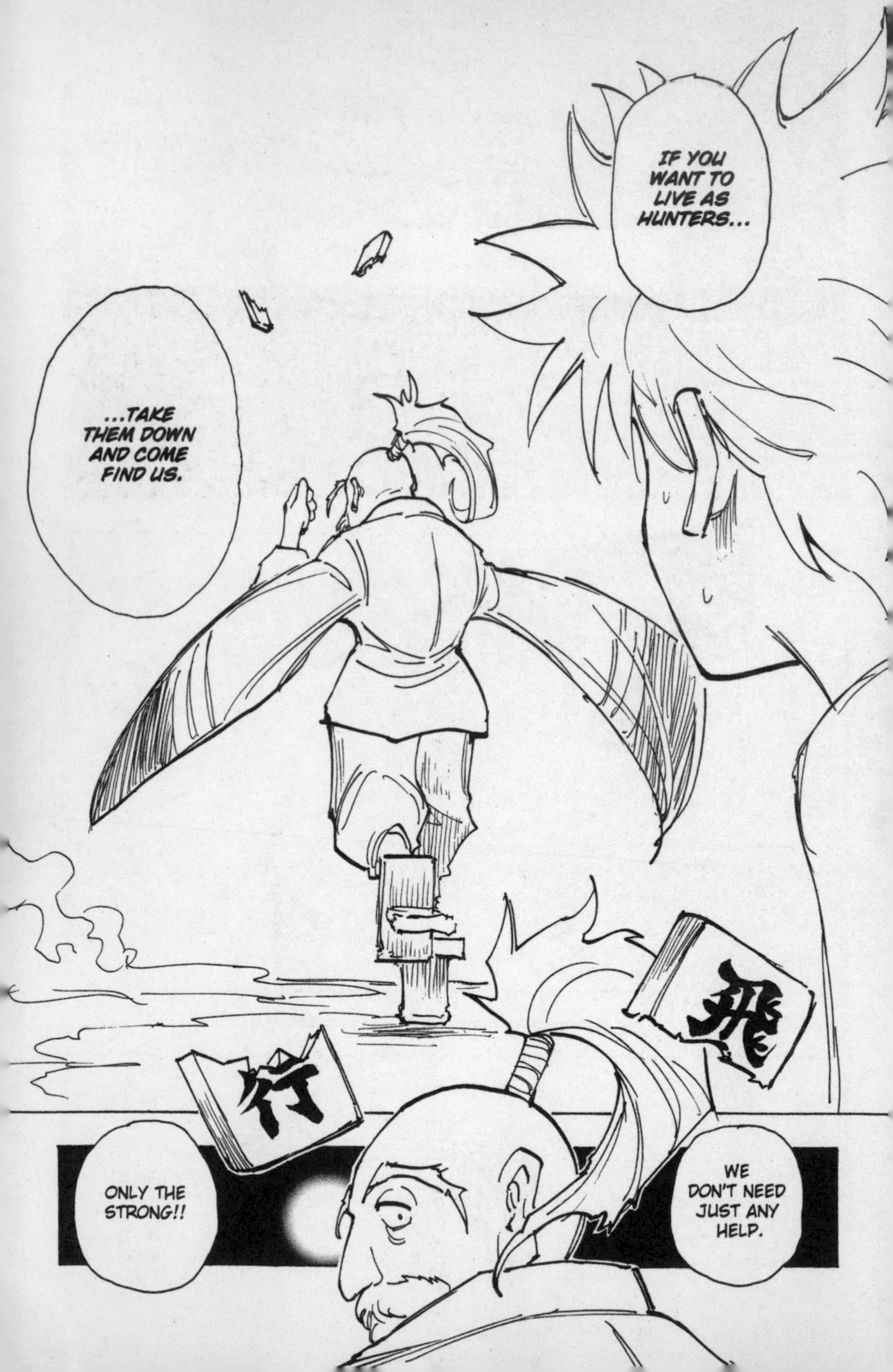
IF YOU WANT TO LIVE AS HUNTERS...
...TAKE THEM DOWN AND COME FIND US.
飛
行
WE DON'T NEED JUST ANY HELP.
ONLY THE STRONG!!

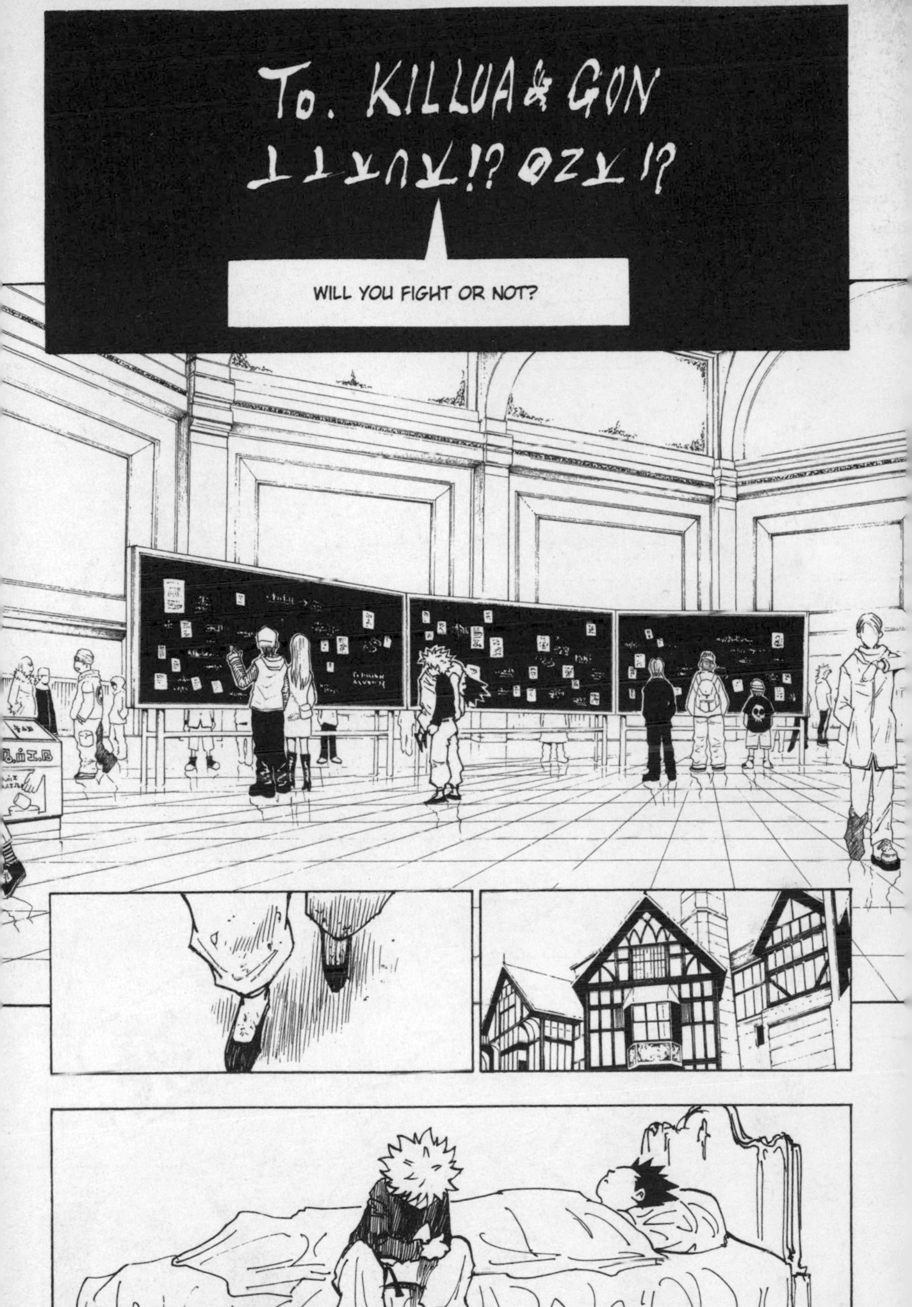
To. KILLUA & GON
WILL YOU FIGHT OR NOT?

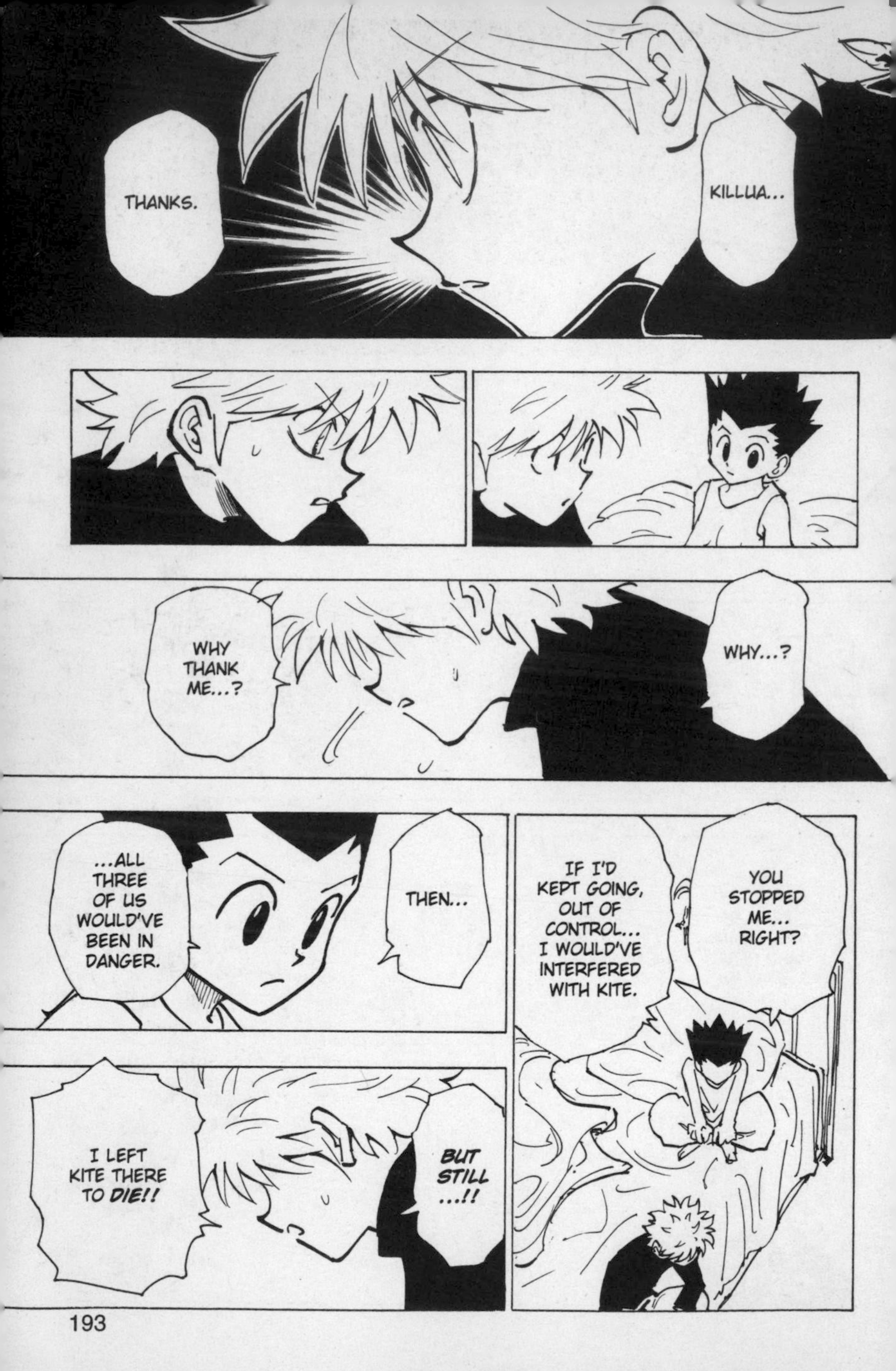
KILLUA...
THANKS.
WHY...?
WHY THANK ME...?
YOU STOPPED ME... RIGHT?
IF I'D KEPT GOING, OUT OF CONTROL... I WOULD'VE INTERFERED WITH KITE.
THEN...
...ALL THREE OF US WOULD'VE BEEN IN DANGER.
BUT STILL ...!!
I LEFT KITE THERE TO *DIE!!*

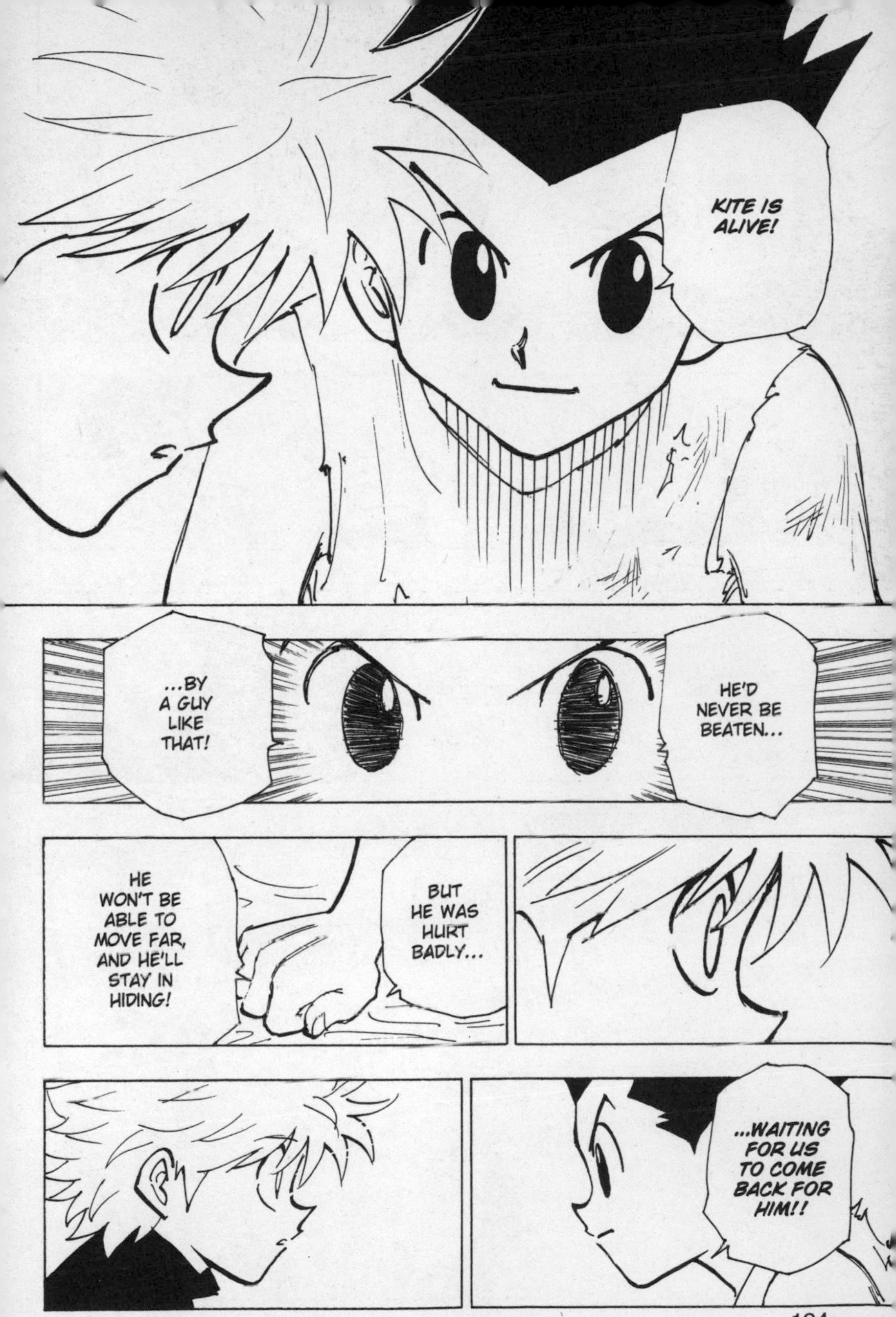
KITE IS ALIVE!
HE'D NEVER BE BEATEN...
...BY A GUY LIKE THAT!
BUT HE WAS HURT BADLY...
HE WON'T BE ABLE TO MOVE FAR, AND HE'LL STAY IN HIDING!
...WAITING FOR US TO COME BACK FOR HIM!!

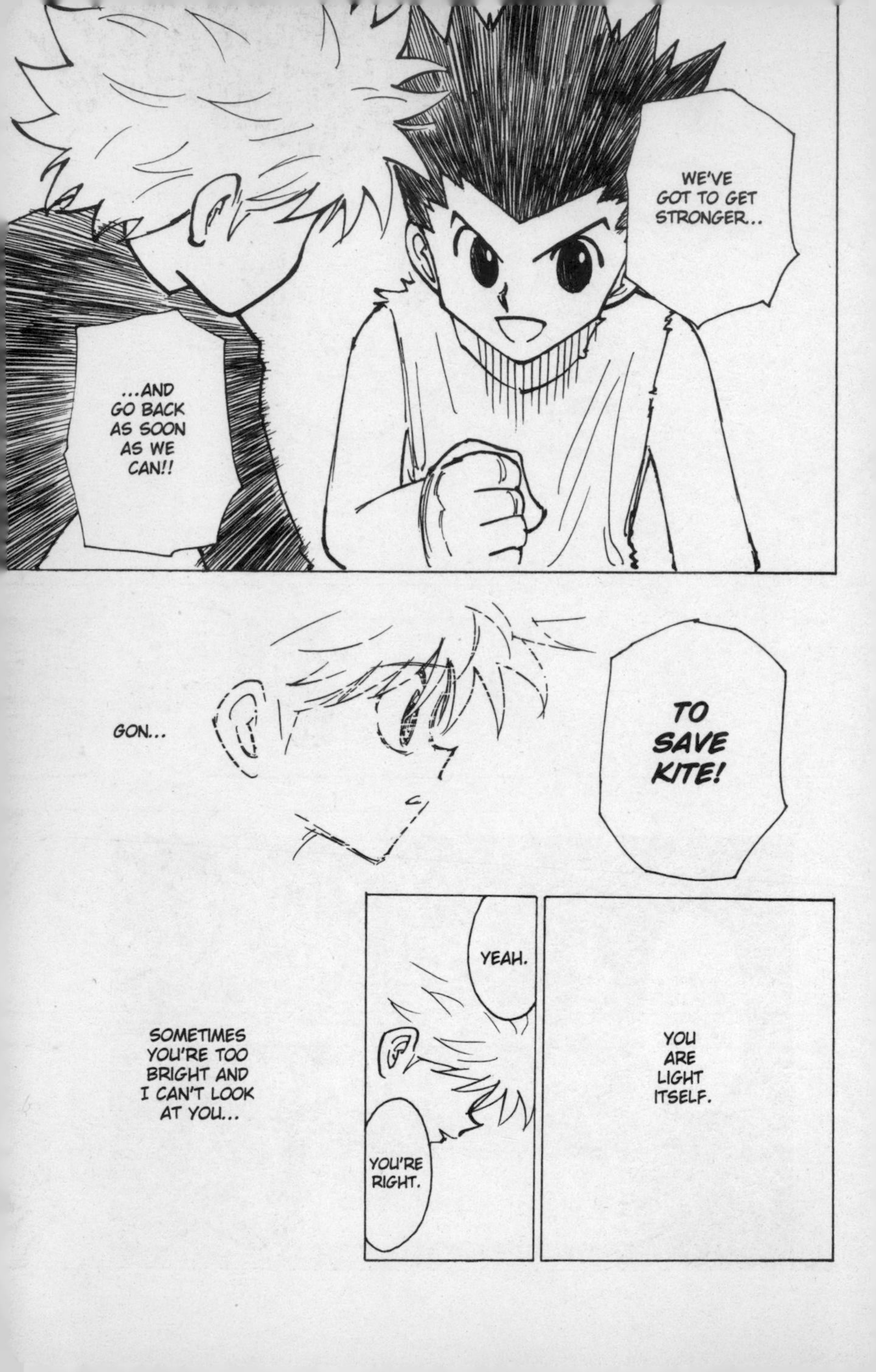

WE'VE GOT TO GET STRONGER...
...AND GO BACK AS SOON AS WE CAN!!
TO SAVE KITE!
GON...
YOU ARE LIGHT ITSELF.
YEAH.
YOU'RE RIGHT.
SOMETIMES YOU'RE TOO BRIGHT AND I CAN'T LOOK AT YOU...

BUT CAN I STILL...

STAY BY YOUR SIDE...?

LET'S GO!

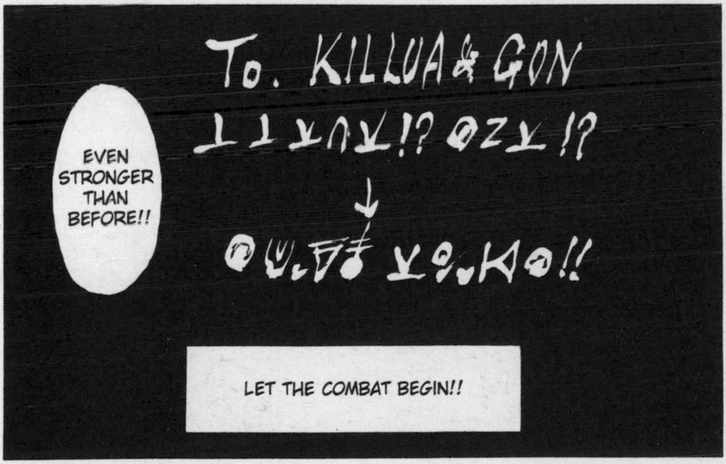
To. KILLUA & GON
EVEN STRONGER THAN BEFORE!!
LET THE COMBAT BEGIN!!

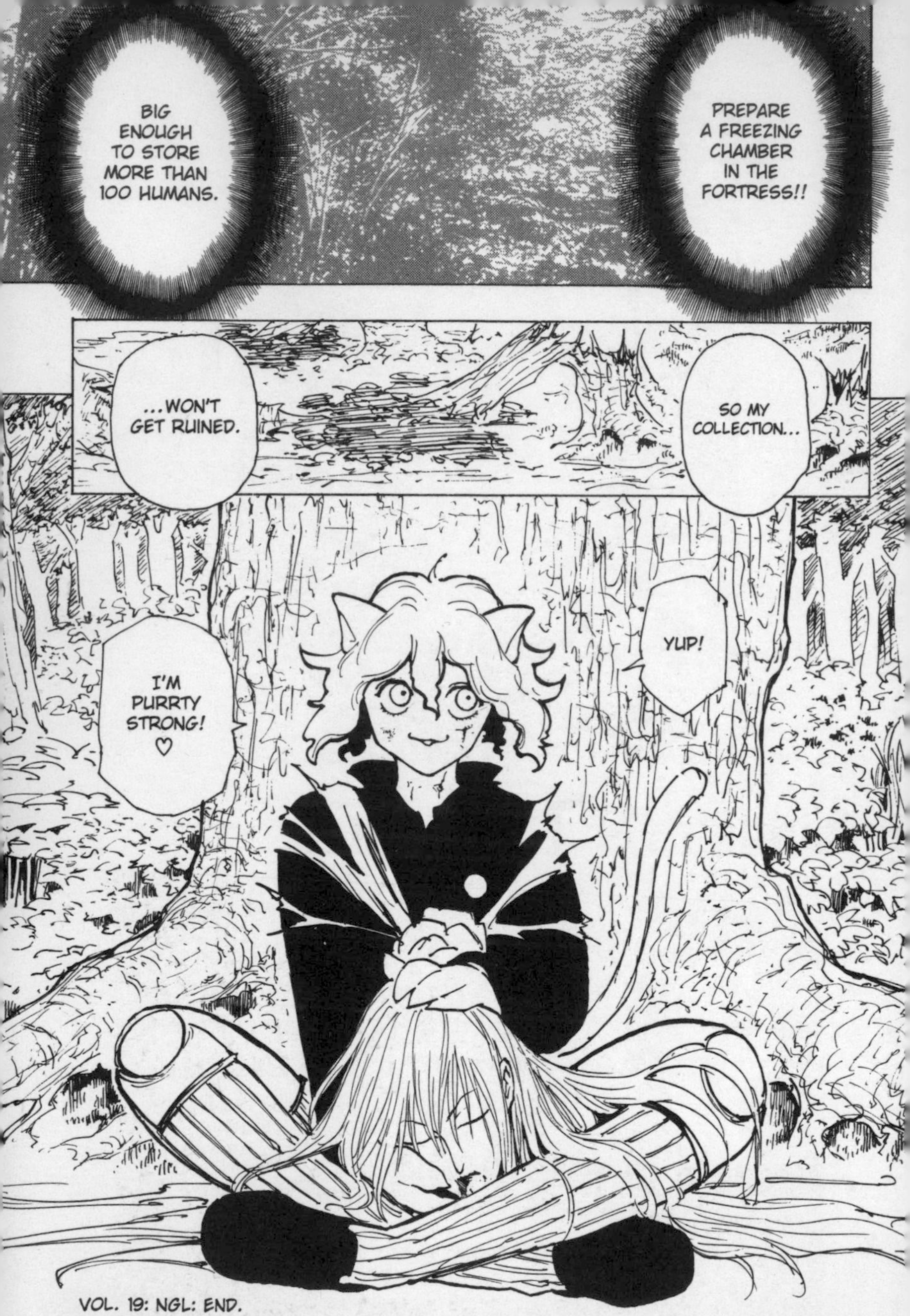
PREPARE A FREEZING CHAMBER IN THE FORTRESS!!
BIG ENOUGH TO STORE MORE THAN 100 HUMANS.
SO MY COLLECTION...
...WON'T GET RUINED.
YUP!
I'M PURRTY STRONG! ♡

VOL. 19: NGL: END.

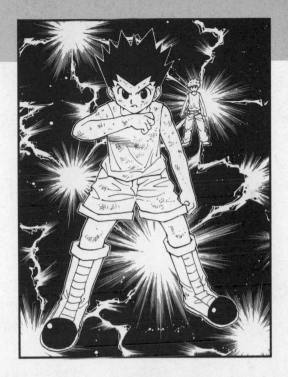

Coming Next Volume...

Gon and Killua have a new foe to fight—Knuckle! Good name for a brawler! They have just one month to fight, so it's back to training again! This time it's the basics—they have to increase their baseline stamina *just* to get to Knuckle's level! When the fight is on, Gon tries a risky move and passes out! Hard to fight when you're unconscious! What's gonna happen to our spiky-haired hero?!

Available in May 2008!

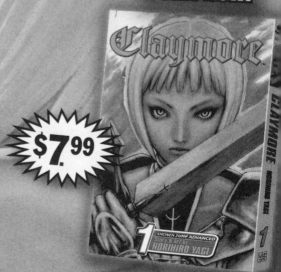

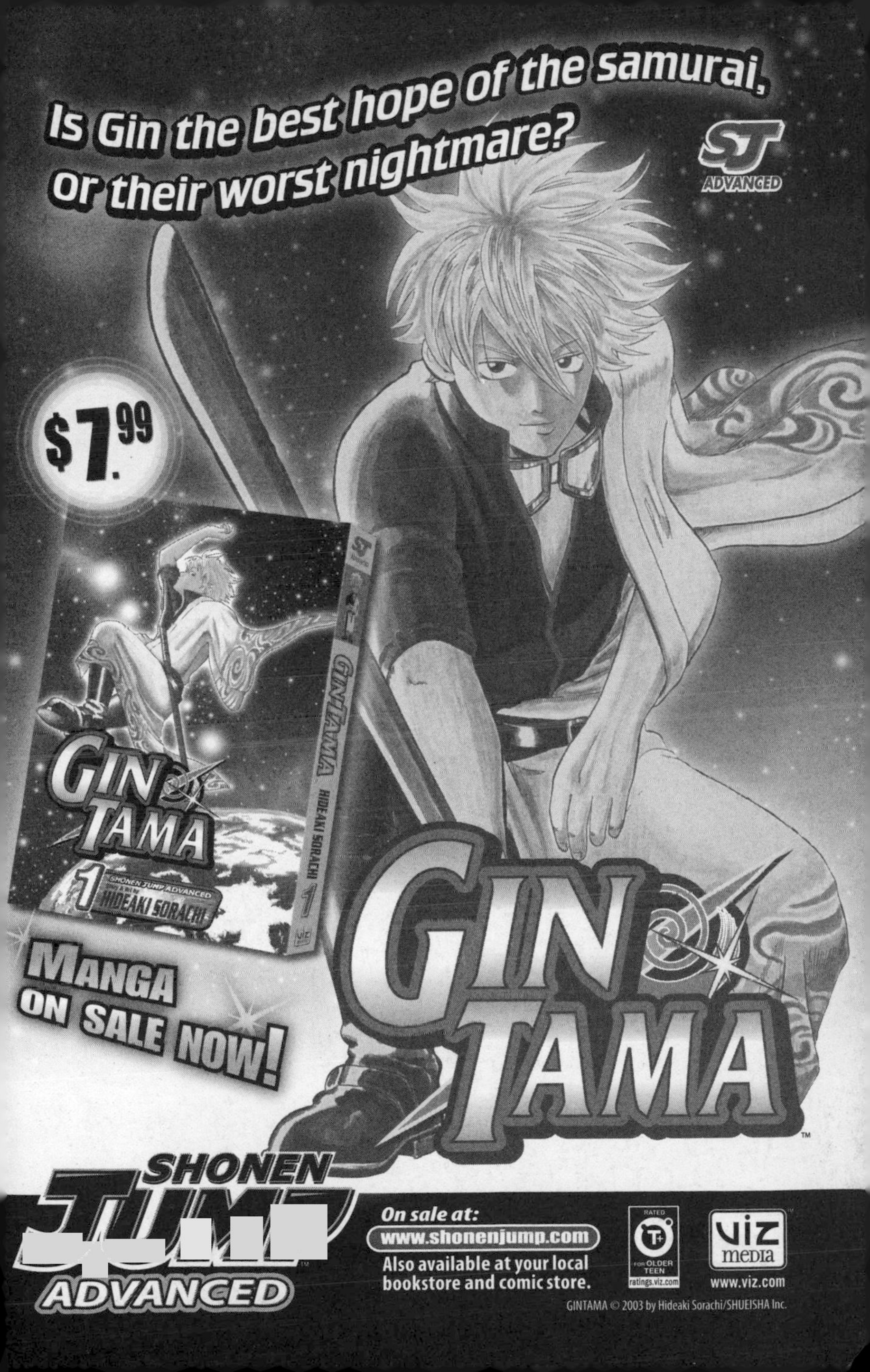
Is Gin the best hope of the samurai,
or their worst nightmare?
SJ ADVANCED
$7.99
GIN TAMA
1
SHONEN JUMP ADVANCED
HIDEAKI SORACHI
MANGA ON SALE NOW!
GIN TAMA™
SHONEN JUMP ADVANCED
On sale at:
www.shonenjump.com
Also available at your local bookstore and comic store.
RATED T+ FOR OLDER TEEN
ratings.viz.com
viz media
www.viz.com
GINTAMA © 2003 by Hideaki Sorachi/SHUEISHA Inc.

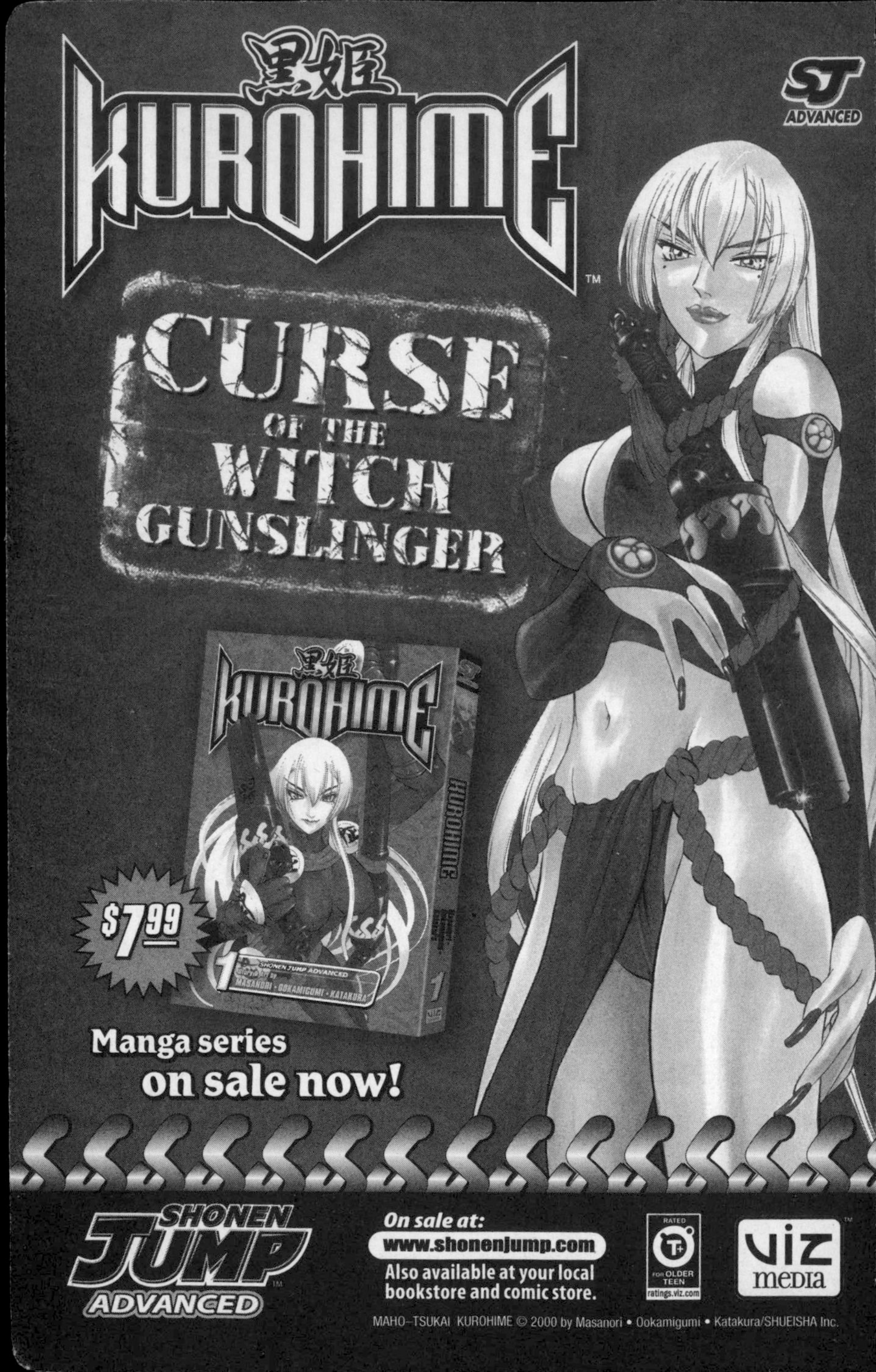

黒姫
KUROHIME
CURSE OF THE WITCH GUNSLINGER
$7.99
Manga series on sale now!
SHONEN JUMP ADVANCED
On sale at:
www.shonenjump.com
Also available at your local bookstore and comic store.
RATED T+ FOR OLDER TEEN ratings.viz.com
viz media
MAHO-TSUKAI KUROHIME © 2000 by Masanori • Ookamigumi • Katakura/SHUEISHA Inc.

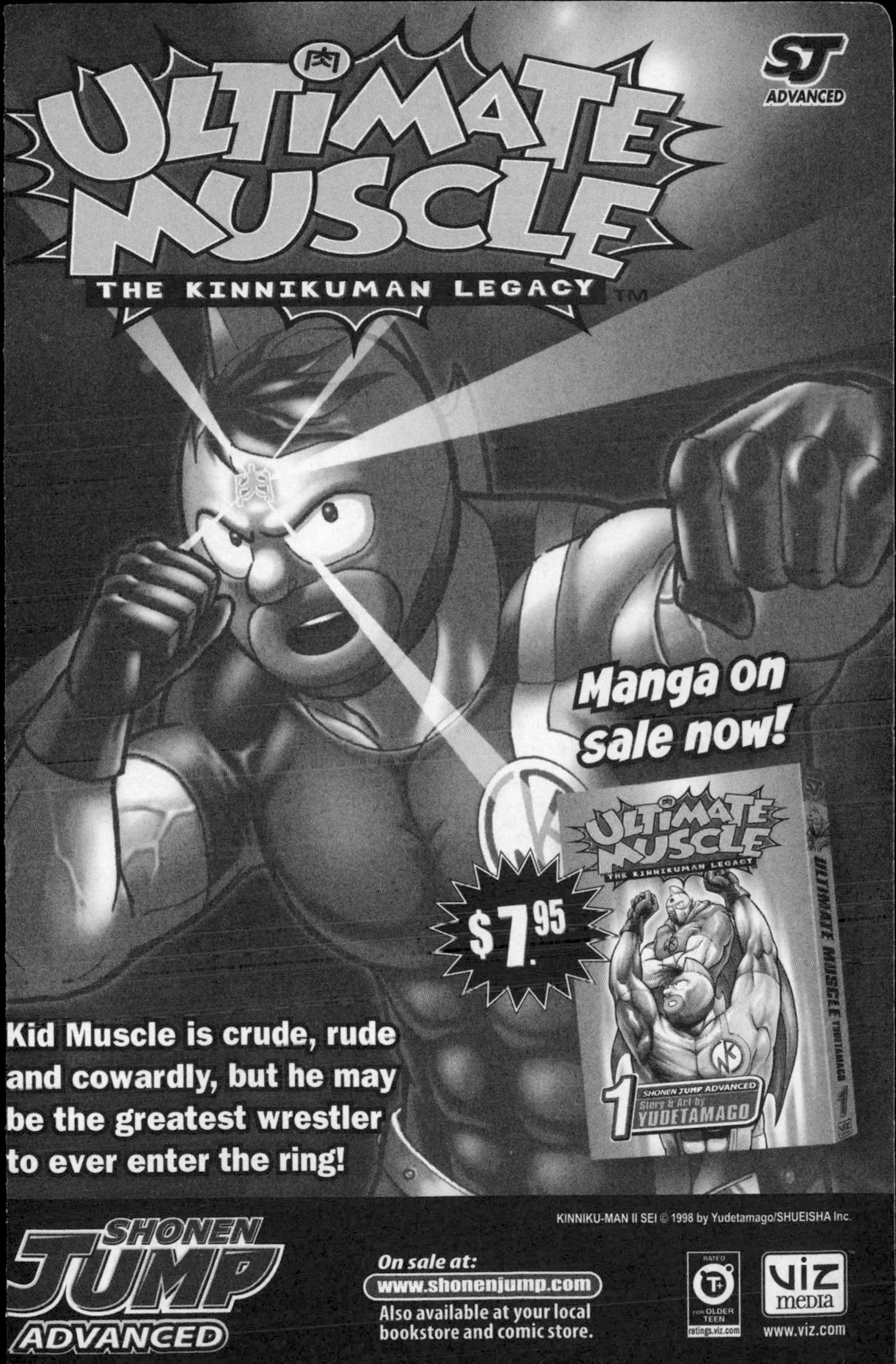
SJ ADVANCED
ULTIMATE MUSCLE
THE KINNIKUMAN LEGACY™
Manga on sale now!
ULTIMATE MUSCLE
THE KINNIKUMAN LEGACY
$7.95
ULTIMATE MUSCLE YUDETAMAGO
1 SHONEN JUMP ADVANCED
Story & Art by
YUDETAMAGO
Kid Muscle is crude, rude and cowardly, but he may be the greatest wrestler to ever enter the ring!
KINNIKU-MAN II SEI © 1998 by Yudetamago/SHUEISHA Inc.
SHONEN JUMP ADVANCED
On sale at:
www.shonenjump.com
Also available at your local bookstore and comic store.
RATED T+ FOR OLDER TEEN
ratings.viz.com
VIZ media
www.viz.com

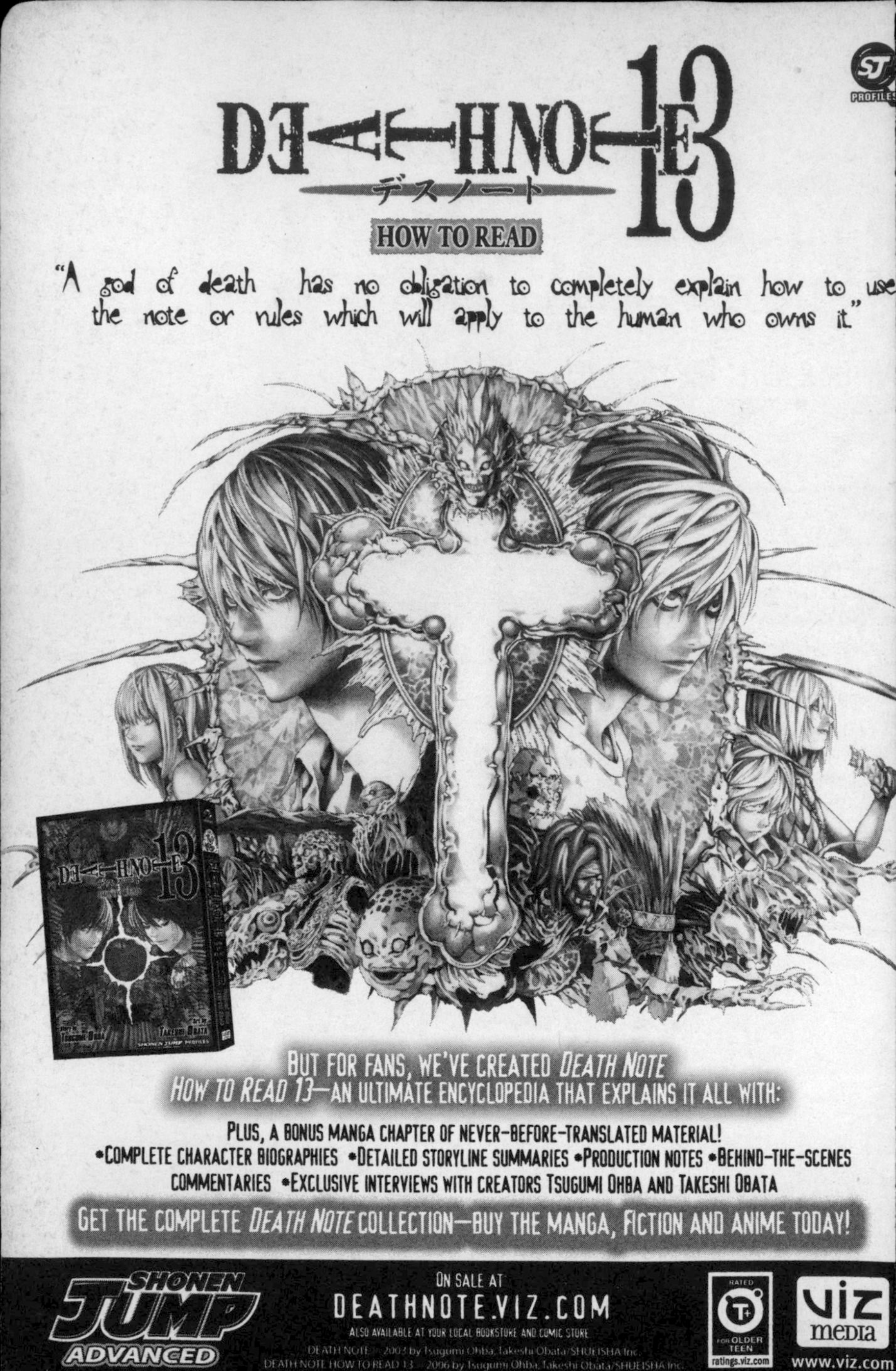
SJ PROFILES
DEATH NOTE 13
デスノート
HOW TO READ
"A god of death has no obligation to completely explain how to use the note or rules which will apply to the human who owns it"
DEATH NOTE 13
BUT FOR FANS, WE'VE CREATED DEATH NOTE HOW TO READ 13—AN ULTIMATE ENCYCLOPEDIA THAT EXPLAINS IT ALL WITH:
PLUS, A BONUS MANGA CHAPTER OF NEVER-BEFORE-TRANSLATED MATERIAL!
•COMPLETE CHARACTER BIOGRAPHIES •DETAILED STORYLINE SUMMARIES •PRODUCTION NOTES •BEHIND-THE-SCENES COMMENTARIES •EXCLUSIVE INTERVIEWS WITH CREATORS TSUGUMI OHBA AND TAKESHI OBATA
GET THE COMPLETE DEATH NOTE COLLECTION—BUY THE MANGA, FICTION AND ANIME TODAY!
SHONEN JUMP ADVANCED
ON SALE AT
DEATHNOTE.VIZ.COM
ALSO AVAILABLE AT YOUR LOCAL BOOKSTORE AND COMIC STORE
DEATH NOTE © 2003 by Tsugumi Ohba, Takeshi Obata/SHUEISHA Inc.
DEATH NOTE HOW TO READ 13 © 2006 by Tsugumi Ohba, Takeshi Obata/SHUEISHA Inc.
RATED T+ FOR OLDER TEEN
ratings.viz.com
viz media
www.viz.com

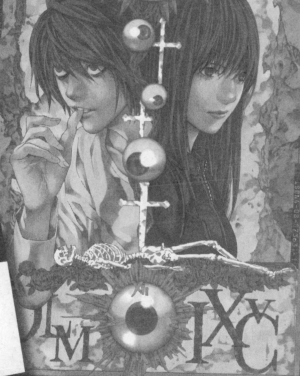

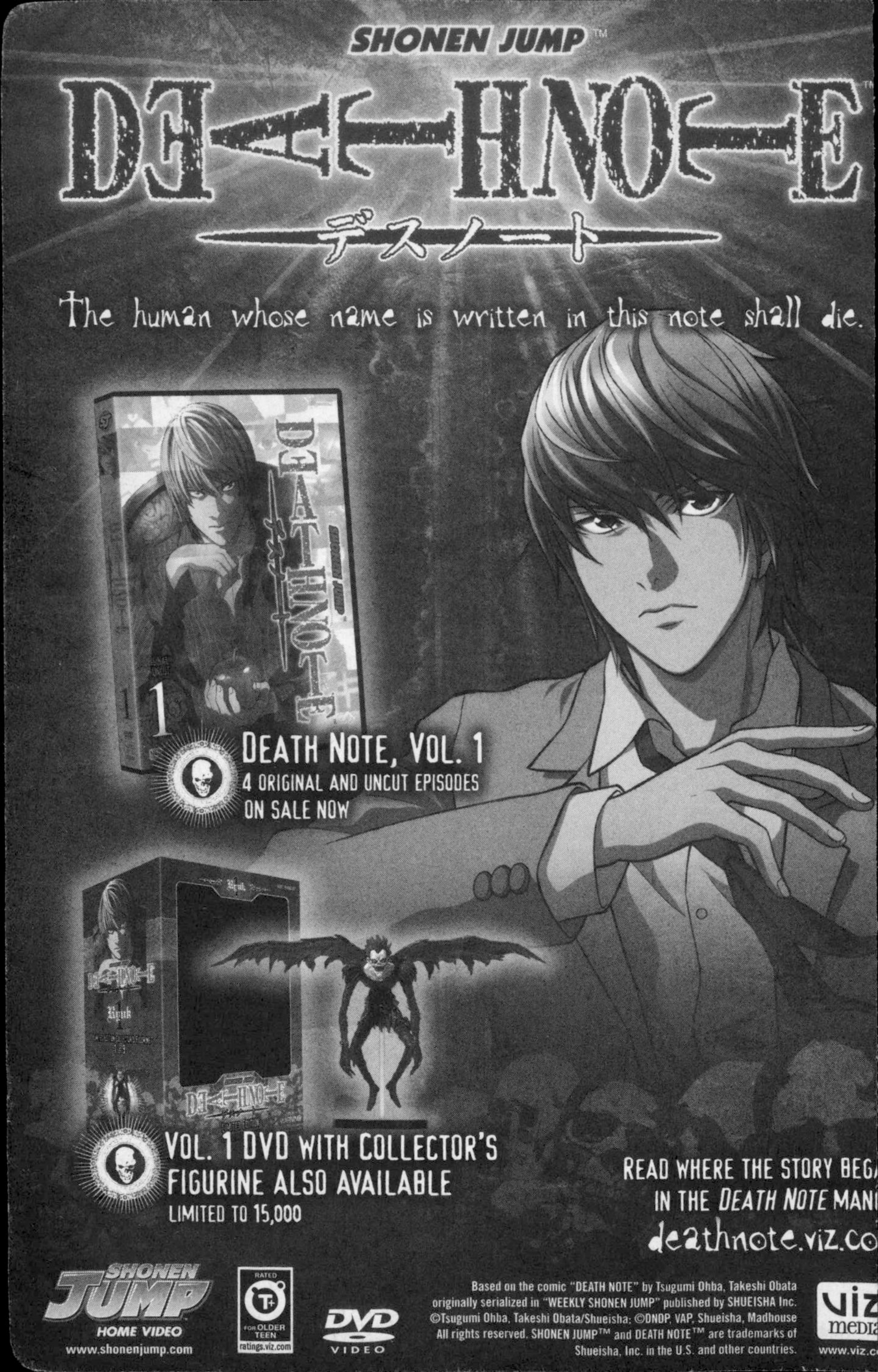
SHONEN JUMP™
DEATH NOTE™
デスノート
The human whose name is written in this note shall die.
DEATH NOTE, VOL. 1
4 ORIGINAL AND UNCUT EPISODES
ON SALE NOW
VOL. 1 DVD WITH COLLECTOR'S
FIGURINE ALSO AVAILABLE
LIMITED TO 15,000
READ WHERE THE STORY BEGA
IN THE DEATH NOTE MANG
deathnote.viz.co
SHONEN JUMP
HOME VIDEO
www.shonenjump.com
RATED
T+
FOR OLDER TEEN
ratings.viz.com
DVD
VIDEO
Based on the comic "DEATH NOTE" by Tsugumi Ohba, Takeshi Obata
originally serialized in "WEEKLY SHONEN JUMP" published by SHUEISHA Inc.
©Tsugumi Ohba, Takeshi Obata/Shueisha; ©DNDP, VAP, Shueisha, Madhouse
All rights reserved. SHONEN JUMP™ and DEATH NOTE™ are trademarks of
Shueisha, Inc. in the U.S. and other countries.
viz media
www.viz.c

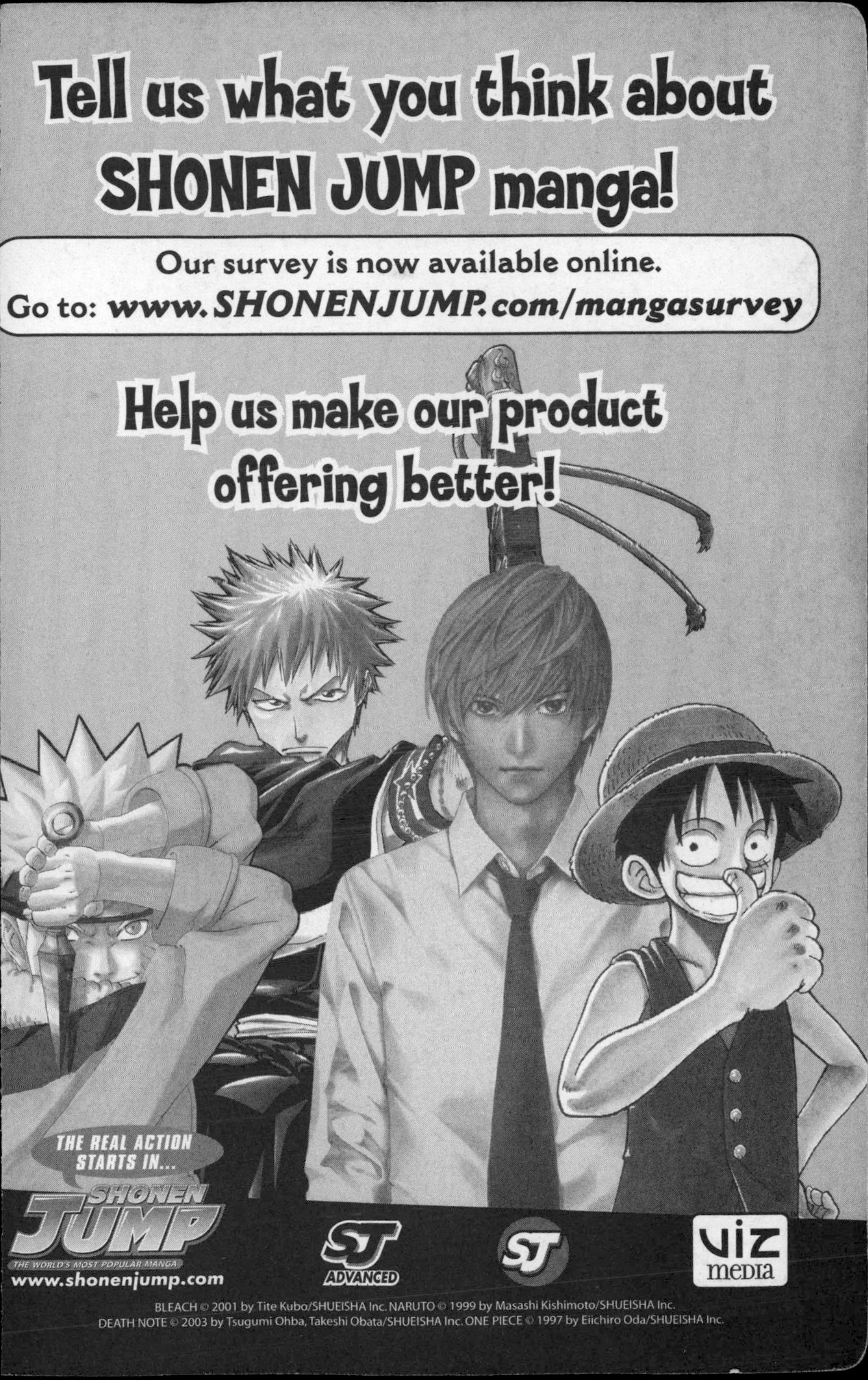
Tell us what you think about
SHONEN JUMP manga!
Our survey is now available online.
Go to: www.SHONENJUMP.com/mangasurvey
Help us make our product
offering better!
THE REAL ACTION
STARTS IN...
SHONEN JUMP
THE WORLD'S MOST POPULAR MANGA
www.shonenjump.com
SJ
ADVANCED
SJ
VIZ
media
BLEACH © 2001 by Tite Kubo/SHUEISHA Inc. NARUTO © 1999 by Masashi Kishimoto/SHUEISHA Inc.
DEATH NOTE © 2003 by Tsugumi Ohba, Takeshi Obata/SHUEISHA Inc. ONE PIECE © 1997 by Eiichiro Oda/SHUEISHA Inc.

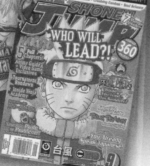
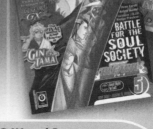

Save **50% OFF** the cover price!

D0207217

SHONEN JUMP

THE WORLD'S MOST POPULAR MANGA

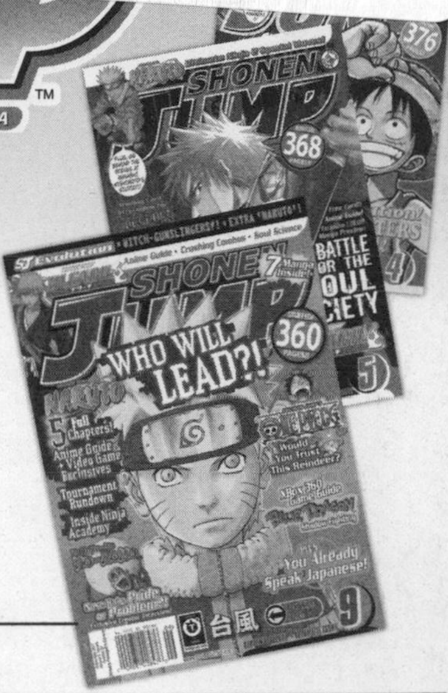

Each issue of SHONEN JUMP contains the coolest manga available in the U.S., anime news, and info on video & card games, toys AND more!

☑ **YES!** Please enter my one-year subscription (12 HUGE issues) to **SHONEN JUMP** at the LOW SUBSCRIPTION RATE of **$29.95!**

NAME

ADDRESS

CITY   STATE   ZIP

E-MAIL ADDRESS   P7GNC1

☐ **MY CHECK IS ENCLOSED** (PAYABLE TO SHONEN JUMP)   ☐ **BILL ME LATER**

CREDIT CARD: ☐ **VISA**   ☐ **MASTERCARD**

ACCOUNT #   EXP. DATE

SIGNATURE

CLIP AND MAIL TO ➡

SHONEN JUMP
Subscriptions Service Dept.
P.O. Box 515
Mount Morris, IL 61054-0515

RATED
T
TEEN
ratings.viz.com